Choice & Coercion

Gender & American Culture

Choice & Coercion

Birth Control, Sterilization, and Abortion in Public Health and Welfare

Johanna Schoen

The University of
North Carolina Press
Chapel Hill & London

Designed by Heidi Perov
Set in Cycles and TheSerif
by Keystone Typesetting, Inc.

Manufactured in the United States of America

Publication of this work was aided by a generous
grant from the Z. Smith Reynolds Foundation.

The paper in this book meets the guidelines for
permanence and durability of the Committee on
Production Guidelines for Book Longevity of the
Council on Library Resources.

■ *Library of Congress Cataloging-in-Publication Data*

Schoen, Johanna.
Choice and coercion: birth control, sterilization, and
abortion in public health and welfare / Johanna Schoen.
p. cm.—(Gender and American culture)
Includes bibliographical references and index.
ISBN 0-8078-2919-6 (cloth: alk. paper)
ISBN 0-8078-5585-5 (pbk.: alk. paper)
1. Birth control—Government policy—North Carolina—
History. 2. Sterilization, Eugenic—North Carolina—History.
3. Abortion—Government policy—North Carolina—History.
I. Title. II. Gender & American culture.
HQ766.5.U5S36   2005
363.9'6'09756—dc22
2004017632

cloth   09 08 07 06 05   5 4 3 2 1
paper   09 08 07 06 05   5 4 3 2 1

In memory of Walter Schoen, 1927–1994,
and for Sabine Schoen

Contents

Illustrations and Figures

Acknowledgments

I wrote this book to give a voice to a group of women who are usually rendered silent, both in historical writing and in today's society. Doing so would not have been possible without the help of many people who, over the years, lent their support and expertise. All of those who helped deserve my immense gratitude.

My greatest intellectual debts go to Reinhard Doerries, Jacquelyn Hall, and Rosalind Petchesky. While I was still at the University of Hamburg, Reinhard Doerries awakened my interest in American women's history, taught me that I have something to say on the subject, and told me that if I wanted to become a professional historian I should leave Germany and never come back. I have never regretted taking his advice. Jacquelyn Hall and Rosalind Petchesky provided me with examples of outstanding scholarship. Both taught me to think broadly while paying attention to the details. Jacquelyn guided this project from its early dissertation stages into a book and throughout the process provided unwavering support and insightful criticism. In addition, she served as such a model as advisor and friend that I can only hope to emulate her example in my own work. Ros Petchesky served as a mentor while I was a Social Science Research Council (SSRC) Sexuality Research Fellow, taught me to think globally, encouraged me to ponder all of those issues that lay somewhere between right and wrong, and helped me to figure out what I wanted to say about women's reproductive rights.

At various stages, financial support from the National Endowment for the Humanities, the American Philosophical Society, the Iowa Arts and Humanities Initiative, and the University of Iowa Old Gold Fellowship helped with the research and writing of this book. The Sexuality Research Fellowship Program of the SSRC, with funds provided by the Ford Foundation, offered me the luxury of three semesters off from teaching during which I could focus my attention on redrafting the dissertation into a book.

This project would have been impossible without the help of numerous archivists. My thanks go to the staff of the North Carolina State Archives, especially to Edward Morris, who alerted me to the existence of the Eugenics Board records, and to the many staff members who, during the summer of 1996, spent time redacting the Eugenics Board minutes for me. In addition, Mary Barnes and Beatrice Allen at the Old Records Center of the State Archives spent endless hours helping me through finding aids, lugging boxes, and making photocopies. The staffs of the University of North Carolina's Southern Historical Collection and North Carolina Collection, of the Sophia Smith Collection at Smith College, of the National Archives, and of the Rare Books Room at the Countway Medical Library in Boston all provided advice and help.

A number of people did everything possible to help me focus on this book by keeping the realities of life as far away from me as possible. Jim Alexander spent years keeping the Immigration and Naturalization Service off my back as well as he could, and he finally helped me obtain permanent residency. Jackie Hall, Ros Petchesky, Robert Berdahl, Stanley Katz, and Catherine Stimpson all vouched for my work with the INS. Nichelle, Bob, and Izaac Thompson kept my son, Joshua, happy during the last several summers of intensive writing.

Many people talked to me about women's reproductive health and shared memories about their work. Thanks go to Elsie Davis, Elizabeth Bryant, Elizabeth Baker, Jenny Cloer, Dorothy Hicks, Eleanor Anderson, Wallace Kuralt, Murlene Wall, Ed Chapin, Ann Wolfe, Jakob Koomen, Chuck Hendricks, Jerry Hulka, Chuck deProsse, and Takey Crist. Meeting them has been a privilege, and our conversations made this research much more rewarding. Amy Scott discovered that I wrote about her mother, provided me with information about her mother's childhood, and sent me a photograph at the very last minute.

A number of people helped in both practical and intellectual ways with the research for this book. Karen Holden spent many months entering data from thousands of sterilization cases into a database, laying the groundwork for a statistical analysis of North Carolina's sterilization program. My research assistants at the University of Iowa, Deb Garbison, Lisa Outlaw, Karrissa Haugeberg, and Anita Gaul, patiently transcribed many hours of oral history interviews. Kevin Begos showed interest in the research findings and made sure that the story of eugenic sterilization found the larger audience it deserved. Bob Korstad generously shared his own work with me and on numerous occasions helped behind the scenes. Diane diMauro and the fellows of the SSRC's Sexuality Research Fellowship Program provided an important intellectual community and turned me into the historian I am today. The history department at the University of Iowa offered amazing institutional support, a stimulating intellectual environment, and many friends.

At various stages of the project, friends and colleagues read portions of the manuscript, offered invaluable criticism and advice, and saved me from making embarrassing mistakes. Thanks go to Laura Briggs, Molly Ladd-Taylor, Susan Smith, Scott Nelson, Cindy Hahamovitch, Allan Steinberg, Barbara Ramusack, Paul Greenough, Ros Petchesky, Linda Gordon, and Linda Kerber. Eileen Boris, Regina Morantz-Sanchez, and Gail Bederman read the entire manuscript, offered many useful suggestions, and pushed me to go even further. All of them helped to make this a much richer book.

None of my work would have been possible without the support of my family and close friends. Kathy Nasstrom, Cindy Hahamovitch, Scott Nelson, and Michaela Hoenicke have supported me and this project since I began graduate school. Cristina Green opened her home to me during my various research trips. Sarah Farmer taught me that running can clear one's head. Jackie Rand, Ken Cmiel, Tal Lewis, and Despina Stratigakos reminded me that there was a life aside from the book. Jackie Blank fed me many lunches and listened patiently as I shared the latest drama about life and work. Allan Parnell and Ann Joyner provided me with a home away from home complete with strong coffee, rejuvenating dinners, and evenings in the hot tub. Takey Crist offered enthusiasm and support, was willing to answer hundreds of "last" questions about medicine, and provided me with access to all of his papers. My family in Germany, Dagmar and Heri in Berlin, and the extended Heineman clan on the East Coast provided important diversions and much love. All have not only been exceedingly supportive of my work but also exceedingly polite as the years we spent with this project dragged on and on and on.

From the very first time we discussed this project, Sian Hunter, my editor at the University of North Carolina Press, has shown unwavering support and offered sound advice. Pam Upton, David Hines, and my copyeditor, Ruth Homrighaus, patiently assisted with all the details. Their help and straightforward approach eased my attempts to negotiate the world of academic publishing considerably. Working with them has been a joy.

Lisa and Joshua Heineman have lived longer with this book than anybody else has. When constructing a sentence in the English language was still a challenge for me, Lisa helped me write my very first seminar papers on this topic. Over the years, she and Josh have shown tremendous patience, intellectual insight, love, and humor. When all else failed, Josh "pretended to care" in such a convincing manner that it made all of us laugh. They deserve all my love and appreciation.

Abbreviations

ABCL	American Birth Control League
ADC	Aid to Dependent Children
AFDC	Aid to Families with Dependent Children
AID	Agency for International Development
ALI	American Law Institute
BCFA	Birth Control Federation of America
D&C	dilation and curettage
DNS	Division of Negro Services
EMIC	Emergency Maternal and Infant Care program
FDA	Food and Drug Administration
FPI	Family Planning Incorporated
FSA	Farm Security Administration
IPPF	International Planned Parenthood Federation
IQ	intelligence quotient
IUD	intrauterine device
NAACP	National Association for the Advancement of Colored People
NCMH	National Committee for Maternal Health
PPFA	Planned Parenthood Federation of America
RS	rupees
WMS	Women's Medical Service

Choice & Coercion

A Great Thing for Poor Folks

In 1948, Estelle, a twelve-year-old African American girl from Pittsburgh, had her first encounter with abortion.[1] Without examining her, a physician had concluded that she was four months pregnant. An irregular period and, most likely, Estelle's race had been enough evidence for him to diagnose pregnancy. Actually, Estelle had not been pregnant, and eventually she began menstruating again. Her first real pregnancy occurred in 1957, and at the age of twenty-one Estelle gave birth to her first baby. After the delivery, she tried to obtain contraceptives but found that as a single woman she was ineligible. Her second baby followed in 1958, and her third in 1959. In 1961, when she discovered that she was pregnant for the fourth time, she tried to secure an abortion. It took her a while to find an abortionist, and when she finally located one, the abortionist informed her that her pregnancy was too far along. Estelle had no choice but to have another baby.

After the delivery, Estelle married and again tried to obtain contraceptives. This time, however, she met the resistance of her husband, who refused to sign the required form. Within four months, Estelle was once again pregnant. Right away, she contacted her abortionist and terminated the pregnancy, only to find herself pregnant for the sixth time in 1962. Her husband had just lost his job, and there was no money for another abortion. Estelle tried a number of home remedies to terminate the pregnancy but was unsuccessful, and she had another child. Sick of her frequent pregnancies and overburdened with five children, a rocky marriage, and no money, Estelle sought sterilization. Her physician, however, refused to perform the operation.

Estelle concluded that she had no other option but to forge her husband's signature to get a diaphragm. But using the diaphragm was nearly impossible. Her husband objected and beat her whenever he noticed that she was using the device, and in 1963 Estelle found herself with a tubal pregnancy. When her physician removed her ovary, Estelle begged him for a sterilization—without success.[2] Her sixth baby was born in 1964, and one year later she was pregnant again. After Estelle received a particularly severe beating from her husband in her seventh month of pregnancy, her seventh baby was born prematurely.

Estelle had had enough. For the second time, she forged her husband's signature, this time to obtain birth control pills. Then she bought a gun and practiced shooting in the basement to keep her husband away from the pills. With this safeguard in place, she was able to protect her birth control pills from her husband and herself from pregnancy for the next seven years. By 1970, however, Estelle had become a diabetic, and she had to stop taking the pill. Instead, she got an intrauterine device (IUD), which gave her a severe infection. After the removal of the IUD, she was again without contraceptives, and she promptly found herself pregnant. Fortunately, by this time she could get a legal abortion for medical reasons. The following year, she had another abortion—her last. Shortly afterward, her husband divorced her.

Estelle's story poignantly demonstrates women's struggle for reproductive control. While she turned to birth control, sterilization, and abortion in an attempt to control her reproduction, Estelle found that she was largely unable to prevent unwanted pregnancies. Her husband and her health professionals repeatedly denied Estelle what we have come to understand as her reproductive rights—her ability to control when and under what conditions to become pregnant and bear children. Poor and black, Estelle frequently lacked the resources that might have allowed her to gain access to birth control, sterilization, and abortion. This book is about women like Estelle. The state, I demonstrate, alternately offered and denied poor women access to birth control, sterilization, and abortion, and women negotiated with their physicians as well as with health and welfare officials in their attempts to control their reproduction.

Access to birth control, sterilization, and abortion was, as one African American woman commented after her sterilization surgery, "a great thing for poor folks."[3] But poor women were rarely able to gain access to these technologies on their own terms. Other groups—philanthropists, policy makers, health and welfare professionals—also had an interest in the control of poor women's reproductive capacities and thought reproductive technologies "a great thing for poor folks." But the terms under which they offered poor women access to them frequently kept control in the hands of health and welfare officials. The title of the introduction thus alludes to the double-edged application of reproductive technologies: they could extend reproductive control to women, or they could be used to control women's reproduction.

Health and welfare officials regulated poor women's access to birth control, sterilization, and abortion for most of the twentieth century. Concerned about maternal and infant mortality and convinced that alcoholism, sexual promiscuity, and poverty were hereditary, officials across the country began in the 1920s and 1930s to offer access to reproductive technologies through public health and welfare programs. Women sought reproductive control, but did so within clear limits. Sometimes, methods of reproductive control could offer women greater autonomy. Women gained reproductive control, for example, when state officials began to offer birth control through North Carolina's public health clinics and when, several decades later, state legislators enacted a voluntary sterilization law and liberalized North Carolina's abortion law. But birth control, sterilization, and abortion found legislative support partly because supporters used eugenic rhetoric and arguments for population control to promote them. Women lost reproductive autonomy when social workers threatened pregnant women on welfare with sterilization and attempted to tie offers of financial help to the use of contraceptives. North Carolina's record on reproductive health evokes the Jekyll-and-Hyde nature of state involvement in such matters. "The operation" (sterilization) that violated a young girl in the name of eugenics brought relief to her overburdened mother; the jellies and foam powder that visiting nurses offered may have aided family limitation, but they hardly substituted for a broader public commitment to women's health and to their reproductive control. The state of North Carolina presents an exemplary case study of what Rosalind Petchesky has called "the tension between the principles of individual control and collective responsibility over reproduction."[4]

Four groups of people influenced the nature and delivery of reproductive policies throughout the twentieth century. First, medical and social scientists offered theories about the origins and characteristics of poverty and proposed solutions that involved the control of reproduction. Birth control and sterilization, concluded University of North Carolina professor of social work George H. Lawrence after an investigation of poverty in Orange County, North Carolina, were crucial to eliminating the state's health and social problems. Second, leading health and welfare professionals as well as financial sponsors shaped public policy and influenced the nature of reproductive services. Clarence J. Gamble, heir of the soap firm Procter and Gamble, distributed and tested cheap birth control methods in North Carolina's public health clinics and elsewhere and advocated eugenic sterilization. Third, the state and county officials who implemented public health and welfare policies shaped the delivery of reproductive services. George H. Cooper, director in the 1930s of maternal and child health programs in North Carolina, took Gamble's offer of free contraceptive sponges and foam powders and tried to convince his county health officers to distribute the devices. He and his colleagues in the health and welfare professions influenced the accessibility of birth control, sterilization, and abortion and shaped the character of women's reproductive health services. Finally, the poor and minority women targeted by the programs responded to them. Edith Turner, for instance, wrote to the North Carolina State Board of Health to ask for contraceptive information. Her interest in birth control and the responses of other poor and minority women to the programs, in turn, influenced the programs' implementation, the policy-making process, and theories about the causes of and treatments for poverty.

While all four groups shared the goals of improving infant and maternal health and reducing poverty, they disagreed about women's ability to control their reproduction and the desirability of giving reproductive control to women. Moreover, none of the groups' members held a unified position. Philanthropists and policy makers argued with each other about the precise goals of reproductive policies. Some held that poor and uneducated women lacked both the motivation and the intelligence to use contraceptives and argued that resources should be channeled into the development of a birth control method geared specifically for the poor. Others felt that women merely lacked access to good contraceptives and health care and would frequent birth control clinics if such services were available. Health professionals also disagreed about the details of policy implementation and about the desirability of extending full reproductive control to women. They argued, for instance, over whether any woman requesting birth control should be given access to contraceptives or whether women needed to be married and to already have several children before they could get access to contraceptive advice. Women, too, lacked a unified response to, or experience with, reproductive technologies. Some sought sterilization, others did not. Some volunteered for contraceptive trials to gain access to birth control, while others objected to being the subjects of what they felt was medical experimentation.

As a result, policy implementation lacked cohesion, leading to the creation of a patchwork of programs with great disparities and contradictions between them. While health professionals might have coerced women to use IUDs, for instance, they barred women's access to both abortion and elective sterilization. Women at times used the programs for their own purposes and in ways that contradicted the intentions of policy makers and health professionals. Lacking access to elective sterilization, for example, some women applied for eugenic sterilization through the North Carolina Eugenics Board, even though this necessitated that they be diagnosed as feebleminded.

Sexual, class, and racial conflicts shaped negotiations over reproductive control. Women's ability to control their sexuality and the terms and conditions of motherhood stood at the center of debates about birth control, sterilization, and abortion. Class and race background determined whether women had access to reproductive health care, whether they came into contact with state sterilization and birth control programs, how they were treated by the representatives of these programs, and how they experienced sexuality and reproduction. Assumptions about the links between sexuality, class, and race shaped public perceptions of women's sexual behavior, policy debates surrounding issues of sexuality and reproduction, the formulation of reproductive policies, and the delivery of services to patients. Policy makers and health and welfare professionals frequently assumed that poor single mothers—particularly if they were African American, Hispanic, or Native American—lacked the ability to function properly as mothers and that they should be discouraged from further childbearing. Middle-class white physicians and female social workers based decisions concerning women's reproductive futures on middle-class assumptions about working-class and black women's sexuality. Many white, male researchers and health professionals assumed that poor and minority women were unable or unmotivated to use contraceptives properly and encouraged the development and testing of cheaper contraceptives and contraceptives that were outside the control of female patients. Women negotiated with an overwhelmingly male medical profession, while an overwhelmingly male legislature regulated access to reproductive technologies. But gender, race, and class were not clear dividing lines in these debates, as any individual could be found on either side of a particular discussion.

Finally, concerns about racial discrimination shaped both the contemporary discourse about women's reproductive experiences and the historical understanding of those experiences. Black nationalists frequently voiced suspicions that birth control for African Americans was equivalent to race genocide. Such allegations raised legitimate concerns. Critics pointed to the real abuse and coercion perpetrated by some family planning programs that targeted minorities for involuntary sterilization. They criticized persistent racial discrimination in access to health care, disapproved of the lack of minority representation on family planning boards, and expressed wariness about the attraction that family planning programs held for many racists. And they found an echo in academic circles in the 1970s, as mainland socialist feminists began to write about abuse as the defining experience that poor, nonwhite women—both in Puerto Rico and on the mainland—had with sterilization.[5]

With the rise of the feminist health movement in the 1970s, historians and feminist scholars turned their attention to the history of women's health. Early works described male physicians who, in the process of medical professionalization, began to specialize in women's health, pushing aside female healers and midwives. Women's bodies came under the control of male professionals who used both their medical knowledge and medical and reproductive technology to reinforce and justify women's subordinate status in society.[6] Publicity surrounding sterilization abuse raised awareness of coercive reproductive policies not only in the United States but also in Puerto Rico, India, Bangladesh, Brazil, and elsewhere.[7] Scholars emphasized the role that governmental policy could play in limiting women's reproduction at home and abroad when both welfare policies and foreign aid tied the receipt of benefits to the control of reproduction.[8]

But not all scholars agreed that the history of women's reproduction was only a story of women's victimization or that all medical technology was harmful to women. Historians pointed out that alliances between female reformers and the medical profession, for instance, had resulted in the legalization of birth control, ultimately increasing women's reproductive control. Moreover, hoping to improve their health, women had sought access to both professional medical care and medical technology, negotiating with usually male physicians over the terms and conditions of such care.[9] Others argued that while African American women had been victims of a racist health care system, they had tried to negotiate with health care providers, had pushed white professionals to extend more care to African American populations, and had established alternative institutions to provide services within their own communities.[10] Similarly, while criticizing heavy-handed or coercive population control programs in developing countries, feminist health activists around the world pushed Western governments and international aid agencies to extend material and structural support for comprehensive women's health services and established nongovernmental organizations to provide services in developing countries.[11] Finally, feminist scholars and historians cautioned that medical technology did not hold only one meaning for all women. Rather, it was the larger social and political context surrounding the technology and the options available to women confronting the technology that determined whether it restricted or enhanced women's reproductive control.[12] The acknowledgment that technology has multiple meanings and that women's health care was and is the result of negotiations between women, medical professionals, and the state led to a reconsideration of women's experiences as patients. Historians began to pay closer attention to the ways in which women exerted control over their health and reproductive care, pointing to both the extent and the limits of women's agency.[13]

Analyzing the role that birth control, sterilization, and abortion have played in public health and welfare programs of the twentieth century brings issues of control and agency into sharp focus. Geared toward a population that lacked access to private health care, state services directly affected poor women's experience of sex and its consequences. North Carolina was among the first states to integrate reproductive technologies into its public health and social welfare programs. The state introduced the nation's first state-supported birth control program in 1937; it had one of the longest-lasting and most active state sterilization programs; and during the 1960s, it was among the first states to pass a voluntary sterilization law and to reform its abortion law. Implemented at the local level by county health and welfare officials, state programs and policies existed on a continuum. At their best, public health birth control programs, voluntary sterilization, and therapeutic abortion provided poor women with access to reproductive health services and to a variety of contraceptive methods. At their worst, health and welfare officials sought to control women's reproduction, coercing women to agree to eugenic sterilization or the insertion of an IUD as a condition for receiving welfare payments for their children.

An examination of birth control, sterilization, and abortion at the local level shows the interworkings of contraceptive programs and highlights political and social factors that influenced the delivery and character of the services. My ability to analyze the policy-making process, however, is limited by the fact that the North Carolina legislature does not keep written records of its legislative sessions. Trying to understand the motivations of state legislators who debated, formulated, and funded reproductive policy is difficult, sometimes impossible. In fact, during most of the period under discussion, such issues were considered to be private and were not debated publicly. Only in the early 1970s did sexuality and reproduction emerge as a topic for public discussion that sparked the interest of newspaper reporters and voters.

This book places the story of North Carolina into a national and global context, pointing to continuities and discontinuities between, among other places, North Carolina, Florida, New York City, Puerto Rico, and India. North Carolina was not a local exception, nor did its process of policy formulation and implementation take place in isolation. Rather, the negotiations surrounding reproductive care mirrored those in other parts of the country and the world. Whether rural mill villages and sharecropping areas or urban centers, whether United States, Puerto Rico, or India, certain factors linked all of the places under investigation: economic underdevelopment, poverty, perceived overpopulation, and a demographic otherness made them ripe for the scientific and sexual experimentation of philanthropy. These factors also made them areas underserved by social and medical services, with populations eager to negotiate for reproductive care.

Despite these similarities, location matters. Social policies played out differently in different places. Race and class relations varied, as did the meaning of sex, reproductive control, and motherhood. Moreover, reproductive policies were defined at the center for the periphery, embedded in a framework of us versus them. And while those on the periphery influenced policy formulation and implementation, they remained locked there, always on the receiving end of social policy. This study draws attention to both the parallels and the differences between reproductive policies at home and abroad.

■ Public Health and Welfare in the Jim Crow South

Throughout the twentieth century, American health and welfare policies in general, and reproductive health policies in particular, were shaped by two contradictory forces: a progressive, democratic impulse that sought to give everybody an equal start in life, and a conservative distrust of any program aimed at helping the poor. Hoping to provide all with an equal chance, health and welfare officials established programs for poor whites and blacks across the South. They did so, however, within a larger political context of deep suspicion toward any services for the poor. In fact, as a whole, the South was slow to address the health needs of its poor population. Some states advocated the improvement of health services for blacks in order to safeguard the health of whites. In general, public health work in the South was inadequately organized, and services to African Americans in particular were governed by a policy of neglect.[14]

While it took most southern states until World War I to awaken to the poor state of health of their populations, North Carolina stood out for its early concern for public health. In 1877, the state established the State Board of Health to advise lawmakers on matters affecting the health of its citizens. Although the board initially had little power and few resources, in 1909 the General Assembly increased the board's annual appropriation and authorized the hiring of the first full-time health officer, Dr. Watson Smith Rankin, dean of the Wake Forest medical school. For fourteen years, Rankin oversaw the rapid growth of public health activities. Support from the Rockefeller Sanitary Commission to eradicate hookworm disease stimulated a decade of innovative public health campaigns.[15]

Under Rankin's leadership, the North Carolina State Board of Health broke long-standing tradition by offering equal services to blacks and whites and departing from fee-for-service medicine by providing free medical treatment through public health officers. Rankin and his health officers advocated a democratic approach to public health work. In their tonsil and adenoid clinics for North Carolina's schoolchildren, for instance, public health officers treated all children together, regardless of their parents' ability to pay. Such efforts attracted national attention and put North Carolina at the very forefront of progressive public health work.

Rankin's advocacy of equal provisions for blacks and whites also established him as a promoter of the modern welfare state. Guaranteeing equal opportunities to all citizens by providing equal treatment to all was important, Rankin believed, in the effort to modernize the South and its citizens. As Robert Korstad has pointed out, long before the participants in national debates about governmental intervention grappled with questions about means-tested versus universalistic health care, Rankin and his colleagues defended their public health approach. Wartime enthusiasm for national fitness and the desire to develop both a healthier citizenry and a more efficient workforce contributed to the willingness of legislators and of North Carolina's private physicians to support Rankin's policies.[16] And even after opposition from local elites and doctors mounted in the mid-1920s and Rankin's public health crusade ran out of steam, the notion that public health officers should take responsibility for the basic health of all citizens continued to strongly influence public health policies in the state.

The progressive impulse notwithstanding, a deeply conservative strain severely hampered state assistance to the poor. Most state legislators and county commissioners across the South were unwilling to support taxation to fund social welfare programs. North Carolina was no exception. In the early 1930s, when the Great Depression led to the collapse of tobacco and cotton prices and the foreclosure of farms and local banks, the state still had no program of relief for the poor. Existing relief efforts were cobbled together by local private charities and county funds. The State Board of Public Welfare merely coordinated its county-funded and county-operated welfare boards and directed federal funds to the localities.[17]

As a result, throughout the New Deal era, North Carolina politicians were ambivalent about Roosevelt's economic recovery plans. A pervasive pro-business ideology and a states' rights tradition hampered attempts to centralize relief efforts and provide financial assistance to the poor. Politicians and business leaders were reluctant to give up local control and feared that relief measures were overgenerous, a threat to cheap labor, and harmful to recipients. In consequence, the state spent the 1930s debating how little, not how much, the state government could do to fight poverty and economic decline. Between 1929 and 1933, the state began to drastically cut its appropriations for poverty and welfare programs. Appropriations to the State Board of Health alone fell by 55 percent. At a time when an increasing number of people found themselves unable to pay for health care, health agencies all over the South lost much of their capacity to provide public care. Appropriations for public assistance funds fared similarly poorly. Throughout the 1930s, North Carolina refused to match federal relief funds. Although state spending on public assistance programs was similar to that of other southern states, it compared unfavorably to the national average.[18]

As a result of state governments' unwillingness to address the structural causes of poverty, economic backwardness continued to characterize the South. During the 1940s and 1950s, a group of politicians dedicated to economic growth replaced the old planter elite. Their ability to attract military spending, research contracts, and funds for business development led to the emergence of a dual economy that ignited growth at the top and tolerated poverty at the bottom. When national attention returned to the poor in the 1960s, poverty in the South seemed just as severe as it had been in the 1930s. Thirty-seven percent of North Carolina's residents, for instance, had incomes below the federal poverty line. Half of all students in the state dropped out of school before obtaining a high school diploma, and one-fourth of adults twenty-five years of age and older had less than a sixth-grade education and were for all practical purposes illiterate.[19]

Like the New Deal, the War on Poverty opened up opportunities for the establishment of a new wave of progressive health and welfare programs. In 1960, John F. Kennedy was elected president, and Terry Sanford was elected governor of North Carolina. Sanford, along with the liberal wing of the state's Democratic Party, devoted his administration to diversifying the economy, improving public education, and reducing state dependence on low-wage manufacturing. Southern leaders, however, continued to reject antipoverty programs that steered resources away from business development.[20] While the South embraced federal welfare for business, welcoming all development-oriented initiatives and enthusiastically supplying matching funds for highways and downtown shopping centers, it rejected welfare for the poor. In 1963, Sanford and a well-connected coalition of business and educational leaders established the North Carolina Fund to attack poverty and racial discrimination. As a private, nonprofit corporation, the fund was able to bypass hostile conservative lawmakers by relying on foundation and federal grants rather than state appropriations. Seeking to empower the poor, the fund's volunteers tutored children and adults, counseled high school dropouts, served as advocates for access to health care and better housing, worked in county health departments, renovated homes, installed sanitary privies, and helped develop community water systems.[21] As the only statewide antipoverty agency of its kind, the North Carolina Fund played a notable role in shaping the Great Society initiatives of the Johnson administration. By 1968, however, the fund and the national War on Poverty were under siege. Liberal Democrats were in retreat as progressive social policies fell victim to racial divisions and to lawmakers' continued refusal to come to terms with the structural causes of poverty.[22]

The tension between progressive health and social policies and a generally tightfisted approach to public assistance provided the context in which North Carolina's reproductive health policies were developed and implemented. The progressive spirit of the New Deal was the backdrop for the establishment of North Carolina's public health birth control program in 1937, and the War on Poverty in the 1960s was accompanied by the implementation of progressive family planning programs. Throughout the period under discussion, family planning advocates understood the ability to control reproduction to be a fundamental right of all women, regardless of their capacity to pay for medical services. This democratic attitude was not limited to family planning programs, moreover, but extended to the passage of a voluntary sterilization law and the reform of the state's abortion law during the 1960s. Together, these policies significantly increased women's reproductive control. At the same time, however, the creation of a state welfare system during the Great Depression went hand in hand with the establishment of a eugenic sterilization program under the Department of Public Welfare. And the expansion of the welfare state in the 1950s and 1960s brought with it a significant increase in eugenic sterilizations and coercive family planning programs. Even the liberalization of the state's abortion law was motivated in part by the hope that access to abortion would lead to a reduction in births among welfare recipients.

While reproductive health policies were designed to provide an equal chance for all, such policies also found support because they promised to lighten the state's burden from the "socially useless."[23] The state seemed to acknowledge access to birth control, and later to sterilization and abortion, as basic citizenship rights. But these rights came with a responsibility: health and welfare officials expected women to have children within marriage and to limit the number of children they bore according to their families' financial means. Those unable or unwilling to exercise this responsibility placed themselves outside the body politic.[24] If the birth control program was for those responsible and intelligent enough to take advantage of it, the eugenic sterilization program and coercive family planning policies were for those unable to control themselves.

■ From Local to Global: Continuities and Discontinuities

North Carolina's reproductive policies were part of an international experiment with family planning. Ever since the rise of the welfare state in the late nineteenth century, governments of the Atlantic world have been participating in a global conversation about health and welfare initiatives.[25] The international women's movement became a major conduit for women's health and welfare initiatives. New philanthropic institutions such as the Rockefeller Foundation, the Carnegie Corporation, and the

Russell Sage Foundation became active and innovative players, and state and federal governments quickly emerged as participants as well.

The same people and institutions advocated and implemented contraceptive programs at home and abroad. Scientists visited international conferences to debate eugenic theory, and governments looked to each other as they formulated and implemented eugenic sterilization programs. Margaret Sanger, Clarence Gamble, and other representatives of national birth control organizations discussed the need for family planning at home and abroad. They tested contraceptives in North Carolina and many other parts of the nation and sent their diaphragms and foam powders to Puerto Rico, India, and other parts of the world. Women crossed state lines and international borders in search of birth control and abortion. And by the late twentieth century, the United States influenced international reproductive health policy by, for instance, tying American family planning aid to foreign health care providers' compliance with the gag rule, which prohibited health care providers from discussing abortion with their clients.

Conceptions of foreign aid and population control mirrored the domestic links between welfare and family planning. Just as the discourse surrounding welfare depicted recipients as excessively fertile and in need of family planning, the discourse surrounding foreign aid depicted developing countries as excessively fertile and in need of population control. Not only domestic welfare dependency but also the persistent nature of poverty in developing countries attracted the attention of policy makers, who sought to establish postwar stability by controlling population growth. Nevertheless, no policy idea had the same impact in every context. Every policy came burdened with extensive baggage, including strong gender assumptions, modern notions of race and eugenic improvement, public attitudes toward the poor and toward women's sexuality, and other assumptions that accompanied different economic settings and political systems. Timing and location, then, both mattered. Combining a close local analysis with a discussion of the international context will help us to more fully understand the similarities and differences between various family planning initiatives.

The Role of Agency and the Writing of History

In the late 1980s, Linda Gordon called for a reevaluation of the ways in which women's historians described poor women's interactions with the state and the helping professions. Wanting to move away from a histo-riography of social control that characterized women as victims of the state, the medical profession, or social workers, Gordon urged historians to pay closer attention to women's agency—the ways in which women sought to exert control over their own lives and the lives of their family members. Women, Gordon cautioned, could be simultaneously "victims and victimizers, dependent and depended on, weak and powerful."[26] Only a broader understanding of their actions would allow us to appreciate clients as active participants in the welfare system who both shaped and were affected by the interventions of social workers.[27]

But discussing agency is complicated by the fact that those whose agency historians seek have often left behind no sources to study. Histo-rians thus have to locate "agency" in the sources created by the very state representatives and health and social work professionals who were seek-ing to exert control over women, prompting further debates over the question of whether poor women did indeed have a voice that can legit-imately be recorded as theirs.[28] Indeed, in the case of medical history, a general lack of access to patient records as historical sources compounds historians' difficulty in locating any information about patient response.

Writing about women's agency means that we reconstruct not only how women responded to birth control, sterilization, and abortion but also why they acted as they did. It also means that we have to acknowledge our historical subjects as complex people in a way that is not always comfortable. It means, for instance, grappling with their strengths and their weaknesses, their achievements and their mistakes, without falling into the trap of blaming the victim. Finally, it means showing our histor-ical subjects enough respect to try to understand why they made choices that we might consider bad. Why, for instance, did they join contraceptive research trials when we feel that joining was not in their best interest because such trials exploited their health and their bodies? Why did they listen to the wrong medical advice of a neighbor over the better advice of a sympathetic physician? What did they perceive their choices to be?

Because of the complexity of agency, close attention to it will at times introduce a tension between our understanding of our subjects' agency and their own. How are we, for instance, to write about the life of Mabel Scott, whose self-perception might be at odds with our reading of her story? In 1968, at the age of thirteen, Scott was sterilized under North Carolina's eugenic sterilization program. Her sterilization followed her delivery of a baby outside of marriage; her pregnancy was the result of a rape. Never informed about the surgery, Scott did not realize what had happened to her until she tried to become pregnant during her first marriage. In the mid-1970s, she decided to sue the North Carolina Eugenics Board over her sterilization. "I wanted to do something about it," she remembers. "I felt like, you know, it was wrong. What they were doing was inhuman." Her decision to sue the Eugenics Board was a strong sign of agency on her part, and it contributed to the abolition of the state sterilization program. But Scott lost her suit. She summarizes her experience: "I was powerless. I was powerless over my own body, my mind. I was powerless over everything and I still am powerless."[29] Is Scott a hero of her own life? She does not think so. Agency and empowerment are not part of her memory and evaluation of her story.

Like so many others, Scott's is a story made up of multiple competing narratives, none of which we should privilege. It recounts both agency and victimization coexisting in parallel but different universes. From Scott's perspective, nothing can change the past and the injustices done to her, under which she suffers to this day. From a different vantage point, however, her reality of victimization becomes simultaneously a narrative of agency; Scott sued the Eugenics Board and constructed a narrative of her past to tell others about the wrongs done to her. Sensitivity to these multiple vantage points helps us appreciate just how complicated women's stories can be.[30]

This is neither a story of the state or the medical profession exerting power over female patients nor a story of strong women rising above all odds. Rather, it demonstrates that women's reproductive health is an outcome of intricate negotiations between everyone involved in the debate, formulation, and implementation of health policy. Despite the existence of real power differentials between policy makers, public welfare workers, philanthropists, physicians, and the recipients of birth control, no one ever possessed total control, and all participants shaped every outcome in the process of negotiating women's access to birth control, sterilization, and abortion in North Carolina.

■ Telling Medical Stories

Reproductive technologies, like other medical technologies, are never value-free, but gain their meaning from the larger cultural and political context in which they emerge, the circumstances under which women encounter them, and the intentions with which health professionals grant women access to them.[31] Reproductive technologies can be both liberating and oppressive, and medical technologies and interventions can hold a number of different meanings simultaneously. As Keith Wailoo reminds us, "the drama of technology in medicine is not a simple narrative—it involves many conflicting stories."[32]

Neither physicians nor patients shared a single view of birth control, sterilization, or abortion. They disagreed with each other about the conditions that might justify women's access to reproductive technologies. While some physicians were willing, for instance, to offer abortion as a "therapeutic" procedure to women who sought to end unwanted pregnancies for personal reasons, other physicians criticized such procedures as operations "of convenience." Deeply mistrustful of women's motivations for obtaining abortions, the latter group advocated the termination of pregnancy only in cases in which urgent medical conditions made pregnancy and childbearing dangerous. Similarly, while some women sought birth control pills as an effective form of contraception, others resisted taking the pill because of its side effects, sometimes criticizing physicians for pushing the pill and jeopardizing women's health in the process. In addition, the meanings that physicians and patients attributed to reproductive technologies sometimes changed over time. Women might have rejected the IUD early in their childbearing years but desired the device years later. Physicians might have been inclined to perform abortions during times of economic hardship such as the Great Depression but adopted a less favorable view of the procedure during the pronatalist postwar period.

Both patients and physicians constructed medical narratives—often at odds with each other—to help them explain and interpret the meaning of medical technologies and the medical experiences that went with them. As Jack Pressman has pointed out, the modern period is characterized by a gap between scientific and lay cultures.[33] This split becomes particularly apparent when we listen to the medical narratives that poor women and their families created as they confronted reproductive technologies. Frequently lacking basic sexual and reproductive knowledge about how these technologies worked and what impact they might have on their bodies, patients attributed symptoms to unrelated causes, establishing connections between events that were physiologically unrelated but seemed closely connected from the patients' viewpoints. Patients experienced reproductive technologies in the context of all of their medical experiences, leading them to construct medical narratives meaningful to them but in stark contrast to the scientific view of the technologies. Mabel Scott, for instance, links her sterilization surgery to a whole host of other medical problems. As a result of the surgery, she explains, she had hemorrhages, developed fibroids and other tumors, and needed a total hysterectomy. In addition, she argues: "I have never enjoyed my body and I can't. . . . [I am] asexual. I'm not male or female." "This is what they did," she summarizes. "They castrated me."[34] While a physician would argue that Scott's subsequent medical problems with hemorrhages, fibroids, tumors, and hysterectomy were in the medical sense unrelated to the sterilization surgery, in her subjective experience as a patient all of the conditions were related. And while one might hypothesize that her inability to enjoy her body and her sexuality stems from the years of sexual abuse that surrounded her sterilization, she sees these problems, too, as originating from the surgery. Patients' understandings of causality in their medical experiences did not necessarily bear any resemblance to the medical facts as defined by medical practitioners. Nevertheless, the stories were very real to the patients. Reconstructing these stories means being mindful of the existence of parallel "realities,"—in this case, the reality of a medical history at odds with the self-perception of a historical subject, the reality of a subject's medical narrative at odds with science.[35]

But a larger social, political, and economic context lends additional meaning to Scott's evaluation of her surgery. Scott, in 1968 a poor black teenager thirteen years of age, pregnant as a result of a rape and sterilized against her will, came to understand the story of her surgery against the backdrop of the civil rights and women's rights movements. While the civil rights movement drew national attention to racial discrimination, the rise of the women's health movement articulated the notion that women have reproductive rights. In the early 1970s, other cases of sterilization abuse involving young, poor, black women led to a national outcry against such cases, which was followed by the formulation of sterilization guidelines to guard against the continuation of such coercive practices. Finally, Scott's own medical problems further influenced her negative evaluation of the surgery. This entire context shaped her understanding of her experience. In contrast, while a white woman sterilized against her will in the 1930s might also have experienced the surgery as oppressive and might possibly have blamed it for her subsequent unrelated medical problems, she would have been unlikely to see it as a violation of her personal rights—a concept that, in the context of reproductive health, only emerged in the late 1960s.

Physicians and health professionals, for their part, had their own explanations of the causalities of symptoms and diseases, treatments and outcomes. While their medical interpretations did not always agree with those of their colleagues, they gained a legitimacy that patients' narratives rarely had. In our efforts to understand patients' experiences, we should be careful not to privilege the scientifically correct account of a medical event over one that is scientifically improbable. At the same time, we need to remain mindful that diseases are not just social constructs but also physiological phenomena. And while the scientific understanding of disease and the meaning of medical interventions changed over time as old technologies gave way to new ones, modern treatment methods replaced the "outmoded," and new diseases emerged while old ones ceased to exist, our stories must make physiological sense.

When patients and physicians came together to negotiate over health care, patients did not merely adopt the medical explanations provided by the experts. Rather, they argued with health professionals over the causes and appropriate treatment of their diseases. While North Carolina Eugenics Board members might have held, for instance, that a patient's feeblemindedness had been passed on from previous generations, family members argued that poverty, deprivation, and overwork were to blame for the weak mental state of their loved one. When Eugenics Board members proposed sterilization as a solution, family members refused to see the value in the surgery and argued that sterilization candidates should just be left alone. In the interactions between physicians and patients, however, it was the scientific story, rather than the patient narrative, that held greater authority.

Ultimately, the services patients could expect to receive were shaped not only by the interactions between physicians and patients but also by the larger social and political context surrounding medical care. In this context, philanthropists and policy makers, health and welfare professionals, and local social workers and public health nurses set the broad parameters in which patients and physicians negotiated about reproductive health. Concerned less with science and more with politics, bureaucracy, and dominant ideologies of proper womanhood, they set the stage for women's access to birth control, sterilization, and abortion, both enabling and limiting the negotiations between physicians and patients.

In the summer of 2002, I received a phone call from Kevin Begos, a journalist with the *Winston-Salem Journal* who was interested in the history of eugenic sterilization in North Carolina. What started out as a couple of innocuous phone conversations became, within the next several weeks, an intense collaboration that stretched over several months. I decided to open my research findings and source materials to Begos, who spent several days at my dining room table reading through thousands of summaries of sterilization petitions to which I had gained access in the course of my research. In addition, he and his team of reporters interviewed sterilization survivors, tracked down physicians, and investigated aspects of the program that I had chosen not to pursue. In December 2002, the *Winston-Salem Journal* published a weeklong series chronicling the history of eugenic sterilization in North Carolina.[36] The series had a tremendous impact. North Carolina's governor, Mike Easley, immediately issued a public apology. In August 2003, North Carolina became the first state in the nation to institute a program of restitution to sterilization survivors in the form of health and education benefits.[37] In addition, North Carolina legislators finally eliminated the state's eugenic sterilization law, which, while inoperative, had still been on the books. This attention came at a time when other states were confronting similar legacies and debating how to respond appropriately.[38]

From the perspective of a scholar, the public debate surrounding state sterilization programs raised troubling questions about the interpretation and lessons of history. While my interest in the newspaper series and in collaboration with Begos stemmed from my larger sense of responsibility toward those who had for decades been rendered voiceless, I ultimately had to realize that I had no control over the way their stories were rewritten, perceived, and discussed. "Unless we know history," the series' authors noted, "we cannot in the future avoid errors that were made."[39] But the history I knew and the errors I thought should be avoided were not necessarily the same history and errors the *Winston-Salem Journal* saw in this story or the same history and errors that readers gleaned from the series. Ironically, this realization rounded out a process for me that started with my interest in competing narratives. I tried to make sense of the competing stories of women, physicians, health and welfare professionals, researchers, and others. The result is a narrative that competes with other interpretations about the errors and lessons of this history. Who in this story was victim and who was agent, who was a perpetrator of wrongs done and who a hero, belies easy classification. Their voices and my understanding of their narratives make up this book.

CHAPTER ONE

Teaching Birth Control on Tobacco Road and in Mill Village Alley

The History of Public Birth Control Services

In 1941, Josiah B. testified to his congregation, "The devil has been to my house and tempted me in my weakest spot."[1] The devil—in the form of public health nurse Lena Hillard—was touring Watauga County in the western part of North Carolina to offer condoms to all women of childbearing age. Josiah, who was deeply torn between his moral objections to contraception and his wife's desire to accept the nurse's offer, sought spiritual help in his effort to solve this dilemma. He eventually acquiesced to his wife's wishes.

Throughout the early 1940s, Lena Hillard offered condoms and a contraceptive foam powder to every resident of Watauga County. As part of a study of the reliability of foam powder and Trojan condoms, she distributed the contraceptives to her clients, gave instructions on their use, and kept careful records of the number of pregnancies among their users. Financed by philanthropist and birth control activist Clarence J. Gamble, this so-called condom project was only one of many programs to bring birth control to poor populations.

The notion that the state should provide birth control information to the poor dates back to the emergence of the birth control movement in the early twentieth century. Under the leadership of Margaret Sanger, the early birth control movement sought the repeal of the Comstock Law of 1873, which prohibited the dissemination of birth control or information about birth control through the U.S. mail. Women, Sanger argued, needed access to birth control and the ability to control their own fertility. But the progress of the radical, broad-based birth control movement was hampered by a conservative medical profession that deemed birth control immoral, thought Margaret Sanger too radical, and feared any government involvement in medical matters. By the 1920s, Sanger had grown frustrated with the movement's slow progress and had begun to work to forge a professional alliance with the medical establishment. Hoping to gain broader support, she began to emphasize eugenic and economic arguments, increasingly grounding her claims for the legalization of birth control on the ideal of racial progress and efficiency.[2]

The 1930s witnessed a struggle over the professionalization of the birth control movement, while the New Deal offered unprecedented opportunities for the delivery of contraceptives to the poor. Physicians replaced laywomen activists in the national birth control organizations and in local clinics. Hard economic times, rising popular demand for contraceptives, and a 1936 court decision removing all federal bans on the distribution of birth control contributed to physicians' greater willingness to provide contraceptive information to their patients. At the same time, expanding welfare rolls increased state and federal governments' interest in the distribution of birth control to the poor. Starting in the late 1930s, state public health programs and federal relief agencies became actively involved in the distribution of contraception.

With the removal of legal prohibitions of the dissemination of birth control, a patchwork of services emerged to address the contraceptive needs of poor women. Public, private, and nonprofit organizations participated in the establishment of a range of birth control services. Both federal and state governments began to provide family planning through public health clinics and traveling birth control nurses. Researchers supported by national birth control organizations and private philanthropies established contraceptive field trials. And some physicians provided poor women with birth control advice in their private offices.

Humanitarian, eugenic, and economic concerns converged in the complex set of factors that motivated health and welfare professionals' involvement in the delivery of birth control. They were genuinely concerned with maternal and child health and hoped to improve women's access to health and contraceptive services. At the same time, most health and welfare professionals shared the view that the poor possessed a number of undesirable qualities that they were likely to pass on to the next generation. They hoped that limiting the reproduction of the poor would provide a scientific solution to poverty and poor health and would improve the quality of the race. Birth control advocates also emphasized that the distribution of contraceptives among the poor would save taxpayers money by controlling state expenses for social services.

During World War II, legislators sharply curtailed spending for health and social services, rolling back many of the programs that had expanded during the New Deal. Maternal and child health improved, and health professionals, resenting government involvement in matters of medicine as an unwanted intrusion into the profession, lost interest in public health birth control programs. Public welfare officials stepped into this gap. Concerned with swelling Aid to Dependent Children (ADC) rolls, they began to look to birth control as a means to limit poverty. In the 1960s, population control rhetoric and the development of a new generation of contraceptives increased both funding for family planning programs and the possibility of abuse. While some programs advocated women's right to reproductive control, others sought to control poor women's reproduction.

Clinics existed on a continuum between two extremes. On one end were clinics whose officials saw contraceptives as an integral part of public health services that, if offered along with prenatal and postnatal care and increased supervision of the state's midwives, would improve the health of mothers and infants. Spacing children, officials at these clinics held, was essential to women's health and contributed to the birth of healthier babies. By the 1960s, officials of some clinics even expressed the belief that women had a right to reproductive control. On the other end of the continuum were clinics that offered only contraceptives. Supporters of these clinics held that general health care services would divert funds needed more urgently for birth control work. Since they deemed it most important to reach as many women as possible, the officials at these clinics stressed quantity over quality by providing only basic services to a larger number of women. In the 1930s and 1940s, such clinics offered simple contraceptives in order to reach as many women as possible. These contraceptives did not require a physician for fitting and thus could be distributed by visiting nurses or through the mail and used safely by a woman with minimal sanitary facilities. By the 1960s, these clinics moved to the use of contraceptives such as the IUD that required little client cooperation; control over the insertion and removal of these forms of birth control lay with physicians rather than their patients.

Most of the women who took advantage of state-supported birth control programs lacked access to the most basic health services. The quality of their experiences with birth control programs depended in part on the extent to which officials integrated contraceptive advice into broader health and social services. Neither minority nor poor white clients of the birth control programs necessarily experienced the contraceptive offers as a form of state control. Nor did they usually see eye to eye with the largely white, middle-class professionals who ran the services. Instead, they had their own agendas, often unanticipated by public health and public welfare officials. These women welcomed the services, participated in them, and helped shape the contraceptive programs. Black health and social work professionals demanded better health and contraceptive services for African American women and occasionally even adopted eugenic rhetoric. They repeatedly challenged public health officials and influential whites to increase their outreach in black communities.

This chapter captures the diversity of delivery systems so typical of the American welfare state by analyzing several birth control programs around the country. It examines North Carolina's public health birth control program and the efforts of the Farm Security Administration (FSA) to offer family planning as part of the New Deal. It follows Florida physician Lydia DeVilbiss, who during the height of the Great Depression distributed contraceptives from her private office. And it explores the "Negro Project" of the Birth Control Federation of America (BCFA) and the efforts of pediatrician Joe Beasley to bring family planning to Louisiana's poor population.[3]

The proliferation of a variety of birth control services such as those described in this chapter marked the development of a welfare state that drew on the government, private, and nonprofit sectors.[4] The geographic inequalities so familiar to us in today's welfare programs have their origin in such services: the lack of a coherent delivery system resulted in a patchwork of services of uneven quality. This chapter's focus on a variety of programs also allows for a fuller understanding of client experiences. Although, for instance, the archival sources in North Carolina offer little material on the politics of race in public health birth control programs, the records of the BCFA Negro Project tell the story. And while the records of the Negro Project are silent on questions of client reception, the sources of the FSA speak volumes.

■ Infant and Maternal Health in the Early Twentieth Century

High rates of infant and maternal mortality alerted health professionals in the early twentieth century to the need to improve infant and maternal health. In 1915, around 10 percent of all infants in the U.S. birth registration area—but 20 percent of infants of color—died before they were one year old. Approximately six white and ten nonwhite women died for every thousand live births between 1900 and 1930.[5] Mortality rates were exacerbated by the general ill health of poor women. Many suffered from hookworm and other intestinal parasites, malnutrition, and malaria. Health conditions for African Americans were particularly dire. In the mid- to late 1930s, about 35 to 40 percent of adult black males in the South were either "fairly sick or just about to be" in any given year. It is safe to assume that black women were in no better health. Indeed, poor women who survived childbirth often suffered from long-lasting and debilitating injuries that resulted from frequent pregnancies, deliveries, and abortions without sufficient medical care.[6]

The inaccessibility of medical care even in cases of serious disease contributed to high infant and maternal mortality rates. Poor roads often made even a distance of ten miles an insurmountable obstacle to medical care, and medical and nursing care was usually unattainable for women living outside of towns. In 1932, the Committee on the Costs of Medical Care issued a report entitled *Medical Care for the American People* that demonstrated that medical resources, while plentiful enough, were not distributed according to need, but rather according to patients' ability to pay for services. For instance, while New York, a relatively wealthy and urbanized state, boasted 1 physician for every 621 individuals, in extremely poor rural counties the physician-to-population ratio sometimes exceeded 1 to 20,000, and some areas had no practicing physicians at all. Furthermore, although southern state boards of health were responsible for serving black as well as white residents, they usually reserved services for whites. Until the late 1930s, poor southern blacks rarely received medical attention for any of their ailments, and many died without having once seen a physician.[7] As late as 1941, sociologists Arthur Raper and Ira Reid estimated that half of the South's people were unable to pay for medical care, leading one commentator to describe the South as "a belt of sickness, misery, and unnecessary death."[8]

Patients who had access to medical care often encountered doctors and nurses who lacked basic skills. Early-twentieth-century reports indicated the poor quality of American medical education in general and of education in obstetrics in particular. Without adequate teaching facilities, most schools trained students of obstetrics on mannequins. A 1912 survey found that in over half of the schools in the sample, students saw three or fewer cases of childbirth. As a result, more childbearing women died from improper obstetrical operations than from infections caused by midwives.[9] One critical physician accused his colleagues of frequently hastening labor, needlessly intervening in delivery, and disregarding the need for sterility. Careless physicians, he warned, not only contributed to maternal and infant mortality but also hurt the reputation of the entire medical profession.[10] No wonder, then, that many women showed little respect for physicians.[11]

Physicians concerned with improving their professional reputations and winning patients who normally used midwives as clients placed the brunt of the blame for high mortality on the presumed ignorance of black midwives and their poor black and white clients. "The disease that tops the list with us," one physician lamented, "is ignorance, complicated by poverty." He characterized most childbearing women unfavorably: "Their homes and labor beds are unbelievably unsterile. There are no screens and usually no lights. In other words, these pregnant women make little or no preparation for their delivery—by engaging a doctor, keeping their bodies in health, or preparing their delivery rooms."[12]

In the early twentieth century, health professionals began to single out lower infant mortality rates as an index of regional achievement and pride.[13] State boards of health adopted a variety of measures to improve infant and maternal health. Together with officials from the U.S. Children's Bureau, North Carolina's health officers and physicians developed a series of responses ranging from the establishment of infant and maternal health centers to the regulation of midwives. The state's interest in maternal and infant health grew out of state health officer Watson Smith Rankin's outreach efforts to improve the health of North Carolina's citizens. In 1920, the North Carolina State Board of Health began a systematic effort to instruct pregnant women and mothers throughout the state about the value of professional medical services. The Bureau of Maternity and Infancy sent out monthly letters to all expectant women reminding them of the role physicians should play in pregnancy and delivery.

Despite their attempts to convince mothers of the need for medical care, physicians recognized that many rural women, particularly in the South, would continue to hire midwives for their deliveries. In the 1930s, approximately one-third of the deliveries in North Carolina, for instance, were attended by midwives—69 percent of births among African American women and 12 percent of white births. So prevalent were midwives' services that in 1933 there were nearly twice as many midwives as physicians in the state. Midwives' reputation was inevitably linked to the fact that most of them were black women serving the black community. "Many of these women are ignorant and dirty," the director of the North Carolina Bureau of Maternity and Infancy, Dr. George H. Cooper, charged in a private letter.[14] In a public speech, he argued, "They represent the lowest class of midwives, and also their work [is] among the lowest and most sordid class of our population."[15]

Since they could not abolish midwifery, health officials hoped to train midwives and to exclude those whose skills they found unsatisfactory by instituting licensing requirements. With the 1921 passage of the Sheppard-Towner Act, which provided grants to states to meet the health needs of expectant mothers and newborns, the North Carolina State Board of Health began to organize maternal and infant health clinics for poor women. Nurses conducted classes on prenatal care and infant hygiene, made home visits to pregnant women and women with infants, and instructed midwives. In order to reach out to both black and white mothers, the state public health office also prodded county health departments to employ black nurses.[16] After the 1929 repeal of the Sheppard-Towner Act, however, funds from Washington were discontinued, and only a skeleton of the new services survived. Nevertheless, the state remained committed to improving maternal and infant health, and when, in the early 1930s, legislators cut appropriations to the State Board of Health by 55 percent, they still made a permanent appropriation for maternal and child health work. With the passage of the Social Security Act in 1935, officials developed a comprehensive statewide plan for maternity centers. County public health officials began to offer clinics for prenatal and postnatal care. By 1939, the State Board of Health had established prenatal centers in 43 out of 100 counties; these centers cared for about 16 percent of the state's pregnant women.[17]

Educating mothers and midwives and providing prenatal and postnatal care, however, could not solve the whole problem. Too-frequent and too-early pregnancies contributed to women's poor health and to high infant mortality rates. While the infant mortality rate for children born up to twelve months apart was 147 per 1,000 births, it sank to 98 or lower for children born more than twelve months apart.[18] Young mothers were at particular risk, and the low age of marriage in rural districts of the southern states exacerbated the problem. "I find these young girls distressingly ignorant of the means to protect themselves against untimely childbirth," one physician lamented. "Many of them have diseases which would make childbirth almost certain death."[19] There was only one solution to too-frequent pregnancies: contraception. Birth control instruction, health officials concluded, had to be an integral part of maternal and infant health programs.

While health and welfare professionals considered birth control essential, they assumed that poor women lacked both the intelligence and the motivation to use the diaphragm, the most effective contraceptive in the 1930s. Moreover, the diaphragm was relatively expensive. In the mid-1930s, a diaphragm and a tube of jelly cost from four to six dollars, and this excluded the cost of medical consultation and fitting. By comparison, a dollar purchased a dozen suppositories, ten foaming tablets, a dozen condoms, or up to three two-ounce douching units.[20] Historian Linda Gordon has pointed out that the diaphragm was a "rich-folks' contraceptive," difficult to use without privacy, running water, and a full explanation of fitting—luxuries not available to many American women.[21] Birth control nurse Doris Davidson bemoaned the problem to Elizabeth Barclay, field director of the American Birth Control League (ABCL).

> We all know the ever-present need for a simpler method for unintelligent, illiterate, lazy and poverty-stricken patients. Although the diaphragm method may provide greater safety in the hands of the intelligent patient, it often acts in just the opposite way in the hands of the unintelligent patient, no matter how carefully she may have been instructed. This type of patient, (and I am referring to the low-intelligent strata found by the hundred[s] in North Carolina, South Carolina, Tennessee and West Virginia) can learn a thing one moment and unlearn it the next with bewildering rapidity. Often by the time the poor creature has arrived back in her home, she is uncertain about technique and therefore hesitant in applying it. . . . If we are going to help this low-grade patient, do we not have to meet them on their own level?—give them something which is EASY for them to apply, and which they can readily understand?[22]

In order to reach the poor, health and welfare professionals advocated both the development of easy-to-use contraceptives and the distribution of birth control through public health channels. Fitting and educating women about the use of a diaphragm could take up to forty-five minutes, an amount of time most physicians were unwilling to spend on patients who could not pay for the consultation.[23] Researchers hoped to develop a birth control method so easy to employ that it could be used by patients who had neither the desire, the education, the privacy, nor the sanitary facilities to carry out more complicated procedures. Contraceptive foam powders and jellies met these conditions and had the additional advantage of making pelvic examinations, which were assumed to deter many women from seeking contraceptive advice, unnecessary. Although it was unclear whether these methods were as effective as the diaphragm, many researchers considered it more important to reach a large number of women than to provide the most reliable contraceptive. Davidson's letter continued: "There is the important problem of reaching MORE patients in a given time. With simpler methods, the reaching of greater numbers is assured. . . . If the jelly method or the sponge-foam method does not insure as high a degree of protection PER SE, the scales would be balanced, and more than balanced on the other hand because greater NUMBERS of patients would be reached and protected."[24]

■ Reaching the Poor: Family Planning in Public Health

Contraceptive field trials drove the development of public health birth control programs around the country. In 1923, Robert Latou Dickinson, a New York gynecologist who lobbied his colleagues to promote contraceptive and sex education, joined with Margaret Sanger in establishing the institutional framework for the distribution and testing of contraceptives. Together, they founded the National Committee for Maternal Health (NCMH) and the Birth Control Clinical Research Bureau and began to systematically test the efficiency of contraceptive products.

Funding for contraceptive research during the 1930s and 1940s was severely restricted, however, especially funding for the testing of simple contraceptives that could be delivered by nonmedical personnel. Early research in this area was financed by private individuals and philanthropists such as Clarence Gamble. Between 1930 and 1970, the social legitimacy of reproductive and contraceptive research increased, and after overpopulation was perceived as a social problem in the mid-1950s, more funding sources materialized. By the 1950s, contraceptive research programs had attracted the attention of corporate foundations, and by the 1960s they had the financial backing of the federal government. The proliferation of funding sources resulted in an explosion in the number of family planning programs and in the expansion of trials into developing countries. This change was accompanied by a shift toward more "respectable" contraceptive research that emphasized hormonal methods and methods requiring physician intervention. Delivery of services remained largely unregulated and continued to be driven by private, public, and nonprofit groups. It was at the intersection between contraceptive research and the welfare state that women negotiated for reproductive control.[25]

During the 1930s, when a vast array of commercial contraceptive products flooded the market, testing greatly expanded. Under the auspices of the NCMH, Clarence J. Gamble and others like him established birth control programs in some of North America's poorest regions. To receive contraceptives for a nominal fee, researchers entered into agreements with pharmaceutical companies to test their products. With the help of nurses and local doctors, such trials tested foam powder in North Carolina and Puerto Rico, condoms in the Appalachian Mountains, contraceptive jelly in Logan County, West Virginia, and, in the 1950s, the birth control pill in Kentucky and Puerto Rico. Health professionals tested a wide range of products, followed each other's progress, exchanged formulas, and recommended or discouraged the use of one product over another. Researchers commented on each other's tests and negotiated with doctors, nurses, and women over the policies and practices of contraceptive trials.[26] Scholars have often condemned the individuals who performed such testing for exploiting poor women as research subjects. Noting that the trials usually offered unreliable (and sometimes dangerous) contraceptives to women who were insufficiently informed about the risks and lacked access to alternative birth control methods, historians have remarked on the race and class politics involved.[27] But to dismiss the trials as exploitative is to fail to explain the appeal they held for the many women who decided to participate in them.

Researchers' zeal to develop simpler contraceptives was driven by the desire to help solve problems of poverty and poor health rather than the wish to provide women with greater self-determination.[28] Their emphasis on the simplicity of the method, moreover, meant both that research was driven by stereotypes about poor women and that it further reinforced those stereotypes. Researchers' focus on the development of cheaper and more "effective" contraceptives meant that the reduction of the birthrate, rather than the improvement of women's health and self-determination, became the measure of success. In fact, the bias in favor of simpler birth control methods worked as a strong counterforce to the development of health and support services that might have increased women's reproductive control. Researchers and health professionals assumed that if simple methods failed in clinical trials, women's lack of intelligence, rather than the poor quality of the method or the lack of other support systems, was to blame.

One of the most active physician-researchers during the 1930s was Florida physician Lydia DeVilbiss. In 1929, she opened her Mothers' Health Clinic in Miami and began to advise black and white clients in the use of birth control while testing both folk remedies and commercial contraceptive products. Throughout the 1930s, DeVilbiss tested the use of condoms, the withdrawal method, suppositories, jelly, douches, pessaries, IUDs, and the sponge and foam powder method. In addition, she offered sterilizations and vasectomies and searched for a form of contraceptive immunization.[29]

DeVilbiss began to offer her services during a period of rising poverty and diminishing resources. During the 1920s, and particularly after the onset of the Great Depression in 1929, most poor and minority women lacked the financial resources to seek medical care even during pregnancy and delivery. A single serious illness could plunge families into irretrievable indebtedness. Even if families called a doctor, they were frequently unable to follow the recommended therapies or to pay for any follow-up visits. Poverty also limited women's ability to obtain birth control, sterilization, and illegal abortion. Frequent pregnancies, deliveries, and abortions without sufficient medical care increased the odds of miscarriage and other "female troubles" and contributed to high maternal mortality rates.

Throughout the Great Depression, DeVilbiss searched for ways to provide patients with otherwise inaccessible care and lobbied for the integration of birth control advice into public health and public welfare services. While she repeatedly complained that poor and minority women lacked the interest or the intelligence necessary to prevent conception, her belief in African Americans' inferior intelligence did not interfere with her firm commitment to provide equal access to services; in fact, it might account for her commitment.[30] To advise those who lacked transportation or child care, DeVilbiss sent visiting nurses into the homes of poor women. Since the commercially available products were too expensive for her patients, DeVilbiss drew up her own substitutes and, in cooperation with Philip Stoughton, a commercial supplier of contraceptive jellies, foam powders, and sponges, developed a foam powder that she reported was enormously successful.[31] At the request of several prominent African Americans, she opened a clinic in Miami's black neighborhood in 1935 and employed a black female physician to run it. In the mid-1930s, when due to the overcrowding of city and county hospitals many of her patients who wanted sterilizations were unable to get them, DeVilbiss began to experiment with cauterization as a form of sterilization.[32]

DeVilbiss's services constituted the only source of health care and contraceptive advice for many Florida women. By the mid-1930s, she was serving 1,490 white and 765 black patients in Miami and had opened additional clinics in West Palm Beach, Sarasota, and Tampa. Many of her patients lived in extreme poverty and under conditions that discouraged the regular use of birth control. Clinic progress reports contain repeated references to patients who had lost all their belongings, including their birth control supplies, when a storm swept their houses away.[33] While clients' poverty made it easy for DeVilbiss to take advantage of women's vulnerable position and to use them to test new contraceptives, it also meant that DeVilbiss's services and commitment to accessible contraceptive care were crucial to her patients. Although it is unclear how DeVilbiss treated her patients, her services were badly needed, and her practice was extremely busy. The fact that African American community leaders approached DeVilbiss rather than another Miami physician to open a birth control clinic in the black neighborhood indicates both their limited choices and their expectation that DeVilbiss's services, regardless of their potential drawbacks, could be of value to the African American community. At the same time, the fact that she withdrew funding from the clinic for African American women after it had been in operation for only two years points to the limits of her clients' influence over the services she offered. Her expressions of disappointment in "southern darkies" and her belief that they could only work under white supervision make clear that the provision of valuable services could go hand in hand with racist attitudes.[34]

DeVilbiss's willingness to provide a range of contraceptive services, however, was the exception during the early 1930s. Until 1936, access to contraceptives and the research of new devices was hampered by the Comstock Law. All this changed with the 1936 decision in *United States v. One Package of Japanese Pessaries*, which legalized the distribution of contraceptives. The U.S. Court of Appeals ruled that the medical prescription of contraception for the purpose of saving a life or promoting the well-being of women was not condemned under the Comstock Act. The decision had tremendous ramifications for the establishment of birth control services throughout the country. Finally, individual health professionals as well as state and federal government agencies felt that they could get involved in family planning, even if it was only on an unofficial basis. The court decision was followed by the establishment of state birth control

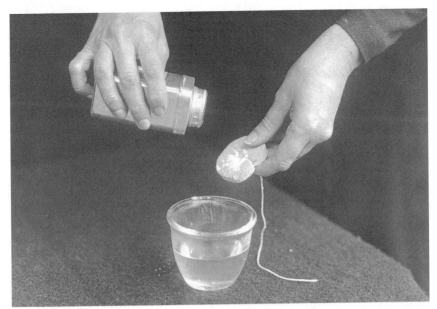

Sponge and foam powder. (Courtesy of Countway Medical Library)

services in North Carolina, South Carolina, and Alabama, the extension of birth control services by the Farm Security Administration, and the development of a new mode of testing: large-scale contraceptive field trials.

In 1937, Boston philanthropist and birth control activist Dr. Clarence Gamble approached North Carolina health officials to discuss a marriage between contraceptive research and a public health birth control program. Gamble had developed a spermicidal foam powder that, if applied to a moist sponge and inserted into the vagina before intercourse, promised to provide an easy method of birth control. Looking for a rural area in which to test his contraceptive, he offered to pay the salary of a nurse who would carry out birth control work if the North Carolina State Board of Health would promote the use of his foam powder through local public health centers. In March 1937, Gamble employed Frances R. Pratt as his nurse, and Pratt set out to organize birth control programs in North Carolina's public health clinics. "It was like manna from the sky," one social worker rejoiced.[35]

North Carolina was among the first locations of Gamble's large-scale research projects in population planning, and the project encapsulated his multifaceted involvement in the politics of reproduction. Born in 1894 in Cincinnati, Ohio, Gamble grew up with his three siblings in a family that was a pillar of Cincinnati society. He went to Princeton and to Harvard

Medical School. Upon graduation, he won one of the most coveted internships at Massachusetts General Hospital under Richard Cabot, the father of medical social work. Influenced by his parents' model of Christian stewardship, Gamble decided that a research career would provide him with the best opportunities to dedicate his life to human service. His inheritance made it possible for him to define his own research interests, while science promised to offer him a means of establishing an identity and a sense of worth.[36]

Two principles guided Gamble's career in birth control: a firm belief in eugenics and a desire to stretch his philanthropic financial contributions as far as possible. Gamble believed that the differential fertility between classes was a fundamental source of social disorder. Birth control and sterilization, he argued, would strike at the root of the matter. Throughout his life, he supported both eugenic sterilization and the development of simple contraceptive methods, which he thought more suitable for poor women than the diaphragm. In fact, as a fervent eugenicist, Gamble not only promoted contraceptives to reduce the reproduction of the poor but also offered cash prizes to those Harvard College alumni with the largest number of children.[37] Foam powder, Gamble argued, could be dispensed by nurses or social workers rather than physicians, reducing the overall cost of providing birth control and increasing the number of women who could be reached with the same amount of money.

Throughout his career, Gamble participated in almost every important experiment in population control and initiated, organized, or financed a considerable number of them. The effectiveness of his work, however, was limited by his impatience, his abrasive style, and his prejudices against those of other social classes and cultures. Eager to support programs when he saw fit, Gamble frequently clashed with officials of the national birth control organizations whose priorities did not always match his own. While his independent wealth allowed him to bypass other birth control activists with whom he disagreed, his tendency to strike out on his own if projects did not go according to his wishes led to constant tension within the movement. In addition, his effectiveness as an engineer of social change was held back by his lack of empathy for and understanding of the poor women who were the potential users of his products. Personal research interests dominated his approach to the work and blinded him to the needs of the poor. The programs he supported mirrored his approach, focusing on statistical results while ignoring the health needs of poor women.

North Carolina's birth control program spread rapidly during the first

Clarence J. Gamble.
(Courtesy of Countway
Medical Library)

two years. With the permission of state health officers, Frances Pratt
traveled from county to county seeking to convince local public health
officials to incorporate the distribution of contraceptive foam powder and
sponges into their regular health department activities. Health officials
who agreed to cooperate made a request for funding to the State Board of
Health, which in turn provided the money to inaugurate the program in
that county. Health officials received free supplies of foam powder and
were asked to collect data on its acceptability and reliability. Although
clinics were free to advise women in the use of other birth control methods, all but one clinic offered foam powder only.[38] Pratt instructed county
public health nurses in using the powder, and they held birth control
clinics for mothers at public health department offices. By March 1938, the
State Board of Health operated 36 birth control clinics in 33 of the state's
100 counties and had reached 641 women. One year later, the state had 62
centers in 60 counties serving 2,000 patients, and by 1946, 93 counties
participated in the contraceptive tests. Of 478 birth control clinics reported in the United States in December 1938, 97 were public health department clinics, and more than half of those were located in North Carolina.[39]

To emphasize the legitimacy of their work, officials described the dis-

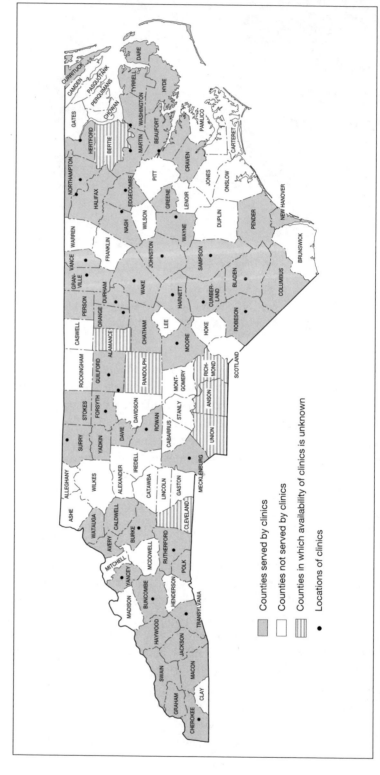

North Carolina counties with birth control services, 1939.

Counties served by clinics

Counties not served by clinics

Counties in which availability of clinics is unknown

• Locations of clinics

tribution of birth control in the objective language of science while dis-associating it from any notion of women's self-determination. Birth control, they argued, was a service as essential to the protection of women's reproductive health as any other medical procedure. Any association with Margaret Sanger and the national birth control organizations, they feared, would mark the birth control program as a radical attempt to encourage women to cease childbearing altogether. For North Carolinians, sponsorship by Gamble was crucial to dissociating the work from Sanger. Dr. George Cooper explained the situation to the president of the West Virginia League for Planned Parenthood:

> There could be an infinite amount of trouble in administering this program if it were in the hands of fanatical people or propagandists and people who lack sound medical information and judgment. We have quietly assumed and published the fact that this part of the program of public health work is just one small item but an important item and that the work of this character for married women is just as important . . . to protect her health and maybe her life as it would be to do a curettage or sew up a lacerated cervix. In other words, as long as the program is held on a sound scientific public health and medical basis, it cannot be criticized.[40]

Birth control, health officials emphasized, was not intended to offer an alternative to motherhood. Rather, it promoted healthy mothers.

As public health officials in North Carolina negotiated with Gamble about birth control, the federal government, too, opened the door to family planning. Officials of the Farm Security Administration—one of several New Deal agencies whose purpose it was to provide for the "bottom third" of Americans—turned to the BCFA to help finance an FSA contraceptive program.[41] And in 1937, FSA agents, home supervisors, and public health nurses began to offer contraceptive advice to their clients and to residents in migrant labor camps across the country. Since the U.S. government did not officially endorse birth control services, the program ran semiofficially. One FSA official put it this way: "We are doing this service as emissaries of the Lord, if you please, and never as emissaries of Uncle Sam, who does not officially know we are doing it."[42]

Farm Security Administration officials, too, encouraged the distribution of contraceptives as part of a larger preventive and educational program for their clients. The integration of birth control advice into public health programs, officials held, served as evidence of a "civilized, enlightened and a forward-looking citizenship" that knew to turn to science and medicine to cope with urgent public health needs.[43] Both FSA officials and North Carolina public health officials stressed the medical and eugenic contributions of birth control. To be eligible for the programs, women had to be indigent.[44] In addition, public health nurses and FSA agents trying to identify potential clients for contraceptive advice were to evaluate the individuals' family histories for insanity, feeblemindedness, and epilepsy; to look for the presence of syphilis, gonorrhea, and tuberculosis; and to consider whether a mother's physical condition might improve with family planning. Patients had to be married, and if they were in basically good health, to already have several children, usually three or four. Women with medical problems that made pregnancy dangerous were considered to be ideal patients. The *North Carolina Health Bulletin* portrayed women who "pleaded for contraceptive advice" as victimized by health hazards to which they had been "exposed by contraceptive innocence." Articles described patients with epilepsy, patients who had had "13 pregnancies and only 4 living children," and patients who were in their "10th pregnancy and bedridden with cardio-renal disease," as well as patients who had been inmates of mental institutions, patients whose husbands were convicted criminals, and patients whose husbands suffered from alcoholism or chronic diseases.[45]

The tension between the progressive spirit and the conservative distrust of direct government aid to the poor influenced early birth control programs. While the prolonged nature of the Great Depression and rising government spending for relief led many to worry about the creation of a permanent relief class, controlling the birthrate of families on relief promised to keep the growing welfare state in check. George H. Lawrence, professor of social work at the University of North Carolina and a fervent advocate of birth control, described concerns about the swelling welfare rolls in an early call for support for birth control:

> Relief families are reproducing out of all proportion to the general population. . . . Leaders in every field are becoming more verbal and outspoken. "Isn't it true that relief families as a group have an extremely high birth rate?" "Isn't the government feeding and maintaining large numbers of families whose outstanding characteristic is that they are producing more babies than ever before?" "Doesn't this mean increased dependency, more suffering, and an even greater tax burden?" "Doesn't this state of affairs add to the despair of such families and create a situation where it is less probable that they can be rehabilitated?"[46]

Whatever the health-related benefits of public birth control services, health and welfare professionals made it clear that such services also made economic sense.

Moreover, officials argued that birth control played a crucial role in helping the poor escape poverty. Family limitation, they held, was necessary for economic rehabilitation. "There are three major factors working against rehabilitation," one farm supervisor remarked: "drought, grasshoppers, and babies." She continued, "This program holds out hope as nothing else has. The first two factors are seasonal, but we have had a year round season of pregnancies."[47] In fact, FSA leaders considered medical care programs in general to be a vital element in the agency's overall rehabilitation mandate. One FSA pamphlet put it this way: "A family in good health was a better credit risk than a family in bad health. So far as the government was concerned the program was simply a matter of good business."[48]

Despite their concern about births among the poor, officials felt that economic hardship alone should not disqualify parents from bearing and raising children. Thoughtful and responsible parents at any economic level, they argued, should be able to plan for families of at least three or four children.[49] Parents should not cease to reproduce, but should limit their families to a size that would allow them to provide financial security to all of their children.

Despite officials' often disparaging attitude, many poor women not only appreciated the contraceptive advice they received but were able to exert some influence over the distribution of contraceptives. Those who received birth control within the context of a research trial often feared the termination of the trial; the tests, after all, provided them with both their only access to contraceptives and at least a minimum of health care. When Lena Hillard began to distribute condoms as part of the Watauga County study, many of the women she approached were eager for birth control information. Indeed, despite the fact that condoms suffered from a bad reputation, women in about 50 percent of the households she visited agreed to participate in the trial.[50] Interest rose even more with the American entry into World War II. "Since the rubber shortage," one report noted, "we can hardly keep Trojans!" The author continued, "I wouldn't be surprised if our patients aren't hoarding them."[51]

Frequently, women behaved as educated consumers, complaining about side effects, comparing contraceptives, and demanding one birth control method over another. Migrant women in Arizona's FSA camps, for instance, did "not like diaphragms, reporting *always* inability to buy jelly, and frequently 'discomfort,' 'stuffiness,' or actual pain."[52] Some contraceptive researchers took women's complaints seriously, modifying the formulas of contraceptive jelly or foam powder to reduce irritation and increase women's comfort with the methods. Lydia DeVilbiss, for instance, carefully examined patients, questioned them closely about their experiences with contraceptives, and hired her own pharmacist to test and change formulas as she found it necessary.[53] Officials at other clinics, however, lacked equipment and staff to perform gynecological examinations and investigate the causes of women's dissatisfaction.

Even when they participated in large field trials, women were sometimes able to influence trial procedures. Having learned from neighbors and from Hillard herself that Hillard distributed not only condoms but also foam powder and jelly, women regularly demanded the contraceptive of their choice, regardless of research protocol.[54] While some such demands reflected women's personal preferences, patients also responded to recommendations from neighbors and friends. Figuring that it was more important to help women prevent conception than to fulfill the formal requirements of the field trial, Hillard and her assistant occasionally deviated from the protocol, allowing women to continue the use of condoms rather than switch to foam powder.[55] At other times, however, both the nurses and the patients felt painfully restricted by trial regulations. Hillard, who discovered that her own reputation and trustworthiness was closely tied to the quality of the birth control method she distributed, found the fact that she had to distribute an unreliable contraceptive so unbearable that she contemplated quitting her work. The news of method failure traveled quickly and immediately influenced women's choices. After finding four of her foam powder patients pregnant, Hillard complained to Gamble that such results would make it difficult for her to convince women to use foam powder. Having been left at the age of sixteen to care for ten younger siblings when her mother died in childbirth, Hillard understood how tragic another pregnancy could be and was likely to empathize with her clients. "There are many cases that can not easily forgive a nurse who gives a poor material for such a very, very important purpose," she reminded Gamble. "It is very tragic for some mothers to get pregnant. . . . In all cases they have been nice to me but I had rather have them not so nice and keep the confidence they have had in me." Hillard asked Gamble to "reconsider" his decision to stick with the foam powder tests, and she threatened, "If you don't I may quit and raise babies and rabbits. . . . Maybe it is time for me to quit when we can't agree any more."[56]

Lena Hillard in the mid-1930s.
(Courtesy of Amy Scott)

A nurse's control over her work was limited by the goals of the researchers directing the program. Gamble's interest in the Watauga project was not in the prevention of pregnancies but in the testing of contraceptives. "It is disappointing to hear the pregnancies are developing in the group of mothers using foam powder," he responded to Hillard. But he continued: "I don't think, though, that the time has yet come to switch to another method. . . . It's very important to have enough mothers and enough time in your series. In previous tests it has never been possible to say whether the pregnancies were due to failure to use the method or failure of the method to protect. . . . If the foam powder is found to be an unsatisfactory method that will protect a lot of mothers from being given it. If it turns out reasonably well it may make it possible to furnish many mothers protection who otherwise wouldn't have any."[57]

Assumptions about poor women's inability to use contraceptives properly were pervasive, and they tainted health authorities' interactions with clients. Although many of the methods were still experimental, researchers and health officials tended to blame patients for the methods' failure rather than to question method effectiveness. In fact, the research protocol for the Watauga study specified that Hillard should record method failure as a failure of the patient even if the patient claimed to have used the method consistently and correctly: "If the patient conceived while using contraception, that is, without having stopped [the use of the contraceptive], then she 'failed' whether she used it regularly or not."[58] Although clients repeatedly complained to county health officials about the high rate of failure and the unpleasant side effects of the foam powder, and although the majority of clinics eventually switched to diaphragms, state health officer Roy Norton concluded in 1957 that the main cause of failure continued to be the patients' neglect or carelessness.[59] Health professionals' prejudices and lack of both trust and interest in clients contributed to their indifference to their patients' well-being, ultimately raising the risk that they would jeopardize women's health. Occasionally, bad experiences with contraceptive tests led women to distrust the medical profession as a whole. Physician Virginia South, for instance, who traveled the Appalachian Mountains for the BCFA to educate women about contraception, reported that one of her patients refused to use the foam powder South distributed because the patient thought it might be an experiment.[60] Since many researchers assumed that women lacked intelligence, they failed to recognize that their research subjects were no less compliant than research subjects in other medical trials. Indeed, many women did pay attention to the instructions on contraceptive use and became conscientious users.

If mothers feared receiving unreliable contraceptives, many feared the termination of the field tests even more. For those women for whom field tests represented their only access to birth control, the completion of a trial could have devastating consequences. Lena Hillard reported of one mother who had heard, incorrectly, that Hillard had stopped doing birth control work: "She told her husband that she would simply catch a hen and take it to the store and sell it in order to get money to buy some Trojans." Hillard commented: "It is true that a lot of our mothers are not financially able to pay $.50 for three Trojans. Yet, it is encouraging to see that some will be willing to sacrifice their chickens and eggs in order to stop babies from coming."[61]

Researchers rarely addressed the ethical issues involved in the termination of contraceptive trials. Gamble and Gilbert Beebe, a demographer hired by Gamble to help with the design of contraceptive field tests, were not only unconcerned with women's access to birth control after the completion of the tests but also saw it as their responsibility to cease distribution of the contraceptives. Beebe assured public health authorities in North Carolina on this point: "When the experiment reaches a conclusion, the present service will terminate, having provided useful data for health officers and others interested in contraceptive service from the standpoint of methods. What the Board of Health might then undertake in the area would, of course, be a matter for the Board to decide. . . . The public health responsibilities in North Carolina lie with the Board, with yourself and others of official position. It goes without saying that we have no right, and I may say that we have no desire, to operate a service which you feel threatens your work."[62]

But not all researchers showed such a lack of concern for women's ability to prevent conception. Occasionally, researchers acknowledged that contraceptives had become central to women's lives and felt responsible for the reproductive futures of the women who had been willing to test their products. When Raymond Squier of the National Committee for Maternal Health made preparations for the conclusion of a contraceptive jelly trial in Logan County, West Virginia, he planned for the continuation of birth control advice to trial participants. The Logan County trials ran from June 1936 to August 1939 and were the largest field trials of a chemical contraceptive ever completed in the United States; they involved 1,345 women. Squier reported to local health authorities in Logan County: "Although our project has been scientific, as an experiment in population, not for contraceptive services as such, we are keenly aware that we have been instrumental in acquainting a number of women with what virtually is a new way of life, so far as control of reproduction is concerned. In other words, there are women in Logan County who through us have come to rely upon contraceptive jelly for the spacing or avoidance of pregnancy, and who want to have the availability of this material continued. We think, and hope that you will agree, that it is humane and proper that such women continue to use this material if they so desire."[63] Squier went on to suggest that the NCMH should supply every physician in Logan County with free contraceptive jelly to distribute to women who asked for it. Physicians would be encouraged to charge women twenty-five cents per tube, with the money to be retained by the physician in appreciation for his cooperation. The fee would also, Squier noted, "induce a desirable psychological effect on the applicants."[64] It is an ironic sign of the delicate relationship between private physicians and contraceptive researchers that the women who had lent their bodies for testing were now to be asked to pay a fee for the jelly, while Logan County's private physicians were to receive what amounted to a financial reward for tolerating birth control.

■ African Americans and the Birth Control Movement

If birth control services for white women were fraught with stereotypes about poor women's presumed inability to use birth control properly, prejudices about black women's lack of intelligence frequently reinforced health officials' belief that funding birth control programs in black communities was a waste of money altogether. Many philanthropists and health professionals believed that African Americans lacked the intellectual capacity to use any form of birth control. Elsie Wulkop, a social worker who collaborated with Gamble to establish small contraceptive field trials, commented on the attempt to educate African Americans about birth control, "It impresses me as being almost like trying to get sheer animals to conform."[65] Clarence Gamble, Frances Pratt, and many public health officials assumed that black women lacked the intelligence to use anything but the simplest contraceptives. Even sympathetic professionals regularly assumed that African Americans were not interested in birth control and would not avail themselves of the methods because they were too complicated, or that patients would not accept or carry out recommendations.[66] Frequently, such attitudes provided an excuse for the absence of programs for African Americans.

Sources indicate that some health officials might have found birth control programs appealing as a form of population control. One article suggested that birth control programs were targeting the poor and uneducated. "The South," the article announced, "is teaching birth control on tobacco road and [in] mill village alley."[67] Another much-cited 1939 article recounted that one county health officer in North Carolina did not think his county needed contraception. The author reported: "He was asked to check his vital statistics. When he discovered that Negroes were accounting for 85 percent of the births he quickly changed his mind."[68]

Most health officials, however, thought it unnecessary to provide any services at all for African Americans. As a result, African Americans were more likely to be underserved than to be the target of population control programs.[69] While two-thirds of North Carolina's counties had at least one birth control center by November 1939, the counties with large African American populations had fewer centers than the rest of the state.[70] In some county health departments, it was left to the few black public health nurses—in 1950 less than 1 percent of North Carolina's nurses—to provide maternal and infant health services to black clients.[71] Some officials cited white clients' refusal to attend the same facilities as blacks as an excuse for excluding African Americans from services. Others offered segregated services in the hope that such accommodation to local customs would attract the largest number of both black and white clients.[72] In times of scarce resources, however, health officials not only deemed any allocation for African Americans unnecessary but also feared that allocating scarce funds to African Americans would provoke opposition. When the BCFA offered North Carolina health officials funds to sponsor a birth control pilot project for the black community in 1939, Dr. George Cooper declined them, saying, "A public health program limited to the Negro race will most certainly stimulate opposition to the entire project."[73] In other words, contraceptive programs were a valued service, and like all other valued services they were reserved disproportionately for whites.

To control their reproduction, African American women were even more dependent on home remedies and on abortion than white women were. Until the mid-1940s, the black press printed copious mail-order advertisements for douche powders, suppositories, preventive antiseptics, and vaginal jellies that promised to destroy "foreign germs." In addition, black couples relied on over-the-counter one-size diaphragms marketed under the name "Lanteen," on the placing of petroleum jelly and quinine over the uterus, and on withdrawal. The lack of reliable birth control information meant that many African American women limited the number of their children by resorting to illegal abortion.[74]

While black women found it harder to gain access to birth control than white women did, their greater poverty and poor health made frequent pregnancies even more dangerous and meant that they were more likely than whites to need contraceptive services. Black mothers died at twice the rate of white mothers. Out of 250,000 African American babies born alive each year in the early 1940s, more than 22,000 died in their first year of life, a rate 60 percent higher than that for white babies. Syphilis—which caused 25 percent of the 18,000 stillbirths among African American women each year—and tuberculosis were five to six times as prevalent among African Americans as they were among whites.[75] Black physician Dorothy Ferebee warned: "The Negro is saddled with problems of disease, poverty, and discrimination which menace not only his welfare, but the welfare of America. The existing medical and socio-economic problems of the Negro race are, therefore, problems of the nation."[76]

Ferebee and other African American professionals looked to birth control for an answer to such pressing health problems. While black physicians warned that birth control could not cure all of the health and economic problems facing African Americans, they insisted that spacing births could reduce the maternal and infant death rates, improve maternal health, reduce the spread of venereal and other diseases, and raise the standard of living by enabling parents to adjust family size to match family income. Pregnancy spacing, Ferebee promised, would "do much towards general welfare improvement" and would be "a major step towards health and happiness."[77]

Within the black community, however, birth control was a controversial subject. Black nationalists such as Marcus Garvey argued that the strength of the African American community lay in its numbers and charged birth control programs for blacks with race suicide.[78] Nevertheless, many black health and welfare professionals advocated the use of birth control and assured African Americans that it was not the goal of planned parenthood "to limit the number of Negro births in this country, but to assure the birth of more healthy babies who [would] live to grow up."[79]

Starting in the 1920s and accelerating in the 1930s, African American laywomen, with the help of black health professionals, forged the National Negro Health Movement to address the dire health needs in black communities. Activists cleaned black neighborhoods, repaired buildings, educated black communities about health issues, and conducted health clinics, examinations, and inoculations. They also pushed public health services to hire African American nurses and physicians. In the 1920s, funding from the Sheppard-Towner Act allowed public health programs across the country to increase the number of salaried public health nurses considerably. Indeed, due to the progressive leadership of Watson Smith Rankin, in North Carolina this expansion had already started in the 1910s and included the hiring of black public health nurses. By 1917, the state health department listed ten African American public health nurses, and by the early 1920s, virtually every county health department employed one or two black nurses.[80] With the onset of the Great Depression, interest in black health activism increased. The federal government institutionalized black health work as part of the New Deal with the establishment of the Office of Negro Health Work and paved the way for growing interaction between government and private initiatives in black health. Funding from the Julius Rosenwald Fund, for instance, enabled state health departments in Virginia to hire black public health nurses. These women played a key role in organizing health clubs and establishing maternal and infant health clinics for black mothers.[81]

While segregation and discrimination continued to bar black women in most parts of the country from access to contraceptive services, in some locations community efforts led to the establishment of a remarkable system of integrated care for black and white mothers. One birth control nurse reported that the state of Virginia in general, and Dixie Hospital in Elizabeth City in particular, had a reputation for having "the best inter-racial spirit."[82] The hospital of the University of Virginia in Charlottesville offered contraceptive services to black and white women. In Atlanta, black and white women could seek birth control information from the Atlanta Tuberculosis Association, the Good Samaritan Clinic, and the Wesley Memorial Hospital at Emory University. With the help of the BCFA, citizens in Asheville, North Carolina, Roanoke, Virginia, and Wheeling, West Virginia, established services for both white and black patients in 1930. In Florida, Lydia DeVilbiss offered birth control advice to black and white women starting in 1929 and, at the request of the black community, opened a clinic in Miami's black neighborhood in 1935. And when in the late 1930s North Carolina and South Carolina began to deliver contraceptive services through their county public health clinics, they offered these services to both black and white women. Black women's need for health services was so great that they tended to take advantage of birth control clinics regardless of any contempt or paternalism they might have encountered there. Moreover, public health officials found that black patients tended to maintain better contact with clinics than did white patients. Still, one observer noted that the clinics established for black women were really "a 'drop in the bucket,'" as the South was "so vast in its area and its need . . . so very great."[83]

Aware of the tremendous health and contraceptive needs of black women, Margaret Sanger secured funding to launch an educational campaign among African Americans. In 1938, she convinced Albert Lasker, a medical philanthropist, to donate $20,000 for the establishment of a Division of Negro Services (DNS) within the BCFA. From the very beginning, however, Sanger's vision of the so-called Negro Project clashed with the BCFA's. Sanger envisioned a broad grassroots campaign under the direction of African Americans that would educate the members of black communities about birth control, allowing them to start their own services independent of potentially hostile whites.[84] Once out of Sanger's hands, however, the project became, according to Linda Gordon, a "microcosm of the elitist birth-control programs whose design eliminated the possibility of popular, grassroots involvement in birth control as a cause."[85] Federation officials and Gamble did more than resist African American control of the project. Gamble argued explicitly for the need to control the reproduction of poor African Americans: "The mass of Negroes, particularly in the South, still breed carelessly and disastrously, with the result that the increase among Negroes, even more than among whites, is from that portion of the population least intelligent and fit, and least able to rear children properly."[86] Rather than invest in a grassroots education campaign, the BCFA followed Gamble's advice and established "demonstration clinics." Such clinics, in offering birth control services to black women, served as a kind of social science laboratory, demonstrating that even African Americans could be taught how to use birth control successfully and confirming the value of birth control in improving health conditions among blacks.[87] Sanger found this approach both narrow and outside the realm of the federation's responsibilities. Feeling that there was no further need to demonstrate black women's ability to use contraceptives, she concluded: "The idea of nurses going out to send mothers to the South Carolina birth control centers just makes me laugh. The state should be doing that at its own expense."[88]

Despite Sanger's opposition, the BCFA launched demonstration clinics in eastern South Carolina's Berkeley County and in Nashville, Tennessee, in 1940. The economic and health conditions of African Americans were poor in both locations. Berkeley County had a population of about twenty-seven thousand people, 70 percent of them African American; the majority of them were tenant farmers with an average cash income of less than $100 per year. Illiteracy rates were high, nobody subscribed to magazines or newspapers, and very few homes had a radio. Since the typical home was more than five miles from a paved road, and thus during the rainy season homes were nearly inaccessible, most residents lacked access to Berkeley County's public health clinics.[89] Nashville—home to Meharry Medical School, which trained over 50 percent of the nation's black physicians— had a death rate among African Americans twice as high as that of the white population. Incidence of both tuberculosis and syphilis among African Americans was mounting in Nashville, and the health conditions of black residents in the city approximated those of African Americans in the nation as a whole. Rather than establish new services, the DNS demonstration clinics expanded previously existing services in the hope of reaching larger numbers of African Americans.[90] Over the course of the following two years, the two Nashville clinics, staffed by black physicians, averaged a total of six monthly clinic sessions and advised a total of 638 women, while Berkeley County nurses held an average of eight monthly clinic sessions and advised 1,008 women. Both projects relied mainly on the sponge and foam powder method, although both also advised some women in the use of contraceptive jelly.[91]

The birth control services established as part of the Negro Project had a profound impact on many women in Nashville and Berkeley County. For most patients, these services represented their first contact with the medical profession, and the physical examinations they received revealed a number of serious health conditions. Pelvic disorders, syphilis, and anemia were common, and many of the patients were referred to family physicians or hospital clinics for further treatment.[92]

Health officials and the BCFA considered the demonstration project a success. By the end of the testing period, 520 women in Berkeley County and Lee County, South Carolina, and 354 women in Nashville had succeeded in preventing pregnancy during the previous twelve to eighteen months. Women, officials in South Carolina reported, had cooperated fully with the program and were so eager and grateful that health officials had trouble meeting the demand for services. Since the Nashville women were on average twenty-four years old, had already had 3.89 pregnancies, and had 3.12 living children by the time they reached the clinics, many felt strongly about the prevention of further pregnancies. The final report praised the two demonstration projects for proving "that properly guided child spacing measures [could] be practiced by even the most disadvantaged groups and that they [would]: bolster maternal and child health, reduce high death rates among mothers and children, check the spread of venereal and other diseases, help lift the family standard of living . . . [and] raise the health standards of the whole community." It concluded, "The cost of extending public health programs to include child spacing services is minute when weighed against the possible ultimate price of impaired health, delinquency, dependency, and death."[93]

Although health officials and the BCFA considered the Negro Project a success, a number of problems contributed both to a low number of patients at the Nashville clinics and a high dropout rate at both locations. Within two years, 45 percent of the Nashville women had dropped out of the program, and in Berkeley County the dropout rate reached 70 percent after eighteen months. Bad roads, bad weather, and a lack of transportation, clothing, and child care prevented many mothers from reaching the birth control clinics. Fearing opposition, moreover, health officials refused to publicize the services, and many women never learned about their existence. Clinic attendance in Nashville rose when officials began to provide transportation and child care and adjusted clinic hours to accommodate patients' work schedules.

The sudden cancellation of the Berkeley County demonstration project indicates that white health officials continued to view contraceptive and medical services to African Americans as dispensable. While it is unclear what happened to the demonstration project in Nashville, Robert Seibels, the director of the South Carolina program, concluded at the end of eighteen months that he had demonstrated the success of the Berkeley County clinic, and he discontinued the project. Remarking on the achievements of the program, the program report concluded of the 302 remaining participants: "The majority could have been kept active if there had been sufficient field force to keep in touch with them and see that they were supplied with materials."[94] With Seibels's termination of services, however, field force and supplies were no longer available, and the 302 women were left with only those rudimentary services that had proven so inadequate prior to the establishment of the demonstration clinic. By 1942, a report indicated that officials at only fourteen of fifty-two public health clinics in South Carolina had met with BCFA representatives in the previous three years to discuss contraceptive programs. Between 1939 and 1942, public health officials had referred fewer than five patients per county annually to contraceptive clinics. Only half of these patients had, to the knowledge of local officials, received satisfactory attention.[95]

Such a halfhearted approach to providing contraceptive services for the black community was the rule rather than the exception. White professionals who sponsored birth control services for African Americans repeatedly changed their minds about these services and terminated financial support for a variety of reasons.[96] Even when clinics did not close down, a lack of funding often forced them to provide inadequate services. A 1945 report on the Harlem Clinic noted that its planned parenthood work "was far from adequate." It explained: "The majority of Harlem residents are not aware of the Center's existence. Clinic sessions, three each week of two hours each, are insufficient for the number of patients who wish to use the services. . . . At the present time many persons who come seeking service find that the Center is closed or that the telephone is unanswered and give up in their attempt."[97] The clinic was not simply hard to reach. It also lacked publicity and formal agreements with local hospitals and physicians to ensure that postpartum patients or women with medical problems in need of contraceptive advice would be referred to it. Moreover, the clinic was understaffed and only able to provide the most basic services to clients. This might have been sufficient for experienced contraceptive users, but it was inadequate for women whose health problems, educational backgrounds, and personal situations required more intensive attention to make them successful birth control users. The mere existence of a clinic guaranteed neither access to contraceptives nor quality service.

Aware of shortcomings in existing clinics and of the need to do more, black professionals welcomed the services offered by the DNS and actively participated in them. Aside from establishing demonstration clinics, the DNS also conducted extensive educational programs, contacting African American physicians, nurses, teachers, and other professionals around the country to offer technical and professional materials for contraceptive education and services. In addition, the DNS publicized family planning through black schools and colleges, the Urban League, the National Association for the Advancement of Colored People (NAACP), the National Council of Negro Women, and other civic groups, and it also prepared materials for the black press. African Americans welcomed these services and took advantage of them, and black health professionals volunteered to accept patients needing free child-spacing assistance.[98] "I do not know of any movement that is more worthy of support than this one," one African American FSA field worker in North Carolina wrote to Sanger. "None of us want 'Race Suicide' but 'Planned Parent-Hood' I think is the logical thing to do. I should appreciate you sending me a list of Negro physicians in North Carolina and county health officers, and any special literature for Negroes that might be available. You may depend on my cooperation."[99]

In addition, African American health and welfare professionals frequently challenged their white colleagues to do more. Estelle Massey Riddle, a member of the National Council of Negro Women and of the DNS National Advisory Council, which had been established to facilitate interracial cooperation, argued that despite all the efforts at interracial cooperation, the DNS had not succeeded either in extending services to African Americans or in involving African Americans in birth control campaigns. She wrote: "There are too few people, white and Negro, to take the program to the people. There is much misunderstanding between different racial groups and a rising tide of racial antagonisms due to the war. Better biracial understanding is desperately needed."[100] Members of the advisory council repeatedly challenged the federation to train and hire black professionals, involve the black community in the planning of birth control campaigns, and integrate contraceptive advice with medical services rather than treat the need for family planning advice and the need for health care as separate problems.[101] The federation leadership, however, remained unwilling to spend money on any of these efforts; it chose instead to limit its support to setting up further demonstration clinics, largely ignoring the advisory council's suggestions. By the late 1940s, the Planned Parenthood Federation of America (PPFA), which had absorbed the BCFA, finally hired two African American consultants—Mary Langford and Grace Hale—to aid local groups in providing services to minority populations. While it met a long-held demand, this move, along with a shift in PPFA policies that relegated responsibility for African American birth control needs to local affiliates, also isolated those working within the black community even further from the rest of the PPFA.[102]

■ Clients and Staff: Allies or Opponents?

Women who had struggled for years to control their reproduction often appreciated contraceptive services and took advantage of them regardless of health officials' motivations. In desperate need of the most basic health and contraceptive attention, many women visited birth control clinics even if they were aware of officials' condescending attitudes. They negotiated with health care providers about the contraceptives offered and used the services for their own purposes, but they did not necessarily agree with health officials' views about contraception.

To be sure, those who requested birth control information agreed with health officials about the potentially devastating social and economic consequences of having too many children. Their requests for birth control testified to the physical strain of constant childbearing. One mother wrote: "Since I married I've done nothing but have babies. . . . I do think there's a limit for it, for my health has begun to fail fast, I have congested ovaries and with my first baby my womb lacerated terribly bad. That is giving me lots of trouble now. . . . And too my legs and thighs hurt almost constantly. I don't know why unless it is caused from 'coitus interruptus' as that method is used lots. We know it is dangerous, but I've tried suppositories, condoms, douche, a pessary, and everything I've heard of but none have kept me from conceiving. My husband and I are only normal beings."[103] Mothers described a wide variety of physical ailments that they attributed to constant pregnancies and childbearing, and they complained of the social isolation and economic hardship they experienced when having to take care of many children. The woman quoted above continued her letter:

> I have done nothing but . . . keep house and do the routine work that
> goes with that. . . . I'm completely shut in. I never go to the church,
> Sunday school, visiting, shopping, or anywhere except occasionally to
> see my mother and father who are very old and feeble. . . . I have never
> rebelled at motherhood and no one on earth is more devoted to their
> home and children than I am. . . . I feel like I've had enough children.

My husband is 52 years old and his health is failing fast. He has no income except from the farm which is so uncertain and a failure some years. I do know that at my age I'll have several children yet unless a preventive is used. . . . We are not able financially to have more babies, as its a terrible time to make 'ends meet' as it is. In fact we haven't made them meet a year since we've been married.[104]

Women wished to limit their families' size for the same reasons public health officials wanted them to: to gain some control over the consequences of frequent childbearing. But while women complained about the burdens and isolation that accompanied large families, they made it clear that they could both appreciate their families and desire birth control. In fact, they believed that contraceptives would enhance their enjoyment of motherhood.

The success of birth control programs depended on health officials' ability to offer integrated services that could attract women with the promise of both contraceptive advice and attention to their overall health and well-being. Misinformation, superstitions, and health problems all posed obstacles to the prevention of pregnancy. Contraceptive services needed to be integrated into a larger program of health services, and women needed both careful education and regular follow-up.

Often afraid of becoming pregnant again, women struggled for years to prevent conception. One FSA study found that almost half of the women questioned had previously tried to prevent pregnancy. Withdrawal was the most common method used. Others included one-size diaphragms, contraceptive jelly, salt in capsules, Lysol douches, and methods procured from Sears, Roebuck catalogs and traveling peddlers. Although women often had faith in the capsules and potions they had procured, success rates were low.[105] Most of the contraceptive devices used were notoriously unreliable. Even highly motivated women, moreover, could find it difficult to use contraceptives in crowded home conditions in which parents and children might share a bedroom, if not a bed. Finding themselves pregnant, women frequently turned to illegal abortions in their quest for reproductive control.

Limited knowledge and false beliefs about the reproductive process made it difficult for many women to use birth control successfully. A study conducted by a Louisiana family planning program in the 1960s concluded that respondents' ignorance about reproduction was extreme. Although women knew that sexual relations and babies were related, few knew why.[106] Women's lack of knowledge about the reproductive cycle also meant that many feared that birth control might harm their health. FSA nurses reported, for instance, that women in migrant camps were suspicious of contraceptive advice. One migrant mother, for example, had not come to the contraceptive clinic after hearing that foam powder was actually designed "to make your organs strong, so you'll have more babies."[107] Some women feared that the use of birth control might cause diseases such as cancer and tuberculosis or might permanently damage their reproductive systems. Since contact with a birth control clinic was often a woman's first introduction to the medical profession, and since it frequently entailed a gynecological checkup during which other diseases were often diagnosed, women might have thought that diseases discovered during medical exams were caused by the use of contraceptives.

Health professionals tried to avoid situations that might lead to misconceptions about the effects of birth control. Willie C. Morehead, a birth control nurse with the BCFA who taught FSA field staff in the South how to advise clients on birth control, advised agents not to give contraceptives to pregnant women: "If this woman should go out and do a heavy day's work and miscarry, as a result, whether she had ever opened that package of contraceptive or not, that would start the tale that we . . . handed out an abortificant [sic]."[108] Only careful education could help women correct these misconceptions and become successful users of birth control.

The continued prevalence of misconceptions about birth control among the clinic clientele indicates that staff frequently failed to adequately counsel women. Some health professionals used a plastic pelvis model, diaphragms, and sample packages of foaming sponges and contraceptive jelly to demonstrate how to use the products they distributed.[109] Most health professionals, however, did not carry plastic pelvis models around with them, and the majority of women never got such detailed instructions. Women were more likely to be visited by an agent who determined their interest in birth control, explained the basics of the female reproductive system, and left them with a sponge, a package of foam powder, and instructions, "something in hand to start the habit."[110] For clients who had no experience in the use of birth control, this method of imparting contraceptive advice must have raised more questions than it answered.

The most pervasive problem birth control clinics faced when advising poor clients, however, was apathy. Clients whose lives and livelihoods had traditionally been controlled by forces beyond their reach—be they landlords, banks, or nature—frequently lacked confidence in their own ability to control such major events as conception and pregnancy. One client explained: "Before I started taking the pills I had a child every year; I wasn't satisfied until I was pregnant. There wasn't any point in starting a job because I knew that I would soon be pregnant. There was nothing to keep me from getting that way, I felt I might as well go ahead and get it over with. There was nothing in life but more children."[111] Repeatedly, Virginia South found herself without any patients after having spent a week or two traveling around the mountain villages in Appalachia and talking to women about birth control.[112] To reach these clients, health and welfare professionals had to offer careful education and counseling. Class differences further complicated patient education, as even the most idealistic staff members often grew impatient with clients' fatalistic attitudes. Morehead explained to her FSA field workers that they were responsible for "teaching these people a glimmer of social responsibility to society as a whole, and [to] their own families in particular. Getting them to the point where they [could] understand that they [were] the architects of their own miserable estate[s], and that they, and they alone [could] apply the remedy."[113] At one time or another, most health and welfare professionals shared her impatience and frustration. We do not know either how often clients could detect such attitudes or, if they detected them, what impact they might have had on the clients' ability to successfully participate in contraceptive programs.

Some patients, of course, opposed birth control. They argued that they had "had their number that God planned for them," or they were suspicious of the medical profession.[114] The general distrust of anything "against nature" and the belief that birth control was a sin further impeded women's use of contraceptives. Husbands also sabotaged efforts to prevent conception, putting holes in diaphragms, throwing them out, or forbidding their wives to use birth control.[115] Some women found it difficult to incorporate the use of birth control into unsettled sexual lives, while others feared unsatisfactory marital relations. Wives, Morehead warned, often lacked sufficient strength to convince husbands of their need for family planning. Referring to the poor rural farm families who became clients of the FSA and thus targets of the birth control program, Morehead complained: "The lower we go in the social and economic strata of society, the more subservient the woman is to the whims and opinions of her mate."[116] She warned FSA agents not to ignore husbands when educating clients about birth control: "We have wasted our time and our breath and our material if we have sold only the mother on this service, for we are not going to get cooperation from that family unit in the use of this material unless the husband is seeing this matter in just the same light that his wife sees it."[117] Men's opposition, Morehead advised, was often based on ignorance, selfishness, or misconceptions about the difference between birth control and abortion, and it was best met by a man-to-man talk between FSA agent and husband. The clients Morehead encountered in California and Nebraska did not substantially differ in their socioeconomic backgrounds from the clients of birth control programs in North Carolina, West Virginia, Tennessee, or other largely white, poor, rural areas. Despite her frustration, her advice to FSA agents stands out for its sensitivity about the need to convince husbands as well as wives of the value of contraception.

Sources suggest that many patients appreciated contraceptive advice and took advantage of birth control services despite advocates' prejudices. Many women became committed to birth control, were careful to renew contraceptive supplies in time, and made plans to purchase contraceptives should the free supplies be stopped.[118] Even women who had trouble using a method consistently or who had become pregnant despite the use of birth control did not necessarily give up on contraceptive use. Reports of the Nashville clinic indicate, for instance, that a quarter of women who had become pregnant despite the use of birth control came back after delivery to have their diaphragms refitted.[119]

Similarly, many physicians and birth control nurses respected their patients, valued their work, and were gratified when patients accepted contraceptives and used them successfully. Health professionals often supported the distribution of contraceptives through public health and welfare channels as an important health measure. Moreover, for rural general practitioners, the FSA health initiative was a "financial shot in the arm" at a time when county, state, and philanthropic resources were overwhelmed by the collapse of the national economy. Before physicians' income began to grow dramatically in the period after World War II, the financial status of rural physicians was often precarious, and many country doctors were forced to barter with their patients for fees and to go into debt. These physicians found that New Deal programs allowed for the extension of medical and contraceptive care to the poor without taxing their own meager resources.[120]

Finding appropriate personnel was essential to good family planning services. Health and welfare professionals not only had to know about the mechanics of contraceptive devices, they also had to be comfortable providing sex education and following their clients' progress, which involved soliciting clients' questions and advising them about how to integrate the use of contraceptives into their sexual lives. Meticulous follow-up was necessary to help couples gain the knowledge and confidence required for successful contraceptive use. "Nothing we put them to doing will they do and do consistently unless we stay behind them with persistent supervision," Morehead reminded her agents. She continued: "You have got to stay behind them about it[,] keeping them reminded that this can be a valuable service to them. We ask each Home Supervisor to carry a notebook for this purpose with a page allotted to each woman in the service, putting down that woman's name and the date on which she secured the service. Then each time you go into that home, we are asking you to follow through with, 'By the way, Mrs. Jones, are you using that material we procured for you? Are you finding it satisfactory?' "[121] Not everyone felt comfortable discussing such intimate topics. The FSA expected that all its agents would educate families about the use of birth control. Morehead reported, however, that some FSA agents objected to this task. One protested "that he felt that 'no gentlemen' should be asked to discuss a man's wife with him and that while he understood that women gathered together to discuss their husbands[,] that 'gentlemen' never discussed their wives."[122]

Of course, some health and welfare professionals either opposed the distribution of contraceptives through public health services as a governmental intrusion into the medical profession or classified the dissemination of birth control as immoral. Some doctors feared that the free distribution of contraceptives would endanger their private practices by taking patients away. Others considered the distribution of contraceptives to be tampering with God's work and worried that birth control would lead women to betray their role as housewives and mothers. "Let them have children, that's what they're here for," one physician responded to Virginia South's birth control campaign in West Virginia and Kentucky, and he threatened to have South indicted for discussing birth control in public.[123] Other health officers never requested birth control and indicated on questionnaires that they were "not interested" in the service. Clinic staff opposed to the dissemination of birth control could effectively boycott entire programs by refusing to refer patients for contraceptive advice, withholding contraceptive information, or misinforming patients.[124]

The earliest institutional opposition to state-supported birth control programs came from the U.S. Children's Bureau. Under the leadership of Katharine Lenroot, the bureau consistently refused to fund the dissemination of birth control advice and threatened to cut funding for maternal and infant health programs in any state that disseminated contraceptive advice through public health clinics. Lenroot, who bitterly recalled that the maternal health programs established by the Sheppard-Towner Act of 1921 had been allowed to lapse in the late 1920s, expressed the fear that the inclusion of birth control services would again jeopardize her programs to promote maternal and child welfare. Even after D. Kenneth Rose, director of the ABCL, arranged for a White House meeting with Lenroot, representatives of other interested agencies, and Eleanor Roosevelt in October 1941, Lenroot held steadfast in her opposition. It was not until the 1960s that the Children's Bureau began to make grants for contraceptive services in local health programs.[125] Thus officials of the Children's Bureau and the U.S. Public Health Service told Dr. George Cooper, who promoted infant and maternal health in North Carolina, to "keep his hands off birth control" when Gamble's North Carolina birth control program was inaugurated.[126] Other states were threatened with the withdrawal of federal funds if they established state-supported birth control programs.[127]

Of course, some contraceptive programs received the wholehearted support of public health and welfare agencies' staff members and from outside agencies. Occasionally, outside agencies even decided to emulate programs they observed.[128] But at other times, health and welfare agencies gave no approval—or gave only tacit approval—to efforts to disseminate birth control, hampering the programs considerably.[129] Birth control clinics across the country had to contend with a lack of support from both state and private health and social service agencies. Clinic personnel complained about the stifling effect that opposition from Catholic agencies had on private and state-supported birth control clinics. In Pennsylvania, for instance, the Department of Public Assistance, fearing opposition from the local Catholic diocese, which provided crucial assistance to the department's clients, forbade social workers to mention birth control even when women asked about it. Fearing the loss of their jobs, few social workers were willing to violate these regulations.[130] Hospitals, in turn, often refused to refer postpartum patients in need of birth control to local birth control clinics. Such a lack of cooperation could lead to a shortage of client referrals; it could also prevent the staff of birth control clinics from making arrangements to refer clients who needed medical treatment to cooperative hospitals.

A lack of interest in birth control could be just as stifling as outright opposition to it. While Willie Morehead conceded that many physicians were beginning to realize the value of contraceptive services, she complained that "too few" advised clients about birth control unless the clients requested the information.[131] Moreover, physicians lacked essential knowledge. Morehead found, for instance, that only one-third of the 322 physicians she interviewed were familiar with the diaphragm. Training doctors about contraception, she concluded, was "the most glaringly demanding need" she encountered in her work.[132]

The inadequate training of family planning workers contributed to a low acceptance and success rate among clients. As a result, some programs began to tighten requirements for outreach workers. The FSA began to demand that outreach workers have both medical and contraceptive training and possess an intimate knowledge of rural life. Such workers, Morehead concluded, should be nurses, should have known wifehood and motherhood, should be mature and dignified, and should inspire confidence in those they instructed about family planning. Morehead also advised that new personnel should receive extensive field training under an experienced colleague.[133]

In the end, however, health officials' fear of opposition hurt the birth control programs more than any actual opposition did. Constantly worried about the possibility of protest, officials frequently refused to publicize birth control programs in any meaningful way.[134] As a result, potential clients never learned about the existence of the services, and clinics operated far below their capacities.

To guard themselves against opposition and possible retaliation from the Children's Bureau, health officials also frequently separated the distribution of birth control from maternal and child health services. By doing so, they ensured that birth control services would not be integrated into a general health program for mothers. Birth control advice became separated from larger maternal health programs, and women in need of medical services who appeared at birth control clinics had to be referred elsewhere. Staff who lacked a commitment to issues of maternal health were less likely to make such referrals. In addition, many clinics were poorly housed and offered inadequate medical services.[135]

The very separation of birth control from maternal and child health services encouraged a mindset that emphasized controlling the reproduction of the poor rather than extending reproductive control to poor women. Some nurses and health officers, to be sure, continued to view their contraceptive work as an important contribution to maternal health. Others, however, attracted more by the eugenic and economic promises of birth control, lost sight of the health aspects and made the control of dependent populations a goal in itself. Staff members often lacked enthusiasm and dedication and complained about their clients. The women, North Carolina state health officer Roy Norton lamented, "seem[ed] to be highly resistant to considerations which usually motivate[d] a couple to family planning, such as desire for a higher standard of living, the higher status of the woman, and medical conditions."[136]

The limited outreach of many programs and officials' lack of dedication frustrated philanthropists such as Gamble. The establishment of clinics in more than sixty counties in three years, Gamble admitted to North Carolina officials in 1940, was a real accomplishment. But he complained: "We really haven't reached every mother, and until then I won't be content. . . . In spite of North Carolina's multiple distributing centers the number of mothers instructed in the last year had been less than in Texas where the public health system had given no help. . . . The limitation of the number of mothers instructed may . . . come from the fact that not enough mothers know that the service is available."[137] Gamble, who always viewed his financial contributions as "seed money" that he hoped would attract further aid from other sources, was annoyed by health officials' refusal to publicize the North Carolina program and to seek outside funding. In March 1940, he ended his financial support, and Frances Pratt resigned as the program's birth control nurse.[138] After Gamble withdrew from the program, county health officers tried to secure money from other sources. Some sought appropriations from their county commissioners; others obtained donations from local individuals and organizations or took money from their regular health department contingency funds. A few clinics had patients pay what they could. The program continued to grow until the late 1940s, and then it began to dwindle for lack of funds.[139]

Structural changes in the mid-1940s contributed to a waning interest in public health birth control programs. Many health professionals were drafted for military service, and farmers abandoned their communities for the armed forces or for urban wartime industries. Public health services were left with only rudimentary staff, and many of the programs and initiatives introduced during the New Deal suffered considerable cutbacks. As the American economy prepared for war, the lingering effects of the Great Depression dissipated. The FSA birth control program broke down in the early 1940s when a lack of funds for family planning left FSA agents without any contraceptives.[140] Increasing hospital regulation of obstetrics practices and the development of antibiotics to treat infection, transfusions to replace blood lost in massive hemorrhaging, and prenatal care to identify many potential high-risk cases all improved maternal health, while the control of infectious diseases lowered infant mortality rates.

Finally, by the end of the decade, physicians had successfully replaced midwives as the attendants at childbirth. World War II produced a large demand for hospital care. Trying to meet a medical care crisis in the vicinity of military bases, legislators passed the Emergency Maternal and Infant Care Program (EMIC) in 1942 to provide free hospital, maternal, and infant care for dependents of servicemen and to bring hospitals up to minimum standards. Many women who had previously delivered at home could now do so in the hospital. By the end of 1946, EMIC had handled almost thirty-eight thousand maternity cases in North Carolina alone. And although EMIC ceased in 1947, the passage of the Hill-Burton Act in 1946 continued its work by providing funds for the establishment of a system of national hospitals and public health centers. This development, combined with the growth of group hospitalization plans, meant that southerners of both races began to enjoy access to modern hospital care that they had never had before.[141] By 1950, 88 percent of deliveries nation-wide took place in the hospital, up from 55 percent in 1940.[142] With the majority of women now seeking the advice of physicians during preg-nancy and delivery, physicians' professional interests in birth control, which had driven their initial involvement in its free distribution, waned.

▪ Family Planning Moves into Public Welfare

As health professionals' interest in contraceptive services declined, family planning captured the attention of public welfare officials. World War II had helped to pull the United States out of the depression, but the rising economic tide did not carry everyone along with it. Pockets of deep pov-erty persisted, and many of the most vulnerable, especially women, chil-dren, and the elderly, continued to need help. The so-called rediscovery of urban poverty in the early 1960s put their problems back into the national spotlight. During the 1950s and 1960s, ADC (after 1962 known as Aid to Families with Dependent Children, or AFDC) expanded dramatically; it served 803,000 families in 1960, compared with 372,000 in 1940. At the same time, unwed mothers replaced widows as the stereotypical ADC re-cipients. Federal pressure to include formerly excluded minorities in the program, as well as climbing fertility and divorce rates and a rising unem-ployment rate among women, contributed to the growth of the ADC pro-gram. These changes made poverty a politically volatile topic during the 1950s and 1960s. As payments to ADC mothers and their children sky-rocketed in the 1950s, many people came to believe that the high number of births to unwed ADC mothers was to blame.[143] Welfare officials looked to birth control for a solution to persistent welfare dependency. State-supported family planning programs became central in the effort to limit the birthrate among women dependent on welfare. Offering contraceptives to ADC mothers, welfare officials hoped, would reduce nonmarital births, curb public expenditures, and break the cycle of poverty. Public provision of contraceptives got a new lease on life.

The new attention to family planning was accompanied both by changes in contraceptive technology and by a shift in emphasis from family planning to population control. The development of the birth control pill and the IUD inaugurated a new generation of contraceptives whose use was separated from sexual activity, making contraception easier and more reliable than ever before. Family planning programs across the country found that the distribution of oral contraceptives in particular led to an exponential rise in the number of their patients.[144] At the same time, fears of overpopulation reinforced the view that poor women did not responsibly limit their pregnancies. By the early 1960s, newspapers across the country were linking the threat of world Communism to a growing world population and an increasing scarcity of resources, and they were calling on the U.S. government to make a commitment to international population control in an effort to achieve both social and political stability around the world. Already in the mid-1950s, a fund-raising letter of the Planned Parenthood Committee of Pittsburgh claimed that there was a direct link between poverty, high birthrates, and the threat of Communism: "The greatest breeding ground for Communism is Poverty and Poverty is generally the result of excess population. J. Edgar Hoover recently stated that Crime costs every American family $495.00 per year. Have you ever stopped to consider how much the 'unwanted' children of poor and ignorant parents are costing you and the community in increased Relief load, State medical and Mental Care, Juvenile Delinquency and Criminality? . . . There is a critical need for the expansion of this work [birth control] in American Slums and other areas."[145] The argument that population control was necessary for the stability of American society appealed to many who supported the revival of family planning in the 1960s. The federal government began to encourage and then to require the extension of family planning services to all women, and it increased funding opportunities for birth control programs at home and abroad.[146] With the passage of the 1967 amendments to the Social Security Act that mandated federal expenditures for family planning, the federal government expressed its commitment to a domestic family planning policy.[147]

Despite the federal commitment to family planning, however, services remained of uneven quality. While the new funding sources for family planning resulted in the emergence of hundreds of new family planning services across the country, the lack of an infrastructure within which to distribute contraceptives and implement services at the local level forced granting agencies to rely on the private and nonprofit sectors to make family planning services available.[148] Moreover, with the proliferation of programs and funds, both the accessibility of contraceptives and the likelihood of coercion increased. Programs simultaneously increased women's reproductive control by making birth control more accessible and controlled women's reproduction by pushing poor and minority women to use contraceptives whose effects could not easily be controlled.

Because public health departments were frequently unwilling to get involved in family planning, efforts to establish such services in the 1960s often originated in public welfare departments or in privately funded public health initiatives. Under the leadership of Wallace Kuralt, who served as director of the Mecklenburg County Department of Public Welfare from 1945 to 1972, Charlotte, North Carolina, inaugurated its birth control program in 1960. Across the country, experiments with new family planning delivery systems followed.

Kuralt's philosophy about social work was shaped by his experiences during the New Deal. Born in 1908 in Springfield, Massachusetts, he came to North Carolina to attend the University of North Carolina at Chapel Hill, graduating with a business degree in 1931. After experiencing some difficulty finding a job in the midst of the Great Depression, he finally got a position as a typist with the Emergency Relief Administration. From there, he moved on to work with the Works Progress Administration in Fayetteville and eventually returned to the University of North Carolina to get a degree in social work. In 1945, he became the director of public welfare in Mecklenburg County, a position he held until his retirement in 1972.

Throughout his tenure with the Department of Public Welfare, Kuralt argued for the importance of preventing poverty and championed an active role for the government. Rather than merely hand out relief checks, he established a whole range of social services, providing day care centers for the children of welfare recipients, setting up a pilot program for legal aid to the poor, hiring homemakers to give women who were ill or who had other emergencies help with child care and household duties, and hiring women from Charlotte's poor communities to educate their neighbors and friends about the services the department offered.[149] In addition,

Wallace Kuralt Sr. (Courtesy of *Charlotte Observer*)

he instituted a groundbreaking family planning program and successfully lobbied both for the passage of a voluntary sterilization law and for the reform of the state's abortion law.

The birth control pill had not even received the approval of the Food and Drug Administration (FDA) when Kuralt read about its promise in a *Reader's Digest* article. He immediately called Dr. Elizabeth Corkey of the Mecklenburg County Department of Public Health, who promised to help him establish a family planning program. In 1960, the two departments opened a joint family planning clinic that offered women access to a whole range of contraceptive devices, including the pill. Both clients and social workers were more than eager to obtain the improved birth control methods. Not only did clients approach social workers asking for the birth control pill, social workers were also happy to use the pill themselves.[150]

As had been the case during the 1930s and 1940s, research interests provided an important impetus for the establishment and funding of new family planning programs in the 1960s. One of the most dramatic examples was the creation of Louisiana's Family Planning Incorporated (FPI), founded by Tulane University pediatrician Joe Beasley. Tulane University researchers hoped to establish a model family planning program to prove that poor women were both willing and able to use contraception.[151] Between 1965 and 1972, FPI offered comprehensive family planning services in Louisiana. Taking advantage of funding available for agencies concerned about overpopulation, FPI became a national and international model for privately delivered public health services and comprehensive family planning programs for the poor.

Both Beasley and Kuralt espoused the rights of women to control their reproduction. "The inability of a woman to control her fertility," Beasley argued, "deprives her of a real right and a real power."[152] Choice, Kuralt argued, meant "not only freedom to choose the method of family planning, but freedom to participate or not participate."[153] The emphasis on choice contributed to an approach that highlighted the importance of women's reproductive plans. Welfare officials pointed out that after more than two decades of governmental involvement in contraceptive services, family planning remained inaccessible to most poor women. As a result, low-income women continued to have more children then they wanted.[154] Poor women, these officials concluded, had a right to the same access to medical and contraceptive care that middle- and upper-class women had.

But Beasley and Kuralt recognized that public and political support for family planning programs depended in part on their ability to couch the goals of family planning in economic terms. One of the most persuasive arguments for family planning, especially among politicians, was that it had the potential to reduce health and welfare costs. In public speeches, both men reiterated that for every dollar spent on family planning, the state would save money. "The public," Kuralt noted, "has been incensed about real and mythical costs associated with illegitimacy." If society really cared about the costs of relief, damage to children born fatherless, and psychological injury to unmarried mothers, Kuralt and Beasley concluded, it had to provide for liberal family planning services.[155] A savvy politician, Kuralt had a keen understanding of the conflicting political forces behind progressive family planning politics. In order to convince his conservative county commissioners to fund family planning, Kuralt drove them to Charlotte's housing projects so that they could observe poverty firsthand. Family planning, he suggested to them, was much cheaper than supporting unwanted children.[156] To demonstrate the success of birth control, Kuralt pointed to the experience in Mecklenburg County. Before the establishment of Charlotte's family planning program, Mecklenburg County's ADC rolls had grown by three hundred names—at a total added cost of $90,000—each year. Three years after public family planning programs had been put in place, Kuralt's department had been able to stabilize the number of individuals on ADC, while throughout the rest of the country the number of ADC recipients had continued to rise rapidly.[157]

Officials in both Louisiana and Mecklenburg County recognized that contraceptive services needed to be integrated into comprehensive medical and social services. Their patients received contraceptive counseling along with sex education, annual breast and pelvic exams, and screening for cervical cancer. The Louisiana clinic also began to offer an annual physical exam, transforming the family planning clinicians into the clients' family doctors. If necessary, clinics referred clients for further treatment or to infertility specialists. Some staff members most likely also helped patients secure abortion services.[158] Clinics adopted a "cafeteria type of approach," letting patients choose among a variety of contraceptives. Officials recognized the need for intensive outreach and follow-up. Both programs hired outreach workers who advertised clinic services in their respective communities, and both clinics placed a high priority on the training of staff members. Patients with medical problems or those who had missed appointments received particularly close follow-up. Finally, clinics offered help with transportation and babysitting, educated clients about home economics, distributed food, and invented recipes for inexpensive, nourishing meals.[159]

Such a comprehensive approach attracted an unprecedented number of clients. In Louisiana's Orleans Parish alone, the clinic had registered 17,459 families by 1969. Eighty-five percent of patients remained active after eighteen months.[160] Mecklenburg County's Dr. Elizabeth Corkey estimated that the service had reached about 50 percent of the public welfare caseload. Women frequently approached social workers to ask about the family planning program and request the pill.[161] Such success proved wrong those officials who had assumed that poor women were unwilling or unable to use contraceptives consistently. Kuralt exulted:

Our experience and modern methods of Planned Parenthood have demonstrated the fallacy of a great many myths that circulate in our society today. The women of poor families do know when they want to stop having children. These women do have concern for their children; they are capable of participating, and they will take advantage of modern planned parenthood methods when they become acquainted with the methods and become convinced that this is a method that will meet their particular needs. . . . We are happy to say that we have had no complaints of any source about our program and we have nothing but "happy customers."[162]

Notwithstanding Beasley's and Kuralt's successes, some health and welfare officials remained convinced that poor women were unable or unwilling to prevent conception. "I tried the [birth control] pills," the health director of North Carolina's Robeson County complained. "I know these people and they don't take them like they ought to."[163] For these professionals, the improvements to the IUD that were made in the 1960s seemed to promise that family planning programs would be able to achieve more ambitious goals. By taking reproductive control out of women's hands and putting it into the hands of physicians, who had to insert and remove the plastic coil, the IUD, some believed, had the potential to "solve the problems of over population in the lower social groups."[164] For some, reducing poverty became synonymous with preventing births to ADC recipients. In fact, Andrea Tone observes that proponents of the IUD routinely identified the device as one particularly suited for women deemed impoverished, irresponsible, and too prolific. Its low price and ease of use made it equally attractive to women and to population controllers, albeit for very different reasons.[165] Remaining skeptical about poor and minority women's ability to control conception, some health and welfare officials pushed contraceptive methods that did not require women's daily cooperation and neglected the supporting health and welfare services that made Kuralt's and Beasley's programs so successful.

Particularly in areas with significant minority populations, white policy makers were receptive to programs that promised to reduce the birthrate among the nonwhite population. In North Carolina's Robeson County, for instance, welfare officials decided to offer only the IUD in a family planning program "aimed at holding down the number of children born into poor families, especially those receiving welfare grants."[166] And in Louisiana, politicians of the racist States' Rights Party came to the spirited defense of Beasley's birth control program.[167] Some welfare officials tied the receipt of social services to women's participation in family planning programs. Although such policies were illegal, the North Carolina Department of Public Welfare decided in 1968 to require women on AFDC to receive birth control instruction.[168] After six months, welfare officials were forced to drop the requirement.

In the 1960s as in earlier decades, the focus on reducing poverty promoted the separation of contraceptive advice from general health care services and caused many clinics to be staffed by personnel who frequently failed to give patients adequate attention. One report stated: "Many indigent women in North Carolina are given contraceptive service . . . and then are never rechecked if even followed outside the clinic. For many there is no information about their continued use of contraception or even about the occurrence of complications or dissatisfaction."[169] Despite the success of programs such as Mecklenburg County's and Louisiana's FPI, services across the country continued to be of uneven quality. While the shortage of health facilities and clinics' meager financial resources contributed to the creation of a family planning delivery system patched together from public, private, and nonprofit sources, the general lack of oversight, regulation, and clinic standards also meant that local attitudes and the motivations of individual health care providers determined the character of each clinic.[170]

Even women who had access to private physicians were often unable to receive the contraceptive advice they sought. Many physicians remained hostile to the idea of providing birth control, particularly if their patients were young and unmarried. Clinics frequently imposed their own eligibility rules, limiting contraceptive advice to married women with at least one child, for instance.[171] After finding herself pregnant, one female college student complained that she had been unable to obtain birth control. Planning to become sexually active with her fiancé but seeking to delay pregnancy, she had sought contraceptive advice from the Student Infirmary at the University of North Carolina. The treating physician refused, however, to help her. She explained: "First of all, he told me that he didn't give contraceptives, and that the infirmary itself didn't give contraceptives out to unmarried people. And then he said did I want to talk about it, or had I already made up my mind [to become sexually active]? And I said that I had pretty much made up my mind. And he said, 'Well you know I like sex just as much as any other normal person.' And then he said, 'It's like a glass of wine, you don't guzzle it, in the same way you don't use sex to excess.' "[172] Students frequently complained that they did not know where to obtain birth control advice, that they were worried their parents

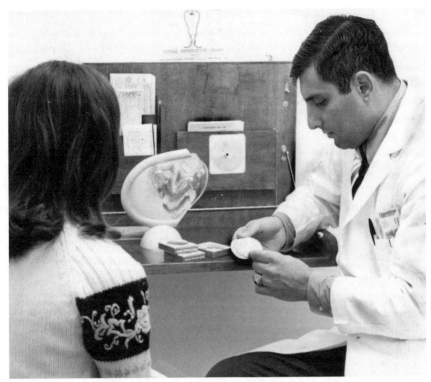

Takey Crist explaining birth control methods to a patient in the Health Education Clinic, ca. 1970. (Courtesy of Takey Crist)

might find out, or that they were refused help when they did seek it.[173] Only after the university established the Health Education Clinic in the early 1970s were students able to seek both sex education and birth control advice regardless of their age or marital status.

Although lack of access, rather than coercive policies, continued to be the more common problem, the new prominence that family planning gained in the 1960s created tensions between white supporters of the new programs and many African Americans. Clinics that hoped to offer successful family planning programs, one black physician warned, needed to ensure that African Americans were heavily represented in their policy-making bodies.[174] The low participation of white clients in some programs seemed to bolster the charge of racial genocide regardless of whether segregation resulted from the targeting of black clients for family planning or from the continued refusal of white women to visit integrated services.[175]

With the rise of black militancy, all family planning programs came under suspicion. In 1968, black militants burned down a family planning clinic in Cleveland and forced the temporary closing of family planning clinics in Pittsburgh.[176] One prominent black Pittsburgh physician charged all government-supported birth control programs with being "an organized plot to cut down the Negro birthrate."[177] While not representative of general black attitudes, such charges were sure to capture headlines. Aware that supporters of public contraceptive programs exploited racial stereotypes to promote the distribution of birth control, public health and welfare officials were jittery about the exposure of racist rhetoric. Some denied charges of racial genocide. Others gained the support of black clients, who fought for the reopening of clinics.[178] In Louisiana, Beasley promoted one critic into top management and hired others as staff members. While the integration of critics into already existing programs could successfully enhance diversity and ensure that weak aspects of birth control services would be improved, Beasley's move aggravated already existing tensions between an increasingly remote managerial staff on the one side and family planning advocates and their clients on the other, eventually leading to the closing of the program.[179]

Despite the politicized nature of family planning, however, by the late 1960s government-supported family planning programs had assumed a permanent character. As Kuralt's and Beasley's programs demonstrated, Johnson's Great Society allowed family planning activists to link federally funded contraceptive programs to local antipoverty programs and to secure support for the delivery of birth control through both government agencies and private organizations. While federal programs remained uncoordinated and frequently underfunded, and while local programs continued to be subject to the political fate of the particular institutions delivering services, family planning had become established policy.[180] With the rise of the women's health movement in the late 1960s, a new group of activists increasingly framed the demand for family planning in terms of women's reproductive rights, including their rights to access to abortion and to protection from sterilization abuse and coercion.

The growing support for birth control as a palliative for poverty also extended government commitment to international programs to control population growth. By the mid-1960s, the U.S. government endorsed international birth control aid as vital to national security, and in 1965 the Agency for International Development (AID) began to support family planning projects overseas. Initially, funds were reserved for research, training, and communications, but by the end of the decade AID had also become involved in the distribution of contraceptives. Operated by organizations such as the Population Council, the International Planned Parenthood Federation, and the Pathfinder Fund, these programs attracted many of the same people who were involved in family planning at home, and they mirrored the patchwork quality that characterized delivery of birth control in the United States.[181]

■ Conclusion

Throughout the twentieth century, humanitarian, eugenic, and economic concerns motivated health and welfare professionals to establish state-supported birth control programs for the poor. Public health services launched their birth control programs as part of a comprehensive public health response to poor infant and maternal health. Health officials hoped to reduce infant and maternal mortality rates and improve infant and maternal health by offering mothers the opportunity to space the birth of children farther apart. The distribution of contraceptives was only one part of well-rounded maternal health programs that also included prenatal and postnatal care and the provision of basic gynecological services.

But offering birth control to poor women also seemed attractive for economic and eugenic reasons. Officials hoped that the distribution of birth control to the poor would reduce the birthrate among those currently on relief. This would not only curb the growth of the dependent population, whose offspring were considered to be undesirable, it would also help to control poverty. Whatever their individual beliefs, officials recognized that economic and eugenic arguments were particularly powerful in attracting support for birth control programs.

From the very beginning, however, the lack of a real delivery system hampered the distribution of birth control. As a result, family planning programs across the country were pieced together by a range of different providers: private physicians, state public health services, and nonprofit agencies all participated in the development of family planning programs. Throughout the period under discussion, private funds supplemented government programs that did not have the resources to act. Clarence Gamble paid for a birth control nurse to facilitate the development of birth control programs in North Carolina's public health clinics; Albert Lasker financed birth control services for African Americans; private foundations funded Joe Beasley's FPI. Occupying a middle ground between public and private, these services participated in the shaping of a welfare state that influenced social hierarchies by addressing questions of rights and entitlements, bodily integrity, and dependence.

Once implemented, public health birth control services straddled the divide between offering women reproductive control and seeking to control women's reproduction. Whether the services increased or limited women's reproductive autonomy often depended on the extent to which officials integrated the dispensation of contraceptive advice into more general health and social services. When birth control advocates merely provided women who lacked access to the most basic health services with contraceptive supplies, the help was insufficient. Health problems, lack of education, and the absence of a support network often proved powerful obstacles to women's successful use of birth control. To truly increase women's reproductive control, birth control clinics needed to offer sex education, medical care, and ongoing support and follow-up. Moreover, clinics had to be accessible to working women and to those living in remote rural areas.

While many programs were able to offer women the health and contraceptive services necessary, they were frequently fraught with race and class prejudices. Stereotypes about poor and minority women's presumed inability to properly prevent conception pervaded both the research and development of new contraceptives and the delivery of contraceptive services. Throughout the twentieth century, most research on contraceptive technology was driven by the assumptions that poor women lacked the intelligence and the motivation to use existing contraceptive devices and that future development should concentrate on contraceptive methods that were easier to use and that required less user participation. As a result, researchers neglected considerations of women's self-determination.

Moreover, researchers who understood women's lack of success with any given birth control method as a technical problem that could be solved by the development of the "perfect" contraceptive failed to pay attention to those support services that might have helped women to become more successful users of birth control. Sex education, adequate follow-up visits in patients' homes, and "continuing program[s] of community education on the benefits of planned parenthood and the availability of the clinic" were essential to the success of contraceptive programs.[182] However, those were precisely the kind of services deemed expendable in public health work.

During the 1930s and 1940s, public health workers' narrow focus on providing birth control resulted in contraceptive field trials that swamped poor and minority women with inexpensive and often unreliable birth control methods such as foam powder. By the 1960s, research had turned to the development of methods that could succeed without women's active participation. Contraceptive devices such as the IUD eventually placed greater control over women's reproduction into the hands of the physicians who had to insert or administer the methods. As the development of birth control devices progressed, the potential for abuse inherent in the new methods increased. While women still had control over the methods used in field trials during the 1930s and 1940s and could stop using them any time they wanted, the users of IUDs had to rely on physicians to remove the devices. This trend continued with the development of Norplant, Depo-Provera, contraceptive vaccines, and Quinacrine in the following decades.

The turn to population control simultaneous with the launching of the War on Poverty in the 1960s finally led to an official government commitment to family planning. Once family planning was part of official government policy, funding for it increased significantly. But the lack of a real delivery system resulted in the proliferation of new birth control programs of uneven quality. Operated under the control of the public, private, and nonprofit sectors, these new programs continued to provide uneven services, contributing to inequities between communities, regions, and states. Some of the family planning programs emerging in the 1960s demonstrated a real commitment to providing women with reproductive control, while others continued to seek control over women's reproduction. Renewed interest in family planning in the 1960s allowed people such as Wallace Kuralt and Joe Beasley to take advantage of new funding sources, implementing programs that put women's reproductive plans at their center. Their visions, however, fell at the progressive end of a range of services; at the other end were services that aimed to control women's reproduction. Ironically, the increase in funding not only eased women's access to family planning but also increased the likelihood of coercion in the services available. A lack of oversight over family planning programs and a social context in which many continued to feel ambivalent about women's ability to make responsible decisions concerning their reproduction contributed to this development.

Although clients were not blind to the race and class prejudices that underlay many family planning programs, they valued contraceptive information, took advantage of the services offered, and bargained with authorities over the conditions of contraceptive advice. Clearly, some women suffered negative consequences from their participation in the contraceptive trials, and some found the attitudes of health and welfare professionals so humiliating that they decided to forgo their contraceptive advice. Others, however, found that birth control introduced them to a new way of life—one unthreatened by frequent pregnancy and childbearing. Public family planning services could play a crucial role in leveling the playing field by providing much-needed access to birth control information to poor and minority women. They used the services to improve their quality of life, and they found allies in local health authorities who lobbied for their interests.

Women's lack of access to decent health and contraceptive services, their poverty, their race, and their gender significantly influenced their decisions to participate in contraceptive field trials or to take advantage of even imperfect birth control programs. Their choices were conditioned by their lack of alternatives. They took advantage of the services in a social and economic context that denied them access to safe, effective, convenient, and affordable methods of birth control and to equitable social, political, and economic conditions under which to make choices.[183]

CHAPTER TWO

Nothing Is Removed Except the Possibility of Parenthood

Women and the Politics of Sterilization

On February 10, 1965, Nial Cox, an eighteen-year-old black unwed mother, was subjected to a tubal ligation under a North Carolina statute providing for the sterilization of the mentally diseased, the feebleminded, and the epileptic. Although she had never been tested for any of these afflictions, her surgeon's discharge summary described Cox, who would later become a nurse, as an "eighteen-year old mentally deficient Negro girl."[1] Three months prior to the surgery, Cox had given birth to a daughter. She and her daughter lived with her siblings and their mother, Devora. While Nial Cox received no welfare benefits for her daughter, Devora did receive benefits for herself and for Nial's brothers and sisters, which meant that she was in regular contact with the local welfare department. For several months before and after Nial gave birth, Devora's social worker, Shelton Howland, had insisted that Nial would have to be sterilized. If Nial and her mother refused, Howland threatened, Devora and Nial's siblings would all be stricken from the welfare rolls. Faced with the loss of her entire income, Devora finally consented. The local social service agency petitioned the North Carolina Eugenics Board for the operation, and three months after her baby was born

Nial was sterilized. It was Nial's nonmarital pregnancy and her mother's welfare dependency rather than Nial's intellectual capacities—or even her own dependency—that earned her the label of "feebleminded" and made her one of over eight thousand people sterilized between 1929 and 1975 under the authority of the North Carolina Eugenics Board.

Historians and social scientists, stressing the operation's irreversible and permanent effects, have emphasized the coercive nature of the sterilization of poor and minority women.[2] Throughout the late 1960s and the 1970s, the publicity given to cases of sterilization abuse raised awareness of its prevalence in the United States and in Puerto Rico, India, Bangladesh, Brazil, and elsewhere.[3] By the late 1970s, a number of political organizations lobbied against sterilization abuse in legislatures and contributed to the passage of federal sterilization guidelines in 1978 that recognized involuntary sterilization as a violation of civil and human rights.[4]

The case of Nial Cox demonstrates how sterilization could restrict women's reproductive autonomy and underscores its peculiarly sexist, classist, racist, and coercive character. Sexual behavior, race, and class background constituted major factors in the identification of the so-called feebleminded. A concern with sexual behavior led social workers to focus on those whose deviation from the desired norm was particularly obvious and disturbing: sexually active single women. Eighty-five percent of those sterilized in North Carolina were women, and half of them were single and had given birth to one or more children outside of marriage. Class and race were critical factors in the identification of potential sterilization cases: the members of poor and rural families were particularly likely to be perceived as feebleminded. The link between mental deficiency and sexual immorality seemed especially close in the case of African American welfare recipients. In the eyes of those who implemented the sterilization program, the presence of children outside marriage served as an indication of women's emotional immaturity and mental retardation even when —as in Nial Cox's case—the woman was able to take care of her children. Given changing attitudes toward sterilization in the late 1960s and the 1970s, however, and given the circumstances of Cox's case, it is no surprise that Cox's sterilization became part of a lawsuit that focused on the question of whether the sterilization program in North Carolina constituted an attempt at "racial genocide."[5]

The eugenic sterilization program did not function only as an assault on women's reproductive autonomy. Ironically, it also offered access to a form of birth control that women desired. One woman who eagerly sought a contraceptive sterilization was Shirley, a white woman who was thirty-six when she petitioned to be sterilized.[6] Shirley had met her first husband in 1950, when she was twenty. In the early 1950s, she gave birth to two children. But her husband was an alcoholic and a poor provider, and Shirley, engaged in a fifteen-year battle against schizophrenia, put her children up for adoption and eventually left the marriage. After her divorce, she became pregnant for the third time. She gave this child, too, up for adoption. In November 1957, she married a marine. Although Shirley did not want to have more children, her second husband pressured her to become pregnant again. By the time her fourth and last child was born, her husband was stationed overseas. Shirley tried to juggle the demands of motherhood with her mental illness but was only able to care for her child when her husband was around to offer help. In May 1963, she attempted suicide and was committed to a psychiatric hospital. She was released in July, just as her husband was leaving for Okinawa, Japan. Overwhelmed with the responsibility of caring for her son, Shirley gave the child to a friend and committed herself to a psychiatric hospital in February 1964. Her child was placed in foster care, and during the next two and a half years, which Shirley spent at the hospital, she had little contact with either her husband or her son. Her husband rarely wrote and only visited a couple of times. Once or twice he took Shirley to see the children, but each such visit precipitated a deterioration in Shirley's mental condition.

At the hospital, Shirley learned about the possibility of sterilization. Eager to end her constant fear of pregnancy and to aid her recovery, she sought the operation prior to her release from the hospital. In the summer of 1966, Shirley and her physician petitioned the North Carolina Eugenics Board for Shirley's eugenic sterilization. The board, however, refused to authorize Shirley's sterilization on the ground that her husband objected to the procedure. Although he had been conspicuously absent during her two and a half years at the hospital, although Shirley's history of mental illness was clearly connected to her inability to cope with the responsibilities of parenthood, although she had proven unable to care for her children, although she was likely to become pregnant again once she was released from the hospital, and although she urgently desired the operation, the Eugenics Board turned down Shirley's petition. To the board members, the factors in favor of an operation did not outweigh Shirley's husband's desire to have more children and his hope that his wife might someday be "cured of not wanting children," allowing him to reestablish his family. In the deliberations of the Eugenics Board, the patriarchal prerogative of a husband who misunderstood his wife's mental illness as a lack of interest in her role as wife and mother outweighed his wife's desire for reproductive control.[7]

As Shirley's eagerness for the operation demonstrates, while sterilization could threaten women's reproductive autonomy, some women very much desired this form of birth control. Until the 1960s, contraceptives were largely limited to diaphragms, douches, foam powders, and condoms. While the diaphragm was considered the most reliable, women had to be fitted for diaphragms, to be taught how to use them, and to have the privacy and the necessary sanitary conditions to feel comfortable with them. Douches and foam powders were less reliable, and men frequently objected to using condoms. Only with the introduction of the birth control pill and the IUD in the 1960s did women gain access to contraceptives that separated the use of birth control from the act of sexual intercourse, making successful contraception much easier for women who found it hard to plan ahead or whose partners were uncooperative. But birth control pills had to be taken every day, and both the pill and the IUD could have serious side effects. Although the risks of major surgery accompanied female sterilization, the unreliability of other contraceptives and the inaccessibility of abortion made sterilization an attractive option for women from all class and ethnic backgrounds. State restrictions on access to sterilization were thus as disempowering for those women denied access to the operation as state promotion of the operation was to women coerced or pressured into sterilization.

Until the 1960s, sterilizations for reasons other than eugenics were not governed by law. The decision whether or not to perform the operation was left to the discretion of individual physicians, who often considered sterilization to be an operation of convenience, mistrusted women's ability to decide responsibly when to cease childbearing, and felt that husbands should ultimately decide whether and when their wives should become pregnant. As the former chairman of the Department of Obstetrics and Gynecology at the University of North Carolina facetiously noted, "The [fallopian] tubes belong to the husband, both the left and the right."[8] Most physicians established complicated parity formulas to govern access to the operation, requiring, for instance, that women have already given birth to four children by the age of thirty in order to qualify for sterilization. While privileged women could seek sterilization from the private physicians of their choice, poor women were forced to seek help from public health and welfare departments. In North Carolina, this meant that poor women who wished to be sterilized had to bargain with welfare officials and petition the members of the Eugenics Board, the same people who sought out "undesirables" for eugenic sterilizations whose voluntary nature was at best questionable.

The history of sterilization, then, reminds us not only that the same operation could both restrict and enhance women's reproductive control but also that the restriction of women's reproductive control could take many forms. As the contrast between Nial Cox and Shirley demonstrates, it was not the technology of sterilization itself that determined whether women saw the operation as repressive or liberating but the context in which the technology was embedded.[9] The state of North Carolina restricted Nial Cox's reproductive autonomy by denying her the opportunity to bear children; it restricted Shirley's reproductive autonomy by denying her the opportunity to cease bearing children. I have chosen the term "opportunity" here to emphasize that women did not have a legally codified right to control their reproductive capacity in general or to choose sterilization in particular. In fact, Nial Cox and Shirley sought control over their reproductive capacities during the mid-1960s, at least a decade before the notion that women have reproductive rights was fully articulated in the United States. In emphasizing the importance of reproductive rights for all women, I would argue that the state denied both women the "right" to reproductive autonomy. However, my goal here is to analyze Cox's and Shirley's situations within their historical context, a context in which such rights had not yet been articulated.

While poor and minority women were more susceptible to coercive sterilization and more likely as a group to suffer from sterilization abuse, women's race and class background alone did not determine the meaning sterilization held for them. Poor and minority women did not share one outlook or one experience in regard to the surgery. Some poor women and women of color actively sought sterilization. Rather than being the victims of coercive eugenic policies, they used those policies and programs for their own ends. Those ends, however, were hardly unrelated to race or to class. The fact that some women could only gain access to sterilization through the eugenic sterilization program speaks to their lack of resources. As the case of Shirley demonstrates, moreover, gender relations further complicated this picture. Given poor women's vulnerable position and the history of racism, class bias, and coercive practices in sterilization programs, the self-determination of women who turned to the eugenic sterilization program is all the more remarkable.

A certain flexibility in the meaning of sterilization could ease women's access to the surgery. While women might be unable to obtain an "elective" sterilization for contraceptive reasons, physicians were sometimes willing to perform the surgery if serious health problems justified a "therapeutic" sterilization. Similarly, welfare officials unable to provide clients with elective or therapeutic sterilizations could petition the state's Eugenics Board for "eugenic" sterilizations. Just as women's access to abortion could depend on whether the procedure was classified as elective or therapeutic, access to sterilization could change as the definition of the surgery changed.

State-sponsored sterilizations were a national, indeed an international, phenomenon. Yet the events that led to each individual sterilization occurred at the local level. An in-depth analysis of North Carolina's sterilization program allows us to understand these local events. In some ways, North Carolina's history with birth control, sterilization, and abortion is unusual. Not only did the state introduce the nation's first state-supported birth control program, it initiated more state-sponsored sterilizations per capita than any other state, and it was among the first states to pass a voluntary sterilization law and to reform its abortion law in the 1960s. Moreover, its sterilization law was the only one in the country that permitted welfare officials to petition for the sterilization of their clients, and the state greatly expanded its sterilization program in the 1950s and 1960s, when eugenic sterilization programs in most states ceased.

Despite the unique attributes of its reproductive policies, however, many of their features could be seen in other states. Many states attempted to control public expenditures by limiting the reproduction of welfare recipients. The interplay of race, class, and gender in the implementation of reproductive policies in North Carolina mirrored tensions in other locations. Across the country, public health and welfare officials, medical professionals, and research scientists were intimately involved in reproductive policies, and several other states expanded eugenic sterilization after 1950.[10]

His excitement about the promise of eugenic sterilization moved Clarence J. Gamble to write a poem on the topic. The poem celebrated North Carolina's eugenic sterilization program by contrasting the fate of a happy sterilized "moron" couple with that of a "moron" couple fated to give birth to generations of feebleminded children, grandchildren, and great-grandchildren. Gamble intended the North Carolina Human Betterment League to use the poem, which he wrote in the mid-1940s, in its promotional materials. League members, however, found the piece in poor taste and worried about the public backlash it might produce. They quietly ignored it. When the Department of Social Services donated its papers to the North Carolina State Archives, the poem went along. I have used it to introduce this chapter's subsections.

■ Eugenic Science and the Making of Eugenic Sterilization Laws

Once there was a MORON, *that means / A person who wasn't very bright. / He couldn't add figures / Or make change / Or do many things / An ordinary man does.*

In April 1932, the Board of Commissioners of Forsyth County, North Carolina, authorized the eugenic sterilization of Mary Brewer. Such an operation, the commissioners held, was in Brewer's best interest and in the interests of Forsyth County and the public in general, since any future children born to Mary Brewer were likely to be "of the same [low] degree of mentality as the children she now has" and "would undoubtedly become public charges."[11] Mary Brewer, a twenty-eight-year-old married white woman with five children, did not want to be sterilized, and she appealed her case to the North Carolina Supreme Court. Arguing for Brewer's sterilization, a member of the juvenile court testified at the hearing that "the conditions in [Brewer's] home were bad." The witness elaborated: "The children were dirty, the house was dirty. I think the first time I went into the home was at ten o'clock in the morning, and if anything had been done toward breakfast or cleaning the house it could not be noticed."[12] Neighbors and social workers agreed that Mary Brewer did not "[keep] a home like a mother should." She "didn't seem to care whether the children were there or whether they were clothed or fed." "I think," one social worker concluded, "Mary Brewer is incompetent to handle her own affairs. I think her mind is deteriorating."[13] In addition, a psychologist testified that Mary Brewer—who had attended school only until the third grade—had the "mental age" of a seven- or eight-year-old. Brewer's low intellectual ability, poor housekeeping skills, and already-proven tendency to procreate, the state argued, made her sterilization necessary.

North Carolina's attempt to sterilize Mary Brewer was part of a nationwide effort to eliminate feeblemindedness and the social problems that accompanied it by drawing on both the latest findings of eugenic science and the development of intelligence testing. Eugenic science gained the ear of policy makers in the last quarter of the nineteenth century, when many feared that immigration and the development of birth control threatened a strong United States dominated by a native-born white population. During the 1910s and 1920s, eugenicists helped to shape legislation that aimed to stem this perceived threat by restricting marriage, controlling immigration, and sterilizing members of the community whose offspring they considered to be undesirable. A U.S. Supreme Court decision in 1927 that upheld a Virginia court order to sterilize seventeen-year-old Carrie Buck for her supposed feeblemindedness encouraged promoters of sterilization programs throughout the United States. The Court was persuaded not only that Carrie Buck and her mother were feeble-minded but that Carrie Buck's seven-month-old daughter had inherited the family's feeblemindedness as well. From 1927, it was within the power of any state (unless specifically forbidden by its own constitution) to enact sterilization legislation. The Supreme Court decision was followed by a wave of new sterilization laws, and by 1929 thirty states, including North Carolina, had passed sterilization laws inspired by eugenic science.[14] From the passage of the first sterilization law until the mid-1970s, when the last states ceased operating their sterilization programs, over sixty-three thousand people nationwide received eugenic sterilizations. California led the way with almost twenty thousand sterilizations between 1909 and 1953; it was followed by North Carolina, which performed over eight thousand sterilizations between the late 1920s and the mid-1970s, and Virginia, which performed over seven thousand sterilizations in the same period.[15]

North Carolina's eugenic sterilization law, passed in 1929, fit squarely with state public welfare policies and the desire to save public funds. Introduced by a former member of the Burke County Board of Public Welfare, the law permitted the sterilization of individuals who were "mentally diseased, feeble minded, or epileptic" and whose sterilization was considered to be "in the interest of the mental, moral, or physical improvement of the patient or inmate or for the public good."[16] During the initial years after the law was passed, state officials made only half-hearted use of it. But in 1932, Mary Brewer's lawsuit resulted in the redrafting of the state sterilization statute and the formalization of sterilization procedures. The new law, introduced by a member of the Board of Directors of Caswell Training School, a state institution for the mentally retarded, established a state Eugenics Board composed of the commissioner of public welfare, the secretary of the State Board of Health, the chief medical officers of the State Hospital in Raleigh and of an institution of the feebleminded or the insane, and the attorney general of North Carolina. Housed within the Department of Public Welfare, the board received petitions for sterilization from the state's penal and charitable institutions and from county superintendents of public welfare, and it voted on the authorization of these petitions.[17] As the only state in the nation that gave social workers the power to file sterilization petitions, North Carolina's eugenic sterilization program represented the state's financial interest in sterilization more clearly than any other state's program did.

The wave of sterilization legislation in the 1910s and 1920s mainly addressed what eugenicists termed "inheritable feeblemindedness." During the first decades of the twentieth century, eugenic theorists thought that feeblemindedness was the result of defective "germ plasm." This defective germ plasm, eugenicists believed, was carried from generation to generation. As the existence of bad germ plasm could not be diagnosed medically, one could recognize feeblemindedness only by its social symptoms, which included poverty, promiscuity, criminality, alcoholism, and illegitimacy, phenomena that were considered to lie at the root of many social ills. As eugenic scientists considered feeblemindedness, and thus undesirable social behaviors, to be hereditary, sterilization seemed to offer an easy medical solution to complex social problems.[18]

Thanks to the development of intelligence testing in the 1910s, scientists felt confident that they could measure mental capacity and confirm the diagnosis of feeblemindedness to which certain social problems pointed. Eugenicists believed that IQ tests were an infallible tool for the diagnosis of feeblemindedness, lending the diagnosis scientific legitimacy and authority.[19] Testing allowed sterilization programs to be implemented that required authorities to provide quantified verification of any diagnosis of feeblemindedness. An IQ rating of seventy and below allowed health and welfare professionals to quickly identify the feebleminded and to move from diagnosis to "treatment."

Health and welfare authorities not only followed eugenic theory when implementing eugenic policies but had their own interests in the programs. Although they usually lacked formal training in eugenic science, they shared with eugenic scientists a common set of assumptions about the meaning of degeneracy and heredity. Their work in public health and welfare led them to hope that eugenic sterilization could aid in the fight against social ills. State-sponsored sterilizations were thus driven as much by the consensus among these professionals as they were by the theories of eugenic scientists.

Indeed, Martin Pernick has argued that the definition of heredity in eugenic theory was a broad one that reached far beyond genetics. In both common usage and in some scientific literature, calling a trait "hereditary" meant that "you got it from your parents," regardless of whether it was transmitted by genes or germs. Pernick points out that this expansive definition was based not on wrong science but in broad moral concerns. Attributing something to heredity meant holding the parents morally responsible for having caused it, not necessarily specifying the technical mechanism through which parental responsibility operated. By this definition of heredity, being eugenically fit meant not just having good genes but also being a good parent, raising good children, and promoting good health for future generations.[20] In the context of growing concern about the ability of those deemed feebleminded to raise their children without state intervention, this broader understanding of eugenics allowed for state involvement.[21]

■ Implementing Eugenic Sterilization: Constructing the Feebleminded

And when the children grew / Up and went to school / They couldn't learn / Very fast / Because they had inherited poor minds from their parents. / They had to repeat MANY / GRADES in the school, / And never learned very much / And never were able to / GET A JOB.

With the passage of the state's eugenic sterilization law, health and welfare officials in charge of implementing the program began to bring their own policy goals to the table. Since the directors of mental institutions as well as social workers could submit sterilization petitions, these goals ranged from controlling welfare spending to improving the health of sterilization candidates to easing institutional overcrowding by sterilizing and then releasing inmates of the state's training schools. Having identified an individual as being in need of eugenic sterilization, petitioners put together sterilization petitions that contained information about clients' social, medical, and eugenic history and submitted the applications to the North Carolina Eugenics Board. At monthly board meetings, Eugenics Board members would review these petitions and vote on sterilization decisions. Once the board authorized a petition, the case was assigned to the hospital closest to the patient, where staff surgeons performed the sterilization. While some hospitals and surgeons might have been more likely than others to come in contact with eugenic sterilization, the surgeons assigned to such cases had no special link with the state sterilization program; they encountered the sterilizations as part of their regular workload.

Sterilization candidates or their legal guardians had to consent to a sterilization. If they failed to do so, the Eugenics Board would call a hear-

Minutes - December 20, 1960

17. ████████████████m

    It was the unanimous decision of the Board that this person is feebleminded, and sterilization was ordered in accordance with the petition.

18. ██████████

    It was the unanimous decision of the Board that this person is feebleminded, and sterilization was ordered in accordance with the petition.

19. ████████████████Am

    It was the unanimous decision of the Board that this person is feebleminded, and sterilization was ordered in accordance with the petition.

20. ████████████e

    It was the unanimous decision of the Board that this person is feebleminded, and sterilization was ordered in accordance with the petition.

21. ████████████

    It was the unanimous decision of the Board that this person is feebleminded, and sterilization was ordered in accordance with the petition.

22. ████████████y

    It was the unanimous decision of the Board that this person is feebleminded, and sterilization was ordered in accordance with the petition.

23. ████████████y

    It was the unanimous decision of the Board that this person is feebleminded, and sterilization was ordered in accordance with the petition.

24. ████████████m

    It was the unanimous decision of the Board that this person is feebleminded, and sterilization was ordered in accordance with the petition.

25. ████████n

    It was the unanimous decision of the Board that this person is feebleminded, and sterilization was ordered in accordance with the petition.

26. ████████████

    It was the unanimous decision of the Board that this person is feebleminded, and sterilization was ordered in accordance with the petition.

Minutes of Eugenics Board meeting.

ing at which family members could voice their opposition to the procedure. Some family members took advantage of this opportunity and came, with or without lawyers, to voice their objections or to seek further clarification about the surgery. If, following the hearing, board members still believed that eugenic sterilization was advisable, they could authorize the surgery over the patient's or the patient's guardian's objections. Most patients and guardians, however, did not attend the hearing. In these cases, a hearing served as a legal formality that allowed the Eugenics Board to authorize a sterilization despite the lack of consent. Theoretically, the state had the power to force individuals by court order to submit to the surgery once it had been authorized. In practice, however, state authorities were hesitant to resort to outright force. If patients did not submit to sterilization orders, state authorities either rested the cases or filed new petitions at a later date in the hope that families would change their minds.

The involvement of social workers, in particular, meant that the state sometimes attempted to take control of the reproductive future of entire families, spending many years in pursuit of this goal. In fact, as the story of the Bodwin family demonstrates, the success of such state interventions often depended on the continued persistence of state authorities, particularly in the face of opposition. In 1934, the Orange County Department of Public Welfare filed petitions for the sterilization of Emily Bodwin and two of her six children, Laura and Patrick.[22] George H. Lawrence, at that point the county commissioner of public welfare in Orange County, was a fervent supporter of the state's new eugenic sterilization program. His staff had administered IQ tests to all Bodwin family members and had concluded that the entire family was feebleminded. Emily's husband, Tom Bodwin, also had a number of health problems. He was a hunchback, he had a marked tremor in his body, and he had a cataract developing in his right eye. The Bodwins, however, did not share the welfare department's excitement about eugenic sterilization. They refused to consent, and after the Eugenics Board ordered the surgeries anyway, they left the county.[23]

Over the next decade and a half, state authorities repeatedly filed petitions for the sterilization of the Bodwin children and eventually succeeded in sterilizing four of them. In 1937, authorities in neighboring Chatham County, where the Bodwins had moved, caught up with the family and filed a new sterilization petition for Laura Bodwin. Emily Bodwin had died in the meantime, and Tom Bodwin—probably overwhelmed with the care of six children—consented both to Laura's surgery and to the suggestion that several of his children be placed in state training schools.[24] This move was significant, because state training schools frequently served as gateways to eugenic sterilization. Three years later, authorities filed a sterilization petition for fifteen-year-old Pamela Bodwin, Laura's younger sister, who had been placed in Samarcand Training School and was now eligible for parole. Arguing that Laura's sterilization had permanently "injured her health," Tom Bodwin refused to consent to Pamela's sterilization. The Eugenics Board called a hearing and authorized the surgery over his objection.[25] In 1943, the board received a new petition for nineteen-year-old Patrick, an inmate at Caswell Training School whose sterilization had initially been authorized in 1937. Patrick, the petition indicated, had an IQ of thirty-nine and was considered to be "a sex problem." The county welfare department also petitioned for the sterilization of ten-year-old Alison, who was the youngest child in the Bodwin family. Alison lived in a foster home, had completed second grade, and had a tested IQ of fifty-six. Again, Tom Bodwin refused to consent. This time, he hired a lawyer, who appeared with older daughter Laura at the hearing. Tom Bodwin's attorney explained to the Eugenics Board that Tom did not object to the sterilization of Patrick but that he refused to consent to Alison's sterilization on the grounds that she was too young for such a procedure and that she was currently living in a safe and moral environment. Testifying to her own health problems and to the fact that she had given birth to a child after her own unsuccessful eugenic sterilization, Laura argued, "I think that she is too young—for a ten year old child to have this operation."[26] Eugenics Board members seemed to agree. They authorized Patrick's sterilization but postponed Alison's petition indefinitely.

But if a sterilization petition for a ten-year-old girl raised questions about the value of the surgery, a sterilization petition for a teenage girl was sure to gain a much more sympathetic hearing. In 1947, after waiting five years, the Department of Public Welfare in Chatham County filed a new petition for the now fifteen-year-old Alison. This petition described her as easily disturbed and as "so immature in behavior and development that she [was] not capable of protecting herself."[27] Again, Tom Bodwin refused his consent for the surgery. Again, he hired an attorney who, along with Alison, Laura, Pamela, and Tom himself, attended the hearing. While his continued objection to Alison's sterilization delayed a decision on the case for another six months (in the meantime, Chatham welfare authorities agreed to perform additional psychological tests, which found that Alison had a mental age of six), the board finally authorized the sterilization in May 1948.[28] The surgery was performed two months later.[29]

Authorities' extensive interest in the Bodwin family stemmed from their belief in the hereditary nature of mental illness and deficiency. Eugenics Board members explained to sterilization candidates and their families that mental illness and deficiency were passed on from one generation to the next and warned that mental conditions, if ignored, would lead to a progressive deterioration of the hereditary quality of coming generations.[30] As one board member cautioned, "The further it goes, the worse it gets."[31] Sterilization promised to provide a solution to this problem. Following the lead of eugenic scientists, health and welfare professionals as well as Eugenics Board members focused on the hereditary history of the families of sterilization candidates, and petitions often noted if relatives of sterilization candidates suffered from mental afflictions.[32] As the case of the Bodwin family illustrates, once authorities had identified a family with mental disease and deficiency, they frequently sought to sterilize more than one family member.[33]

Unimpressed with the scientific framework of these arguments for sterilization, family members and their attorneys often questioned the very diagnosis of mental illness or deficiency. "She was not feebleminded when she left home," objected one mother to the diagnosis of her seventeen-year-old daughter, who had been committed to Samarcand Training School. "When they found she was feebleminded, why didn't they tell me then? I was down there every visiting day. I didn't see anything different about her then than at home."[34] Family members and attorneys puzzled over the invisibility of mental disease and deficiency and argued that candidates for sterilization looked intelligent and attractive. Many believed that feeblemindedness and mental illness should have visible symptoms similar to other diseases. Some objected that feeblemindedness and mental disease could only be passed on if a parent showed acute symptoms during the period of the child's conception, pregnancy, or delivery. One father explained, for instance, that while his younger daughter was feebleminded, his older daughter was not, because only the younger girl had been born after his wife "went bad."[35] Such beliefs indicated clients' lingering perception that embryos could be "marked" if the mother experienced a particularly traumatic event during conception or pregnancy. They also reflected clients' attempts to understand a mysterious affliction by comparing it to diseases more familiar to them.

Even if they accepted a diagnosis, family members of candidates for sterilization frequently objected to board members' claim that the diagnosed condition was hereditary. They pointed to their personal family histories to prove their point. "She hasn't had any children that were illiterate or feebleminded—all in good health," explained Mr. Greene's representative at the sterilization hearing of Mrs. Greene, a mother of eleven.[36] Others suggested that the success of some family members indicated the hereditary potential in their family lines: "While there is some that is mentally diseased on her mother's side, she has some intelligent people on her side too, attorneys, etc.," one witness declared of a sterilization candidate.[37] Board members conceded that a mental condition might skip a generation or two, raising the possibility that any epileptic, mentally ill, or feebleminded parent might give birth to a child "perfectly strong and perfectly able to take care of itself."[38] They warned, however, that this was unlikely.

Refusing to accept eugenic explanations for patients' mental troubles, family members often pointed to environmental factors instead. Mothers argued that their daughters had been under a bad influence. "Her mind was all right," explained one mother about her daughter, but "she got to running with bad girls."[39] Relatives and their attorneys protested that clients were not feebleminded, but that they lacked formal education.[40] Others held that overwork, deprivation, and unsuitable living conditions had led to patients' mental problems.[41] The sister of a sterilization candidate argued that her family's insanity was rooted in deprivation and dysfunctional family structures. "Our family insanity don't run in the brains," she explained. "My aunts had children too fast. That had effect. My mother and sister yonder all come from abusation [*sic*] in the family which I won't go into here which brought on all this."[42] Searching for an explanation for her sister's mental condition, she asked the Eugenics Board members, "Don't you think that it is an evil spirit and heart as much as anything that causes insanity?"[43]

Eugenics Board members and candidates' families did not limit their discussions to issues of heredity and environment, however, but also discussed social and economic factors. Indeed, class background played an important role in identifying the mentally defective. Eugenic scientists emphasized the inability of the feebleminded to compete economically with others around them. Feebleminded persons, one official definition read, might be "capable of earning a living under favorable circumstances, but [were] incapable . . . of competing on equal terms with their normal fellows."[44] The members of poor rural families were particularly likely to be perceived as feebleminded. In the 1930s, when the United States was struggling in the midst of the Great Depression, health and welfare officials across the country conflated welfare dependency with feeblemindedness and suggested that sterilization might provide a solution. A host of local studies seemed to confirm the close links between poverty, rural isolation, and feeblemindedness. The 1937 *Study of Mental Health in North Carolina* reported: "Scattered rural communities in poor 'marginal' lands, with low standards of living and low levels of cultural-intellectual development show high frequencies of apparent mental deficiency."[45] A study of mental illness, mental deficiency, and epilepsy conducted a decade later found that most of those classified as mentally deficient had demonstrated their incompetence by receiving some type of financial assistance from the state. The report listed some of the costs the state bore for these individuals: "This has been in the form of general assistance, old-age assistance, ADC, boarding home placement, institutional care in homes for children, free medical care and hospitalization, and employment on the projects of the WPA and in Civilian Conservation Corps camps. In addition to this, there is the cost of court hearing, sentences served in the county jail, training schools, State prison, and the road camps."[46] In fact, the author's description of working-class men and women as "potentially mentally ill, mentally deficient, and epileptic persons" gave socioeconomic status practically a diagnostic character.

As a result, most clients of eugenic sterilization programs were poor.[47] Of those recommended for sterilization in North Carolina, the majority made their living by farming, selling tobacco and other crops, and sawing wood. One-fourth were considered unable to work, and 63 percent received some form of welfare benefits.[48] Often, it was the illness or desertion of the male breadwinner that plunged families into poverty. Housing conditions were poor. Residences were overcrowded, in ill repair, barely furnished, and lacking conveniences.[49] Conditions like those in which a family of seven lived—a dilapidated trailer with a lean-to built onto it located in a wooded area with standing water—were not unusual.[50] As both a cause and an effect of their marginal economic status, many patients and family members also lacked formal education. Especially among the parental generation, illiteracy was still quite common during the 1930s and 1940s.[51] Confronted with the need to make a living, many people felt both intimidated by the educational system and unconvinced of the value of formal education. Parents frequently kept their children at home to help on the farm or around the household. Many children missed school because their parents lacked funds to pay for books or shoes.[52] As concern about persistent poverty and accompanying welfare costs grew, so did the number of eugenic sterilizations performed.[53]

The case of Mary Brewer demonstrates both welfare officials' concern with clients' economic competitiveness and their unwillingness to consider present circumstances and past employment histories in their clients' favor. Mary Brewer had supported herself, her parents, and her eleven siblings from the age of ten until she married by working in a hosiery mill, a cigarette factory, and a knitting mill. She had quit work only after marriage and the birth of five children forced her to stay home. In 1932, the worst year of the Great Depression, when 28 percent of the nation's households lacked a single breadwinner, she found herself unemployed. Despite her employment history, the superintendent of public welfare in Forsyth County saw in her present inability to find paid employment a symptom of feeblemindedness. "When they reach that state [of feeblemindedness,] they are rarely ever self-supporting," he argued. "They usually make their living by begging."[54]

An inability to hold a job and a history of welfare dependency were not only indications of feeblemindedness but could in themselves constitute reasons for sterilization. Across the country, health and welfare professionals advocated the sterilization of "charity cases."[55] To convince candidates and their families of the desirability of the surgery, members of North Carolina's Eugenics Board frequently stated that they wanted to prevent the birth of children who might become financially dependent on the family or on the welfare department.[56] They inquired about families' financial resources, the kind of work they did, how much they earned, whether they had ever received relief payments or help through the WPA, and how much they had received. The state, board members emphasized, had a financial interest in sterilization. As one board member argued, "[Patient] is a state charge and to protect herself and the state we feel that this operation would be for the best."[57] In fact, board members claimed that the real or potential financial dependence of patients gave the state a right to consider sterilization, and they asked family members who objected to sterilization to prove that a patient was "perfectly capable of taking care of herself or of any children she might have [and] that any children she might have would be able to take care of themselves."[58] Such proof, of course, was impossible for anyone to render.

Families responded by arguing that they did not fear the burden of potential offspring and that they were well able to take care of themselves and of any children who might arrive in the future. "My daddy has his own home and money in the bank and I have money in the bank, too, so we don't have to worry about her financially as for now until she gets married," Pattie's mother assured the Eugenics Board after Pattie had given birth to a child outside marriage and a petition was submitted for her sterilization.[59] Not surprisingly, many patients and family members recognized that social workers sought patients' sterilization because of their families' welfare dependency. Some even complained that social workers had tried to coerce consent to the operation by withholding welfare payments.[60] But even if they were unable to point to their savings or property, many families argued that they worked hard and should be left alone for that reason.[61] Protesting the sterilization of his thirty-year-old cousin, who was an inmate at the State Hospital in Raleigh, one man argued: "I don't see why she needs no sterilizing. She's been with me ten years. She stays at home and works all the time. Sent her over here [to the hospital] because she worked too hard. She did the cooking and washing and all the work."[62] When one board member objected that he "never knew hard work made people nervous," the cousin countered: "You just never done any. Try it and see."[63]

Occasionally, a family succeeded in forestalling a sterilization authorization by pointing to income and savings that would allow it to support both the sterilization candidate and any other potential children. Pattie's mother was able to convince Eugenics Board members that savings would allow her and her father to support both Pattie and Pattie's illegitimate child, leading board members to postpone Pattie's sterilization petition.[64] Similarly, Mr. Greene was able to convince Eugenics Board members that his wife did not need to be sterilized because he worked on a farm and was able to take care of her and his five children.[65] In fact, in this case, the importance allotted to Mr. Greene's ability to financially support his family seemed to outweigh a number of other problems in the family. The petition charged Mrs. Greene with sexual promiscuity and welfare dependency; it argued that she was incapable of caring for her children and that she had taken food away from them and burned them as punishment. It also noted that Mrs. Greene had given birth to eleven children, six of whom had died. Although Mr. Greene and the supporters who accompanied him to the Eugenics Board hearing assured board members that Mrs. Greene was a good mother, of good morals, and, given her age, unlikely to have many more children, neither he nor the Eugenics Board members ever addressed the circumstances under which six of his children had died. In this case, Mrs. Greene's age and good reputation in the community and Mr. Greene's ability to financially support the family weighed heavily enough to avert her eugenic sterilization.

Patients' sexual misbehavior provided another indication of mental disease or deficiency. Here, too, public health and welfare professionals followed the lead of eugenic scientists, who identified sexual behavior as a root cause of deviancy. One researcher who was deeply concerned about the relationship between feeblemindedness, sexuality, and deviant behavior was zoologist Charles B. Davenport. With the help of the Carnegie Institution, he established the Station of Experimental Evolution at Cold Spring Harbor, Long Island, where he set up research programs in human genetics. Davenport argued that sexually immoral people were also afflicted with criminality and feeblemindedness. The release of erotic energy that accompanied sexual climax, he claimed, resulted not only in continued sexual licentiousness but also in violent outbreaks of temper and in derivative crimes.[66] Prostitutes, criminals, and tramps, he argued, lacked the genes that allowed modern human beings to control their primitive and antisocial instincts and thus to develop civilization.[67] Their sexual excitability also differentiated the feebleminded from those with normal mental capacity. The feebleminded, eugenicists argued, were "addicted" to sexual orgasms that further perpetuated their idiocy. Robert Dugdale, author of *The Jukes*, the first of a number of studies that described degenerate families, warned of the feebleminded's "precocious sexual excitability" and advised "sexual training from early childhood."[68] Fornication, Dugdale concluded, was the main occupation of the feebleminded, and it was accompanied by prostitution, bastardy, pauperism, and crime.

But the feebleminded's sexuality was believed to do more than fuel other deviant behavior. Eugenicists found that the sexual lives of the feebleminded also posed a threat to the gene pool of the general population. Indeed, eugenicists concluded, ironically, that the feebleminded were more dangerous the more intelligent they became. While eugenicists believed that sexual activity between the "low grades" and "normal minded" people was inhibited by the physical repulsiveness of the "low-grade" feebleminded, this was not the case for relations between the "high-grade" feebleminded and the "normal minded." "Attractive morons abound in the community," one publication warned, illustrating the danger with photographs of two young women who were inmates of a state training school. It explained, "Girls like these, who come from defective stock yet who are trained sufficiently to pass for normal by those with superficial judgment, are the greatest menace to the race when returned to the community without the protection of sterilization."[69] Ninety-nine percent of the "high-grade" feebleminded, the 1926 *Report of the Committee on Caswell Training School* warned, lived outside mental institutions and were "mixing and mingling with the general population."[70] These feebleminded people were said to be "uncontrolled, and to a considerable extent uncontrollable."[71]

Echoing eugenicists' descriptions of the feebleminded's inability to con-

"MARY. Attractive Morons abound in the community. These two are in a training school for the feeble-minded."

"MILDRED. In her family there is insanity, alcoholism, mental deficiency, and epilepsy. MARRIAGE DOES NOT MERELY UNITE TWO INDIVIDUALS BUT IT UNITES TWO FAMILY LINES, as the offspring generally prove."

These two photographs appeared in Marian S. Olden, *The ABC of Human Conservation*, with captions as shown above. (Courtesy Southern Historical Collection, folder 77, series 1, box 2, Human Betterment League Papers)

trol their primitive instincts, health and social work professionals maintained that individuals who engaged in sex outside of marriage lacked the self-discipline to control their sexual urges. A 1948 study of forty people sterilized under North Carolina's eugenic sterilization program found a close connection between feeblemindedness and sexual delinquency: twenty-two of the forty people were known to be sex offenders, while nineteen had been diagnosed as sexually promiscuous. Other sexual delinquencies among this group included incest, "trespassing[,] including being a peeping tom," "abduction, adultery, . . . bastardy, crime against nature, indecent exposure, prostitution, seduction, using a hotel room for immoral purposes," and "uncontrolled sexual desire."[72] But if eugenic scientists understood sexual activity outside of marriage to point to larger problems of feeblemindedness, health and welfare professionals elevated the symptom to be worth treating in and of itself. One Eugenics Board member explained that sterilization could be performed on people who were "mentally disordered, mentally defective, or promiscuous sexually."[73] Among the case histories that include information about patients' sexual histories, 80 percent of the patients were identified by the petitioners as promiscuous.[74] Since sexual activity outside of marriage was particularly disturbing in women, they became the main target of sterilization programs. Sixty-one percent of eugenic sterilizations nationwide and 84 percent in North Carolina were performed on women.[75] Seventy-three percent of those sterilized in North Carolina were either unmarried or were separated from their spouses.

Health and welfare authorities, moreover, understood a wide range of behaviors to be sexual, to indicate patients' lack of judgment, and to point to mental defects. Especially for women, both sexual activity outside of marriage and behaviors that could be understood as precursors to sex were seen as indications of feeblemindedness. One board member explained to the mother of a seventeen-year-old who had repeatedly run away from home and who upon her return tested positive for venereal disease: "Her conduct . . . is some indication of a rather unstable mind. You know, no girl who is well aware of her best ways of living runs away from home like she did. . . . people who roam around [the] country are more than apt not to be normal people."[76] Clients' sexual activities became even more problematic if they involved partners of a different race. Social workers and Eugenics Board members interpreted interracial sexual activities as an indication of patients' inability to distinguish between the races, which they read as a clear indication of mental disease or deficiency.[77]

Family members, however, objected to the stigma of sexual promiscuity that eugenic sterilization carried and argued that sterilization candidates did not deserve to have such a reputation. "She has never been a filthy girl," the mother of one candidate protested.[78] Many parents denied that their children had had any sexual experiences, while others argued that their children had been unwilling participants in sexual activity.[79] Still others conceded that their daughters might have engaged in sex outside of marriage but argued that the girls now regretted their conduct and had promised to abstain from sex outside of marriage in the future. Opposing the sterilization of her eighteen-year-old daughter, Pattie's mother assured the board members that Pattie's out-of-wedlock pregnancy had been a mistake and that Pattie had changed her ways. "She is doing real good," Pattie's mother testified. "She is behaving herself, . . . stays at home and tends to her own business and she helps me. . . . She knows she made a mistake and she promised me faithfully she wouldn't do it again."[80] Emphasizing her daughter's domestic and mothering skills, Pattie's mother also assured the board that Pattie had male supervision from her grandfather to enforce proper behavior. Pattie, in turn, promised the board that she did not intend to remain a single mother but planned to get married, that she would refrain from sexual activity until marriage, and that she would follow the wishes of her future husband when considering whether to have additional children. The board decided not to order Pattie's sterilization with the warning that her case would be reconsidered should she fail to keep her promises. One board member warned, "You will get another chance. You might come before us again if things don't work out."[81]

For a family to convince the Eugenics Board not to forcibly sterilize one of its members, then, the ability to counter the claim that the family member had a genetic condition was secondary. More important was the family's ability to assure board members of its economic independence, of the morality of the candidate's conduct, and of the proper control and discipline of the candidate in the home. Pattie's mother successfully convinced board members that Pattie would have no more children outside marriage, that she would pose no financial burden to the welfare department, and that she would willingly submit to parental authority. In contrast, the father of thirteen-year-old Kim Miller was unable to convince Eugenics Board members of his ability to protect, control, and financially support his daughter, and thus he failed to forestall Kim's sterilization. The county welfare department had suggested Kim for eugenic sterilization after removing her and her younger sister from their father's home, where Kim had received a beating that left her with bruises all over her body.[82] Kim's mother was an inmate in a state mental institution. Lacking any other option, the child welfare worker responsible for Kim placed her in the county home. There, Kim spent her days locked in a room to prevent her from interacting with the prisoners and workmen in the vicinity. This situation was far from ideal, and after five months the child welfare worker finally decided to return Kim to her father. Fearing that Kim might be coerced into having sexual relations and might become pregnant, however, the welfare worker sought Kim's sterilization before her return. Kim's father objected. He argued, "If she is insane, it is from being locked up five months. It would run anybody crazy."[83] He charged the Eugenics Board with wanting to "butcher her up and experiment when she is innocent" and complained that the social worker should leave him and his children alone and turn her attention to a neighborhood boy, Charlie, whom he charged with picking on his daughters, pushing Kim down, pulling her under a building, and threatening her with a knife.[84]

Board members, however, failed to address the issue of Charlie and worried instead about Mr. Miller's alcohol consumption and his inability to either control his children or provide for them. Mr. Miller explained that he drank "once in a while" but that he had never been drunk or been in court.[85] Asked how he earned his living, Mr. Miller responded: "I am not doing anything. . . . Neighbors give me something to eat." He added that he would "go to work" to provide for his daughters. At the center of the hearing, however, was the issue of parental discipline. Board members were worried about Mr. Miller's apparent inability to control his daughters. Alluding to Mr. Miller's complaints about Charlie, one board member warned: "If you continue to object [to the sterilization] and if we do not go ahead, you are going to have trouble all the time. You know you can't afford that." Mr. Miller defended himself: "I have tried to train them right. I whipped them for disobeying. This thing started because I was correcting my own child."[86] But board members remained unconvinced that Mr. Miller could provide for his children and protect them from the advances of neighborhood boys. They authorized Kim's sterilization over Mr. Miller's objection.

Mr. Miller's inability to avert the sterilization of his daughter stands in contrast to the more positive outcome of hearing cases in which family members were able to convince Eugenics Board members that they were able to control and support the sterilization candidates, making sterilization unnecessary. While Pattie's mother could point to the family's savings and Mr. Greene to his income from the farm, Mr. Miller failed to convince Eugenics Board members that he was indeed able to earn a living and to support his children.[87] And whereas Pattie's mother could point to Pattie's willingness to submit to the authority of her grandfather, Mr. Miller seemed unable to control himself and his children. Not only did he beat his children—a form of parental authority that indicated his lack of control and that board members were likely to find inappropriate—but his complaints about Charlie further reinforced board members' impression that Mr. Miller did not know how to protect his daughters from the Charlies of the world and that his daughters needed the protection of sterilization.

Every family chose similar grounds on which to base its arguments against eugenic sterilization. No witness wasted many words on the question of whether the sterilization candidate in fact had a hereditary condition. Rather than focus on eugenic theory, all based their arguments against the procedure in terms of broader economic and social concerns. Despite the fact that Eugenics Board members and the families of sterilization candidates came from vastly different economic and educational backgrounds, they shared the same language and understanding of the nature of eugenic sterilization cases. All knew that money and sex, rather than eugenics, lay at the heart of the matter.

■ Seeking the Protection of Sterilization

And after a while he met a / GIRL / She, too, wasn't very bright, / but they liked each other. / And she, too, had been to / CASWELL for training / And had a JOB and a / Surgeon had PROTECTED / Her from UNWANTED / CHILDREN, without / Making her different in any other way from other women.

Despite the punitive aspect of sterilization, health and welfare professionals understood it to be a benevolent protection and a direct aid in the prevention of poverty, neglect, and sexual abuse. The secretary of the Eugenics Board noted in the early 1960s, "I also plan to look carefully at people who live in dreadful living conditions (substandard housing, crowded families, etc., where poor standard of conduct may flourish) to determine if sterilization of the family members would help to prevent the situation from worsening."[88] Addressing reproductive issues and acknowledging the vulnerability of children in general and the sexual vulnerability of young girls and mentally disabled women in particular, health and welfare professionals saw sterilization as a form of progressive state intervention. Sterilization, social workers believed, not only offered protection from unwanted pregnancy, illegitimacy, and poverty, it could also protect children from abuse, neglect, and undesirable sexual behaviors and experiences.[89] In fact, supporters of the program often used "protection" as a euphemism for sterilization.

Eugenics Board members frequently encountered sterilization candidates who suffered from such serious mental illness or retardation that they were indeed unable to take responsibility for their children. Twenty-three percent of sterilization candidates had been diagnosed with some form of mental illness, and many of them suffered from auditory and visual hallucinations, delusions, or depression. Martha B., a twenty-nine-year-old mother of four who had been diagnosed with schizophrenia, claimed her children were dead, showed no interest in her newborn child, and confused her husband with her sister-in-law. She laughed and talked to herself, repeatedly tried to run away, threatened to kill family members, and attempted suicide. All of these problems, social workers felt, made her unable to give proper care to her four children, and they suggested that

Martha be sterilized.[90] Lillie P., a forty-two-year-old woman diagnosed with moderate mental deficiency and psychotic reaction, thought she had no hands, feet, or eyes, was obsessed with the idea that she was burning up, had delusions of persecution, and said that her nurses wanted to kill her.[91] And thirty-two-year-old Carla M., diagnosed with schizophrenia, was unable to do housework because she had difficulty breathing, coughed up blood, and had somatic delusions, including the belief that her body was rotting away while her brain was still alive. The superintendent of the State Hospital at Morganton recommended her sterilization.[92]

Many health and welfare professionals perceived a close link between pregnancy, childbearing, and child raising on the one hand and mental illness on the other: the events and responsibilities associated with motherhood were believed in some cases to precipitate a mental attack.[93] One board member explained, "There is a weakness mentally. That weakness is accentuated by childbirth."[94] Sterilization promised to relieve the stress of pregnancy, ease the responsibility of motherhood, and prevent the recurrence of a patient's mental attacks and consequent readmission to a mental hospital.

But health and welfare professionals not only worried about the suffering that mental conditions might cause their patients, they also feared that patients' mental illnesses or retardation might lead them to physically harm their children. In fact, a number of patients did threaten their children's safety or severely neglect or abuse them.[95] Twenty-six-year-old Alma H., diagnosed with schizophrenia, felt so overwhelmed by her responsibilities as a wife and mother that she had homicidal feelings toward her three children, particularly when they cried. The petition for her sterilization stated, "It is considered dangerous for her to be around them."[96] Since Alma was anxious about becoming pregnant again, her relations with her husband were tense. The staff at Dorothea Dix Hospital suggested her sterilization. David O., forty-two years of age with four children ranging in age from four to sixteen, had shot at his wife, threatening to kill her and the children and to burn down the house. Following this incident, David was diagnosed with epilepsy, and physicians suggested his sterilization.[97] And twenty-three-year-old Nellie S. suffered from schizophrenia and, "in a spell of mental disorder," tried to poison her seven children, who ranged in age from four months to eight years old.[98]

Sometimes, a patient's mental illness resulted in such severe child neglect as to cause the death of a child or children. Twenty-one-year-old Bertha M., diagnosed with mental retardation, was the mother of a four-month-old and a four-year-old. After her younger child died as a result of neglect, the Department of Public Welfare explained that Bertha herself was a half-grown child who needed "someone . . . responsible to care for and guide her," and the department petitioned for her sterilization.[99] Occasionally, parents killed their children. Ethel W., a forty-year-old mother of seven, suffered from depression and killed her two youngest children.[100] And twenty-seven-year-old Pattie M., diagnosed with mental retardation, was so immature that she was incapable of caring for any of her three children. After she killed her third child soon after its birth, the other two were placed with relatives and put up for adoption.[101]

Lacking resources and support, many mentally ill patients became clients of a sterilization program that masked their problems but failed to provide a real solution to them. Until the early 1950s, the lack of effective medication meant that many mentally ill patients had little hope of getting better. Since the operational standard of mental well-being was restoration to productive citizenship, returning mentally ill patients to a condition that allowed them to resume their family responsibilities was the ultimate goal of intervention. In the absence of treatment that might have actually cured patients, and at a time when abortion was illegal and contraception often inaccessible or too difficult for those suffering from severe mental illness or retardation to use, health and welfare professionals looked to sterilization to make the best of often tragic circumstances. Sterilization, then, was not advertised as a medical cure but as a way to partially salvage a dire situation. Reducing the financial and emotional stress that came with parenthood and limiting the number of children who might suffer because of a parent's mental illness or retardation appeared a prudent and humane thing to do.[102]

At the same time, however, the psychiatrists who staffed many of the state hospitals and who were responsible for petitioning for the sterilization of their inmates were among the first group to distance itself from the use of eugenic sterilization. While institutional petitions constituted the majority of sterilization petitions until the early 1950s, after 1954 there was a marked drop-off in institutional sterilizations. Sixty percent of those sterilized before 1950 but only 29 percent of those sterilized between 1951 and 1966 were inmates of state mental institutions. After 1954, institutional sterilizations sank to 17 percent of all eugenic sterilizations.[103] With the introduction of effective medications beginning in the 1950s, the focus of treatment for the mentally ill shifted drastically from institutional warehousing and shock therapies to drug therapies, resulting in a significant decline in institutional populations.[104]

While sterilization seemed to offer one kind of protection by treating

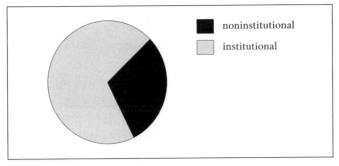

Figure 1. Sterilization petitions, 1933–1949

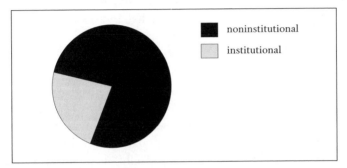

Figure 2. Sterilization petitions, 1950–1966

the person with the potential to do harm, another kind of protection was aimed at potential victims of sexual abuse. Many parents shared with health and welfare professionals the fear that their mentally retarded children might become victims of rape and sexual abuse. Health and welfare professionals hoped, somewhat illogically, that the sterilization of feebleminded children would protect them from sexual abuse. Anxious about their daughters' inability to protect themselves and afraid that they might not be able to provide sufficient supervision to protect them against pregnancy, parents joined social workers and health and welfare professionals in seeking sterilization as a safeguard.[105] In the imagination of parents and social workers, then, sterilization promised much more than it could deliver. Some parents hoped that sterilization would cure their children's mental problems. One welfare official reported of the mother of a severely retarded son: "She was under the impression that an operation of this type would give him a new mind. . . . She thought it was going to make him a perfectly normal person."[106] Others had more realistic expectations about the permanency of their children's mental conditions but hoped that sterilization might protect their children not only from pregnancy but also from rape and incest. One social worker urged the sterilization of a twelve-year-old girl after reporting that there had been "several attempts by older boys to molest [the] patient, and one of the stepbrothers [had] been caught engaging in sex play with her." The social worker continued, "She cannot understand what can happen and does not know how to protect herself."[107] Sterilization, mother and social worker hoped, would protect the girl.

Some parents took advantage of sterilization to hide incest and rape. One father sought the sterilization of his fourteen-year-old daughter after admitting that he had incestuous feelings for her. The social worker who filed the petition reported: "The mother had patient carefully examined by a physician who reported that she had had intercourse. . . . The parents wish sterilization for patient as they are afraid she will become pregnant."[108] A mother wished for the sterilization of her fourteen-year-old son, who, she and the social worker acknowledged, was capable of forcing others into sexual acts. "The community," the social worker wrote, "is fearful of him since he is fully developed sexually. . . . [He] is always in close proximity to his sister and since supervision is lacking, the possibility of incest is always present." Although they acknowledged that the boy had the potential to use force, they sought his sterilization as a "positive protection to avoid [his] being falsely accused in the community."[109] Sterilization, they hoped, would protect the boy from the accusation of rape by making his wrongdoing difficult to prove. This understanding of sterilization was not only a result of an intellectual confusion on the side of parents and social workers. Eugenics Board members, too, valued the sterilization of sexually aggressive men because it promised to make these patients "safe in society so that if [they] made an attack [they] would be harmless."[110] Such arguments rested on the assumption that the danger to society did not lie either in the attack itself or in the physical or psychological harm it caused its victims, but rather in the possibility that it might cause pregnancy.

Sterilization, of course, offered no protection against rape, incest, or any other sexual act. By preventing pregnancy, however, it made illicit and unwanted sexuality invisible. The value of sterilization lay less in its protective character than in its ability to enable people to believe that certain sexual acts had not taken place. Incest-related sterilization, moreover, had very different effects on girls and boys, since girls were thought to be incest victims, while boys were seen as potential assailants.[111] Girls who were protected against pregnancy by means of the operation were still vulnerable to rape and incest. Justifying the sterilization of female victims of incest, authorities blamed girls for their sexual experiences, marked them as sexual deviants, and undermined their future sexual credibility.[112] Sterilizing boys accused of incest, by contrast, permitted them to continue their behavior. Preventing them from impregnating women, in fact, reduced the likelihood that they would be charged with deviant or even criminal sexuality.

The sterilization program's focus on sex contributed to its advocates' failure to recognize and confront internal contradictions in it. "Nothing is removed except the possibility of parenthood," one pamphlet assured its readers about the consequences of eugenic sterilization.[113] While the Eugenics Board repeatedly emphasized that sterilization did not affect sexual pleasure or introduce any other changes in clients' sexual lives, many sterilization petitions indicate that social workers and board members indeed expected sterilization to cause changes in patients' potency and their level of pleasure. Thus sterilization was recommended to control promiscuity—that is, sex outside of marriage—and to protect clients from sexual abuse, which was considered to be a result of clients' radiant sexuality. Moreover, the perception of sterilization as protection from mentally ill or mentally retarded parents on the one hand and from sexual abuse on the other provided a powerful justification for the surgery while masking the fact that there were no real solutions to mental illness and retardation.

■ From Genes to Socialization:
Eugenic Sterilization in the Postwar Era

And because they loved / Each other, they married / And WERE HAPPY just as other couples are. / Both kept on with their / Jobs so they were still / SELF SUPPORTING.

While health and welfare professionals had high hopes for eugenic sterilization, the eugenic science that underlay it did not go unchallenged. Starting in the 1920s, geneticists, anthropologists, physicians, and psychologists began to engage in research that eventually undermined eugenic science's basic assumptions. Geneticists, for instance, criticized pedigree studies as an inaccurate way of tracing hereditary defects and during the 1920s and 1930s laid the foundation for population genetics. Psychologists attacked IQ tests as an inaccurate measure of an individual's abilities. Anthropologists charged that the term "race" was too vague to be a useful concept; they explained that it could only have biological significance—

and thus tell researchers something about the processes of heredity—if it described a uniform, closely inbred group. Since this was not the case for human beings, anthropologists charged that arguments based on the concept of race as a distinct characteristic were unscientific. Environment rather than heredity, Franz Boas concluded, determined human development.[114] A 1936 report on sterilization laws issued by a committee of the American Neurological Association concluded that compulsory sterilization laws lacked a scientific basis.[115]

Many of these critiques, however, were directed at other scientists, and until the 1940s eugenic policies were not challenged directly. Research took years to complete, and scientists, wary of engaging in political fights, posed their challenges in academic journals that failed to reach the policy makers and legislators responsible for the formulation and implementation of eugenic programs. Moreover, eager to confirm the validity of biological explanations for racial differences, many scientists ignored the growing body of scholarship that challenged such explanations, and they continued to search for the biological roots of social problems.[116] Direct challenges to eugenic policies were rare and did not necessarily extend to restrictive policies such as eugenic sterilization. Geneticist Dr. Herbert Jennings, for instance, criticized eugenicists' support of the 1924 Immigration Bill but in 1930 still believed that feeblemindedness was caused by a single germ pair and thus could be easily controlled through sterilization. Abraham Myerson, a neurologist at Tufts University, published the first series of attacks on the theory that feeblemindedness was hereditary in 1928. But rather than suggest that eugenic sterilization be abolished, he recommended that the procedure be made voluntary in nature. Only in the 1940s did Lionel Penrose disprove the notion that most retarded persons were born to retarded parents.[117] Even when scientists directly attacked eugenic sterilization programs, as Herbert Mueller did at the Third International Congress of Eugenics in 1932, they did so in a scientific surrounding, and thus their critiques had little effect on public attitudes. And if slow scientific research muted criticism of eugenics in the 1920s, the devastating economic effects of the Great Depression and high rates of unemployment and poverty contributed to a climate in the 1930s in which both scientists and the general public were unwilling to dismantle programs that seemed to promise a solution to poverty and poor health.[118]

By the 1940s, nevertheless, eugenic theory had been undermined. With the onset of World War II, interest in eugenic sterilization began to decline. The country finally pulled out of the Great Depression, and wartime production led to full employment and a drastic reduction of the welfare rolls. The shortage of surgeons during the war caused a sharp decline in the number of sterilization operations performed, and news of sterilization abuses in Nazi Germany helped to discredit the practice. In 1942, the U.S. Supreme Court struck down an Oklahoma law that had provided for the sterilization of thrice-convicted felons. Although this decision did not overturn *Buck v. Bell*, the 1927 Supreme Court decision that had upheld Virginia's sterilization law, it did set a new precedent for judicial decisions. In most states, state-ordered sterilizations had ceased completely by the late 1940s. But this decline was countered by an expansion of sterilization programs in Georgia, North Carolina, and Virginia. In 1944, these states were responsible for sterilizing 285 patients, 24 percent of the nation's total. In 1958, by contrast, they sterilized 574 patients, 76 percent of the nation's total.[119]

The expansion of North Carolina's sterilization program paralleled the expansion and professionalization of public welfare services in North Carolina under the leadership of Ellen Winston. In 1944, Winston took over as state commissioner of public welfare, a position she held until 1963. Born in Bryson City in western North Carolina, she had grown up in a liberal democratic home. Her father practiced law, and her mother engaged in volunteer social service work. In 1930, Winston received a Ph.D. in sociology from the University of Chicago. There, she was strongly influenced by teachers such as William Ogburn, Robert Park, and Ernest Burgess who emphasized process and change over fixed social structures and encouraged their students to think eclectically. During the New Deal era, Winston served as a social economist and technical editor for several federal agencies in Washington, D.C., and contributed to a number of studies of social welfare, poverty, and population policy.[120] Her experience during this period, which was characterized by a strong government and by professional social services performed by an idealistic group of intellectuals, influenced her perception of the appropriate shape of government service.

During her tenure as commissioner of public welfare, the improvement and diversification of welfare services and the professionalization of the public welfare staff dominated Winston's concerns. Winston strove to provide equal services to white and black recipients and to expand the range of services available. During the 1950s, when ADC recipients were increasingly being blamed for rising illegitimacy rates and for draining public funds, she steadfastly defended the program and its recipients while also aggressively promoting eugenic sterilization. Convinced that having too many children was in the interest of neither ADC families nor

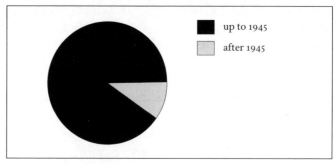

Figure 3. Sterilizations in California

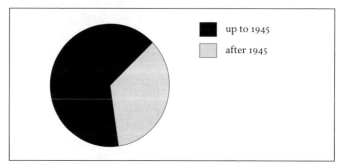

Figure 4. Sterilizations in Virginia

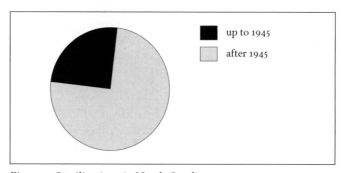

Figure 5. Sterilizations in North Carolina

the state, she promoted sterilization as one of several solutions to poverty and illegitimacy. Soon after taking office, she sought an appropriation for a full-time Eugenics Board secretary and began to work to expand the program. Throughout her tenure, she attended monthly Eugenics Board meetings and remained one of the staunchest supporters of the program. Her personal and professional support of eugenic sterilization, combined with the unusual role the North Carolina Department of Public Welfare played in the execution of the program, contributed to its expansion in North Carolina during the 1950s and 1960s.

As challenges to eugenic sterilization programs were mounting across the country, supporters of the programs embarked on a massive publicity campaign to argue for the programs' continuation and expansion. The effort to retain support for eugenic sterilization was supported by Birth-right, an organization devoted to the promotion of eugenic sterilization and the distribution of sterilization statistics, and financed by Clarence J. Gamble, who had also been instrumental in financing local birth control and sterilization clinics across the country.[121] Undisturbed by the wave of criticism from within and outside the field, a small but vocal group of health and welfare professionals across the country formed coalitions with local philanthropists, ministers, women's clubs, and professors from local universities to lobby for the continuation of state sterilization programs.[122] Starting in 1945, sterilization supporters initiated newspaper campaigns to explain the continuing need for sterilization to the general public.[123] "Alarming Mental Deficiency Rate Confronts State" warned the headline of the first article in a newspaper series promoting sterilization in North Carolina. The article spelled out the consequences of a high rate of mental deficiency for national defense: "14.2 out [of] 100 Men are Rejected [for military service]."[124] With defense projects forming a major state priority, the series' author asserted the following day, the state lacked money to invest in the feebleminded and the mentally ill.[125] She noted: "It is a peculiar paradox of human nature that while the best stock of our people is being lost on the battle fronts of the world, we make plans for the betterment and the coddling of our defectives."[126] Sterilization, the article suggested, was the "key in solving [the] problem of feeblemindedness in the state."

Although the secretary of the North Carolina Eugenics Board conceded in 1944 that "we do not know precisely to what extent mental defects and psychopathic conditions are inherited," the board's supporters lumped poor heredity and bad environments together and emphasized the devastating influence of both on children.[127] To justify the continued operation of eugenic sterilization programs, officials promoted a loose variation of hereditary theories. While health and welfare professionals had argued earlier that social problems were passed on from generation to generation via genetic transmission, they now held that the same undesirable qualities were passed on through socialization; regardless of the mechanism, they believed that the continued use of eugenic policies was warranted. One social worker explained: "While it cannot be objectively demonstrated that mental retardation or mental illness is inherited, children, generally speaking, must live in the environment into which they are born. . . . Deprivation results then in decreased function of the individual and you have the same result as when there is actual brain damage to cause the retardation."[128] As a Birthright publication generalized, sterilization prevented "the birth of children who would have a bad heredity or a bad environment or both."[129] While socialization replaced genes as the medium, the inheritance of undesirable qualities remained inevitable.

Although eugenic science was discredited by the 1940s, the policy goals behind the programs remained. Eugenic sterilization programs continued both to offer a medical solution to hereditary feeblemindedness and to cut welfare rolls by reducing the number of children born to welfare recipients. Thus as welfare rolls grew in the 1950s and 1960s, eugenic sterilization programs in a few states expanded. Continuing such programs became particularly appealing in the postwar period, when sex outside of marriage and rising illegitimacy rates seemed to threaten the stability of the American family. Eugenic sterilization, Winston suggested, could be used to combat the problem of illegitimacy.[130] The "rediscovery" of poverty in the early 1960s further fueled concerns about the reproductive capacity of poor families and solidified the link between illegitimacy and innate immorality.[131] In fact, social workers pathologized the environment of poverty itself, pointing out in one eugenic sterilization case, for example, that a patient had a "personality disorder . . . in keeping with her environment."[132] The focus on the "culture of poverty" replaced hereditary theories as a justification for eugenic sterilization and other measures while demanding similar interventions.[133] By the 1950s, social policy had refashioned the theoretical foundations of eugenic sterilization to meet its purposes.

Fears about the rising cost of the ADC program led to a significant shift in the racial composition of those targeted for eugenic sterilization. The proportion of state-sterilized patients in North Carolina who were African American rose from 23 percent in the 1930s and 1940s to 59 percent between 1958 and 1960 and finally to 64 percent between 1964 and 1966.[134] While the discriminatory welfare practices of the 1930s and 1940s had excluded African Americans from ADC programs and left them largely outside social workers' sphere of influence, federal pressure and a series of new requirements relating to the implementation of ADC resulted in black women's inclusion in social service programs, bringing them into closer contact with social workers and thus with state-supported sterilization. Nationwide, the percentage of welfare recipients who were African American rose from 31 percent in 1950 to 48 percent in 1961. The addition of Hispanics to the rolls produced a nonwhite majority among welfare recipients in the 1960s. It seemed especially pressing to save funds considering the "prevalence of illegitimacy among the lower-class Negro population" and the perception that most nonwhite unwed mothers had "no means of support except through public assistance."[135] While the fertility rates of both black and white women rose steeply, peaking in 1957, black women's fertility exceeded that of white women. Black women were also much more likely to be separated, divorced, or widowed, which affected the number of black women in need of ADC. The public association between ADC and black female recipients was thus particularly close.[136]

The emphasis on illegitimacy in the black community and on the presumably uncontrolled sexual behavior of black women reinforced racist stereotypes about the hypersexual black woman—the Jezebel character.[137] As a larger number of African Americans became ADC recipients, the focus on ADC families reflected racial tensions. The discourse about ADC mothers blamed black single mothers for urban plight, poverty, and social unrest. Emerging in the context of the powerful family ideology of the 1950s and continuing in the "family values" rhetoric of recent decades, this discourse shifted attention away from the structural causes of poverty and crime and placed the blame for urban poverty and social unrest at the feet of African American women.[138] "The expectation was that black people were not able to take care of themselves. They were all illiterate, retarded," recalled an African American social worker who encountered the eugenic sterilization program in the 1960s.[139] Social workers acknowledged that there was a connection between fights over desegregation and negative views of ADC mothers.[140] Resentment of African American single mothers and the presumed burden they placed on the state culminated in a number of legislative proposals aimed at controlling the reproduction of ADC recipients.[141]

To intensify the fight against poverty, Ellen Winston, North Carolina's commissioner of public welfare, recommended in 1951 that the state expand its use of the eugenic sterilization program by following up on ADC families in which one family member had been sterilized to determine if other members might benefit from the surgery.[142] This new policy not only led to an increase in the number of noninstitutional sterilizations but also to a sharp rise in the number of women sterilized who had given birth to children prior to having the operation. The proportion of noninstitutional sterilizations rose from 23 percent between 1937 and 1951 to 76 percent between 1952 and 1966. Sixty-six percent of patients sterilized in

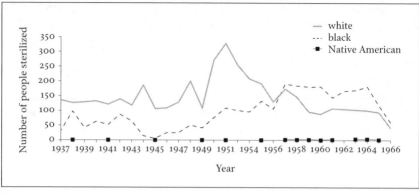

Figure 6. North Carolina sterilizations, by race

the 1950s and 1960s had had children prior to their sterilization, and 52 percent of them had given birth to these children outside marriage.

The new emphasis on socialization drew particular attention to the behavior of teenage girls. Social workers considered girls reared in impoverished and immoral environments to be likely to perpetuate the pattern set by their parents. The superintendent of the Alabama hospitals for the insane warned in 1946: "Practically every County Welfare Department can testify to the fact that they often have problems through the juvenile and other courts involving single girls and young women with illegitimate offspring [because] the mothers, being mentall[y] deficient, are irresponsible." Sterilization, he suggested, "would provide some remedy."[143] Almost formulaically, social workers emphasized the inadequate supervision daughters received from their mothers; they argued, "Sterilization will prevent additional children who will never be able to realize any potential they may have because adequate care will be denied them and will restrict the third generation who are caught in this cycle of poverty and neglect."[144]

Describing a patient as sexually uncontrollable, then, became petitioners' most successful strategy for convincing Eugenics Board members of the necessity of sterilization. The sterilization petitions for Ella T. demonstrate the growing emphasis that social workers placed on clients' sexuality in order to convince the Eugenics Board to approve sterilizations. In 1964, the welfare department in Bladen County filed the first sterilization petition for fourteen-year-old Ella. The petition noted that Ella had been born out of wedlock, her mother had been murdered, and she was living with her grandmother and aunt, who were said to be concerned about her. The petition stated: "Ella has been a problem in the school and commu-

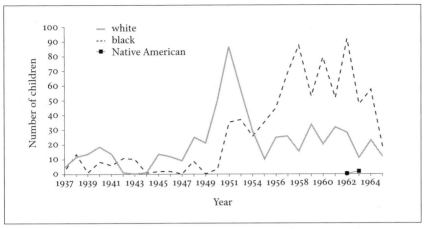

Figure 7. Number of children born to patients prior to sterilization petition

nity but is now said to behave in a more acceptable fashion. She attends the sixth grade in school but is unable to learn, profiting only from the companionship of her class mates. The grandmother wants sterilization for Ella because she feels that this will give protection against unwanted pregnancies since there are ample opportunities for sexual relationships despite supervision."[145] Given that Ella was only fourteen, lived in a supervised environment, and seemed to show no interest in sex, however, board members denied the petition. Four months later, they received a second petition for Ella's sterilization that emphasized her sexuality and her inability to support herself financially. Now fifteen years of age, Ella, the petition noted, was showing increased interest in boys. Since she was unable to "take care of herself," had "never been employable," and could not support herself financially, her grandmother and the petitioning social worker sought sterilization as a "protection for her since she [was] quite interested in boys and [could not] constantly be watched."[146] Disregarding these combined economic and sexual concerns, the Eugenics Board again denied the petition. It seems most likely that board members remained unconvinced of Ella's interest in sex. The petition filed the following year left no doubt about Ella's status as both a sexual aggressor and a sexual victim. It noted: "[Ella] not only wanders about causing trouble. She is fully developed physically and has begun to show a decided interest in boys. She often sneaks out of the house unnoticed and goes about the neighborhood looking for boys. The grandmother states that if she is left alone for even a short period of time it is necessary to run the boys away from her. The grandmother and aunt feel that it is only a matter of time before she becomes pregnant. Both feel that sterilization is in the best interest of this retarded child who cannot care for her own needs let alone those of another person."[147] This time, board members approved the petition.

As Ella's case demonstrates, it was not only health and social work professionals but also parents and other relatives who wished for the sterilization of teenage girls. Some guardians, like Ella's grandmother and aunt, worried that sterilization candidates would never be able to take care of children, and, fearing the burden of having to care for additional children, they sought sterilization to prevent their charges from becoming pregnant. Others were already caring for both their daughters and their daughters' children. To avoid having to care for yet more grandchildren in years to come, they asked for their daughters to be sterilized.[148] The sterilization of sexually active daughters, moreover, could protect a family's reputation.[149] In fact, one Eugenics Board member pointed out that "problems which many parents encounter with daughters when they reach puberty [could] be controlled by surgery."[150] Some parents, unable to control their daughters, were only too glad when the Department of Public Welfare stepped into the picture. All the relatives of eighteen-year-old Martha B., for instance, found her "out of control" and were unwilling to take her in. To both her aunts and her mother, sterilization seemed a good solution.[151] While some parents were careful to weigh all their options and to consult their children when considering sterilization, others looked to sterilization more for their own convenience and gave little thought to the implications that the surgery had for their children's futures.

■ Seeking Sterilization

And there weren't any children's / Mouths to feed—although / They wouldn't have / Known why if / The operation hadn't / Been explained to them. / And with just the two in the / Family, they kept on / Being SELF SUPPORTING */ And they were very thankful they lived in* NORTH CAROLINA.

Despite the many sexual and racial stereotypes that shaped the eugenic sterilization program throughout the course of its existence, a substantial number of women from all economic and ethnic backgrounds actively sought sterilization. Not wishing to postpone childbearing or space their children more widely, women seeking elective sterilization felt strongly about putting an end to their childbearing years.

For the poor, the prominent role of social workers in North Carolina's eugenic sterilization program increased the threat of involuntary steriliza-tion, but it also extended the promise of sterilization to those who sought a permanent form of birth control. In fact, information about the opera-tion often spread by word of mouth. Women learned about it from rela-tives or friends and knew to approach social workers if they desired the surgery.[152] Of roughly 8,000 sterilization petitions filed in North Carolina between 1929 and 1975, I found 468—446 petitions for the sterilization of women and 22 for men—filed between 1937 and June 1966 that I would consider petitions for an elective sterilization, sometimes referred to in the records as "voluntary sterilization." In a third of these cases, the clients initiated the request for the operation; in the remaining cases, they responded enthusiastically when a case worker informed them of the availability of sterilization. During the 1960s, up to 20 percent of the board's annual caseload consisted of clients who asked to be sterilized.[153]

The overrepresentation of black women among those seeking elective sterilization through the Eugenics Board speaks to the greater difficulty they faced in securing access to health services and contraceptive clinics. About 70 percent of those seeking sterilization electively were African American, while African American women made up 38 percent of the Eugenics Board's overall caseload and about 30 percent of North Car-olina's population. Women seeking sterilization through the eugenic ster-ilization program were on average 27 years old and had had 4 children at the time of their petition. Black women tended to have had more children in a shorter time span (4.4 children compared to 3.4 children for white women) and to seek sterilization at a younger age (at the age of 26.5 compared to 28 for white women). Forty-three percent of African Ameri-can petitioners, but only 28 percent of white petitioners, had had 5 or more children at the time of their petition. Black women not only had greater difficulty gaining access to elective sterilization by private physi-cians, they also found it more difficult to obtain reliable contraceptive advice, which left them with more children at a younger age and with the eugenic sterilization program as their only alternative to continued child-bearing.[154]

Poor women who sought sterilization shared middle-class ideals about family size. Most already had a number of children and felt that they had fulfilled their role as mothers. One mother of ten argued, "I've had my pile. I've done my share."[155] Many of the petitioners had tried a number of birth control methods and found them unsatisfactory. Some complained of unpleasant side effects, while others had become pregnant despite the use of birth control.[156] A number of the women lived under conditions that discouraged the use of birth control. They lacked their husbands' cooperation or simply found it difficult to "follow through with birth control pills."[157] All hoped sterilization would solve their contraceptive troubles.

Women who sought sterilization through the Eugenics Board tended to be the poorest of the poor, and many petitioned for the operation because they felt unable to provide for the children they already had. More than two-thirds of the 446 women who petitioned for elective sterilization lacked the financial support of a male breadwinner.[158] In the 187 cases for which information about the petitioners' financial background is available, 43 percent had income from farm, domestic, or other unskilled work, and 42 percent received welfare benefits (usually ADC).[159] Even those who received assistance often found it impossible to make ends meet. One petition noted of a mother of nine whose husband had deserted her five years earlier, "Even with assistance given the children are . . . hungry to the extent that they eat out of garbage cans."[160] Housing conditions were equally poor. Case files from the 1960s tell of families that lacked electricity and plumbing. Some lived in shacks so poorly furnished that family members either had to share beds or to sleep on the floor.[161] Financial problems often accompanied a host of other difficulties: alcoholism, the desertion or imprisonment of spouses, poor health, and a lack of health care were typical of the problems that many women who sought sterilization through the eugenic sterilization program had to deal with.

Health problems contributed directly to many women's decision to seek sterilization. Constant childbearing and inadequate health care not only caused women to feel physically and mentally overburdened, but more serious illnesses often became aggravated by too-frequent pregnancies and childbearing. Many petitions described individuals like one forty-five-year-old mother of six living children, pregnant for the tenth time, who was "anxious for the operation": the petition stated that she and her husband seemed "neither physically or mentally strong enough to have any more children."[162] Social workers found a host of diseases among their clients, such as asthma, liver ailments, rheumatic heart disease, tuberculosis, mental illness, anxiety, seizure disorders, deafness, and blindness. Often, physicians had recommended the sterilizations and sent their patients to the Eugenics Board.[163] Sometimes the illness of a spouse or other family member triggered the decision to seek sterilization. One woman sought sterilization because her husband suffered from a severe heart condition. A mother of five, she was "quite concerned over what might happen to his young children if he should die." Her social worker hoped that sterilization would prevent the emotional breakdown of the already overburdened mother and limit further strain on this family's already tight budget.[164]

But women did not ask to be sterilized only in reaction to conditions of poverty and poor health. They also expressed their desire for sterilization in terms of their right to enjoy sex without the fear of pregnancy. Such women made sure social workers knew that sex was important to them. One woman explained to her social worker, "Every woman has to have a man."[165] Some women described their specific intimate arrangements in arguing for their sterilization. One woman, for instance, had a disabled husband who could not have sex. She sought sexual satisfaction outside of her marriage and felt that sterilization would improve her family unit.[166] Another had given birth to eight children fathered by her brother-in-law. While she promised to discontinue the relationship every time her social worker objected to it, she probably did so only in an attempt to appease the social worker. As the petition for her sterilization explained, the woman's family saw nothing wrong with the situation. Indeed, the fact that the woman finally sought sterilization to bring an end to her constant pregnancies suggests that she planned to continue the relationship.[167]

For most women who applied for the surgery, health problems, financial concerns, and sexual considerations converged in a complex set of factors that favored sterilization. As the case of Bethany demonstrates, women who sought the surgery frequently battled several different problems at once. A thirty-three-year-old mother of seven, Bethany sought sterilization due to her health and financial problems as well as her lack of a support system. She sought the surgery in 1966 during her stay at Broughton Hospital, where she had been diagnosed with schizophrenia. After marriage and the birth of five children, Bethany and her husband separated in 1960. For the next five years, they had an on-again, off-again relationship that deprived Bethany of regular financial support but left her with two more children. Alone with her seven children, mental health problems, and little support from her family, Bethany was unable to cope. Her monthly expenses regularly exceeded her AFDC grant, and she constantly had to borrow money from neighbors. Housekeeping, cooking, and parenting presented a challenge to Bethany. The accumulation of financial and health problems and the lack of any spouse or relative who might have offered support ultimately led Bethany to seek sterilization.[168] Sterilization promised not only to help Bethany avoid additional financial burdens but also to provide her with some stability, to ease her mental strain, to speed her recovery, and to prevent future mental breakdowns.

Despite their desire for reliable contraception, women did not make the decision in favor of sterilization lightly. Although knowledge of sterilization was widespread, often women spent years in ongoing discussions with spouses and relatives before they decided for the procedure. At least a few women knew about sterilization because the Eugenics Board had authorized their sterilizations earlier but the surgeries had never been performed because the women had, at the time, refused sterilization.[169] In the meantime, their personal situations had changed. One twenty-one-year-old mother of three, for instance, had refused sterilization four years earlier when she and her husband were planning a family. After they married and had three children in less than three years, however, the mother, burdened with the responsibility for her three small children, petitioned for the surgery herself.[170] While some women changed their minds about earlier sterilization decisions, others who applied had wanted the operation for a long time but had met with the resistance of spouses or other family members. Now they had finally been able to convince those around them of the desirability of the operation or had decided to go ahead with the petition over the objection of their husbands or parents.[171]

Once they had decided to seek the surgery, women took an active and often persistent role in securing their own sterilizations. They "shopped around" for a doctor who would sterilize them, asked their public health official for the operation, or referred themselves to the public welfare department for eugenic sterilization. Some asked social workers for help in securing the consent of a parent.[172] One mother and daughter, seeking sterilization for the daughter, hitchhiked from their home in rural Rowan County to the welfare department in Salisbury to be sure they could sign the consent forms as quickly as possible.[173] To ensure that she met all the formalities required for sterilization through the Eugenics Board, another candidate secured her brother's consent for the operation herself rather than leave this formality to the social worker responsible.[174] If, after persistent attempts, the Eugenics Board failed to approve their petitions, women reapplied or sought sterilization for their spouses instead.[175]

Securing sterilization was not easy for women of any economic background, and it was especially hard for poor and minority women. The law made no mention of elective sterilization; it did not forbid, permit, or regulate it. Women could try to convince their physicians to perform a therapeutic sterilization on them. Like therapeutic abortions, therapeutic sterilizations were legal in cases in which pregnancy and childbirth endangered the health or life of a woman. They were intended not to allow women to control their fertility but to protect mothers whose health or life was endangered by future pregnancies, thus permitting them to continue to function as mothers for the children they already had.

The lines between eugenic, therapeutic, and elective sterilization were somewhat fluid. Eugenics Board members, physicians, and those seeking sterilization relied on this flexibility to achieve their goals. Physicians, for instance, could define sterilization for a mother of many children as therapeutic, arguing that frequent pregnancy and childbearing was injurious to women's health, while the woman herself might have viewed the procedure as an elective sterilization to prevent pregnancy. This fluidity provided women with access to the surgery at a time when elective sterilizations were largely inaccessible. Still, in the absence of clear legislation, many physicians feared prosecution under the old English law of mayhem, which declared it a felony to "castrate or maim another" with the "intent to render impotent." They thus refused patients' requests for the surgery as a form of birth control.[176] Whether and how women secured elective sterilization, then, depended on their health and their resources. Middle- and upper-class women could usually find a physician willing to perform the operation. Poor women, however, who were unable to search for a sympathetic physician, were unlikely to be able to secure sterilization without the help of the Eugenics Board.

Physicians' willingness to sterilize women varied over time. Though evidence is scant, it seems that during the 1940s physicians nationwide performed a large number of undocumented sterilizations.[177] This trend accompanied the increased medicalization of pregnancy and childbirth. As physicians gained control over the medical care of pregnant women, they extended control over other areas of women's reproductive health.[178] Doctors' own testimony suggests that no clear lines between medical and nonmedical indications existed for sterilization in this period. A 1944 article in the *North Carolina Medical Journal* listed a host of conditions that might justify sterilization surgery, including kidney disease, hypertension, a history of difficult pregnancies, anemia, and exhaustion.[179] The inclusion of non–life threatening conditions such as mild nephritis (chronic kidney disease) and multiparity (having borne many children) in the list of indications for sterilization suggests that the article's authors saw the surgery as having broader uses than simply to safeguard women's lives. Indeed, physicians often inserted socioeconomic commentary into their discussions of medical indications for sterilization, making it possible for doctors to stretch indications to include socioeconomic reasons for the surgery.[180]

By the early 1950s, the tide had turned. The American College of Surgeons and the American Medical Association began to pressure physicians and surgeons "not to be too free with tubal ligations" and to stop "sterilizations of convenience" at teaching hospitals.[181] This change in attitude, which grew out of a "politically charged, pronatalist atmosphere hostile to female autonomy," was accompanied by attempts to lower the number of therapeutic abortions physicians performed.[182] Local physicians and medical societies rallied to the cause. The *North Carolina Medical Journal* charged North Carolina physicians with abusing therapeutic sterilization. While previous articles had described voluntary sterilization as legal, though ungoverned by law, physicians now warned their colleagues of the illegal nature of the procedure and sharply reduced the list of conditions that justified sterilization. Economic and social factors, the authors warned, did not justify sterilization, and the article advised physicians to refuse women's persistent demands for the surgery.[183] By 1954, the Joint Commission on Accreditation of Hospitals had issued national standards that required physicians to consult with their colleagues if they wanted to perform a sterilization.[184] To keep the number of therapeutic sterilizations low, some hospitals removed the ability to make decisions regarding sterilization from the hands of individual physicians by establishing sterilization committees—similar to, indeed often identical with, abortion committees—that decided on the necessity of the operation. These committees permitted the operation only for women who were clearly mentally ill or physically endangered by childbearing. As Shirley's case demonstrates, however, even the presence of clear-cut indications did not guarantee access to sterilization when male committee members decided women's reproductive futures in a setting devoid of any concept of women's reproductive or sexual rights. Ultimately, doctors saw themselves as deciding in women's best interests, even when they acted against patients' wishes.

Internal policing within the medical profession contributed to physicians' hesitation to perform therapeutic sterilizations. Increasingly, elective sterilizations suffered from the reputation of being sterilizations of convenience, and it ultimately hurt physicians to offer them too freely. In the eyes of many medical professionals, a woman's lack of desire for children was an insufficient reason for, and constituted an abuse of, therapeutic sterilization. Charging women with making up symptoms to obtain sterilization, physicians took a decidedly hostile attitude toward their patients. Even those who supported women's desire to control their reproduction preferred for women to use other contraceptive techniques. "We're plagued all the time by women who are having their second or third child and want you to sterilize them," one physician complained. "They won't bother with birth control, even those who are intelligent and could protect themselves if they wanted."[185]

It is impossible to determine by how much the number of therapeutic sterilizations declined in the 1950s. A survey of North Carolina hospitals taken between 1955 and 1957 reported 5,209 operations among participating hospitals, but no comparable data exist for any other time period. While it is clear that eugenic sterilizations constituted only a small fraction of the total number of tubal ligations performed, the report also demonstrates that obtaining an elective sterilization would have been difficult for most women. Although 69 percent of the seventy hospitals that performed tubal ligations reported that they had no minimum age requirement for the surgery, 64 percent (forty-five hospitals) had parity requirements of four or more children, and 6 percent (four hospitals) performed sterilizations for medical indications only.[186] Indeed, in the discussion following the presentation of the survey results to the North Carolina Medical Society, a number of physicians bemoaned the limitations on access to sterilization and urged legislative reform. Charging his colleagues with operating under a double standard that made sterilization available to middle-class but not to poor patients, one physician called on them to extend sterilization to underprivileged women: "It is particularly painful to find that a hospitalization policy may be an influencing factor in puerperal ligation [sterilization following delivery]. It is also disturbing to find that in some instances the privilege of tubal ligation is not extended equally to all patients despite their race or financial status. . . . our laws should be living laws that can be adjusted to the realities of the present. . . . [If] tubal ligations are going to be performed for convenience or socioeconomic reasons as indeed they are being performed in our state, it should seem that this operation should be covered by the North Carolina statutes."[187] A vocal minority of physicians, aware of the class stratifications in the state's system of medical care, called for equal access to the surgery for all.

In the end, physicians' demand for legal protection and the perceived class injustices in the delivery of the surgery became key issues in legislative reform. In the early 1960s, Wallace Kuralt and a number of physicians successfully lobbied for the passage of a voluntary sterilization bill. Kuralt argued that all women, regardless of their economic background, should have access to a wide selection of contraceptives, including sterilization and abortion.[188] Inspired by both a progressive vision of women's reproductive rights and a conservative desire to control the reproduction of poor and minority women, North Carolina became the first state to legally permit voluntary sterilization in 1963.[189] The passage of the voluntary sterilization law, however, did not necessarily make sterilization accessible to all women. Indeed, as the case records of the Eugenics Board suggest, physicians continued to seek additional legal protection before performing the operation. Although under the new law surgeons could legally sterilize clients who consented in writing and provided the written consent of their spouses, many physicians sought additional approval from the Eugenics Board and continued to refer their clients to the eugenic sterilization program.[190] As the case of Shirley demonstrates, moreover, Eugenics Board members began after 1963 to apply standards of spousal consent to eugenic sterilizations even though the eugenic sterilization law did not require them to do so.

It took repeated legal battles to ensure that sterilization would be included in publicly sponsored birth control services and thus made accessible to the poor. Starting in the late 1960s, women began to sue for their right to obtain elective sterilizations. The most important decision in such cases was probably made in a California case, *Jessin v. County of Shasta*, in which a husband and wife sought sterilization because they already had as many minor children as they could support. The couple alleged that the county was legally required to provide them with surgical sterilization because, due to their poverty, they were eligible to receive health services from the appropriate county public health agency. The plaintiffs won their case. Ironically, however, the inclusion of sterilization in federally funded family planning programs contributed to sterilization abuse.[191]

The lack of clear guidelines both before and after the passage of the voluntary sterilization law in 1963 left the ultimate decision about whether to perform sterilizations in the hands of physicians who varied widely in their approach to the operation, and a woman's access to the surgery was extremely dependent on her ability to find the right physician. Surveys from the late 1940s and the 1950s record criteria for sterilization that ranged from having two children and certain social or psychological factors to having six or seven children. One gynecologist offered sterilization to any patient after her second Cesarean section. Another physician offered sterilization only to men, for whom the surgery was comparatively minor.[192] Occasionally, physicians saw sterilization as an important birth control method.[193] There is evidence that African American physicians, in particular, were willing to sterilize women before constant childbearing had ruined their health. Given the range of physician attitudes, it was essential that a woman who wanted sterilization be able to shop around, which meant that she needed to have the means to visit several private physicians. In addition, women had to be able to pay for the surgery, which in the late 1940s cost between $75 and $100; by the 1970s, fees had climbed to between $300 and $500.[194] Few women could afford to pay for an elective operation. Those black women who gained access to sterilization had often had ten or more pregnancies and were in such poor health that sterilization was deemed therapeutic rather than elective.[195]

Women who desired sterilization but could not obtain one through a private physician turned to their local public health or welfare departments. Officials' willingness to aid women in their search for sterilization depended on their feelings about the procedure and on the availability of surgeons willing to perform sterilizations for noneugenic reasons and for the lower fee offered by welfare departments.[196] Sometimes public health and welfare officials sought sympathetic surgeons who were willing to interpret "therapeutic" in the broadest sense of the word. But other officials lacked the resources or empathy to help poor women obtain sterilization. When this was the case, the only place left for the women to turn was to the eugenic sterilization program.

As sterilizations became increasingly inaccessible after the Second World War, the number of women hoping to secure sterilization through the Eugenics Board climbed steadily. Three-fourths of the 468 patients who petitioned the board for sterilization between 1937 and June 1966 did so between 1958 and 1966, when the number of petitions climbed drastically from ten in 1958 to sixty-seven in 1959 to a high of ninety petitions in 1962. During the 1960s, up to 20 percent of the board's annual caseload consisted of clients who asked to be sterilized.[197]

Despite its emphasis on eugenic sterilization, the state sterilization program was known as a means by which to secure elective sterilization. Physicians and health and welfare officials repeatedly referred women who sought sterilization to the eugenic sterilization program.[198] In some counties, up to 30 percent of the petitions to the Eugenics Board were for elective sterilizations.[199] These numbers not only suggest that residents in counties with a particularly active sterilization program were more likely to know about the program and use it to their own advantage but also that some county welfare officials helped clients who sought access to the operation.[200]

In their petitions to the Eugenics Board, social workers made it clear that women wanted the operation for contraceptive reasons. "Has had thirteen pregnancies and does not want more," one petition read. It continued: "She already has as many children as she can possibly care for.

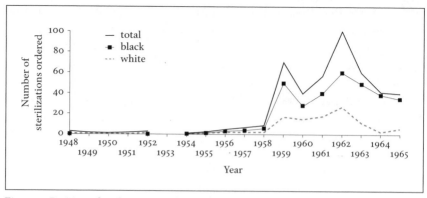

Figure 8. Petitions for elective sterilizations received by the North Carolina Eugenics Board, by race

Sterilization will relieve her of bearing additional children who will be a burden for her."[201] Another petition noted, "Birth control through medical means for the past year has been unsuccessful to the couple and they now request sterilization as a means of preventing additional children being born for whom they cannot care."[202]

The Eugenics Board was not inclined to approve elective sterilizations. It was, however, prepared to authorize the operation if adequate grounds for eugenic sterilization could be found. Just as many physicians and psychiatrists manipulated psychiatric indications to get therapeutic abortions past hospital review boards, some social workers exploited eugenic indications in their arguments for sterilization.[203] Social workers rewrote women's stories to emphasize factors that had always featured prominently in eugenic considerations, such as women's family background, their failure to fulfill middle-class expectations in their roles as housewives and mothers, and their supposedly promiscuous sexual behavior. While it might seem obvious that a woman with many children would be likely to suffer from ill health, to be overburdened with her household responsibilities, and to long for a permanent form of birth control, social workers played down such factors in favor of other arguments for sterilization. Thus the petition for Annie, a twenty-seven-year-old married woman with eight children, stressed that she "complained of many illnesses" and charged her with being "a neurotic type of individual of limited intelligence."[204] The petition contains many clues that Annie was overburdened with the care of her eight children and that she might have suffered from serious health problems: she had had eight pregnancies starting at age fourteen; she had tried to use birth control pills but "appeared allergic to them" and became very sick; and she stated that she felt she would die if she got pregnant again. Nevertheless, the social worker's petition claimed that Annie used her illnesses as an excuse for her failure to either manage her own household properly or work outside the home. To underscore this diagnosis, the social worker observed that Annie's home was poorly kept. While Annie sought sterilization because she suffered from the negative side effects of other contraceptives and needed a permanent form of birth control, the social worker petitioned for sterilization on the grounds that Annie was neurotic and unable to care for her family.

Social workers characterized clients as mentally unstable and searched for similar problems in the clients' extended families to support their sterilization petitions. A family history of mental illness, deficiency, or criminality could serve as an argument for eugenic sterilization in cases in which the client herself presented no symptoms of such illnesses. A petition for twenty-six-year-old Irene, a mother of three who sought sterilization, acknowledged that Irene performed her housekeeping tasks and farmwork adequately. It stated, however, that her relatives had a number of serious problems. The family was allegedly beset with mental retardation; two sisters had been sterilized because of their low IQs; one brother had killed a man; and Irene's mother had a severe speech impediment. Although the petition did not state that Irene had any of these conditions, the petitioning social worker concluded that mental retardation and speech impediments must be hereditary and "that sterilization . . . would prevent additional strain on an inadequate person."[205] Sterilization was justified, then, not because Irene felt that she had enough children and sought a permanent contraceptive but because she was judged eugenically "inadequate" on the basis of her family's multiple problems.

The majority of petitions, however, focused on the clients' sexual behavior. Pearl, a twenty-one-year-old mother of six, had requested sterilization because she felt she did not "need additional children to care for." Her social worker, however, pitched the case differently, noting that Pearl herself had been born outside of marriage and had received no help from her mother in "learning acceptable ways of life." Since Pearl was, the petition stated, "exceedingly slow in reasoning powers and easily led" and made "no effort to curb her sexual desires and [was] very promiscuous with numerous suitors," the social worker supported her sterilization.[206] Similarly, Mattie's request for sterilization found support not because Mattie desired the operation after having given birth to eight children whom she was raising by herself but because the social worker considered

Mattie "too weak to resist putting herself in the position where she might get pregnant."[207]

It is impossible to determine social workers' personal feelings about the contraceptive desires of their clients. There is evidence that some supported their clients' wish for sterilization and found ways to help their clients get the operations they desired. Many female social workers sympathized with, or even shared, their clients' contraceptive desires. In interviews, social workers discussed the excitement that they and their clients felt when the birth control pill became available. Some African American social workers were intimately familiar with the daily struggles waged by their clients, even if they were separated from their clients by class. They served as cultural translators for white social workers, enhancing white social workers' ability to comprehend and to sympathize with the strains under which their largely black clientele lived. It is likely, then, that some social workers formed an alliance with their clients and tried to do everything they could to ensure the success of their clients' sterilization petitions.[208] Aware of the difficulty of obtaining a sterilization and familiar with how the Eugenics Board operated, such social workers employed eugenic rhetoric, increasing the likelihood that their clients' sterilizations would be approved. Other social workers, however, were insensitive to their clients' contraceptive needs but genuinely convinced of the necessity of eugenic sterilization. One former social worker recounted the story of a male colleague who had his entire caseload sterilized.[209] It is unlikely that all the women in his caseload desired the operation. In such a setting, clients were more likely to be coerced to submit to sterilization, limiting rather than increasing their reproductive control.

For those women who actively sought sterilization through the Eugenics Board, however, it mattered little under what pretenses their operations were approved just as long as they were approved. These women expressed relief and gratitude after being sterilized. Their reactions testify to the freedom from anxiety women felt after sterilization; many wished they could have been sterilized years earlier. "People envy me," reported one woman about the reactions of her friends and neighbors. Another summed up her view about sterilization with the remark, "[I] think it's a great thing for poor folks to have."[210]

Opposing Sterilization

And the WELFARE DEPARTMENT / DIDN'T have to feed them / And the SCHOOLS didn't / Have to waste their efforts on / Any of their children who weren't very bright. / And because they had / Been trained at Caswell / And because they had been / STERILIZED, the taxpayers of / North Carolina had / Saved / THOUSANDS OF DOLLARS / And the North Carolina MORONS LIVED / HAPPILY EVER AFTER.

While some people enthusiastically welcomed sterilization and even sought out the surgery for themselves, others opposed sterilization. Often, it is difficult to determine the feelings that candidates and their family members had toward the operation. Responses changed over time and were influenced by family members and neighbors. Moreover, family members did not always agree with one another about the desirability of the surgery.[211] While many sterilization candidates seemed to meet their fate passively, other people struggled to exert control over their own or their family members' reproductive lives.

Since the majority of sterilization candidates lacked formal education, it was often difficult for them to understand the technical language of sterilization petitions. Many candidates for sterilization—and many of their guardians—gave consent without comprehending the nature of the operation.[212] Discussing sterilization among themselves or with neighbors helped families make a decision about sterilization and often strengthened their resolve to protest an unwanted sterilization. "Neighbors think it should not be done," one father told the Eugenics Board members. "Told me to fight it. If anything happened they would come to my rescue."[213]

Candidates and their family members had numerous reasons to object to eugenic sterilization. Many sterilization candidates simply wanted to have more children.[214] Others dreaded the experience of surgery. One woman worried that sterilization would involve "boiling her" as one would sterilize a baby's bottle. Others compared the surgery to veterinary procedures on farm animals. Many family members feared that their relative might die on the operating table.[215] Fears about the impact of sterilization on sexual behavior were also common. Husbands worried that the operation might reduce their wives' desire for sex, while parents worried that sterilization might give their daughters a license to be even more sexually promiscuous. Many people were also afraid that the operation might ruin patients' health.[216]

Candidates' family members frequently questioned the diagnosis of feeblemindedness and the necessity of the surgery. "She is not more feebleminded than anyone in this building," one mother protested of the diagnosis of her daughter.[217] Some people expressed the hope that their own or their relatives' situation would improve with time, making childbirth possible at a later date.[218] Others resented the suggestion of sexual promiscuity that eugenic sterilization carried; mothers argued that their daughters had never been "filthy girl[s]."[219]

Finally, some sterilization candidates objected that the surgery violated their religious beliefs and their personal rights. While the absence of a significant Catholic community in North Carolina contributed to the lack of organized religious opposition to eugenic sterilization, other religious denominations were not necessarily more sympathetic to reproductive control. Some sterilization candidates, then, argued that "the bible didn't say anything about sterilization" and refused their consent because they felt that humans should not "interfere with God's plan."[220] "You are absolutely tearing down the laws of God when you do this," one man accused Eugenics Board members. "God said when he drove Adam and Eve out of the Garden of Eden—did He tell her to go out and be sterilized? God said 'Go out and multiply.'"[221] Many family members worried about the long-term implications sterilization would have for patients' future happiness and argued that patients had a right to their own lives.[222]

Many people's negative view of sterilization was influenced by the fact that petitions were initiated by the staff members of local health and welfare departments, whom clients frequently perceived as antagonistic. One man explained his and his sister's opposition to the sterilization of his brother-in-law, an inmate at the state hospital in Raleigh: "It seems that Mrs. Brown [superintendent of public welfare in Moore County] is the one who wants it done the worst. It seems the welfare department wants to have it done just because they are having to help sister and the children. If Dr. Ashby [patient's physician and a member of the Eugenics Board] had recommended it first, I would have been more willing to have it done, because I have more faith in him."[223] Clients frequently resented social workers for "meddling" in their personal affairs and suspected that sterilization petitions resulted from social workers' personal malfeasance.[224] Since social workers routinely misinformed clients about the nature of the operation, tried to pressure families into giving consent, and resorted to illegal measures such as withholding welfare payments to obtain consent, clients had good reasons to be suspicious.[225] Occasionally, Eugenics Board members agreed that social workers had overstepped their boundaries. But board members themselves were not beyond reproach. At times, they intimidated patients, gave misleading information about the benefits and dangers of the surgery, and claimed that the board was required, rather than permitted by law, to authorize eugenic sterilizations.[226]

Opposition to the program was never organized. However, many attempted to oppose their own sterilizations on an individual basis. They delayed signing or refused to sign the consent forms, revoked consent they had previously given, broke appointments with welfare and health officials, or married if that promised an escape from sterilization.[227] Some individuals moved to different counties or out of state to avoid the hearing and the operation. Others refused to enter the hospital where the sterilization was to occur.[228] Having been warned by her social worker that she would be sterilized if she had another child outside of marriage, one woman hid her next child from the social worker.[229]

Occasionally, families decided to appear before the Eugenics Board to protest a sterilization petition.[230] Because most families were intimidated by the legal formalities and the sensitive nature of the cases, however, only a few actually attended the hearings. Those who came frequently brought relatives and friends for support; some even hired lawyers to speak on their behalf.[231] At the hearings, the families of sterilization candidates protested by challenging diagnoses, questioning the necessity of surgery, and assuring board members that they were well able to support and control sterilization candidates. Some pleaded with Eugenics Board members to give clients another chance. Others challenged board members' smug attitudes and threatened to sue the state.[232] In cases of persistent opposition, the Eugenics Board usually decided to rest the cases in question and occasionally even rescinded a sterilization order previously given.[233] Most candidates, however, submitted to the surgery once it had been authorized.

If sterilization was performed against the wishes of a client and his or her relatives, families were likely to feel ashamed of the experience and the stigma for the rest of their lives.[234] One mother protested both her daughter's sterilization and the blemish she felt it would leave on her family: "I am not feebleminded. Father was not. He was not a drunkard. He didn't drink no more than I do and I certainly don't drink myself. I don't see where they get feebleminded at."[235] Others took exception to the suggestion that they had been unable to control their children, necessitating state intervention in the form of sterilization. "I try to live right and raise my children right," one father objected to the sterilization of his daughter.[236]

But escaping sterilization was not necessarily the only satisfactory outcome for clients and their family members. Some families attended the Eugenics Board hearings because they wanted more information about the surgery or because they sought the advice of medical professionals. In discussion with Eugenics Board members, they became convinced that sterilization might indeed solve some of their problems and consented to the operation.[237] Others, seeking some control over the process, were satisfied to get a second medical opinion, negotiate for a different hospital or surgeon to perform the operation, or receive assurance that someone would be around to help in the home during the period of recovery.[238]

Not only clients but also Eugenics Board members themselves occasionally doubted the value of eugenic sterilization. The first signs of dissent within the Eugenics Board appeared in 1955, when Dr. C. C. Applewhite challenged the program's assumptions about heredity. Applewhite, who represented the secretary of the State Board of Health on the Eugenics Board in the 1950s, commented that "some [had] sentiments against sterilization."[239] Criticizing the sterilization of a twenty-one-year-old expectant mother, he pointed to the dubious assumptions about heredity under which the program operated: "Suppose this baby soon to be born turns out to be a genius. I have been talking with some of these psychiatrists—some pretty smart boys among them. They have their doubts about this matter of heredity."[240] And Worth H. Hester, who represented Attorney General William Rodman at Eugenics Board meetings, reported in late 1955 that Rodman was not "too friendly toward the program" and had remarked on the "great responsibility" that the decisions of the board involved.[241] Many board members felt at least initially uncomfortable with the task of authorizing eugenic sterilizations. They wondered, "Was this the function of the state? Was this a right thing to do? Did we really have all of the data at hand?"[242] The board members, the secretary of the Eugenics Board complained in 1955, lacked "honest conviction for the program."[243]

Ironically, the 1950s, when the Eugenics Board authorized over three hundred cases annually, was a period during which the turnover of board members was high, attendance at meetings was low, and several board members expressed doubts regarding the program's goals. Between January 1934 and June 1966, 113 different board members attended the 500 scheduled meetings. Almost half of all meetings were attended by only three board members rather than the designated five, typically Ellen Winston or her representative, R. Eugene Brown; R. D. Higgins from the State Board of Health; and W. R. Pierce from the state attorney general's office.[244] Some board members, opposed to the program, chose not to attend board meetings rather than to challenge individual sterilization decisions.[245] Often in the minority at meetings, they probably felt powerless to significantly influence the process. Others sent delegates to act on their behalf, many of whom only came to a couple of meetings, making continuity in discussion and decision making almost impossible. While there were some signs of criticism of the program, then, there was even more evidence that Eugenics Board members simply felt apathetic about it.

If low attendance and high turnover made challenges to Eugenics Board decisions difficult, procedural rules further discouraged discussion and fostered apathy. An agenda of thirty sterilization petitions was not unusual for meetings in the 1950s and early 1960s. Board members, however, did not actually read the files of those suggested for sterilization but rather based their votes for or against sterilization on brief case summaries that the secretary of the Eugenics Board or a representative from one of the state's mental institutions prepared in advance. "The members," secretary Ethel Speas remarked, "are all busy with their own work. They . . . have little opportunity to give thought to their responsibility to this other important program. The meetings are as a rule conducted in a hurried fashion because of the pressure of their own programs."[246] The large number of petitions considered at each Eugenics Board meeting, the obvious social and educational distance between Eugenics Board members and sterilization candidates, and the fact that board members never met most sterilization candidates in person contributed to the almost automatic authorization of sterilizations by the board.[247]

The commitment of Ellen Winston to eugenic sterilization meant that even in the face of some board members' apathy, the board was able to sustain momentum. Winston saw the eugenic sterilization program as crucial in the fight against poverty and welfare dependency. Throughout her tenure at the Department of Public Welfare, she not only supported the work of the board but also recommended the expansion of the sterilization program in an effort to "reduce the number of children born to inadequate mothers for whom [the state] provide[d] help through the ADC program."[248] Either she or her delegate, R. Eugene Brown, represented the Department of Public Welfare at virtually every Eugenics Board meeting.

Professional and personal ties among board members further contributed to a sense of camaraderie and common purpose; most board members shared the hope that sterilization could "make things better for . . . the flow of illegitimate children and the circumstances in which they were brought up."[249] Even the program's staunchest supporters, however, were not impervious to change. When in 1962 Dr. Higgins of the State Board of

Health suggested that the Eugenics Board change its procedures to allow all board members to review each individual case together rather than review summaries of the cases, Winston and the secretary of the Eugenics Board welcomed the suggestion and the resulting opportunity to have more discussion of petitions. These changes led to an increase in the number of petitions that were rejected or on which a decision was postponed.[250]

Changes during the 1960s laid the groundwork for the dismantling of state-supported sterilization in North Carolina. The development of more reliable contraceptives, the onset of the civil rights and women's rights movements, and a better understanding of mental disease and deficiency all contributed to a significant shift in board members' perceptions of eugenic sterilization. By the late 1960s, sterilization rates had begun to fall drastically, and in 1974 North Carolina and Virginia both repealed their eugenic sterilization laws (though in North Carolina the now inoperative law stayed on the books until 2003).

The development of the birth control pill and the improvement of the IUD meant that more reliable contraceptives provided an alternative to eugenic sterilization. During the 1960s, public welfare departments across the country became involved in the distribution of contraceptives. The passage of voluntary sterilization laws and the reform of abortion laws in several states further increased access to contraceptive care.[251] While the desire to control the reproduction of the poor lingered, Eugenics Board members began to discourage the use of eugenic sterilization, and health and welfare professionals turned their attention to alternative forms of birth control. By the early 1970s, Eugenics Board members were turning down most sterilization petitions and suggesting that other methods of contraception be considered.[252] Couples who were intent on securing sterilization were advised to seek the operation under the 1963 voluntary sterilization law.

The growing accessibility of voluntary sterilization, however, also increased the risk of sterilization abuse. In 1971, North Carolina's Office of Economic Opportunity finally authorized funding for voluntary sterilization services.[253] But it took the office until 1974 to formulate and distribute sterilization guidelines to ensure that patients would receive adequate counseling and give informed consent. In the intervening years, a number of clinics across the country coerced poor women to agree to sterilization. In 1973, a wave of court cases began to draw national attention to sterilization abuse. In North Carolina, two women sued the North Carolina Eugenics Board over their sterilizations, contributing to public outrage about the past decisions of the board.[254]

The greater choice of contraceptive methods also increased health and welfare professionals' attention to the reproductive desires of sterilization candidates. During the 1960s, Eugenics Board members and social workers began to downplay the fact that the eugenic sterilization law allowed for involuntary sterilization and to emphasize the voluntary aspects of the program instead. While the Eugenics Board secretary conceded in 1968 that there were provisions for involuntary sterilization in the sterilization statute, she emphasized that these provisions were "rarely used, and [that] to all intent[s] and purposes the law [was] a voluntary one."[255] Although the emphasis on the voluntary nature of eugenic sterilization helped to sugarcoat the more subtle coercion that social workers might have employed when seeking consent for the surgery, it also sensitized Eugenics Board members to the existence of such coercion. As a result, social workers and board members began to pay closer attention to the feelings that patients and their families had about the surgery. One social worker wrote of her client, "She has reached the decision to petition for sterilization on her own and has not been forced by the welfare department or the judge."[256] By the early 1970s, board members refused to authorize sterilization if families expressed their opposition or did not understand that sterilization involved surgery.[257]

Finally, both a better understanding of mental disease and retardation and the development of drug therapies in the 1950s opened new opportunities for the mentally ill and retarded. With the introduction of drug therapies, many of the mentally ill were able to move out of mental hospitals and back into their communities. At the same time, a growing understanding of mental retardation resulted in the development of community-based programs that provided both therapy and education.[258] By the 1960s, these developments had begun to cast doubts on the necessity and humanity of eugenic sterilization. Physicians and surgeons who performed eugenic sterilizations increasingly criticized the procedure. Medical students repeatedly raised questions concerning the precise grounds upon which the Eugenics Board ordered sterilizations, and in some instances hospitals delayed the surgery until the surgeons could obtain psychological, social, and medical information about a client. Although advocates for the mentally retarded generally favored easy access to sterilization, awareness grew that the sterilization operation was "not quite like having a tooth pulled," but rather constituted an important intervention in a person's life.[259]

With the help of several new board members and a new Eugenics Board secretary, the Eugenics Board adopted a number of guidelines in 1972 to allay petitioners' growing frustration about the rising number of rejected sterilization petitions. Mental retardation or mental disease, the new guidelines explained, were not sufficient justifications for sterilization, and an IQ measurement alone was considered a questionable indication of mental retardation, especially when the figure was over fifty-five. The growing understanding that factors such as class and race could negatively influence the results of IQ tests complicated the interpretation of the tests for many in the health and social professions. While professionals were frequently unwilling to give up on IQ testing altogether, they became more wary of basing a decision for sterilization on the results of such tests. Eugenics Board members suggested that social workers should provide clear evidence that a patient had had sexual experience and that the risk of pregnancy outweighed the surgical risk of sterilization and should also explain why other birth control methods were considered inappropriate. "Please do not spare our sensibilities by phrases such as sexual acting out, sex play, behaves seductively, etc.," one Eugenics Board member urged. "Specify the facts as known."[260] The new guidelines led to confusion and frustration among the petitioners. After the Eugenics Board had turned down the petitions of two girls and a boy (thirteen and fourteen years old) because the children had shown no interest in sex, one social worker complained, "I am at a loss to understand how the State Board of Eugenics can refute such a qualified recommendation." "These children," he argued, "do not have to be interested in sex. They just have to be easily led by any male who might want to take advantage of them."[261] In the eyes of many parents and social workers, the board had become unwilling to provide the kind of "protection" it had been more than eager to provide ten years earlier.

While many social workers and families voiced their dissatisfaction with the rising number of petitions rejected by the Eugenics Board, criticism of the eugenic sterilization law as outmoded continued to grow on all sides.[262] But board members disagreed about what should replace the legislation. Board member Ann Wolfe, deputy commissioner of mental retardation services, preferred to have no law at all, removing the possibility of state-ordered sterilizations entirely.[263] Board member Bob Rollins, superintendent of Dorothea Dix Hospital, urged petitioners to pay closer attention to the individual rights of the patients and to provide comprehensive treatment.[264] Others expressed reservations about patients' right to counsel. Noting that those who petitioned for the sterilization of their clients were "more enthusiastic" about the surgery than their clients were, Assistant State Health Director W. Burns Jones pointed out that a "restraining voice, looking at the alternatives" was sometimes not "heard until the case got to the eugenics Board." Patients, he urged, should be represented at all stages by a disinterested legal advocate.[265] The National Association for Retarded Children argued that the severity of certain mental handicaps made it impossible for some individuals to make use of temporary methods of contraception or to take advantage of the provisions for voluntary sterilization.[266] A new law, it held, could put sterilization decisions in the hands of community members and the local court system, where the special needs of those suggested for sterilization would be known and better understood.[267]

In April 1974, the Bill for the Sterilization of Persons Mentally Ill or Mentally Retarded was enacted; it put decisions regarding sterilization petitions in the hands of local judges.[268] This new act finally dissolved the Eugenics Board. However, the passage of the 1974 sterilization law was also a sign that the state was not willing to relinquish control over reproduction completely. By delegating the matter to the community level, it removed the stamp of approval that Eugenics Board authorization had given to local health and welfare officials who sought sterilization. But by replacing the authority of the state Eugenics Board with the authority of a local judge, the new law delegated control to the local level, where the needs of sterilization candidates might be better known, but where inequities between one locality and another might also be amplified.

■ Conclusion

During the 1960s, both Nial Cox and Shirley came into contact with eugenic sterilization. Both suffered from a lack of adequate health care services, both sought reproductive control, and both were denied it. But while Nial was denied reproductive control through the state's insistence that she be sterilized, Shirley was denied reproductive control through the state's refusal to allow her the sterilization she desired. Thus while the state refused to give reproductive autonomy to either woman, state sterilization policies played themselves out very differently in their lives.

Shirley and Nial, however, were not just victims of a sterilization program that refused sterilization to one while forcing the other to have the operation. Both women tried to gain control over their reproductive lives. Shirley sought to obtain a contraceptive sterilization by petitioning the

North Carolina Eugenics Board; Nial tried to gain control over the consequences of her involuntary sterilization by suing the Eugenics Board and seeking a declaration that the state's sterilization legislation was unconstitutional. In the end, however, both women were unsuccessful. Shirley never received her sterilization, and Nial lost her lawsuit.

Contrasting the experiences that Shirley and Nial had with North Carolina's sterilization program emphasizes the contradictory meanings that the same program could hold: for one woman, sterilization promised reproductive control; for the other, it embodied the denial of reproductive autonomy. But even more significantly, the contrast highlights how the absence of accessible social welfare and health care services contributed to a situation in which the state could deny reproductive control to both women. Only a social worker's threat to withhold welfare benefits convinced Nial's mother to consent to her daughter's sterilization. And only the denial of access to either birth control or contraceptive sterilization put Shirley in a position in which she had to turn to the Eugenics Board in search of reproductive control.

The state's interest in sterilization changed over time. Initially intended to improve the quality of the race, eugenic sterilization programs marked the first attempt by the state to regulate access to sterilization and to use it in cases in which the control of reproduction seemed to be in its interest. Both eugenic concerns and general problems of poverty and poor health justified eugenic sterilization during its early decades in North Carolina. Health and welfare authorities supported restrictive reproductive policies not only because they took a client's inability to support his or her family as an indication of mental illness or feeblemindedness but also because they wanted to save money. Eugenic sterilization became a way to save the future of the germ plasm and the future of the state's purse.

During the 1950s and 1960s, eugenic sterilization became a way both to regulate undesirable sexual behavior and to control the size of the state welfare rolls. Despite the discrediting of eugenic theory and the growing emphasis on socialization as the medium through which negative traits were passed from parents to their offspring, eugenic sterilizations not only continued in the postwar years but took on a new meaning. As the number of institutional sterilizations declined, a growing emphasis on poverty and sex outside of marriage drew the attention of the Eugenics Board to female welfare recipients who were having sex outside marriage. Health and welfare officials argued that parents were likely to pass poverty, sexual promiscuity, and poor parenting skills on to their children.

But not every diagnosis of mental illness or retardation merely reflected the discourse surrounding women's mothering skills and sexual behavior. Mental illness and mental retardation are not, after all, simply social constructs. Some women, like some men, truly suffered from mental illness or severe mental retardation. Many of them found it difficult to prevent conception, adding the constant threat of pregnancy to already existing mental health problems. In addition, mental health problems occasionally led to child neglect or abuse, making reproductive control necessary. In some such cases, sterilization was an appropriate answer. Although sterilization was only a partial solution among a number of inadequate ones, it could at least prevent a situation from getting worse by assuring effective reproductive control.

The Eugenics Board was charged with evaluating which sterilizations constituted appropriate state intervention and which violated the reproductive freedom of sterilization candidates. This job exceeded the capacity of the Eugenics Board. First, because board members all had regular professional positions, they frequently had their own interests in sterilizations on which they were supposed to vote as disinterested individuals. Second, board members often lacked the knowledge and information to make appropriate judgments about the needs and abilities of sterilization candidates. Third, they were overburdened with such a large caseload that thorough consideration of individual cases was impossible. In this context, the existence of sterilization candidates with serious social and medical problems blurred the line between legitimate state intervention and the abuse of state power. In fact, the very existence of such cases allowed health and welfare professionals and Eugenics Board members to convince themselves that each and every sterilization authorized fell into the category of constructive intervention rather than the category of destructive abuse of power.

A lack of adequate social and health care resources contributed to a situation in which viable alternatives to sterilization were often nonexistent. Rather than solve the problem at hand, sterilization became a Band-Aid solution that promised to prevent further disaster. The sterilization of thirteen-year-old Kim Miller, for instance, demonstrated the lack of appropriate social services. Since Kim's mother was in a mental institution, Kim's social worker felt it was necessary to remove Kim from her home after she had received a severe beating from her father. But the absence of a foster care system, an orphanage, or relatives who might take responsibility for Kim left the social worker with only two placement options: the county home or the abusive father. Since both placements were clearly inappropriate, lacking structure, supervision, and guidance suitable for a thirteen-year-old, Kim's social worker turned her attention from solving the problem of placement to preventing Kim's situation from getting even worse. Convinced that pregnancy would worsen the situation further, she sought eugenic sterilization for Kim. The surgery addressed an anticipated problem—the potential rape or sexual abuse of Kim—rather than remedy the girl's present situation. The Band-Aid quality of such eugenic sterilizations contributed to the inhumanity of the sterilization program.

The state, however, was not the only entity seeking to control access to sterilization. The medical profession had its own interest in sterilization that was sometimes similar to and at other times counter to the interests of the state. Much of the time, physicians supported the sterilization program by lobbying for it, arguing for the sterilization of those deemed mentally ill or feebleminded, and sterilizing those whose surgery had been authorized. Yet physicians and psychiatrists were also among the first to challenge the program. Psychiatrists, in particular, voiced their concerns about the theoretical foundations that underlay the eugenic sterilization program, and starting in the 1950s they stopped referring their patients to the program. Some local physicians also refused to cooperate with superintendents of public welfare in performing eugenic sterilizations. And starting in the 1960s, medical professionals at teaching hospitals challenged at least some eugenic sterilization cases outright.

At the same time, many physicians' opinions about sterilization were shaped by the same conservative and pronatalist position that characterized their attitude toward any separation of sexuality from reproduction. As the debate surrounding voluntary sterilization demonstrates, the medical profession as a whole was reluctant to allow women to choose sterilization for contraceptive reasons. While physicians were more willing to grant women access to the surgery in times of economic and social hardship such as the Great Depression and World War II, the medical profession clamped down on members who continued to provide easy access to sterilization in the pronatalist postwar years. Hospitals established complicated parity formulas to restrict access to sterilization to older women and to those who had had four or five children. Women's continued demand for the surgery, however, led physicians both to criticize the emergence of a two-tier system that allowed privileged but not poor women access to sterilization and to lobby for the passage of a voluntary sterilization law. Physicians did not simply function as the arm of the state when it came to sterilization but participated in negotiations with both the state and female patients over access to and use of the surgery.

Women had no uniform response to sterilization. Instead, their responses to sterilization varied by context and over time. Women did not react as one race or one class. Rather, women's responses were conditioned by their personal economic, social, and family circumstances, their religious beliefs, their health and access to birth control, and their sexual experiences. For some, sterilization was a clear infringement of their reproductive autonomy. For others, it was a procedure very much desired. Moreover, many women's responses to the surgery changed over time. A woman might have looked unfavorably at sterilization at the beginning of her childbearing career, for example, but begun to desire the surgery after having given birth to several children.

Women's attempts to secure elective sterilization through the eugenic sterilization program were both active and reactive. Women reacted to conditions of poverty and poor health. They sought permanent contraception because they felt unable to provide for their children, hoped to escape poverty by limiting the number of their children, or wished to give their children more opportunities than they themselves had had. In addition, they hoped to improve their health by bringing an end to near-constant pregnancy and childbearing. But women also asserted their sexual rights when seeking sterilization. They wanted to continue sexual activity and hoped to increase their pleasure without constantly having to worry about pregnancy. Their actions were not simply, then, reactions to hardship. Rather, they grew out of women's understanding of themselves as sexual beings and of their desire to shape their sexual, social, and economic lives.

Women's choice of elective sterilization, however, was conditioned by their lack of other alternatives. This is not to say that women would necessarily have chosen other contraceptives had they had complete reproductive control. Yet women's lack of access to decent health and contraceptive services, their poverty, their race, and their gender all significantly influenced their decisions to seek sterilization. They lacked the ability to choose from a range of safe, effective, convenient, and affordable methods of birth control in a context of equitable social, political, and economic conditions.[269] Moreover, having to apply for an elective sterilization through the eugenic sterilization program denied women the dignity of obtaining sterilization on their own terms, and it must often have felt humiliating. Women did not base their desire for sterilization on abstract notions of reproductive rights, although some voiced the opinion that they had a right to enjoy sexual relations without the constant threat of pregnancy. Nevertheless, within the constraints that bound their decisions, these women were able to achieve a measure of reproductive control.

Women's use of the eugenic sterilization program to obtain elective sterilization, however, did not change the nature of the program. Women who petitioned the Eugenics Board for elective sterilization constituted a minority of the North Carolinians sterilized under the program. Furthermore, they used the program in ways contradictory to the intentions of those who established and implemented it. Nial Cox's lawsuit against the state correctly drew attention to many of the sterilization program's most significant features, including its coercive nature, its tendency to sloppily attribute intellectual and physical defects to women on the basis of their sexual behavior, and its bias against African Americans and people who received public assistance.

The process by which women could gain elective sterilizations through the eugenic sterilization program reinforced negative stereotypes of women and African Americans—those very stereotypes that made the eugenic sterilization program so oppressive for the majority of its clients. To justify their desire for sterilization, women told stories of ill health, poverty, and overburdened motherhood. Although social workers did not entirely obfuscate these women's narratives, they added elements of their own to petitions, emphasizing their clients' alleged inferiority and promiscuity. Such narratives were shaped by social workers' limited options regarding their ability to obtain sterilization for their clients as well as by their own prejudices against their clients. In highlighting their clients' supposed inferiority and promiscuity, however, social workers further reinforced their own prejudices and bolstered a eugenic sterilization program that played to them.

State-run eugenic sterilization programs targeted members of unpopular social groups for sterilization with the dubious aim of shaping both present and future generations according to the preferences of the privileged. Yet we cannot assume that members of marginalized groups never desired sterilization for their own reasons or that they were simply victims of eugenic policies. Instead, we must recognize that the poor were squeezed from both directions. They were more likely than others to be targeted for involuntary sterilization, but they were also disproportionately denied access to voluntary sterilization. It is not surprising that poor white and black women, in the context of their limited access to health care, faced extraordinary difficulties in obtaining elective sterilization. The supreme irony is that limited access to health care also made the eugenics program one of the few resources available to poor and minority women who sought greater reproductive control.

CHAPTER THREE

I Knew That It Was a Serious Crime

Negotiating Abortion before *Roe v. Wade*

In 1945, eighteen-year-old Sandra discovered that she was pregnant.
A college student in Boston, Sandra knew about birth control but as
an unmarried woman lacked access to contraceptives. Wanting to
end her pregnancy, she approached a pharmacist friend, Ralph, for
help. Ralph gave her pills. Sandra remembered: "I took lots of different kinds of pills, because Ralph tried one kind after another.
None of them worked. It's not that they did nothing. Some made me
sick. One kind gave me terrible diarrhea. But none of them had any
effect at all on the pregnancy. Finally, there were no more pills to try
and I began looking for a doctor or someone who could do an abortion."[1] Through a friend, she got the name of an abortionist, whom
Sandra remembered as extremely dirty. He charged $200 for the
procedure, which he performed on his equally dirty kitchen table.
After the abortion, which was quick and relatively painless, Sandra
suffered from a bad infection. Worried that she might get arrested if
she went to the hospital, she "just waited it out." The following year,
she married her boyfriend, and since neither she nor her husband
wanted any children, she got a diaphragm. However, in 1952 Sandra
found herself pregnant for a second time and again began to look for
an abortion. This time, she got the name of a fancy Park Avenue
doctor in New York City. Sandra remembers her second abortion as

skillful—a regular dilation and curettage (D&C) in the hospital—but extremely expensive.[2] The procedure itself cost $1,000. In addition, there was the cost of travel to New York and an overnight stay in a hotel. Moreover, the physician forced Sandra to have sex with him before he would perform the procedure. Sandra recalled: "By the time I got to the sex part of the 'price tag,' what was I going to do? We had already spent all of the other money. Besides I wanted an abortion and I'd have done whatever it took, at that point, to make it happen. The doctor probably knew that."[3] In the mid-1960s, Sandra had a third abortion, this one performed by her regular gynecologist. While she did not have to have sex with her doctor, she did need letters from three psychiatrists stating that she was mentally unbalanced. In addition, she had to consent to sterilization. "I guess that went with the mental thing," she reasoned. "My gynecologist and the three psychiatrists had to protect themselves, and the message in the psychiatrists' letters was that I would become insane if I were pregnant, or maybe that pregnancy somehow triggered insanity—not just this pregnancy but any future pregnancy. Anyway, I had my tubes tied. It was really not unlike the situation in New York fifteen years earlier. I just did whatever it took to get the abortion."[4]

Sandra's story poignantly demonstrates the role that abortion has played in women's lives, the determination with which they sought the illegal procedure, and the changing conditions under which they were able to gain access to it over the course of the twentieth century. Because women were denied access to safe and reliable contraceptives, abortion was frequently the only hope they had in trying to control their reproduction. But women who lacked access to birth control and sterilization also lacked access to legal abortion. During the second part of the nineteenth century, state legislators across the country passed laws prohibiting abortion except in cases in which pregnancy and childbirth threatened a woman's life. The passage of this legislation marked the beginning of almost a century during which most abortions were illegal. In practice, the legislation divided women who sought abortion into three groups: those who were granted so-called therapeutic abortions for medical reasons, those who sought but were denied elective abortions, and those for whom health and welfare professionals desired abortions for eugenic reasons. Whether abortions were understood as elective, therapeutic, or eugenic greatly influenced their reputation among health and welfare professionals, their toleration in the courts, and, ultimately, their accessibility. This chapter will analyze the competing definitions of abortion and discuss the consequences that the shifting meaning of abortion had for physicians, women, and the state.

For most of the eighteenth and nineteenth centuries, abortions performed before quickening—fetal movement—were not punishable by law, and an abortion obtained after quickening was treated as a misdemeanor rather than a felony as long as the woman who had obtained it did not die. By the middle of the nineteenth century, the commercialization of birth control and access to abortion meant that women were increasingly able to control their reproduction. These changes inspired ambivalent feelings, however, among the populace. Fearing that widespread reproductive control allowed sexuality to move outside the family, social and medical reformers crusaded to restrict access to both abortion and contraception. By appealing to the deep-seated belief that sexual intercourse should be restricted to marriage, they contributed to the passage of state laws during the second part of the nineteenth century that criminalized most types of abortion. The ease with which women could gain access to abortion changed over time and depended on the determination with which state authorities investigated and prosecuted abortion-related injuries and deaths. As historian Leslie Reagan has demonstrated, from the time of its criminalization until the 1930s, abortion was "widely accepted" and practiced in women's homes and in the offices of physicians and midwives.[5] With the onset of the Great Depression, hard economic times meant that many more women sought to delay childbearing. Medical practitioners responded to women's increased demands for abortion, leading to the emergence of physician abortion specialists who began to perform abortions in hospitals and clinics rather than in private offices and homes. By the 1940s, however, the tide of tolerance had turned. More-frequent prosecution of abortion providers restricted women's access to the procedure and pushed illegal abortion services underground. From the 1940s to 1973, the state prosecuted abortionists more aggressively than ever before, systematically raiding abortion clinics, publicly interrogating women who had sought abortion, and humiliating both clients and abortion providers in the courtroom. While this pushed abortion services underground and made it harder for women to locate providers of safe and affordable abortion, women continued to ask for the procedure. Their persistent demand convinced physicians to provide it and led to a mass movement that stretched from the mid-1950s to the legalization of abortion with *Roe v. Wade* in 1973.

Women negotiated for access to abortion just as they negotiated for access to birth control and sterilization. And just as physicians and the state classified birth control and sterilization as elective, eugenic, or therapeutic in order to regulate access to them, they followed this pattern in the case of abortion. Although it is hitherto unexplored, the common history of abortion and sterilization suggests that the procedures were not located on opposite poles; rather, both promised to extend reproductive control to women who sought them while holding attraction for policy makers as tools that promised to control women's reproduction.[6]

The existence of illegal abortion focused the debate surrounding abortion on the dangers that the procedure could hold for women's health and lives rather than on women's lack of access to it. Prosecuting those who provided illegal abortion and restricting women's access to the procedure seemingly protected women from these dangers. As a result, however, the discourse surrounding abortion took place in a medical rather than a reproductive rights framework. Similar to debates surrounding sterilization, the debates surrounding abortion focused on specific medical conditions that might justify a therapeutic or eugenic abortion but remained hostile to elective abortion, which could extend reproductive control to women. In addition, they depicted women as victims of partners and abortionists who manipulated their bodies rather than as agents who chose sexual pleasure and abortion. The paradigm of woman as victim was essential in order for antiabortion laws to be upheld, and it shaped the context and severely limited the conditions under which women could gain access to abortion.

Once abortion was criminalized, the process of securing an abortion from a physician became highly structured and restricted. Abortions were generally illegal and could only be obtained legally if a physician found that the pregnancy or delivery seriously impaired a woman's health or endangered her life. Despite the illegal nature of abortion, however, women continued to seek it, bargaining with their private physicians and shopping around for the desired procedure. But like elective sterilization, elective abortion suffered increasingly from a poor reputation as an operation of convenience, leading the medical profession to police itself in an attempt to lower abortion and sterilization rates as much as possible. In the 1950s, hospitals began to set up abortion committees; like the hospital sterilization committees established during the same period, these abortion committees reviewed women's requests for the operation and decided whether therapeutic abortion was warranted. The highly structured process successfully regulated and limited women's access to abortion.

While women were denied access to elective abortion, and while thera-peutic abortion was tightly regulated, a number of health and welfare professionals sought to pass legislation permitting abortion for eugenic reasons. Legislative proposals for abortion reform highlighted the prom-ise of eliminating the births of babies with birth defects. Physicians push-ing to increase women's access to abortion in the 1950s and 1960s did so under the guise of psychiatric indications that declared certain women too mentally unstable to bear and raise children. As was the case with eugenic sterilization, then, women's access to the procedure hinged on the pres-ence of a mental or physical defect, either in the fetus or in the pregnant mother, that could be avoided through pregnancy termination. Arguing that unwanted children were responsible for a host of social problems, health and welfare officials looked to abortion—just as they looked to birth control and sterilization—as a solution to unwelcome pregnancies. Reformers held that unwanted children were usually born to mothers of questionable competence and were likely to perpetuate their parents' so-cial problems. Financial and eugenic considerations made it desirable for such women to have access to abortion. Advocates of eugenic abortion argued that the legalization of abortion would provide yet another avenue for preventing the birth of children who were likely to perpetuate social problems and become public charges. In their fight for abortion reform, health and welfare officials across the country turned to the same financial and eugenic arguments that justified eugenic sterilization policies and that stood behind the 1960s push for family planning programs.

Despite the appeal that abortion might have held as a social policy measure, the state never sought out women for eugenic abortion as it sought out women for eugenic sterilization and use of IUDs. Women were rarely subjected to abortion against their will. Many proponents of eu-genic sterilization, however, wished to extend eugenic policies to include abortion, allowing, for instance, for the termination of pregnancies in cases in which the Eugenics Board had approved eugenic sterilization for a pregnant woman. Indeed, during the 1960s, at the height of public hos-tility toward ADC mothers, proposals to extend eugenic policies to include abortion found considerable public support and contributed to the pas-sage of an abortion reform bill in North Carolina. The lack of state super-vision of pregnant women might have been responsible for the fact that eugenic abortion programs never materialized in the United States.[7] The appeal that eugenic abortion held for American reformers suggests, how-ever, the common heritage of sterilization and abortion. Depending on the context in which the surgeries were performed, both sterilization and abortion could either give women greater reproductive control or allow for the control of women's reproduction.

Unlike women's experiences with birth control and sterilization, however, many of their experiences with abortion centered around illegal procedures. During the nearly century-long period during which abortion was illegal, women continued to terminate their unwanted pregnancies, usually by seeking underground abortions from laypeople. "The practice with many of these mothers to produce abortions is shocking," one public health nurse noted half a century after abortion was criminalized. She explained: "Many employ a rubber catheter, 'slippery elm,' quinine and turpentine taken internally and inserted into the uterus, [and] 'large pills' (these cost $1.00 each, the name of which they could not tell, though relate that they are very effective, but they could not always get the dollar)."[8]

The most common abortion techniques during this period can be grouped into three categories: noninvasive activity, such as hot baths or strenuous exercise; ingestion of a chemical or herbal substance believed to have abortifacient properties; and invasive mechanical or surgical techniques. Noninvasive activities were attractive to women because they required no medication, surgery, or mechanical invasion, and because they were free. However, they nearly always failed to produce abortion. Once women had exhausted all noninvasive activities, they could choose from an astonishing array of chemical and herbal teas, nostrums, poultices, and pills touted as home remedies for unwanted pregnancy. If these methods failed, women often sought the help of an abortionist.

The quality of service women received in the hands of abortionists varied widely. While some abortionists provided their clients with excellent care, others performed crude operations that jeopardized women's health. Underground abortionists mainly used two catheter techniques. Some inserted a catheter and then removed it almost immediately. When this method is used, the foreign substance the uterus tries to expel is not the catheter but the infection it leaves behind, though in some cases the uterus contracts in response to the irritation caused by the introduction of the catheter. The other, more reliable technique was to insert a catheter and leave it in place until the woman aborted hours or days later. This method is almost always effective, since a catheter is too large and too invasive an object to be ignored by a pregnant uterus.[9]

The introduction of a foreign object and the resulting possibility of infection posed one of the greatest health risks associated with abortion. The catheter could perforate the uterus, causing uncontrolled bleeding,

and the infection introduced to expel the fetus could also spread throughout the entire body, leading to blood poisoning and septic shock. Moreover, a woman who survived a serious infection could become sterile as
a result of scarring in her womb. Thousands of women suffered from
abortion-related injuries and deaths. Before 1950, 1 in every 200 women
who received an abortion died as a result. After 1950, when antibiotics
became widely available, the number fell to 1 in every 316 women. While
the introduction of antibiotics in the 1950s led to an overall decline in
abortion-related deaths, the total proportion of maternal deaths that were
the result of abortion climbed drastically. In the late 1950s, the rate of
abortion-related maternal deaths stood at 25 percent for white women
and 49 percent for black women. Although most women survived their
illegal abortions and suffered no ill effects, women who sought illegal
abortion were well aware of the potential dangers associated with it.[10]

Women resorted to abortion as a form of contraception, to delay childbearing, or to space their children. Particularly in the late nineteenth and
early twentieth centuries, when other birth control methods were not yet
readily available, abortion was often the contraceptive of choice for
women who wished to control their reproduction. Most women who
sought to end their pregnancies did so for socioeconomic reasons. Determined to escape poverty, they saw the control of their reproductive lives
as essential in this effort. Others had poor marriages, had been deserted
by their husbands or boyfriends, had partners who were married to someone else, did not intend to marry the man who had impregnated them, or
had parents who were opposed to their marriage. Many women searched
for abortions because their physicians had warned them not to have more
children, because they sought to avoid the terrors of childbirth, or because
they did not wish to bear illegitimate children. Unlike women who sought
sterilization, most of those seeking abortion expected to have children
sometime in the future after their personal or economic circumstances
had improved.[11]

Writing a history of illegal abortion depends on the historian's ability to
unearth information that others wanted to keep secret. Much of the time,
abortion was not only an illegal activity, it was also an embarrassing and
humiliating event for those involved. If discovered, women who sought
abortion, their male partners, and abortion providers all faced legal prosecution and public humiliation. Because of this, even the records of court
cases related to abortion—the most obvious place to begin constructing its
history—are full of contradictions and unanswered questions. Much of
this chapter relies on the twenty-four abortion cases that reached the

North Carolina Supreme Court between 1880 and 1973. While relatively small in number, these cases offer invaluable evidence about the terms and conditions under which women sought illegal abortion and the state prosecuted those involved in it. Less than 1 percent of North Carolina criminal cases ever made it to the state supreme court. If a defendant appealed his or her conviction in a local court, the appeal would be reviewed by a panel of three judges. If the three judges ruled unanimously in favor of the appeal, the case would then be sent to the appellate court. Only if one of the judges dissented from the other two did the case get a hearing before the North Carolina Supreme Court. Naturally, it took financial resources even to appeal the decision in a case. But a review of the abortion cases heard by the state supreme court indicates that those who got a hearing were not always wealthy people. Still, the nature of the selection process for supreme court cases indicates that the characteristics of the abortion cases that came before the state supreme court did not necessarily resemble the characteristics of abortion cases in the state as a whole. While we cannot draw firm conclusions about changes in state prosecution on the basis of North Carolina Supreme Court cases, then, the cases do allow us to point to broad trends in law enforcement and prosecution throughout the period under review.[12]

Moreover, they also provide us with a number of competing narratives about sexuality, reproduction, and parenthood. At times—as when women asked for abortion, physicians warned about the dangers of the procedure, and the state prosecuted and sentenced those involved—these narratives are familiar. At other times, however, the narratives become unfamiliar and even transgressive. While the state, for instance, was often loath to give voice to women's determination to control their reproduction even by illegal means, the narratives tell of women who not only pursued their own sexual pleasure but also took an active role in seeking abortion. Women's ability to be heard in the courtroom influenced the outcome of their court cases. When women were able to articulate the reasons they had sought abortion, judges and juries, moved by humanitarian concerns, frequently sided with the physicians who had decided to help these women end their unwanted pregnancies. As a result, prosecutors became determined to exclude any testimony that might jeopardize their ability to convict abortion providers. Court proceedings became carefully scripted to exclude the women's points of view. As discussion of women's motivations for seeking abortion and their difficulties in obtaining it vanished from the court cases, women were also stripped of their humanity and turned into the immoral accomplices of their abortion providers.

This chapter tells the story of abortion in a largely rural area.[13] Many of the stories in this chapter are stories of small-town America. To a certain extent, they challenge the perception of abortion as an anonymous big-city phenomenon as they tell of small-town physicians and laypeople who, intimately familiar with women's lives, provided abortions throughout much of the period under discussion. State prosecution, these stories demonstrate, was not as uniform as hitherto assumed. Physicians in small towns were often more familiar with and connected to the world of illegal abortion than physicians in urban areas were. But these cases also tell of the special challenges of keeping abortion a secret in places where everyone was likely to know everyone else's business. Yet in investigating the texture of illegal abortion in rural and small-town settings, we should be careful not to overstate the differences between one locality and another. The impact that illegal abortion had on women's health and lives was as devastating in New York and Chicago as it was in Stantonsburg, North Carolina.

▓ To Have Her Body and Then Cast Her Off: Abortion and Gender, 1880–1930

In 1881, North Carolina passed legislation to make abortion illegal. The new law made it a felony for any person to "willfully administer to any woman, either pregnant or quick with child, or prescribe for any such woman, or advise to procure any such woman to take any medicine, drug or other substance whatever, or [to] use or employ any instrument or other means with intent thereby to destroy such child, unless the same be necessary to preserve the life of the mother."[14] A second statute, intended to protect the pregnant woman rather than the fetus, criminalized the same actions if committed with the intent "to procure the miscarriage of such woman, or to injure or destroy such woman."[15] Conviction under the new laws carried a prison sentence of one to ten or one to five years, respectively. By specifying that abortion was illegal for a woman "pregnant or quick with child," legislators hoped to emphasize that abortion was illegal from the moment of conception, following an 1880 state supreme court opinion that had argued that "the moment the womb is instinct with embryo life, and gestation has begun, the crime may be perpetrated."[16] The 1881 abortion laws remained unchanged until the passage of abortion reform legislation in 1967. The 1881 laws clearly altered almost two centuries of precedent regarding abortion, leading abortion to move underground.

The shift toward the criminalization of abortion was not a smooth one, however. Women and their male partners continued to seek abortion despite the illegal nature of the procedure, challenging the new anti-abortion statutes both in practice and in the courts. Despite women's participation in abortion, however, the law did not allow for the indictment of the woman who received an abortion. By definition, her role was that of the object upon which others acted.

Depicting women as victims of their sexual partners and abortionists as well as silencing women's voices when they articulated their own agency became crucial to the successful prosecution of cases and further stifled any discourse concerned with women's access to the procedure. Regardless of the agency women exhibited in search of sexual excitement and abortion, court cases during this period established a narrative of women who had been tricked by men into sexual intercourse with the promise of marriage. In public discourse, women became passive participants in their own abortion dramas, while men played the active roles. Relegating women to a position of passivity also silenced women's voices in reproductive decisions. That women sought abortion, their reasons for doing so, and the conditions under which physicians were willing to meet their requests only found public acknowledgment when they fit with the paradigm of the abandoned woman.

In fact, the state's early focus on prosecuting male partners rather than abortion providers indicates the existence of a loophole that permitted abortion in certain cases. Since physicians could legitimately perform so-called therapeutic abortions in order to save the life of pregnant women, they could determine when such a procedure was legal and necessary. As Reagan points out, throughout the period of criminalization, medical texts taught physicians which instruments and techniques to use in performing therapeutic abortions and gave them both guidance about and space to debate the conditions that were indications for therapeutic abortion. Social and economic changes as well as advances in medicine led to changes in indications, eliminating some while replacing them with others. The most important indication for abortion in the early twentieth century, for instance, was a pregnant woman's excessive vomiting. But by the 1910s, tuberculosis had replaced excessive vomiting as the leading indication for abortion, and medical advances eventually eliminated vomiting as an indication altogether. Physicians also induced abortion for eugenic and social reasons. As in the case of therapeutic sterilization, then, the literature on therapeutic abortion reveals disagreements and conflicting attitudes. The legal loophole allowed physicians and their patients room to negotiate the conditions under which physicians would terminate a pregnancy.[17]

Until the 1930s, the performance of abortion per se was of less concern to the state than the perception that the sexual partners of women seeking abortion had failed to assume their responsibilities as fathers, husbands, and breadwinners when they impregnated women and then arranged an abortion rather than a marriage. Of the eleven North Carolina Supreme Court cases that dealt with abortion between 1880 and 1939, nine involved the indictment of the sexual partners of pregnant women, while only three included the indictment of the abortionist.[18] Even if the state was unable to prove conclusively that a man had arranged and paid for the abortion of his female lover, the intent to arrange an abortion itself allowed for his conviction. When William Thompson was charged with procuring an abortion for Mary Lee Fuller, it was his biological relationship to Fuller's future child and his intent to "destroy the unborn child" that led to his conviction. Thompson, Fuller testified, was the father of her child. When she told him she was pregnant, he arranged for an abortion and then left town. Fuller protected Thompson until she realized that he was not going to marry her.[19] Although the abortionist testified that it was not Thompson but rather Fuller's uncle who had arranged and paid for the abortion, the state still found Thompson guilty. The decision read: "The evidence is uncontradicted that the defendant William Thompson was the father of Mary Lee Fuller's unborn child, and that upon becoming aware of the pregnancy of Mary Lee Fuller the defendant *definitely made up in his mind* to destroy the unborn child."[20] Even if he had not arranged or paid for the abortion, the prosecution insinuated, his impregnation of Fuller and his intent to arrange an abortion made him guilty. Thompson was sentenced to two to three years' imprisonment.

Weaving a tale of seduction and abandonment, prosecutors depicted women as passive both in the sexual acts that had led to their impregnation and in the abortions themselves. While an indictment did not require that women be depicted as passive objects, the state was more likely to achieve a conviction if the members of juries did not hear testimony regarding the women's interest in abortion. Jacob Slagle's indictment, for instance, described Eva Bryson as entirely passive in her sexual interaction with him. After having paid "marked attention for several years" to Bryson, it argued, "Slagle induced her to believe that he intended to marry her," and Bryson, "being deceived by the said Slagle, . . . on the 27th day of October 1877, was overcome and submitted to one act of sexual intercourse with the defendant." The act, according to the indictment, "was never repeated."[21] Only after finding herself pregnant did Bryson take action and insist that Slagle "[perform] his vow."[22] Even after Bryson's parents intervened and, "reciting their grief and disgrace[,] begged [the] defendant to marry their daughter," however, Slagle refused to honor his vow of marriage.[23] And although testimony indicated in another case, *State v. Thompson*, that Mary Lee Fuller was more than a passive victim of William Thompson—she freely admitted that she had had sex with Thompson despite the fact that Thompson was married to somebody else, and testimony revealed that she visited her abortionist on her own—the prosecutors focused on details most likely to portray her as a victim of Thompson, such as her naive hope that Thompson would marry her and her disappointment when she realized he would not. Men, this narrative implied, seduced women to have sexual relations but never had any intention of taking responsibility for the outcome. Indeed, in *State v. Evans*, one state prosecutor charged defendant Don Evans with "going with [Lucile Belk] and other girls for the purpose of despoiling her, to have her body and then cast her off."[24]

Women's testimony regularly confirmed this narrative of events. Described in court proceedings as "young ladies," they told of boyfriends who had raped them or deceived them into submitting to sexual relations by promising marriage. After finding their girlfriends pregnant, these men had reneged on their marriage proposals, arranging abortions and abandoning their victims. The image of woman as victim was further strengthened in cases in which the woman's father or brother swore out an indictment against her sexual partner.[25]

Despite the power and currency of these narratives, evidence suggests that most women took much more initiative in procuring their abortions than courts were willing to acknowledge. Joseph Crews, accused of arranging an abortion for Florence Kiger, claimed that he had done so only because Kiger asked him for help in obtaining it. Evidence also indicates that Kiger threatened to swear out an indictment against Crews if he did not give her $25 for the abortion. Annie Craft procured $25 from J. L. Sherrill, by whom she was pregnant, and then went to the home of Elizabeth Shaft, where she agreed to pay $150 for an abortion, leaving $20 as a down payment. Unable to convince Sherrill to give her the rest of the money, she returned to Shaft's home, informed her that she had changed her mind, and asked for her down payment back.[26] In addition, women pressured their male partners to marry them, swore out indictments against them, and occasionally resisted or refused taking the abortifacients provided by their boyfriends. Eva Bryson initially refused to take the oil of turpentine and oil of savine that Jacob Slagle offered because she feared "the character of the medicine."[27] Polly Sinclair explained to the court about her boyfriend, Charles Brady: "Brady got some medicine for me and told me I had to take it. I didn't want to send my soul to a place I didn't want to stay for taking medicine to kill a baby. He was more particular about my being pregnant than I was. . . . He said that he didn't want to be in any more disgrace than he was. I cared enough about the disgrace, but not enough to kill the child."[28] And when Elizabeth Shaft refused to return Annie Craft's down payment to her, Craft swore out an indictment for seduction under promise of marriage against J. L. Sherrill and later added a charge of bastardy.[29]

Men and women involved in abortion trials had every reason to downplay or deny outright their involvement with abortion. Men feared that testimony about their involvement would lead to their convictions, while women, who could not be indicted under the state's abortion laws, feared for their reputations. As a result, it is often unclear precisely what role a women or her boyfriend played in arranging a particular procedure. Certainly, some men tried to depict their girlfriends as the true moral culprits. Joseph Crews denied that he was responsible for Florence Kiger's pregnancy but acknowledged that he had inquired about abortion. He had done so only, he insisted, because Kiger had asked for his help. In fact, he maintained that he had warned Kiger that abortion was illegal and that he had never advised her to actually take any abortifacients. Crews's insistence that it was Kiger who had taken the initiative in procuring her abortion could have been either an attempt to deflect responsibility or the truth. The court still found Crews guilty. Some men tried to cast doubt on women's moral character by accusing them of having had multiple sexual partners, making it impossible for the women to prove who was responsible for their pregnancies. When Magnolia Hobson accused John Powell of first raping her and then advising her to drink turpentine to induce an abortion, Powell defended himself by arguing that he had been married twice and that neither union had resulted in the birth of any children. Someone else, he concluded, must have been the father of Hobson's child. In fact, Hobson's testimony indicated that she was at least confused about the rape. Powell, she claimed, had raped her in February of 1919. The baby that she attributed to the rape was born in January 1920. Despite the impossibility of an eleven-month pregnancy, and despite additional testimony that Hobson had been seen in a compromising position with a man other than Powell, the court found Powell guilty.[30]

Between 1880 and 1930, then, a paradigm was established in which the focus of abortion prosecutions rested on male partners rather than on women and their abortion providers. While this focus offered women space to negotiate for an abortion, it silenced their voices inside the courtroom. In fact, it often remained a mystery what the woman in the witness stand thought about abortion. For the court proceedings, it was in fact irrelevant how women felt about pregnancy and abortion. But depicting women as passive objects in legal narratives about an event that they had strong opinions about was crucial to the enforcement of legal statutes that denied women reproductive choices.

■ Both of Them Wanted to Get Rid of This Unborn Child: The Great Depression and World War II

If men's failure to fulfill the responsibilities of husbands and fathers stood at the center of abortion cases until the 1930s, changes in women's role and in their demand for abortion shifted the focus from male partners to women and their abortion providers in the following decades. Starting in the 1920s, the marriage rate declined as more young men and women postponed matrimony or opted to remain single. As the image of the new woman—independent, self-supporting, and aggressive—emerged, the popular image of women's sexual victimization lost currency. Despite the fact that many of these developments were more urban than rural in nature, the social and cultural changes they brought with them affected the discourse surrounding women's sexuality across the country.[31] Women were increasingly expected to be responsible for their own sexual fates, and court cases surrounding abortion mirrored this belief. With the onset of the depression, more and more couples found that poverty and poor health turned pregnancy into an intolerable burden. As hard economic times hit, the demand for abortion rose, and so did state interest in abortionists. The prevalence of illegal abortion clearly indicated that women insisted on their right to interrupt unwanted pregnancies regardless of the legal statutes; it emphasized their active participation in abortion rather than their victimization by it.

Tolerance of illegal abortion remained relatively high as long as women suffered no ill consequences from the interruption of their pregnancies, and many physicians continued to provide abortions and to challenge the boundaries of the law. But as the state sought to reduce the dangers of the operation by prosecuting careless abortionists, prosecutors began to shift their attention from the partners of pregnant women to abortion providers.

Physicians responded to women's increased demand for abortion by liberalizing access to "therapeutic" abortion. A 1936 study by Frederick Taussig of the medical and social aspects of abortion not only listed a number of medical indications that justified therapeutic abortion but included a long discussion of socioeconomic indications for the procedure that was similar to lists of indications for therapeutic sterilization during this period. Calling on physicians to consider both the preservation of "the health of the mother and the integrity and well being of the family," Taussig suggested that a pregnant woman's loss of weight, physical depletion, heavy household duties, and lack of financial resources should factor into a physicians' decision about whether to perform a therapeutic abortion on her. While physicians continued to resist considering what the patient herself wanted, poverty and hunger could now become part of a medical diagnosis. As Reagan points out, Taussig's inclusion of social and economic indications helped to legitimate what was already accepted practice among many doctors. The expansion of acceptable indications was accompanied by the emergence of physician-abortionists who in the 1930s and early 1940s specialized in performing abortions with the knowledge and toleration of the medical profession at large.[32] With these changes, abortion moved out of private homes and practices and into clinics and hospitals.

Medical literature and physician testimony from the 1930s and 1940s demonstrates that the definition of criminal abortion was shifting. Increasingly, it was not the reason for the abortion but rather certain markers of the procedure itself—who had performed it, where had it been performed, how successful it had been—that differentiated a legitimate therapeutic abortion from a criminal abortion. According to many physicians, legitimate abortions did exist and could be recognized by the fact that they were performed by skilled physicians—preferably in hospital settings—without any negative consequences for the patients' health. During Dr. J. R. Brown's trial, Bessie Frye's treating physician contrasted Dr. Brown's procedure with a legitimate abortion: "The proper place to perform an abortion would take place in a hospital and naturally gas or some kind of anesthesia would be used. You scrape the whole thing out while the patient is under gas."[33] Another physician explained at a 1937 trial, "Criminal abortion differs from other abortions in as much as this woman had a perforation or a tear into the womb."[34]

Indeed, there is some evidence to suggest that when abortions were performed in safe environments by skilled practitioners, the state was usually willing to overlook the legal restrictions on the procedure and side with the abortion provider if his reasons for performing it were good ones.

In *State v. Forte*, for instance, Albert Clarke testified that it was Dr. A. V. Forte who had volunteered to perform an abortion after finding Clarke's fifteen-year-old girlfriend, Elmer McClure, pregnant: "He told me to get him $35.00 and he could fix it. I said I wouldn't do nothing to hurt the girl; I had rather go ahead and marry her. He said that in two or three days she would be all right."[35] Clarke agreed, Forte performed the abortion, McClure was indeed "all right," and the North Carolina Supreme Court overturned Forte's earlier conviction on a technicality.[36] Probably reassured by the safe conditions under which McClure's abortion was performed, the judges might also have agreed with Dr. Forte's consideration of the factors in favor of abortion. Testimony revealed that the young couple was in no position to raise a child. The two were unmarried, McClure was still in school, and Clarke seemed to lack the financial resources to support a family. He had to borrow three dollars to pay for McClure's physical exam, a fact that may have contributed to Forte's decision to charge thirty-five dollars for the abortion when the going rate was fifty dollars or more. Finally, Dr. Forte might have feared that McClure and her boyfriend would seek an abortion from an unskilled provider, significantly raising the risk to McClure's health and life, if he did not perform the procedure. It is also possible that Forte's standing as a respected family physician who had recently retired contributed to the judges' decision to overturn the lower court's verdict. Finally, witnesses for the defense were able to provide Forte with an alibi for the entire day during which the abortion was thought to have been performed. While the jury had found Forte guilty despite this testimony, the supreme court judges might have given it greater weight.

The difficulty of verifying the existence of pregnancy conclusively during its early stages also contributed to the toleration of safe early abortions. Pregnancy testing was possible beginning in the 1930s, but it required the injection of the urine of a pregnant woman into a rabbit. These so-called rabbit tests were expensive and thus frequently unavailable; most women who consulted a physician in North Carolina during the 1940s and 1950s did not get a rabbit test. Instead, the physician looked for signs of probable pregnancy such as the bluing of the cervix and the softening of the uterus and cervix. Such signs, however, were not visible until the sixteenth week of pregnancy. It took the development of modern urine tests in the early 1970s for early pregnancy testing to become more widely available. Given that the abortion laws criminalized an abortion for women "pregnant" or "quick with child," it was a matter of some concern whether a woman accused of having procured an abortion had indeed been pregnant when the procedure was performed.[37]

During the 1940s, the difficulty in diagnosing pregnancy and greater leniency in the enforcement of the abortion laws resulted in the overturning of three convictions for abortions performed during the very early stages of pregnancy. Although it had not previously tolerated abortions performed before "quickening" (the first signs of fetal movement, which usually occur between the sixteenth and twentieth weeks of gestation), in the 1940s the state supreme court overturned every case that came before it in which the abortion in question had been performed before quickening. The lawyers for Dr. A. V. Forte argued, for instance, that Elmer McClure's was not a criminal abortion because she had not yet been "quick with child" when it was performed; she was only two months pregnant. Although the authors of the abortion statutes had intended to make abortion criminal throughout the entire period of pregnancy and had hoped to express this intention with the phrase "either pregnant or quick with child," North Carolina's supreme court judges agreed with Forte's lawyer's argument and overturned the earlier conviction.[38] And although the judges had decided in previous cases that the abortion statutes might be interpreted to cover the entire length of pregnancy, not just the time after a woman had become "quick with child," during the 1940s they expressed their toleration for early abortions by arguing that the legislators' intention had really been to criminalize abortions performed after quickening. One decision from this period read: "If 'pregnant' is used in its broadest sense, the 'quick with child' adds nothing to the statute. Instead, it constitutes the injection of superfluous and meaningless language in the law which tends only to confuse. . . . The very purpose of the statute is to protect the child in ventre sa mere after it has reached the stage of development at which it gives evidence of independent life."[39] The notion that the termination of a pregnancy might be permissible as long as a woman was not yet quick with child was so pervasive during the 1940s that one prosecutor, seeking the conviction of a physician-abortionist, felt the need to point out that the woman in question "was not only pregnant, but she was quick with child at least to the extent of five months, if not more."[40]

In contrast, a poorly performed abortion that led to the hospitalization or death of a woman was universally considered to have been a criminal abortion. In all of the North Carolina Supreme Court cases in which a woman had died or been hospitalized after an abortion, the court upheld the lower courts' convictions of the abortion providers. Insofar as prosecutors continued to describe women as victims, they now depicted them as the victims of abortionists rather than of deceptive male partners. Dr. J. R. Brown's attempt to abort the fetus of Bessie Frye, a physician testified for the prosecution, had left Frye acutely ill, with abdominal pain, a foul discharge from the vagina, an enlarged womb, and a temperature of over 101 degrees.[41] Ethel Smith fared even worse. She died after receiving an abortion from Dr. C. C. Stewart. In gory detail, witnesses for the prosecution described her poor medical condition, the decomposed skeleton that doctors had found in her vagina, and the resulting blood poisoning that had spread throughout her entire body by the time she reached the hospital.[42] While such testimony was sure to deter women from seeking abortions, it also demonstrates the importance that prosecutors attached to the quality of an abortion when they assessed its legality. If evidence of the physician's guilt was not enough to convince the jury to convict, the description of his patient's suffering surely was. A prosecutor argued in 1932 that to convict Dr. Brown of Bessie Frye's abortion, which Frye claimed she had not wanted and which had sent her to the hospital, would not only punish Brown for the crime he had committed but would also "be a restraining influence upon him and other quacks who would like to do likewise in the future."[43]

As they turned their attention from sexual partners to abortion providers whose abortions had injured or killed women, state prosecutors confirmed a shift in the meaning of criminal and therapeutic abortion. If women were going to secure illegal abortions, prosecutors seemed to reason, they should be warned of the health dangers and protected from the worst abortionists. As a Pittsburgh district attorney and former police officer remembered, police officers in some areas, with the consent of local prosecutors, even aided women in their search for safe abortions: "Back in the forties, it was not unheard-of for the police officer to act as a sort of intermediary, if you will, and to actually arrange the abortion. . . . Your chief responsibility in those days was to be aware of the community's needs and see that those needs were met in the best possible way. If prostitution or gambling or abortion was a need, you looked the other way, even though they were all crimes. But you only looked the other way for the cleanest and safest operators, because you wanted to meet those community needs in the cleanest and safest way."[44] If women suffered no ill effects from abortions, their abortion providers were likely to evade the attention of police and state prosecutors. If, however, women were hospitalized or died as a result of abortions, their abortion providers were likely to face prosecution.

The shifts in the meaning of abortion were accompanied by changes in the public perception of women's sexuality. By the 1930s, the notion of men's sexual aggressiveness and women's sexual victimization had eroded so far that courts had become more likely to hold women responsible for their pregnancies. The case *State v. Jordon* indicates that women had clearly become culpable partners rather than victims of their boyfriends' seduction and deception in the eyes of the law. While seventeen-year-old Mildred Bennett tried to rely on the traditional seduction narrative when she claimed that she began having intercourse with Mayford Jordon "on the basis that [they] were going to get married," her strategy backfired.[45] In an attempt to discredit Bennett's sexual behavior, Jordon successfully used his own promiscuity to demonstrate how easy it was to have sexual relations with Bennett. As early as their first date, Jordon testified, he "went to loving her up": "I did everything but have an intercourse with her that night and the only reason I didn't do that was that she said she could not that night, that she had just got over her sick period that day. Mildred told me to come back two days later, that she was willing. On Tuesday night, two days later, I dated Mildred . . . and had intercourse with Mildred for the first time. Mildred said she didn't mind, that it was all right."[46] At the same time that state prosecutors turned their attention to abortion providers, then, they were facing growing difficulties in convicting women's sexual partners. Even when Mildred Bennett's father intervened to remind Jordon of his promise of marriage, Jordon refused to marry Bennett. "I didn't feel I should bear the responsibility of I didn't know how many other boys or men," he told the court.[47] Unlike in earlier cases in which the court had sided with parent and daughter, the court now agreed with Jordon and overturned his lower court conviction.

Women's demand for abortion indicated their more active sexual role during the 1930s and 1940s and their belief that they had a right to terminate unwanted pregnancies regardless of the law. It was apparent that some male partners, too, felt their girlfriends should have the ultimate say in the matter and offered their support as a result of this belief. In fact, in the eyes of the courts, men's culpability might have lain in the fact that they were unable (or unwilling) to prevent their girlfriends from asserting this perceived right. According to prosecutors, however, women and men not only lacked the right to terminate a pregnancy, they also chose abortion for the wrong reasons. It was pure convenience and immorality that led women and men to seek abortion. Inconvenience, a state prosecutor charged in 1937, led Don Evans to skirt his responsibility as a parent. Both he and his girlfriend had "wished to protect themselves from the possibility of a child being born, or to protect themselves from any discussion, or any inconvenience, or disgrace, which result[ed] from [Lucile Belk's illegitimate pregnancy] becoming known, and . . . both of them wanted to get rid of this unborn child."[48]

The testimony of both men and women clearly reversed traditional assumptions about male sexual aggression and women's sexual victimization. Many men argued that far from seeking their partners' abortions for their own convenience, they did so with genuine concern for these women's health and well-being. Evans, for instance, not only told the arresting sheriff that he had tried to convince Lucile Belk to seek some other solution to her pregnancy than abortion, he also described the growing concern he had felt about her deteriorating physical condition following the abortion. Truly worried about her health as she got sicker and sicker, he had stayed at her side, pressed her repeatedly to see a physician, finally called one despite her persistent opposition, and volunteered to donate blood after her admission to the hospital.[49] Even boyfriends who had played a less active role during the aftermath of abortions testified to the deep emotional attachment they had to their girlfriends, appearing anything but uncaring. Melton Baker, admitting to the uncle of his girlfriend, Madell Williams, that he had "done very common" when he had had sex with her, explained, "These things overtake you and put you where you don't want to be."[50] After Williams's hospitalization, Baker visited, paid all her medical bills, and apologized to her family for having "done that."[51] Unable to face her family after Williams's death, he skirted the funeral but visited her grave by himself.

Although it went unacknowledged in the courtroom, testimony unmistakably spoke of women's active participation in demanding the termination of their unwanted pregnancies. While prosecutors tried to depict both Lucile Belk and Ethel Smith as victims of botched abortions that eventually killed them, and while they charged Belk's and Smith's boyfriends with responsibility for these crimes, both women seem to have taken the leading role in securing their abortions. Smith claimed in her dying declaration that her boyfriend, Ollie Parish, had initiated her abortion over her objection by taking her to a "negro doctor," but the bulk of the testimony in his trial indicated that it was Smith, not Parish, who had taken the initiative in securing the abortion.[52] Not only did Parish deny having known about Ethel Smith's pregnancy, but four witnesses testified that Smith had been by herself when she asked them for help, and there was reason to think that Parish indeed might not have known about the pregnancy. One physician stated: "She walked in and I asked her what I could do for her. She said, 'I want you to do something for me' and she said, 'I am about three months pregnant and I am in the predicament of being engaged to one young man and another being responsible for my condition.' So I told her I was sorry, but there wasn't anything I could do about it. She was insistent. She begged and persuaded."[53] Similarly, although state prosecutors charged Don Evans with procuring an abortion for his girlfriend, Lucile Belk, Evans argued that it was Belk who had been determined to end the pregnancy. While he admitted that he had helped Belk find an abortionist and had paid for the procedure, he argued that she was the one who had taken the initiative in obtaining the abortion: "I did not suggest that she have an abortion produced or counsel her to have one produced. . . . She went at her own suggestion. She said she had missed two periods and said she had taken medicine and couldn't get rid of it."[54] In fact, before deciding to help Belk, Evans had proposed marriage and had suggested that she tell her parents about the pregnancy. Belk had rejected both suggestions. Evans testified, "She said she had done something before and she could again."[55] Met with such determination, Evans decided to respect her decision and help her through the process. While it was clearly in the interest of male partners on the witness stand to minimize their own role and draw attention to their girlfriends' initiative in obtaining their abortions, several men actually admitted to their role in the abortions and seemed genuinely remorseful.

Even if a woman was determined to end an unwanted pregnancy, difficulties in finding an abortionist, fear of disgrace, and a lack of money combined to compromise her access to medical care in a way that jeopardized her health and life. In fact, as the discourse surrounding illegal abortion presented women as victims of unscrupulous abortionists, it masked the ways in which the illegal nature of abortion truly victimized women determined to end unwanted pregnancies by delaying their access to medical care or denying them access altogether. When Lucile Belk became sick following her abortion, her boyfriend sought to call a physician, but Belk, fearing both detection and additional medical costs, objected. Don Evans explained, "I wanted to call a doctor from the time she first started to having those terrible pains; she did not consent; she never consented to my calling a doctor."[56] He finally called a doctor over her opposition. By that time, it was too late. While Belk had the help of her boyfriend, Ethel Smith's case demonstrates how difficult it was for women who wished to keep their pregnancies a secret from friends and family even to find an abortion provider. Engaged to one man but pregnant by another, Smith, a white woman, feared that white physicians would be unsympathetic to her plight and sought help from black health care providers instead.[57] But it proved difficult for her to find an abortionist in the black community as well. At least one midwife and several physicians turned her away, most likely increasing Smith's sense of despair. One physician testified that Smith pleaded and begged with him. A midwife described Smith as a distraught young woman who implored her for help.

> I saw her on my porch in October. . . . She came and asked me was that where Mrs. Davis lived. I told her no, that Mrs. Davis did not live there, that Alice Minor lived there. She asked me where Mrs. Davis was, and I told her I did not know. She was not in the city, I didn't think, and she told me her business and I told her I was sorry but I couldn't tell her where I could find her, and she asked me couldn't I tell her something, and I told her I didn't have anything to tell her. She told me she had missed three months. She told me she wanted to see Mrs. Davis, she knew she could help her and I told her I was sorry but I couldn't tell her anything about Mrs. Davis.[58]

Without a doubt, having to tell strangers one's "business" and pleading with them for help must have been a humiliating experience.

Black communities were frequently known as places where one might find an abortionist. One black physician recalls: "The black community as a whole—not [just] the doctors—was just more open about abortion than they were in the white community. White women tended to get referred to someone in the black community, midwife or doctor, and a lot of them came, often referred by their own white doctors."[59] Physicians and midwives cooperated closely, with physicians referring patients seeking an abortion to certain midwives who would terminate the patients' pregnancies and then refer the women back to the physicians for aftercare. African American midwives, the physician quoted above remembers, were quite competent and may have offered better abortions than women were able to get in white communities, where some abortionists lacked any medical training: "I don't know what it was like in the white community. . . . I suppose in other communities—maybe white communities—you got dishwashers and mechanics, but in the black community, mine and others, you got midwives who were by and large very good."[60] But even if white women knew to approach African American midwives or physicians for abortion, black health care providers were hesitant to help those without connections to their communities. "I didn't usually just take white folks on faith," one African American midwife who performed abortions for many white women remembers. "Usually when I did a white woman, she was brought to me by a black person I had some reason to trust."[61] We do not know whether Ethel Smith was finally able to convince one of the black health care providers she approached to help her or whether she obtained her abortion elsewhere. There is no reason to assume, however, that white women like Smith necessarily evoked sympathy from black health care providers. Aware of the danger that white women could pose to their medical practices and careers, some might have felt resentment at white women's assumption that black health care providers would help them. Others judged women who lacked connection with and loyalty to the black community to be bad risks for illegal abortion. The African American midwife explains: "I would trust a black person not to betray me where a white one might because of the way blacks and whites feel about what I will call 'the system.' Whites basically expect the system to believe them and to treat them right. Blacks, on the other hand, expect not to be believed by white folks. They don't think they will do well in the system no matter what their role is. As a result, a black patient of mine was less likely to report me to the system because the system would probably somehow punish her as well as me."[62] That the person ultimately charged for performing Smith's abortion was an African American physician with a long-standing practice in the black community, and that several other black health care providers who testified at the trial were humiliated by the prosecuting attorney, confirms that black health care providers had every reason to be wary.[63]

Women's persistence in seeking abortion despite the risks involved provided health care professionals and physicians with a powerful argument in favor of the distribution of birth control. Citing the results of Frederick Taussig's famous 1936 study of abortion, birth control advocates incorporated Taussig's statistics about maternal deaths caused by abortion into their literature advocating family planning. Clarence Gamble argued in 1938: "It is estimated that 700,000 abortions are induced in this country every year. . . . One-fifth of the maternal deaths follow abortions, nine-tenths of these occurring in married women who choose this dangerous method of limiting their families rather than bring another child into the unfavorable surroundings to which it would be destined. . . . Adequate distribution of contraceptive information will decrease the induced abortions and improve that record."[64] And a 1939 form letter from

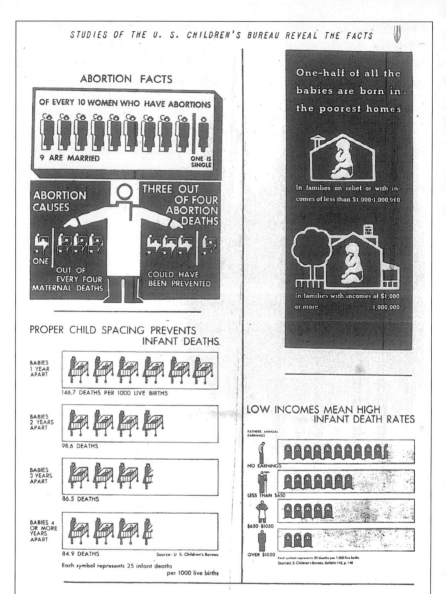

"Birth control prevents needless deaths." BCFA fundraising letter, 1939. (Courtesy Sophia Smith Collection)

the Birth Control Federation of America graphically illustrated the dangers of abortion under the title "abortion facts" and concluded, "birth control prevents needless deaths."[65] The pamphlet implied that women's decision to risk their lives in order to limit their pregnancies and provide a better environment for the children they already had was a socially responsible one. Proper child spacing, the authors argued, prevented infant deaths and allocated more resources to children. Occasionally, physicians even ruminated on the desirability of decriminalizing abortion. One physician, speaking about the problems of infant and maternal mortality in the mid-1930s, informed his audience of North Carolina physicians that in Russia abortions for social reasons were legal. He wondered openly whether Americans should start a war on abortionists or follow the Soviet example.[66]

During the 1930s and 1940s, however, abortion laws faced no legal challenges, and by 1950 tolerance of abortion had given way to intense state repression. In fact, Leslie Reagan has suggested that it was openness toward illegal abortion itself that led to more than two decades of intensified prosecution. With the end of World War II, women faced intense social and ideological pressure to return from work to the home, marry, and bear children. Their sexual conformity to marriage and motherhood became so prevalent that anxiety or ambivalence surrounding pregnancy was considered to be a pathological condition.[67]

■ Raiding Abortion Mills and Syndicates: The Postwar Era

The relative visibility and ease with which women could obtain illegal abortions in the 1930s and 1940s was transformed in the postwar era by public hysteria about the existence of so-called abortion mills. Beginning in the 1940s and stretching into the 1960s, a number of cities initiated campaigns—similar to the moral purity campaigns of the Progressive Era —to crack down on abortion, prostitution, pornography, and homosexuality.[68] Physicians and women seeking abortion were increasingly pitted against each other as more and more physicians refused women's requests for illegal abortion and women began to fear that physicians would report them to law enforcement agents if they confessed to having procured illegal abortions. Silenced in the emergency room for fear of prosecution and harassment, women were also silenced in the courtroom, where prosecutors needed their testimony to convict abortionists but suppressed women's voices when they told about their reasons for terminating a pregnancy. Ironically, women found a new ally in sympathetic medical professionals and psychiatrists, who were the first to articulate the hardship of forced pregnancy and who expanded women's access to therapeutic abortion by making it available for mental health reasons.

In cities across the country, including Chicago, New York, San Francisco, Akron, Detroit, Baltimore, Los Angeles, and Pittsburgh, police officers and prosecutors stepped up raids of abortionists' offices. In many places, the political ambitions of elected officials as well as turnover in and the professionalization of police forces and prosecutors' offices marked the increase in prosecutions of abortionists. Portland, Oregon's antivice campaign, for instance, started in 1948 with the election of a new mayor, Dorothy Lee. While the police force had tolerated abortion providers before Lee's election, with Lee in office it began to conduct sensational raids on brothels, gambling dens, and the city's abortion establishments. Throughout the 1950s and 1960s, abortionists in Portland faced arrest and prosecution. In Pittsburgh, prosecutors arrested abortionists every three or four years to "clean up" the city during mayoral election season. After the election, however, all the abortionists were released, and business returned to usual until the next election season.[69]

Patterns of prosecution and conviction were far from uniform, however. Local prosecutors in one city might be aggressive, while in another city they might look the other way. Evidence suggests that in rural areas where whole communities depended on the medical services of a few physicians, abortionists often continued to operate openly, protected from prosecution. In Ashland, Pennsylvania, for instance, juries refused to convict Dr. Robert Douglas Spencer for the death of one of his patients despite clear evidence that she died while he was performing an illegal abortion. Spencer, a prominent physician-abortionist who, by his own account, performed over one hundred thousand illegal abortions between 1923 and his retirement in 1967, operated with tacit community support. His conviction would not only have meant the loss to the community of a competent abortion provider and physician but also the loss of needed revenue to hotels and restaurants that benefited from the regular visits of out-of-town abortion patients. In the North Carolina Piedmont area, a number of physicians and nurses provided abortion throughout the 1950s and 1960s; they were known to the surrounding medical community and law enforcement agents, but they were never convicted.[70]

Public health considerations also sometimes convinced prosecutors in urban areas to refrain from indicting known abortionists. When in the mid-1950s during Charles deProsse's residency at the Lying-In Hospital in

New York City a group of physicians decided to visit the city attorney to seek his help in imprisoning criminal abortionists, for instance, the city attorney refused to intervene. DeProsse recalled: "He told us that his office was aware of most of the people in the city of New York who were doing abortions. And that as long as they didn't get women into serious trouble, they didn't want to do anything about it. . . . The reason they gave was that if they did . . . it would go down to a lower level of competence, and that more women would be getting into trouble."[71] Similar considerations protected a group of women in Chicago who founded an underground abortion service called Jane that provided about eleven thousand abortions between 1968 and 1973. Though Jane began as a referral service, Jane members eventually learned how to perform abortions themselves. By 1971, they performed the abortions, educated women about their bodies, and offered pap smears and basic pelvic exams—all under the eyes of and with the protection of the police.[72]

If prosecutors were interested in shutting down an abortion provider, however, the very intention of performing an abortion could now lead to conviction. While outside complaints, a woman's death, or her admission to the hospital had previously led to the initiation of abortion investigations, state authorities in many localities now adopted a policy of zero tolerance. "Under the new order," one former police officer remembered, "if you received complaints about abortionists, you went after them, no matter who they were or where they lived."[73] Police officers systematically investigated and set up traps for abortionists, raided their offices, and arrested abortion providers regardless of their professional backgrounds. Once arrested, abortionists became less likely to escape conviction than ever before. In this atmosphere, the North Carolina Supreme Court upheld all lower court convictions of abortionists between 1956 and 1966 even though in four of the six cases the woman in question had suffered no ill effects from her abortion.

Under the new regime, a lack of physical evidence of either pregnancy or abortion was no hindrance to conviction. Both physicians testifying for the state in abortionist Florence Stallworth's trial argued that the diagnosis of Juanita Rozzell's pregnancy on the basis of a physical examination in the sixth to eighth week of pregnancy could have been in error. One of them cautioned that definite signs of pregnancy—x-ray images of a fetal skeleton or auscultation of the fetal heartbeat—were not yet present and could not, in fact, be detected until the sixteenth to eighteenth week of pregnancy. Moreover, the physician who examined Rozzell after her alleged abortion by Stallworth testified that Stallworth's procedure had left no evidence of lacerations or damaged tissue and that he, too, was unable to state with certainty that Rozzell had been pregnant. In spite of these doubts, however, Stallworth was convicted, because Rozzell testified that she had gone to see Stallworth about an abortion.[74] Although North Carolina law specified that a woman had to be pregnant or quick with child in order for abortion to be a crime, North Carolina's supreme court judges now upheld lower court convictions even when it was unclear either that the woman had indeed been pregnant or that the abortion provider had ended the pregnancy.[75]

State prosecutors, aided by the courts and the media, began to pressure women who had obtained abortions to participate in the prosecutions of their abortionists or face prosecution themselves. Police raided abortionists' offices in order to catch patients and bribed and threatened women to elicit testimony against their abortion providers. In exchange for her testimony against her abortionist, for instance, Officer A. A. Mauney put Lillie Mae Rape up in the Hotel Monroe for the duration of the trial even though she lived only eight blocks from the courthouse. Prosecutors tracked down women to testify about their abortion experiences and forced them to submit to gynecological exams for the purpose of collecting evidence.[76] Rather than eliciting sympathy in the courtroom, moreover, women now faced hostile interrogations that implied that they were both immoral and callous for choosing abortion. Although Lillie Mae Rape testified that dire economic circumstances had motivated her to seek an abortion—"I was desperate about it because I worry about my bills"—the prosecutor accused Rape of having been in trouble with the law herself, having had affairs with men other than the father of her child, and having failed to seriously consider the possibility that she was able to afford a fifth child.[77] Harassment of women patients occasionally extended to the hospital, where doctors attending women with complications from abortions gone wrong occasionally told them they were going to die in order to intimidate them into giving details about their abortions.[78]

Court narratives became controlled and highly constructed, depicting the abortionist and the woman seeking abortion as morally suspect while excluding any discussion of the men responsible for the pregnancy or of the reasons why the woman might have sought the abortion.[79] In fact, while in earlier decades women had complained about male partners who failed to lend support, they now seemed unwilling to name the men who had gotten them pregnant or who had helped them obtain abortions. Despite persistent questioning, for instance, Donna Lee Merritt refused to give the names of either the man who was responsible for her pregnancy or the friends who had lent her money for her abortion.[80] The absence of any discussion of male partners gave the impression that women lacked an emotional connection to their sexual partners and heightened the suspicion of female promiscuity, immorality, and callousness. The most likely place for a discussion of a woman's sexual partner or partners to emerge in this period was in the suggestion that it was the woman's promiscuous behavior that had led to her pregnancy and abortion. In some contexts, references to abortion came to function as evidence of women's promiscuity.[81] Reagan points out, "In the past, juries had been understanding, and prosecutors knew that it was nearly impossible to convict accused abortionists unless a woman had died."[82] Fearing that juries and judges who heard women's side of the story might feel sympathy for the women's position and refuse to convict the abortion providers, prosecutors became more and more determined to eliminate such testimony.

In order to police themselves and discourage their colleagues from helping their patients to procure abortions, physicians around the country established hospital abortion committees to determine the necessity of every abortion performed in a given hospital. Similar to the hospital sterilization committees that were also established during this time, the abortion committees discouraged individual doctors from approving or even requesting abortions for their patients and dissuaded women from requesting therapeutic abortions. Some physicians demanded that women submit to sterilization if they wanted to obtain an abortion.[83] By the 1950s, hospitals were competing to have the lowest abortion rates in their regions and states, ignoring the implications their restrictive abortion policies had for women's health care.

The existence of hospital abortion committees also changed physicians' understanding of what constituted a legal abortion. Earlier, physicians had deemed an abortion noncriminal if a medical indication classified it as a therapeutic abortion and the procedure was performed in a hospital setting by a physician. In the postwar period, an abortion became therapeutic, and thus legal, if an abortion committee had approved it. This meant, Reagan notes, that "implicitly, a doctor who had failed to go through a committee had performed an illegal abortion."[84] Two court cases of the 1950s confirmed this shift. In 1951 and 1958, police officers in Baltimore and Detroit raided the offices of doctors George Timanus and Edgar Keemer. For years, both had performed abortions undisturbed. Now they had attracted the attention of prosecutors, who charged them with providing criminal abortions. Timanus and Keemer argued that the abortions they had performed were legal because they had been performed for medical reasons. But prosecutors countered this understanding of legal abortion with testimony by medical experts who described abortions as legal only if they were performed in hospitals, after committee review, and only for physical indications. By performing abortions in their offices without the sanction of committee review, both doctors had violated these unwritten rules. Both were convicted.[85]

These changes in the definition of legal abortion contributed to an atmosphere in which physicians became less willing to argue that a patient's medical condition required an abortion. Therapeutic abortions, Charles deProsse explained, were now reserved for "very, really ill people who shouldn't have been pregnant to begin with."[86] Advances in medical science, including the discovery of penicillin, meant that conditions that might have justified a therapeutic abortion in earlier times were now excluded from the list of acceptable indications for abortion. While new medical indications emerged—research on the risks that rubella infection and the tranquilizer thalidomide posed to fetal development, for instance, suggested new justifications for therapeutic abortion—the overall effect was that the list of indications got shorter.[87]

Even if they could no longer ask physicians directly for abortions, some women were successful in tricking their physicians into performing D&Cs. Jaroslav Hulka remembers a patient who complained to him of irregular bleeding. Assured by her that she could not be pregnant, he decided to perform a D&C and discovered to his surprise that she was, indeed, carrying a fifteen- to sixteen-week-old fetus. He apologized profusely and terminated the pregnancy. He recalls: "I went ahead with it and just felt awful for having interrupted that. But she wasn't feeling nearly so awful. In other words, women were smart, they had to be smart. They didn't come at me and say: 'Do an abortion.' They came to us saying, 'Help us, we are having these symptoms,' hoping that we wouldn't get to the pregnancy just like I did."[88] Women invented stories about their sexual histories in order to convince physicians to perform the desired procedures, and they brought in false urine samples to guarantee negative pregnancy tests.[89] Occasionally, physicians aided women in their attempts to beat the system. In order to help students at the University of North Carolina obtain D&Cs in the late 1960s and early 1970s, obstetrics and gynecology residents would inject blood into the women's vaginas and tell them to come to the emergency room an hour later claiming to have had a miscarriage. Then the residents would perform D&Cs on them.[90]

Increased attention to and prosecution of abortion providers made African American physicians and midwives particularly vulnerable to harassment and prosecution. "A black doctor . . . is just not given the benefit of the doubt in the same way that a white doctor is," one African American physician held. "If Dr. Spencer [the Ashland, Pennsylvania, physician who provided abortions throughout his career] had been a black doctor in Pittsburgh, he simply would not have been treated as he was—either in his practice or in his trial."[91] This was true especially if the woman seeking an abortion from a black physician was white. The physician explained: "Black doctors are going to be real careful about referring a strange white woman to a good midwife unless the white doctor who referred her is someone you know and trust. If the black doctor was going to do the abortion himself, he had to feel really safe—a close friend or relative or a highly reliable referral source. You had to protect yourself from the setup and from the patient who would crumble under pressure."[92]

Sometimes patients exploited the vulnerability of African American physicians and tried to coerce them into performing abortions. Lillie Mae Rape, who was white, claimed that she obtained an abortion from Dr. A. E. Perry, who was black, by bullying him into performing the procedure. Rape testified: "I knew that it was a serious crime for anyone who did it. . . . I had been turned down by another doctor that I had attempted to get to commit the act."[93] Nevertheless determined, Rape approached Dr. Perry: "I told him that I thought I was pregnant and I wanted him to do something about it. . . . He said there wasn't anything he could do about it, and I told him it was a lie, there was, and he said, 'Well, there was something he could do, but he wouldn't guarantee it.' "[94] Perry gave Rape a shot and told her to get quinine capsules. When these did not terminate the pregnancy, Rape returned to Perry's office. Perry again claimed there was nothing he could do, Rape again called him a liar, and Perry told her to bring seventy-five dollars and he would fix her up. When Rape returned with the money two weeks later, she again argued with Perry over whether he would induce an abortion. Eventually, Rape claimed, Perry did so, and she finally miscarried several days later. Perry's narrative of events, although considerably different from Rape's, confirms the sense of vulnerability that the racial dynamics introduced to the negotiation between black male physicians and white female patients. Throughout the trial, Perry denied having performed an abortion on Rape. Rape, he claimed, was accusing him because she was angry at his refusal to perform the abortion. Although he had explained to her that he could not take the professional risks involved, Rape kept returning to his office. On her last visit, she became so angry at his continued refusal that she threatened to "get him."

She sat there in the chair, she cried, and she asked me and begged me. I told her NO. I said, "I have tried to treat you as a lady; I have tried to treat you as a member of the nursing profession which I hold in high esteem." I said, "There are too many dangers and even having you sit here and talk to me." I said, "I want you to leave this room. I want you to leave." I pointed out to her that among other reasons I wasn't too popular in the community, at that particular time. There were, I pointed out to her, that there were people who would like to get something like that so as to prosecute me. After she still did not leave, I still talked to her. She got rather violent. We both began to talk at the same time. I just stood there and talked with her, and she got violent and said that her first approach was to beg me and cry and try to get help, and I told her, "no" it wouldn't work. After arguing for a while she changed her attitude to one of threats and demands. So I proceeded to go back into my examining room in an effort to let her know that I was through. I had threatened to go on out the back door. When I got to the back, well, then she was still talking, and says, "That's all right. I'll get you!" [S]he said that, among other things that I could not clearly discern.[95]

Perry's trial and conviction further confirmed the no-win situation in which both women and physicians could find themselves. Police successfully coerced Rape to give Perry up when, following her abortion, Rape contracted an infection and sought help in the hospital. Perry, in turn, tried to have his indictment quashed by arguing that as an African American physician who was charged with performing an abortion on a white woman he could not receive a fair trial in Union County. Although he successfully appealed his first conviction, he was again convicted in his second trial.

As physicians became more unwilling to provide abortions, most women learned not to approach them with such requests. Sometimes, however, they asked for referrals. DeProsse remembers: "We'd throw up our hands and say, you know, try your luck. . . . Go out of country if you can, go to New York if you can, see what you can do. [We] didn't like that, didn't like having to refer patients that way, didn't like putting them at the risk we were putting them at."[96] Physicians in rural areas were more likely to be able to help than those who practiced in urban areas and at large university hospitals. While physicians in the latter group might have encountered hundreds of women with complications from illegal abortions in the city's emergency rooms, patients in urban areas were unlikely to trust the treating physicians in emergency rooms, who were essentially strangers. Illegal abortionists might operate a block away from the hospital, but they seemed a world apart from legal medical practice. "The medical field was remote," Hulka explains.[97] In small cities, however, where women's private physicians were more likely to treat them if they had postabortion complications, physicians often did know the local abortion providers and were more willing to refer patients to them. In Wilson County, North Carolina, for instance, all the surgeons knew who provided abortions throughout the Piedmont area. One physician remembers a vast network of illegal providers from all walks of life.

There was a man in Sims who ran a bootleg joint when he did abortions. . . . He would do an abortion for $15 or at least he would start the abortion. I had several patients come to me after having abortions started by him. . . . There was a doctor in Stantonsburg who I have personally talked to about what he was doing. He would start the abortion with a solution that came in a tube which was squirted into the uterus. It was similar to what has been referred to as the saline injection. His fee was $50.00. He did a number of them. In Fremont there was a doctor who would actually do a dilation and curettage procedure to produce an abortion. I knew a number of girls who were going to Atlantic Christian College who would go to see this man. His work was always done at night. This doctor would do the abortion and the girls would miss one or two days of school. There was another doctor in Wilson who produced abortions and I saw a number of his patients. These were illegal, dangerous type of abortions. A number of them came to me for follow-up treatment to clear up the infections. . . . Besides the above there was a place in Rocky Mount between the Atlantic Coast-line Railroad Hospital and uptown where a woman would do abortions. In Richmond there were two places where you went and had complete abortion done with an anesthetic illegally. I knew several people in Wilson who went to Richmond. There was a woman, a nurse, in Portsmouth, Virginia that a number of Wilson people went to. She did complete abortions in her home. . . . You probably remember a famous case in Raleigh, Mrs. Broughton, a nurse, who performed abortions. She received wide publicity and attention but never was convicted. Another case which I did not mention above is a man who is now dead. He was a very prominent surgeon in Goldsboro. He catered to the well to do people. I know one man who is now president of a big corporation in North Carolina who took three different girls to this man for abortions. His fee was $300 plus hospital fees. Back in the 40s and 50s this was a fairly good sum of money. . . . In the 40s and 50s there were five other surgeons who also helped in treating illegal abortions here in Wilson. They knew what I have listed above.[98]

Despite the continued existence of such a vast underground network, women found it increasingly difficult to locate somebody willing to perform abortions. One woman recalled her search.

First, I called a friend in Miami who sent me pills which I took that did not affect my pregnancy. Second, I called a friend in Atlanta who knew someone but [they] were no longer in operation. Third, I called a friend in Charlotte who knew a doctor in South Carolina, but the doctor had recently died. Fourth I contacted a nurse friend who did not know a doctor and suggested that I have the baby and adopt it out. Fifth, I contacted another friend who knew someone that was operating out of the hotel at $1,000 per person. Sixth, I contacted a doctor in Winston-Salem which I didn't have any luck. By this time I was very discouraged. I remember I cried all the way from Winston-Salem back to Charlotte which is quite a drive. Seventh, I contacted a doctor in Charlotte which I didn't have any luck. Eighth, I called my doctor in Miami who was very nice and understanding and wanted to help if he could. He told me to call him back the following week. This made me feel a little better. At least I had a little hope, and I almost decided to drive to Miami, but I changed my mind which I am glad I did, because I called back the following week. The only way he could help me would be through an adoption agency. But understanding my circumstances, he agreed that an abortion was the right answer for me. After this phone conversation I was very upset again. Ninth, I contacted a business friend in Atlanta who in the meantime had been to see two doctors he knew, but the answer was no. He had also contacted someone in Tennessee he knew, but no luck. By this time I didn't know which way to go. I was so mentally upset and I was physically sick too, as I had been all along.[99]

Moreover, as prosecutors began to clamp down on abortion providers, women lost what control they had over when and under what conditions they were able to obtain abortions. Prices for the procedure rose, increasingly attracting abortion providers who were interested in the money but lacked competence and professional skills. An adventurous woman with $500 cash might stand at two, four, or six o'clock on any downtown street corner in Arlington, Virginia, wearing a pink dress and be picked up and taken to a clinic for an abortion, a shot of penicillin, and a package of pain medication. This scenario demonstrates the risks women were forced to take if they sought abortion during the 1950s and 1960s. The stories about abortion providers who required their clients to be blindfolded and of drunk practitioners who sexually harassed their patients and performed abortions in dirty rooms all reflect women's abortion experiences during this period.[100]

As abortion became more secret and more expensive, a woman's risk of discovery increased with every person she approached in search of a provider and money to pay for the procedure. When Donna Lee Merritt needed an abortion, she asked two close male friends for help. She later testified: "They gave me the name of a girl who had an abortion. I stopped her on the street and told her my problem and she told me. I did not know her before this."[101] After Thelma Brooks terminated Merritt's pregnancy, Merritt began to refer other women to Brooks: "I told other people about this. Well, the people who lent me money for my own [abortion] knew about it to begin with, and it was discussed later with them and then one of their girlfriends got into trouble and went over again. I mean it was just passed from mouth to mouth and with close friends. I went back to Thelma Brooks' house later somewhere between five and seven times. . . . The purpose of these visits, the ones when I took people with me was to get them abortions, too. I can't say accurately how many there were, about five girls. They came from the different universities all around."[102] As Merritt was unable to control the flow of information, knowledge about Merritt's connections eventually reached a nurse at Guilford College, who notified the authorities and helped to set a trap for Merritt and Brooks.

Many women lost valuable time in searching for an abortion, and the procedure became more difficult—and thus riskier—as pregnancy progressed. Fear of detection limited access to aftercare, which created problems if something went wrong with an abortion. As the story of Annie Anderson illustrates, the isolation that resulted from the secrecy surrounding illegal abortion made the interruption of pregnancy both a dangerous and a terrifying experience for many. Although she had the support of her former boyfriend, Clarence W. Seagle, who accompanied her to the abortionist and stayed at her side during the following days, Anderson was nervous about her abortion and grew increasingly frantic as time went on. Dr. B. O. Choate performed the abortion on Anderson while Seagle waited in an adjoining room. "She was highly nervous and had been crying," Seagle explained about her condition after the procedure.[103]

After performing the abortion on Annie Anderson, Dr. Choate instructed Anderson and Seagle "not to go to another doctor and to get out of town and not to stay in Sparta."[104] Seagle and Anderson stayed an hour away in Elkin. When Seagle became concerned about Anderson's deteriorating condition, he called Dr. Choate to negotiate for medical care. He testified: "I told him that Mrs. Anderson was suffering a lot and could not stand it much longer; and I told him if he didn't do something about it she would go to another doctor."[105] Choate agreed to see Anderson a second time and gave her some medicine, which failed to improve her condition. Seagle and Anderson returned to the hotel, with Anderson "highly nervous and frantic and very restless." Anderson's physical condition continued to deteriorate, and some time in the early morning hours she had a massive hemorrhage. Afraid to leave any traces, she balled up the bloody hotel sheets and towels, scrubbed the bathroom, and changed her clothing. Seagle testified about what happened next.

> I heard her go to the bathroom; it must have been 20 or 30 minutes later she called me. She had turned blue then. I went to the bathroom, led her to my bed in my room and laid her down on it. I noticed that her fingernails were turned pink. . . . At the time she came out of the bathroom she had changed and had on slacks. I don't know why I put her on my bed, I just did. She looked so frightfully bad. . . . The sheets on my bed were bloody; I don't know about hers. After I put her on my bed I ran down and called Dr. Choate. . . . I told him I believed Mrs. Anderson was dying. He said, 'Where is the medicine? What did you do with it?' He said to destroy it. . . . [I] called a local physician as soon as I got through talking to Dr. Choate. . . . She was getting bluer all the time. . . . She passed away about 8 o'clock or 8:10; she passed away before the Doctor got there—Dr. Cooke. She had been dead probably five minutes when he got there. I was present when she died.[106]

The need for secrecy that prevented Anderson from seeking timely medical care also tainted the interactions between physicians and patients when women did make it to the hospital. Asked about the circumstances that brought them to the emergency room, women frequently lied. "I've had many women come into the emergency room and I said, 'What happened?' She said, 'Oh, I fell down the stairs,' or, 'I fell down the bicycle,'" physician Jaroslav Hulka remembers about the 1960s. "One poor woman, there was a catheter still in her vagina. . . . I asked her what happened. And she said, 'I fell down the stairs.' I pulled out the catheter and said, 'Was this on the stairs?' And she said, 'What's that?' I said, 'Well, that's what I found in your vagina.' 'Oh, I don't know how it got there.' Absolutely flat and cool. And I realized this is not a game. This is a serious thing for these women, I wasn't gonna punish them. I just wanted to hear what happened. Well, I didn't have to hear when I saw the darn catheter."[107]

While some physicians did harass women and report them to law enforcement authorities, many were primarily concerned with treating their critically ill patients and were hesitant to accuse women and question them about illegal abortions. Many physicians who suspected that some of their patients had received illegal abortions did not report their suspicions to the authorities. In fact, in order to protect women, some physicians attributed complications such as infections and extremely heavy bleeding to causes other than illegal abortion. Physician Charles Hendricks explains: "Most of these patients who had these severe problems . . . were poor . . . and the poorer you were the more likely people were to say, well, you know . . . they're so damn poor that their hygiene isn't very good. If their hygiene isn't very good, then no wonder they get infected."[108] Sometimes the search for alternate explanations became second nature, making it unclear whether physicians failed to understand how often complications were the result of illegal abortion or whether they refused to make the connection between complications and illegal abortion in order to protect themselves and their patients from inquisitive hospital administrators and law enforcement officers. Even physicians attuned to abortion issues could be surprised to realize after *Roe v. Wade* how frequent illegal abortion had been. As Hendricks concludes, "It isn't that we weren't motivated to find out, but we didn't understand the severity and the frequency with which this was happening."[109] In the end, most physicians were concerned with curing their patients rather than aiding law enforcement efforts. But the silence and deception could both protect women and their physicians and endanger women's health and well-being.

The crackdown on abortionists led to rising rates of hospital admissions and an increase in mortality rates resulting from botched abortions. In Chicago's Cook County Hospital, the number of women treated for abortion-related complications climbed from over one thousand in 1939 to nearly five thousand by 1962, mirroring a pattern in hospitals across the country.[110] One physician described his experiences at a public hospital in the New York area as follows.

There were two gyn wards. They were supposed to have thirty-two beds each, but they had to have beds all up and down the hallways. They were always full [because of illegal abortions]. They must have had one hundred and forty beds in those wards. . . . The residents would get duties of twenty-four-hour periods, and in that period, you'd get ten to twelve admissions. They walked into the emergency room bleeding. . . . [T]he routine was that you accumulated all the women until two o'clock in the morning when all the major surgery was done and the last gunshot wound had been cleared out of the emergency room—then the first-year residents dragged the patients down to the operating room and started doing the D&Cs at two o'clock in the morning. That's when the operating room was quiet. . . . There would be two or three operating rooms going at the same time. Between 2:00 and 6:00 AM you could get a certain number of D&Cs done and clean up the women who weren't septic, scrape their uteruses and get them back upstairs so they could be discharged in a day or two.[111]

As the number of admissions to hospital emergency rooms went up, so did the number of women who died as a result of illegal abortions. In New York City, the number of abortion deaths nearly doubled between 1951 and 1962, rising from twenty-seven deaths per year in the early 1950s to fifty-one deaths a decade later. By the 1960s, as many as five thousand women died annually in the United States as a direct result of criminal abortion, with women of color being nearly four times as likely to die as a result of abortion as white women.[112]

In the face of such dire developments, many physicians not only shielded women from prosecution but sought the expansion of indications justifying therapeutic abortion. As medical indications shifted and declined in importance, physicians increasingly turned to psychiatric indications to justify the termination of pregnancy. Studies showed the growing importance of psychiatric indications in the practice of therapeutic abortion as early as the 1940s, and by the late 1950s mental disorders had become the leading indication for therapeutic abortion.[113] Just as women had themselves declared feebleminded in order to gain access to eugenic sterilization, they had themselves declared mentally unstable to gain access to therapeutic abortion. Similar to social workers and health professionals who in the 1950s and 1960s helped women get eugenic sterilizations by presenting them as mentally ill or feebleminded, physicians and psychiatrists helped women get therapeutic abortions by presenting them as mentally unstable. Unlike the Eugenics Board, however, which suppressed women's voices as they articulated their desire for a life free of pregnancy and childbearing, psychiatrists offered women an opening to voice their goals and desires.

For many women, psychiatric consultations provided a rare opportunity to discuss emotionally complex issues with a mental health professional. Indeed, at their best, psychiatrists provided abortion counseling to their patients at a time when this was not yet part of the protocol. Especially for young women torn between the opinions of family members and sexual partners, it could be difficult to come to terms with an unplanned pregnancy and to decide whether or not to have an abortion. One psychiatrist explained the situation of one of his patients, who felt conflicted about abortion due to the disagreement between her fundamentalist parents, who urged abortion, and her boyfriend, who urged her to break with her parents and keep the baby:

> The patient and her boyfriend thought seriously of marriage, but her parents are immutably opposed because there are three additional younger children in the family and because they feel that a "premature" birth would have a bad influence on the younger children and would be a source of personal and religious embarrassment to them. Consequently, they have told the patient that if she gets married at this point, she must leave their home, leave the community, and have no further contact with them or her younger siblings for three to five years, "at which time maybe people will have forgotten the birth date." Because I found this posture difficult to believe, I arranged to see the parents and literally confirmed what the girl had said to me. They are adamant on this point. . . . The alternative proposed to her by her parents, which is acceptable to them, includes an abortion now, to be followed by an immediate engagement and a marriage sometime this summer.[114]

In light of the patient's emotional dependence on her parents, the psychiatrist recommended that she have a therapeutic abortion.

By taking women's conflicts seriously, psychiatrists were also among the first to articulate the hardship of forced pregnancy. One psychiatrist explained about a patient who worried both about not finishing school and about creating a scandal in her hometown if she were to choose adoption, "If this patient is forced to carry this pregnancy to term it will be a threat to her future educational aspirations. This poses a real threat to her mother's well being as well."[115] Indeed, many psychiatrists supported women's right to choose abortion without labeling them mentally ill or unstable. At the same time, some women realized in their conversations with psychiatrists that they did not want an abortion.[116] Psychiatrists held that their patients should have the choice between ending a pregnancy or carrying a child to term without being forced to take the risks of illegal abortion. "Having the pregnancy continue without marriage is quite unacceptable to this girl," one psychiatrist argued, and he concluded, "I am quite satisfied that she would attempt an illegal abortion if we could not give her a therapeutic abortion."[117] Rather than look for indications of mental distress, psychiatrists stressed that patients were mature and mentally stable enough to choose pregnancy termination. "It is my considered professional opinion," another psychiatrist stated in support of his patient's quest for an abortion, "that there is no contraindication to therapeutic abortion."[118]

Despite the help that psychiatrists could offer women, the system of psychiatric consultation and referral was clearly limited in its ability to assist women in gaining access to abortion. Psychiatrists were quickly overwhelmed with patients seeking consultations for therapeutic abortion, and at times such consultations became a charade, which frustrated both the psychiatrists and the women who went to see them. In fact, many women experienced the requirement of psychiatric consultation as an expensive and even traumatic imposition. One woman, describing her experience and that of three others, complained: "I think $40 for a psychiatric consultation is too high for a student, but the psychiatrist knows that he has us in the bottom of his hand, and we four girls all come to the same conclusion, he made us feel very inhumane and primitive when he was through. I thought he was there to help, but I was only more upset and afraid when I left. Unfortunately, I have another appointment with him at 10:00. I don't want to be treated like a dog again, but there is not much that I can do."[119] Psychiatrists, on the other hand, could become frustrated with patients who refused to engage in serious conversation because they viewed the consultations merely as yet another hurdle to jump through. At the University of North Carolina's Memorial Hospital, for instance, psychiatrists regularly discussed with patients—most of whom were young college students with little sexual and contraceptive experience— why they had become sexually active without using contraceptives. Hoping that one of his patients, a nineteen-year-old dental student who had been sexually active with her boyfriend for five months without using any contraceptives, might understand that sexual behavior carried contraceptive responsibilities, one psychiatrist inquired about her sexual history. When this patient refused to engage in a discussion, he reported with frustration: "During the course of the whole interview the patient's basic attitude was one of covert hostility. After I commented on her attitude, she said that she did not see why I asked her the questions I did, since the interview was 'a formality and I am going to have the abortion so why do you need to know all this.' "[120] Unwilling to play the role of "a formality," he denied the patient's request for abortion. He explained: "[The patient] explicitly denied any symptoms of depression, anxiety, concern, intrapsychic distress or other evidence of stressful experiences. She said that her only reason for requesting abortion was the 'inconvenience' and that she did not see herself as psychologically stressed. . . . I told the patient and her mother that I could find little evidence of intrapsychic distress which would warrant a psychiatric recommendation from me for therapeutic abortion. . . . The data presented to me appears to point to abortion-on-request in the absence of significant psychiatric disturbance."[121] While some psychiatrists did not approve of abortion or only supported pregnancy termination for genuine psychiatric indications, this particular psychiatrist regularly supported the abortion requests of mentally healthy women.[122] His refusal in this case seems to have been due less to his aversion to making an abortion "of convenience" available than to his refusal to participate in a system that reduced him, a trained professional, to playing a role in a charade. It also indicates, however, that he felt somewhat ambivalent about women's reproductive rights, since he was unwilling to support his patient's decision in itself. In the end, he did refer her to a colleague more likely to write a positive letter, and he suggested that the patient and her mother think about some of the questions he had asked.

Psychiatrists were among the first to openly question the system of approving abortions that had developed in the postwar years. Hospitals, they charged, lacked clear standards for determining the necessity of an abortion and discriminated in favor of white, middle-class women who were educated enough to fake acute psychiatric problems. Physicians who treated the growing number of women flooding hospital emergency rooms with complications from botched abortions joined psychiatrists in criticizing the conditions under which abortion was available in the 1950s and 1960s. Exposed to the horror of illegal abortion, a growing number of physicians began to call for legal reform.[123]

■ Lobbying for Abortion Reform

By the 1960s, a number of factors converged to set the stage for abortion reform. Responding to medical complaints about the lack of clear legal guidelines, the American Law Institute (ALI), made up of attorneys, judges, and law professors, proposed a model abortion law in 1959 that would clarify the legal exception for therapeutic abortion and enshrine it in law along more liberal lines.[124] During the following decade, legal and medical organizations promoted the ALI model in state legislatures and in the media.

Demographic changes during the 1960s increased the demand for abortion. Women's rising labor force participation and college attendance contributed to falling birthrates and climbing abortion rates. The ability to delay childbearing took on new importance to women coming of age in the 1960s and led to a shift in public attitudes toward abortion. Women's growing need for access to safe abortion services became painfully evident to the medical professionals who were staffing the nation's emergency rooms and taking care of women who had obtained illegal abortions. The specter of women dying as a result of illegal abortions propelled activists, who hoped to protect the lives of women by making therapeutic abortion more accessible.

Sympathetic doctors and psychiatrists tested hospital rules and utilized health and psychiatric indications to push the boundaries of the existing law. In 1962, the Sherri Finkbine case raised public awareness of the dangers of thalidomide and inaugurated a nationwide debate about the use of abortion to avoid birth defects. The debate not only altered the national consciousness concerning abortion but also played a crucial role in emerging reform efforts. Starting in the late 1960s, the organized feminist movement put pressure on the medical profession and state legislatures to repeal abortion laws. By the mid-1960s, state legislators across the country were debating abortion reform based on the ALI model law, and in 1967 Colorado and North Carolina were the first states in the nation to pass reform legislation.[125]

The first serious initiative for the reform of abortion legislation in North Carolina came from Wallace Kuralt. Kuralt, who had launched a successful family planning program in Mecklenburg County and who in the early 1960s was instrumental in drafting North Carolina's voluntary sterilization law, argued that birth control, sterilization, and abortion should be accessible to all women. In 1967, he approached his friend Arthur H. Jones, who had just been elected to the North Carolina House of Representatives, to discuss the introduction of an abortion reform bill. Reform was needed, he told Jones, to ameliorate the serious socioeconomic problems caused by unwanted pregnancies and the birth of deformed children. Jones, himself interested in reproductive questions, promised to introduce a reform bill during the 1967 session of the legislature.[126]

Jones, who had grown up in Philadelphia and who was a retired senior vice president of North Carolina National Bank, had a long history of interest in and activism surrounding issues of family planning. In 1926, during his sophomore year at Oberlin College, he had formed Ohio's first planned parenthood association. He and other students manufactured contraceptive jelly that they sold at cost to married couples. In a sociology course, he discovered the writings of Margaret Sanger, interviewed her, and wrote his undergraduate thesis on family planning, including a chapter on abortion. In Charlotte, he was active in a host of social welfare organizations, including the Social Planning Council of Charlotte and the Charlotte Mental Hygiene Association. After his retirement, he was elected as a Democrat to the North Carolina House of Representatives, one of the few "Yankees" in North Carolina's General Assembly. His friendship with Kuralt and his wife's experience as a counselor in Charlotte and Mecklenburg domestic courts, where she had almost daily contact with the problems of unwanted children, played an important role in his decision to introduce the abortion bill.[127]

The 1967 movement for abortion reform embodied the tension between Kuralt's and Jones's desire to make abortion available upon request and their fear that a blanket endorsement of abortion would jeopardize the passage of any reform bill. Both men firmly believed that women should be able to decide when and when not to have abortions. "We aimed to make abortion as private an operation as possible," Kuralt explained. "We wanted it to be a decision involving the woman and her doctor and nobody else—as simple as an appendectomy."[128] Since passage of a reform bill permitting abortion on demand seemed unrealistic, both hoped that a bill significantly expanding the indications for abortion would, in effect, give physicians the flexibility to accommodate all abortion requests. Relieving doctors of the fear of prosecution, they felt, would give them the leeway to perform an abortion on any woman who desired one. Designed to conform closely with the ALI model abortion law, North Carolina's proposed abortion statute would permit licensed physicians to perform abortions in cases of "substantial risk that continuance of the pregnancy would threaten the life or gravely impair the health of [a] woman."[129]

Complicating matters further, Kuralt and Jones worried that the debate surrounding legislative reform would revive earlier suggestions that state reproductive policies ought to control the reproduction of ADC recipients. The state had recently weathered a debate about two legislative proposals that sought the compulsory sterilization of women who had given birth to two or more children outside of marriage. Spawned by an outcry against rising welfare costs and by white resentment of black single mothers, the bills had defined women with illegitimate children as "grossly sexually delinquent" and proposed sterilization as a punitive measure.[130] Although the sterilization proposals died in legislative committee, punitive attitudes toward ADC recipients who had children outside of marriage endured. Worried that such attitudes might drive the debate about abortion reform and jeopardize the passage of their bill, Kuralt and Jones chose to disassociate the bill from public welfare in order to avoid the suggestion that abortion, too, might curb births outside of marriage by allowing pregnancy termination for poor (and black) welfare recipients. Similarly, they hoped to avoid allegations that abortion reform was really a form of population control.

The hearings surrounding the abortion reform bill confirmed Kuralt's and Jones's suspicions that legislators opposed abortion on demand. In fact, lawmakers deeply distrusted women's ability to make any decision regarding abortion. They worried that the reform bill might be "simply a convenience bill for those who don't want a child."[131] Opponents raised the specter of women " 'crying rape five months after pregnancy' simply to get an abortion" and devised hypothetical scenarios in which legalization would lead women to seek abortions for selfish monetary reasons.[132] Legislators, it was clear, were opposed to legislation that extended reproductive control to women. When a Durham gynecologist, testifying in favor of legislative reform, argued that the only fault she could find with the bill was that it did not go "far enough," she was accused of favoring abortions of convenience. Another physician who described the bill as the "logical extension of planned parenthood" met with similar disapproval from legislators.[133]

To draw attention away from the implications abortion reform could have for women's reproductive control, supporters of the bill carefully couched the bill as a medical measure that would give physicians urgently needed legal backing for practices that were grossly out of step with the present law. With one exception, all of those who spoke in support of abortion reform were physicians who urged that abortion legislation needed to be brought in line with abortion practice. "I have performed abortions," Dr. Robert A. Ross, a University of North Carolina obstetrician/gynecologist and president of the North Carolina Medical Society, admitted to legislators at a public hearing. He continued: "And I say in all honesty, I have regretted much more the ones I haven't done than the ones I've done. . . . The existing law permits abortions but is not clear on the responsibilities of the doctor in the matter. . . . The proposed legislation clearly defines their responsibilities. . . . Doctors want and need this legislation to back up their responsibility."[134] Another physician, chairman of the medical society's legislative committee, assured lawmakers that physicians across the state had commented favorably on the bill. And Arthur Jones reminded legislators that his bill would not only provide physicians with the legal safeguards they needed to perform necessary abortions, it would also protect women from unskilled abortionists and thus curb high rates of infection, sterilization, mutilation, and death—all serious public health problems caused by illegal abortion.[135]

Despite these efforts, however, the debate focused on two issues at the heart of public welfare policies: public expenditures and the worthiness of particular offspring. While legislators did not address the issue of children born to welfare recipients, they did focus considerable attention on state funding for the disabled. Senator Jack White, who introduced the bill to the state Senate, reminded legislators of a trip they had made to the State Hospital at Goldsboro, an institution for the physically and mentally disabled. The new abortion law, he promised his colleagues, would eliminate "hundreds of 'vegetables' and 'basket cases' now cared for at state expense."[136] Although Dr. Ross testified that physicians could not diagnose physical or mental defects in a fetus—they could merely determine the statistical probability that a baby might be born handicapped—legislators advocated the bill for its vague eugenic potential.

The hope that abortion could be of value as part of state eugenic policies dated back to policy debates of the mid-1940s. One of the first people to suggest the reform of North Carolina's abortion legislation was George H. Lawrence, professor of social work at the University of North Carolina and director of public welfare in Orange County. Lawrence, a longtime proponent of eugenic sterilization and the author of a number of studies of feeblemindedness in North Carolina, was particularly concerned about pregnant women for whom the North Carolina Eugenics Board had authorized sterilization. A revision of the abortion law, he hoped, would make it legal to perform abortions on these women, providing a way to implement state eugenic policies even more comprehensively. Physicians and parents who during the 1940s and 1950s petitioned the North Carolina Eugenics Board to authorize eugenic abortions shared Lawrence's intentions.[137] But while Lawrence's proposal gained a sympathetic ear, the Eugenics Board voted after "thorough" discussion not to sponsor a eugenic amendment to the abortion law in 1967 and in subsequent years refused to consider all requests to authorize eugenic abortion. It is unclear why board members refused to support the amendment. Most likely, they feared that involvement in such a controversial issue as abortion would raise opposition to the entire sterilization program.[138]

While legal considerations might have contributed to the Eugenics Board's unwillingness to get involved in abortion—after all, the board's authority was limited to the authorization of sterilization—medical professionals were also familiar with the use of eugenic indications to justify abortion. Both the rubella epidemic of the mid-1960s and the debate surrounding the Sherri Finkbine case indicated that the threat of fetal defects had emerged as an important consideration in the abortion debate. Sherri Finkbine's husband explained their decision in favor of abortion to the media: "There is a fifty-fifty chance our baby would be a basket case if it were allowed to be born. We feel very strongly about this and believe we are doing the right thing."[139] Jack White's arguments to his fellow senators, then, must be understood in the larger context of an abortion discourse influenced by eugenic considerations.

The abortion bill embodied the tensions between lawmakers' support of the law's eugenic potential and their opposition toward the idea of ceding reproductive control to women. Most legislators hoped to cut public expenditures by controlling the reproduction of those deemed likely to bear inferior offspring. But while they were willing to provide physicians with greater flexibility to make decisions about abortion, they were unwilling to grant women the same decision-making power. The bill finally passed with several amendments that significantly watered down the radical potential of abortion reform. Most important, it imposed a state residency requirement of four months on those seeking abortion and specified that women had to consult with three physicians who were willing to justify the procedure in order to obtain a therapeutic abortion. The law did greatly increase physicians' autonomy in determining whether their patients would benefit from pregnancy termination. But it wrote the cumbersome process of outside consultation into law, stopping short of allowing women and their physicians to decide upon abortion by themselves.

Some physicians took full advantage of the new abortion law and began to offer the procedure to any woman requesting it. Immediately following the law's passage, physicians Takey Crist and Jaroslav Hulka at North Carolina Memorial Hospital, under the leadership of Charles Hendricks, chair of the Department of Obstetrics and Gynecology at the hospital, set out to significantly open women's access to therapeutic abortion. All three men were firm believers in extending reproductive control to women. Hendricks and Hulka, both the sons of physicians, had been trained in the Midwest and Northeast and had spent years caring for women who came with abortion-related complications to hospital emergency rooms. Crist, a native North Carolinian and the child of Greek Cypriot immigrants, had gone to medical school at the University of North Carolina. Having grown up believing that women should be able to choose their destiny just as freely as men, Crist understood early in his medical education that women's ability to do so hinged on their ability to control their reproduction. Despite these physicians' determination to make abortion more widely available in North Carolina, however, opposition to abortion within the department was considerable. "There were tears and yelling and swearing," Hendricks remembers about the first staff meeting at which the issue of abortion was on the agenda. "[One staff member] was shouting, 'If this goddamn department is going to go around doing abortions, I'll be ashamed that I've ever been associated here.' "[140] The bloody nature of the abortion procedure contributed to the uneasiness that many physicians felt toward it. Physician Charles deProsse commented about physician opposition:

> The technique was such that it put a bad taste in the mouth of a lot of doctors with respect to therapeutic abortions. The only thing we had at that time . . . was doing a routine D&C. . . . And doing an abortion by routine D&C was a very bloody procedure, frighteningly so, sometimes. . . . I don't think that without the advent of suction abortion that abortion would ever have been as accepted by the medical practice as it was. . . . A lot of older doctors, when it did become legal, just all they could think of was that horrendous therapeutic abortion regimen that they had gone through, and they just didn't want to do it, didn't want to get involved.[141]

The increase of therapeutic abortions at Memorial Hospital coincided with and was eased by the introduction of vacuum aspiration. In 1967, Hulka traveled to England to observe the use of a vacuum aspiration machine and purchase the first model. Upon his return, he and Crist learned how to use the machine and quickly taught others in the department. To convince his colleagues of the desirability of legal abortion, Crist conducted research on the sexual and contraceptive knowledge of college students at the University of North Carolina, demonstrating that students were sexually active but lacked essential information about reproduction and contraception.[142]

Moreover, Hendricks, in order to comply with the new law, made a significant effort to establish collaboration between obstetrician/gynecologists and psychiatrists, spending considerable time convincing psychiatrists to support women's requests for therapeutic abortion. Personal experience with the effects of unwanted pregnancies was the factor that most frequently convinced physicians and psychiatrists to aid women in need of abortion. Hendricks recalled one psychiatrist, for instance, who "came around" after his unmarried daughter became pregnant. Confused and distressed, he spent hours talking to Hendricks. Hendricks recalled: "We must have had a dozen conversations. He wanted to check about this and that. And she was a student at S., wonderful S. College in Q. And [the psychiatrist] told me about how it was to be at S. and how important it was, and she wasn't married and so on, and on, and on, and on."[143] The effort paid off, however, when this psychiatrist subsequently became a regular consultant for women seeking therapeutic abortions.

As a result of these efforts, the number of therapeutic abortions performed at North Carolina Memorial Hospital in Chapel Hill rose from 8 in 1966 to 164 in 1969 to 616 in 1970.[144] As word spread that physicians were increasingly willing to honor women's abortion requests, many physicians were confronted with patients who would have sought an underground abortion earlier. "When we opened up the doors," Takey Crist recalled about his time at Memorial Hospital, "there was a car in front of my house in the driveway, there was a couple in the living room, there was a couple in the kitchen, there was someone on the phone."[145] At the same time, statistics indicate that Memorial Hospital was an exception, performing up to 60 percent of the total number of abortions in North Carolina during this period.[146] Wanting to relieve themselves of the responsibility of performing abortions, a number of physicians from across the state referred their patients to North Carolina Memorial Hospital. But abortion, Charles Hendricks held, was a community responsibility. Jaroslav Hulka recalls: "Dr. Hendricks, as chair [of the Department of Obstetrics and Gynecology,] would call these people up and say, 'Gee, thanks for your referral for this therapeutic abortion. We certainly will be happy to do it for you. By the way, do you still do hysterectomies or would you like to refer them to us as well? And do you do Caesarian sections? We can do those too. Oh, you prefer to do your own hysterectomies? Why don't you do your own abortions?' And gradually he got the pressure onto the referring doctors to stop referring them and to do their own as part of the practice of obstetrics and gynecology."[147] In the early 1970s, Charles Hendricks and Takey Crist visited county medical societies across the state to convince physicians to perform their own abortions. Crist remembers:

The residents and those that had been in practice that had trained at the University were contacted and said, "Look, do you remember we took care of a lot of your patients on this abortion issue. And so now we are saying it's gonna be a community responsibility. We are not going to take any more. You have a responsibility in your community, and you need to help us." And Chuck would talk to them on the phone, other faculty members would talk to them, and then we did like a little speech, a little visit. And they were encouraged to bring everybody on the medical staff in that particular community hospital to understand what the problem was. And they were told about the illegal abortions from Cheraw [South Carolina], from Durham, the complications, and that, if women had access to family planning and contraception, then you wouldn't have as many abortions.[148]

Even though the increase from 8 abortions in 1966 to 616 in 1970 felt tremendous to those caught in the middle of making it happen, for the majority of North Carolina women abortion remained inaccessible. In fact, immediately after their passage, doubts surfaced about the ability of the new abortion reform laws in North Carolina and Colorado to significantly increase access to abortion and ameliorate the public health crisis caused by botched abortions. At a symposium held by the Department of Obstetrics and Gynecology at North Carolina Memorial Hospital, Allan Guttmacher criticized the North Carolina law's limited indications and its requirement that three physicians had to approve an abortion. The new law, he warned, would "do very little, if anything to reduce illegal abortion."[149] And in 1971, Takey Crist echoed Guttmacher's warnings when he concluded: "The number of illegal abortions in North Carolina has been estimated to be 25,000. Even if reporting was poor, and even if we did in reality perform 5,000 legal abortions last year—still there are 20,000 women being subjected to the risk of death! And for these people the laws might as well never have been passed."[150] If Kuralt and Jones had hoped that physicians would understand the bill as an endorsement of contraceptive abortion, they were disappointed. Echoing the experience of physicians in other states that passed similar abortion reform laws, most North Carolina physicians remained suspicious of women's motivations for terminating their pregnancies and continued to turn away women in need of abortion. Critics complained that the new law was unduly cumbersome and almost as nonspecific as the law that preceded it. Impatient with the ineffectiveness of legislative reform, some physicians grew in

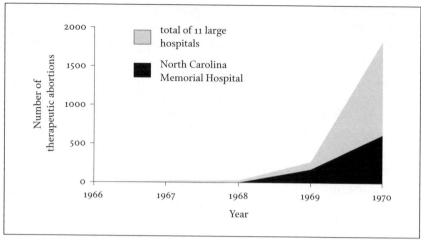

Figure 9. Therapeutic abortions in North Carolina

creasingly willing to "make up" diagnoses that would permit the termination of pregnancy. The result was an explosion of psychiatric indications, which led psychiatrists to be overburdened with mentally healthy patients who sought abortions.[151] One psychiatrist complained, "I would prefer to spend my time with patients who need my skills more."[152] "Finally you ran out of the psychiatrists' energy," Hendricks explained. "The system gets to be overwhelmed. . . . It doesn't mean that the psychiatrists were getting so that they didn't care, or they weren't counseling. They just ran out of energy. They had their academic lives to live and they had their practices to run and so on, and they also had to survive in an environment where eventually, I suppose, somewhere they went to a PTA meeting, someone would say something disparaging about their practice."[153]

Women, too, were not uniformly excited about the conditions under which they could obtain abortions. Those who were fortunate enough to learn about the willingness of physicians at Memorial Hospital to provide elective abortions expressed their gratitude for and relief about the service. Others, however, still encountered physicians who refused to offer help or found that the law's age requirements—women had to be twenty-one years of age or to provide parental consent in order to obtain a therapeutic abortion legally—made legal therapeutic abortion inaccessible to them. And many complained about the cumbersome system that required the time and expense of obtaining outside consultation.[154]

Frustrated by the lack of change, Arthur Jones and a number of physicians tried in 1970 to force further abortion reform through the courts by challenging the constitutionality of the 1967 abortion statute. They asked that the law be declared unconstitutional on the ground that it denied women the right to decide how many children they wanted to bear. While the judges agreed that it was not the state's business to regulate whether a woman practiced contraception or chose to become pregnant, they decided that the real issue in this case was whether the state could assign an embryo or fetus the right to be born. An embryo or fetus should have this right, the judges concluded, and they confirmed the constitutionality of the law. Having failed in the courts, Arthur Jones decided to introduce another reform bill to the legislature in 1971. This time, he asked for the abolition of the cumbersome requirement of outside consultation and for the legalization of abortion for any reason at all within the first twelve weeks of pregnancy.[155]

If abortion proponents in 1967 had been genteel in their avoidance of arguments that posed abortion as a solution to rising welfare costs, they became more forthright during the 1971 debate. Moreover, abortion opponents, who had been largely caught off guard four years earlier, were now prepared to enter the fray. As constituents began to barrage legislators with arguments for and against further reform, a heated exchange developed over precisely those issues that Kuralt and Jones had sought to deflect four years earlier: the worthiness of and costs to the state of raising particular offspring.

This time, supporters of abortion did not shy away from making reproductive rights arguments. Jones was joined by a minority of constituents who sought abortion reform as an aid in women's emancipation. Such arguments resonated with some. When Mrs. Milgrom, a mother, grandmother, and wife of Democratic representative Henry Milgrom, argued at a legislative hearing of the House Health Committee that only a person who could become pregnant was qualified to talk about abortion, she received a burst of applause. Reform advocates pointed to the amount of work involved in child care and the division of labor that defined child care tasks as women's responsibility. Advocates asked legislators to consider the burdens of unwanted pregnancy and the workload of already overburdened mothers when casting their votes. Moreover, constituents emphasized the punitive character of proposals that sought to limit women's access to reproductive control. Sex, one proponent pointed out, should not be viewed as a crime for which the female partner deserved to be punished with childbirth. Repeatedly, constituents held that unwanted pregnancies could have devastating consequences for women's emotional and physical well-being. No man, they concluded, had the right to insist that a woman bear an unwanted child. Legalizing abortion, they hoped, would erase the stigma of premarital pregnancies, put women in control of their childbearing capacities, and eliminate the health hazards linked to underground abortions.[156]

Echoing concerns voiced in the 1967 abortion debate, however, the majority of proponents and opponents of the new bill were not only indifferent to women's emancipation but highly suspicious of women's motivations for terminating their pregnancies. One obstetrician/gynecologist from western North Carolina argued: "The argument based on the so-called right of a woman to bear or not to bear children is clearly fallacious. Granted that a woman has a legal right to be promiscuous, or even to be a prostitute, must she not bear the legal and moral consequences of her action? . . . On what basis can the proposed abortion-on-demand law be justified? It does not appear to utilize good principles of either medicine, or law. Is it to save the life of the mother; is it to preserve the mental health; is it to control the population; or is it pure convenience? I cannot help feeling that it is primarily the last reason."[157]

In fact, rather than focus on women's reproductive rights, the majority of abortion proponents emphasized precisely that factor that had always featured prominently in shaping the state's reproductive policies: the financial cost of unwanted children. Unwanted children, constituents argued, were costly to American society. Being unwanted scarred children emotionally from birth throughout their lives. Deprived of maternal love and care, such children grew up to become social and financial liabilities. "If the mother is immoral and has only concern for herself, then she has spawned another AFDC child or one with perverted and warped values," one supporter of the bill cautioned.[158] Not only were unwanted children likely to become public charges, the supporters of the bill argued, but they might also jeopardize the economic survival of their families, leading other family members to become public charges as well. Moreover, proponents warned, the lack of proper maternal love and care in early childhood turned children into criminals and made them likely to need mental health and penal services. "I have read that Charles Manson was the child of a prostitute. And the product of what I daresay was an unwanted pregnancy," one supporter remembered, topping all efforts to demonstrate the undesirable qualities of unwanted children.[159] Another pointed out: "Unwanted children are a large drain on tax-money. In contrast, an abortion earlier than the 12th week of pregnancy costs only about $25.00."[160] Liberalizing the state's abortion law would offer mothers, particularly those on AFDC, the opportunity to terminate their pregnancies, relieving the taxpayers of the burden of supporting unwanted children. It would also give social welfare agencies the opportunity to pose an ultimatum to AFDC mothers: "Have an abortion or support the child yourself."[161]

Supporters hoped that abortion would not only reduce public spending but also break the cycle of illegitimacy. Many proponents assumed that unwanted pregnancies did not happen to "normal" women but only to women already marked by other undesirable characteristics such as poverty, social irresponsibility, immorality, and carelessness. Such women were likely to provide their children with poor role models and to contribute to the perpetuation of social problems. Because of the poor socialization that resulted, the cycle of giving birth to unwanted children was thought to repeat itself.[162] A liberalized abortion law promised to break the cycle of illegitimacy and to increase state control over women's reproductive lives.

By preventing the birth of unwanted children, then, legalizing abortion —like birth control and sterilization—was supposed to help solve a host of larger social problems. It was hoped not only that abortion could reduce child abuse, neglect, and resulting personality disorders, but also that it could be an invaluable aid in controlling poverty and criminality, saving the taxpayers money. Finally, it was hoped that abortion, in conjunction with sterilization, could prevent immorality: women who sought abortion because they had become pregnant outside of marriage would be deterred from further immoral acts by the threat of ensuing sterilization.

Despite the widespread appeal that abortion reform held for those concerned with public health and public welfare, attempts to further liberalize the 1967 abortion statute failed. Abortion opponents who, caught off guard by the 1967 debate, had remained practically silent four years earlier successfully rallied to support their position in the following years.[163] In 1971 as in 1967, opposition was limited to Roman Catholics, but they had coalesced to form a much more proactive group. Like the proponents of a liberalized abortion statute, opponents of the bill emphasized the worthiness of particular offspring and issues of morality. Less skeptical about the fate of unwanted children, however, they argued that "there is potential good in every life no matter how that life comes into being" and recommended that mothers put their unwanted children up for adoption.[164] Opponents of the bill compared abortion to Nazi euthanasia policies that had eliminated the handicapped regardless of their potential, and they worried about the loss of genius due to abortion. Others feared the consequences that abortion would have on the mental state of women. "Those in the nursing field inform me that a large majority who have an abortion suffer various mental agonies," one opponent informed her senator, and she warned that the liberalization of the law would flood the mental institutions with dependent patients.[165] In addition, opponents were concerned about the larger social implications of liberalized abortion regulations. Believing that social morals were already in great danger, they feared that liberalization would encourage promiscuity, increase the divorce rate, and generally lower the standard of civilization. Abortion, opponents agreed, was murder, and permitting abortion meant usurping God's right to creation.[166] In the end, the opponents of the bill prevailed. Although the House of Representatives approved the bill, at the last minute a number of senators who were thought to support abortion reform switched their votes. The measure was defeated by a vote of twenty-five to twenty-one.[167]

The discourse surrounding the 1971 abortion reform bill offers several valuable lessons concerning reproductive politics. The division of abortion proponents into those who sought abortion to extend reproductive rights to women and those who hoped to cut public spending ultimately weakened support for the measure. Believing that the passage of a reform bill was more important than the reason why such a bill passed, progressive proponents like Kuralt sought to avoid the more controversial arguments on both sides. Most legislators were suspicious of elective abortions, but many supported medical and financial arguments in favor of abortion reform. Kuralt himself avoided making reproductive rights arguments in 1971 much as he had shied away from associating public welfare and abortion reform in 1967. To be sure, his attempts to steer the discussion had contributed to the easy passage of the first abortion reform bill. But while Kuralt's strategy made sense in the context of 1967 North Carolina, it contributed to the failure of the abortion debate to fully develop, allowing unresolved divisions among the proponents of the bill to fester and eventually contribute to the defeat of the 1971 bill. This failure is even more poignant in light of the fact that in response to the 1976 Hyde Amendment, supporters of liberalized access to abortion from both sides of the fence were able to come together to establish a state abortion fund that offered financial help to poor women who desired abortion.

Following the failure of further reform in North Carolina, the practice of abortion in the state continued as it had in previous years. Despite a slow rise statewide in the number of therapeutic abortions performed, Memorial Hospital continued to stand out as the most accessible place in the state to obtain therapeutic abortion, and many women remained cut off from access to legal abortion. The legalization of abortion in Washington, D.C., in 1969 and in New York in 1970, however, led to the emergence of a network of independent abortion clinics. By the late 1960s, a number of ministers across the country had established the Clergy Consultation Service, which provided women with abortion counseling and referred them to safe abortion providers. Starting in 1970, then, physicians and clergy could send women who failed to qualify under North Carolina law to one of the abortion clinics on the East Coast. For about $260, a woman could fly with her partner from Raleigh-Durham to New York City in the morning, get an abortion, and fly back to North Carolina by late afternoon.[168]

In January of 1973, the U.S. Supreme Court decision in *Roe v. Wade* legalized abortion. The decision declared that a woman's right to privacy included the "decision whether or not to terminate her pregnancy."[169] While *Roe v. Wade* granted women the right to choose abortion in consultation with their physicians, it rejected the notion that women had a *right* to abortion on demand. By doing so, it upheld states' right to limit access to abortion if they found that they had an interest in doing so. Women, then, could choose abortion as part of their right to privacy, but states were under no obligation to guarantee women equal access to the procedure. As Rosalind Petchesky has noted, *Roe v. Wade* fit abortion within the market paradigm. Access continued to depend on a woman's ability to find a sympathetic physician and pay for the procedure.[170]

Despite these limitations, *Roe v. Wade* expanded women's access to abortion significantly. The decision removed physicians' hesitation to perform abortions by establishing the legality and legitimacy of the procedure as a method of assuring women's health in the broadest sense of the term. As it was interpreted in the liberal climate of the time, *Roe v. Wade* resulted in the opening of abortion clinics across the country, drastically increasing women's access to the procedure. As a result of legalization, emergency rooms emptied of women seeking treatment for botched abortions, cases of septic shock disappeared, and abortion-related maternal mortality fell to a rate of 0.4 deaths per 100,000 procedures.[171]

■ Conclusion

Throughout the twentieth century, women, physicians, and prosecutors argued about the meaning of abortion, defining and redefining the procedure as elective, therapeutic, or eugenic. Abortion, like sterilization and birth control, could simultaneously provide women with a form of reproductive control and enable the state to limit the reproduction of those whose reproduction it considered undesirable. Which of these roles abortion should play in American society was an issue that inspired much public debate.

Elective abortion never gained wide political support. While women continued to terminate their pregnancies throughout a century during which elective abortion was criminalized, thus claiming their right to elective abortions, even supporters of abortion reform shied away from arguing that women should have access to abortion on demand. *Roe v. Wade* did not grant women a right to abortion, whether in the first trimester or later. However, the decision gave physicians the right to perform abortions, elective or therapeutic, whenever they found the operation necessary. While this did change the legal situation regarding elective abortion, it still meant that a woman seeking an elective abortion had to find a physician willing to perform it. This might seem a mere formality in a context in which women have equal access to abortions because physicians are willing to perform them. At times like the present, however, when more and more physicians hesitate to perform abortions for fear that they will hurt their image, and when medical schools no longer teach the procedure to their regular medical students, women lose their equal access to abortion, and poor women in particular are denied reproductive autonomy.[172]

During the period of criminalization, the availability of abortion depended on state prosecutors' interest in enforcing the abortion statutes and on health professionals' willingness to provide women with the procedure. Throughout the twentieth century, sympathetic physicians have offered to perform abortions at women's request, thus providing women with an important form of reproductive control. In this role, physicians mediated between women seeking access to abortion and prosecutors restricting access to it. Physicians emphasized the necessity of therapeutic abortion for medical reasons and negotiated for more expansive definitions of medical indications for the procedure (as in the shift from medical to psychiatric rationales for it) at times when prosecutors ceased to accept indications that had been acceptable earlier. For a while, physicians successfully set the parameters for illegal but tolerated abortions cleanly performed by qualified practitioners in hospital settings. But the medical profession did not always act as a progressive force, providing women with desired abortions in the face of criminalization and prosecution. Many physicians refused to provide abortions altogether and, after the establishment of hospital abortion committees, participated in the policing of their own profession.

Eugenic ideas had a powerful influence on the liberalization of abortion. The discourse surrounding eugenic abortion, like discussions of the role of eugenic sterilization, reflected larger anxieties about women's sexuality outside of marriage, the transmission of physical and mental defects, and growing welfare rolls. Supporters of abortion reform used arguments similar to those that underlay proposals for the liberalization of sterilization and the expansion of birth control programs. They sought the liberalization of abortion legislation not to provide women with access to elective abortion but to prevent multiple social problems that they believed were rooted in the birth of unwanted children. Health and welfare professionals identified unwanted children and the social problems that accompanied them as a problem of the poor white and black populations —the same social groups that became the target of sterilization and birth control programs. Where costly social programs had failed, health and welfare professionals argued, cheap abortions could solve social problems. Public health and social welfare arguments in favor of liberalizing access to eugenic and therapeutic abortion took precedence over arguments that promoted women's right to choose whether to experience pregnancy and childbirth.

As the discourse surrounding abortion reform demonstrated, however, the categories of elective, therapeutic, and eugenic abortion were not clearly defined but tended to overlap. Proponents of eugenic abortion voiced concerns similar to those voiced by people who supported therapeutic abortion for psychiatric reasons: both groups aimed to prevent future social problems that they expected would result from the birth of unwanted children. At other times, however, physicians defined therapeutic abortion so broadly as to include the elective abortions desired by their patients. It is essentially this overlap of definitions that has given women access to legal abortion.

From a feminist perspective, *Roe v. Wade* seems to have limited women's right to unrestricted elective abortion by placing abortion into a therapeutic framework so that the procedure requires medical justification. In fact, it is the assault on the medical necessity of abortion that has reduced women's access to the procedure. It has been difficult to get abortion recognized as a legitimate therapeutic procedure that should be included in regular health care coverage. Its exclusion from Medicaid coverage, for instance, is possible because abortion continues to be perceived as an elective rather than as a medical procedure—regardless of the therapeutic framework provided by *Roe*. Beginning in 1976, Congress began to reduce the number of permissible medical criteria for the operation, and by the end of the decade Medicaid funding for abortion was reduced to include only cases in which a woman's life was threatened by her pregnancy.[173] Insurance companies followed suit, treating abortion as an elective operation rather than a health-related procedure.

Since the late 1970s, the erosion of medical rationales for performing abortions and the redefinition of abortion as an elective procedure—an operation of convenience—have combined to restrict access to abortion. As Frederick S. Jaffe, director of Planned Parenthood's Center for Family Planning Program Development, argued shortly after *Roe v. Wade*, to define most abortions as "elective" procedures is ipso facto to disqualify them from receiving public or private funding, thus to "win the battle and lose the war."[174] The gap between formal rights to abortion and practical access to it points to socially unequal access to the health care system as a whole.

CHAPTER FOUR

Taking Foam Powder and Jellies to the Natives

Family Planning Goes Abroad

In October 1935, Margaret Sanger boarded a ship bound for Bombay to lobby for family planning in India and to support its fledging birth control movement. She took with her a large inventory of medical supplies and educational tools, including a demonstration film and fifty plastic pelvis models used to instruct women at the Clinical Research Bureau in New York. Sanger's trip to India was not her first sojourn abroad in the name of birth control. In 1922, she had taken a much-publicized trip to Japan, where she had spoken on behalf of family planning. Nor was Sanger the only American birth control advocate interested in promoting family planning outside the mainland United States. While she was touring Japan, Clarence J. Gamble began to support family planning efforts and test contraceptives in Puerto Rico. In the early 1950s, he followed Sanger's lead and established contraceptive trials in Japan, India, Ceylon, and elsewhere.[1]

Sanger's and Gamble's endeavors were part of a larger international effort that extended from the establishment of local birth control programs in Indian and Puerto Rican villages to the organization of international conferences on the future of world population. Early in the twentieth century, scientists developed an institutional infrastructure to link individuals and organizations concerned with the newly emerging field of population studies into an international network. As scientists shifted their focus from eugenics and individual reproduction to analyses of whole populations, the family planning policies of developing nations took center stage.[2] By the time Sanger chaired the 1927 World Population Conference in Geneva, scientists had already organized six international neo-Malthusian and birth control conferences at which birth control activists, demographers, and biomedical scientists from around the world had debated differential fertility rates and exchanged ideas about family planning. This chapter will explore some of these international efforts at family planning to point to both the continuities and discontinuities that emerged as reproductive policies crossed international boundaries.

I focus my attention on Puerto Rico and India for two reasons. First, both countries attracted the attention of a number of the philanthropists and researchers who feature prominently in this book. Second, both countries share certain characteristics that make them particularly suitable for comparison. Population growth in these countries seemed to provide an ongoing threat to their economic, social, and political security and thus to the security of the world at large. As a result, they attracted the attention of international population planners early in the twentieth century and held that attention throughout the 1970s and beyond. Both countries experienced their share of coercive family planning policies within the context of democratic political systems. These two nations, moreover, have received considerable attention from scholars, who have produced a rich body of literature to draw on.

Spawned in large part by the global economic crisis of the Great Depression, the establishment of public health birth control programs to fight against poverty and poor health stood as a sign of modernization not only in the United States but also abroad. Just as American public health officials hoped that science and medicine would curb the high reproductive rates of America's poor, health and welfare officials in Puerto Rico and India turned to scientific population planning in an effort to control birthrates and demonstrate their commitment to modernization. Under the leadership of private philanthropists such as Clarence Gamble, physicians and public health officials abroad established birth control programs for the poor. Closely emulating U.S. contraceptive programs, foreign birth control programs were often embedded in contraceptive field trials, with officials dispensing foam powders, contraceptive jellies, and condoms in order to test their effectiveness. In addition, health and welfare officials in the United States and Puerto Rico turned to eugenic sterilization to limit the reproduction of those considered to be socially undesirable. India also instituted coercive measures, albeit several decades later during its state of emergency in the 1970s.

After World War II, the promotion of population control abroad began to receive institutional support from within the United States. In an effort to establish global stability in the postwar world, American foreign policy supported decolonization efforts and promoted social and economic development in the new nations of Asia, Africa, and Latin America. Economic planners sought the help of demographers, whose development models touted Western-style modernization and political liberalization and linked both to fertility decline. With one-third of the world's population uncommitted to either democracy or communism as of 1945, the fate of developing countries took on special significance in the Cold War period, and "excessive" population growth was seen as a potential threat to U.S. security. Demographers and policy makers feared that rapid population growth would threaten the former colonies with severe resource shortages, economic catastrophe, and political instability. Demographer Kingsley Davis argued, "The demographic problems of the underdeveloped countries, especially in areas of non-Western culture, make these nations more vulnerable to Communism."[3] The solution was direct government intervention to lower the birthrate among the poor at home and in Third World countries.

The opportunity to establish family planning programs with Western help held a number of contradictory meanings for developing countries. On the one hand, local elites frequently subscribed to Western modernization models and thus supported efforts at population control in the hope of promoting Western-style economic development. Health officials and their supporters argued that a country's ability to participate in family planning programs was a sign of modernity and signaled its ability to join the international scientific discourse about population control. Moreover, Western sponsorship of family planning programs frequently provided opportunities to import technologies and services otherwise unavailable into Third World countries. While the imported contraceptive supplies were often untested, inferior, or both, the family planning programs nevertheless provided access to medical technologies and services otherwise out of reach. Health officials who conducted field tests of the birth control pill in Puerto Rico, for instance, were able to negotiate to perform regular biopsies for reproductive cancers on patients, tests that were largely unavailable in Puerto Rico and had to be analyzed in Boston. While the Puerto Rican physicians who supervised the pill trials considered such tests necessary to the evaluation of the birth control pill, access to the biopsies also brought a level of health care to trial participants that was otherwise inaccessible to them. Indeed, the promise of granting access to unattainable medical care motivated health officials not only in developing countries but also at home. Nurse Eunice Rivers, who served as a public health nurse and liaison to the black community for the infamous Tuskegee Syphilis Study, in which African American men who had contracted syphilis were studied but not treated for the disease, argued that trial participants gained significantly as a result of the experiment: "Those people got all kinds of examinations and medical care that they never would have gotten. I've taken them over to the hospital and they'd have a GI series on them, the heart, the lung, just everything. It was just impossible for just an ordinary person to get that kind of examination. . . . They'd get all kinds of extra things, cardiograms and . . . some of the things that I had never heard of. . . . Those people had been given better care than some of us who could afford it."[4] It would be too simple to dismiss Rivers or similarly motivated health officials in developing countries as the dupes of researchers or as individuals who participated in the exploitation of their research subjects. Despite the racial, gender, and medical hierarchies under which they operated, health care professionals such as Rivers and the Puerto Rican physicians who cooperated with research experiments frequently saw themselves as advocates for their patients and acted accordingly. Indeed, their position illustrates the tension in their role as mediators between the medical needs of clients who lacked access to the most basic health services and the demands of researchers who provided access to these services.

Just as American women encountered family planning programs that ranged between those that extended reproductive control to women and those that controlled women's reproduction, Indian and Puerto Rican women's experiences with family planning can be located along that same continuum. But if it is difficult to reconstruct American women's responses, it is even more so in the case of Puerto Rican and Indian women. Nevertheless, the same parameters prevail. Many women sought access to health and reproductive services but found that husbands, religious authorities, health care providers, and others artificially restricted their choices or denied them access altogether. Women made their decisions about contraception and abortion within this limited context. Frequently, choices were far from ideal, but women were not rendered passive objects in their negotiations for health care.

Although international family planning efforts mostly lacked institutional support until the early 1950s, the story of Margaret Sanger and Clarence Gamble illustrates that prominent family planning advocates in the United States were supporting family planning abroad well before the emergence of a population control lobby. The same negotiations that shaped policy implementation and patients' experiences of reproductive policies in the United States also influenced reproductive programs abroad. But while the cast of characters involved in these negotiations overseas was essentially the same as it was in the United States, the unequal power relationship between the United States and both Puerto Rico and India, as well as these nations' economic dependence on the United States, significantly shaped perceptions of family planning efforts from all sides. Thus the relationship between First World philanthropists and contraceptive researchers and Third World health professionals and women has influenced the discourse surrounding birth control and sterilization in the past as well as historians' understanding of family planning efforts in the Third World.

As the United States began to invest in the family planning programs of developing nations, social scientists initiated studies of the success of these programs and their implications for American foreign policy, demographic patterns, and women's health. Reviews were mixed and depended largely on the perspective from which scholars evaluated family planning efforts. Did they curb high birthrates, reduce poverty, improve women's health, offer reproductive choices? What were their implications for foreign relations? Did such programs indeed improve American relations with developing countries and thus contribute to a more stable global environment? Two strands of analysis evolved. The first celebrated growing U.S. investment in foreign family planning efforts. Historians charted a course of progress in which a population lobby led by John D. Rockefeller III and motivated by humanitarian, economic, and security concerns successfully pressured a reluctant federal government to integrate family planning into its foreign and domestic policy agendas. Scientists credited family planning programs with contributing to an overall improvement in maternal and infant health and growing social and economic stability in those countries that were willing to invest in family planning.[5] In contrast, a second strand sharply criticized policy makers for implementing heavy-handed population control policies abroad and decried the establishment of foreign family planning programs as a symptom of American imperialism. It charged the population control lobby with dumping inferior contraceptives in Third World countries, endangering women's health, and denying them reproductive control.[6]

Reproductive politics have always been global in nature, and the fortunes of publicly accessible family planning at home and abroad have remained closely tied together. As news about the coercive character of birth control programs inside and outside the United States raised public awareness of abuse, reproductive rights activists pushed for the adoption of guidelines for these programs and for global recognition of women's reproductive rights. They have made significant strides in convincing policy-making bodies of the United Nations and international conferences on human rights and development to adopt principles for the protection of women's reproductive and sexual rights. However, the gap between the adoption and implementation of such policies has remained large. In addition, the rise of religious fundamentalism inside and outside the United States has created considerable roadblocks to the narrowing of this gap. Finally, domestic restrictions on access to reproductive technologies have had an impact both inside and outside the United States. The Helms Amendment, which prohibits the United States Agency for International Development from using funds to pay for advice in favor of abortion or to pay for the procedure, is only the most obvious example of such a restriction. In our evaluation of reproductive policies, then, we need to incorporate international comparisons to remain mindful of the close link between local policies and global politics and to fully account for policy decisions that have extended both the promise of modernization and the threat of imperialism to a postcolonial world.

■ Birth Control and Sterilization in Puerto Rico

Sexuality lay at the heart of American ideas about the modernization of Puerto Rico from the moment the United States took colonial possession of the island in 1898. Most Puerto Ricans met the American invasion with open arms. To working people, the United States appeared as a liberator from Spanish oppression. To ruling elites, American rule promised economic prosperity while guaranteeing the preservation of social hierarchies and the continued political power of the elite. During the following decades, the United States embarked on a project to modernize Puerto Rico in which sexuality, family, and gender relations featured prominently. Starting with the introduction of civil marriage and divorce legislation and moving on to the institution of policies designed to control venereal disease and reproduction, this modernization project centered on family relations and the position of women in Puerto Rican society.[7] Puerto Ricans welcomed and adopted some aspects of this modernization project while rejecting, ignoring, and adapting others. They participated in the project, negotiating in the process the meaning of modernization and the definition of nationhood.

The modernization of the island, American and Puerto Rican elites argued, was hampered by the island's uncontrolled population growth. Not only did the lack of reproductive control keep the island mired in poverty, it also contributed to poor health and other social problems. Arguing that large families were a cause of poverty and that birth control could make the lives of working-class women happier, Puerto Rican public health advocates—like their mainland counterparts—looked to family planning as a solution. Motivated by the same complex set of humanitarian, eugenic, and economic ideals that justified many mainland birth control programs during this period, Puerto Rican reformers sought to extend access to birth control in order to improve the health and living conditions of working-class families.[8]

In addition, just as North Carolina health professionals advocated family planning as a scientific solution to social and medical problems, Puerto Rican birth control advocates looked to science and medicine as a sign of modernization and progress. But the Puerto Rican conception and implementation of eugenic policies followed the Latin American understanding of eugenics laid out by Nancy Stepan. It called for a preventive approach in which the environment was cleansed of all factors that were damaging to racial health.[9]

In the early twentieth century, Puerto Rican elites established an indigenous birth control movement that quickly attracted attention and support from the mainland. In 1923, the Puerto Rican Socialist Party introduced a bill to decriminalize birth control, and two years later Socialist José Lanauze Rolón founded the island's first birth control group. In the early 1930s, Puerto Rican nurses and social workers took over the cause, creating maternal and child health programs and opening the first birth control clinic in 1932. Three years later, a federally funded birth control program, part of the New Deal, replaced the underfunded and short-lived early birth control clinics. Just as the Roosevelt administration had provided help with the dissemination of contraceptives in the United States through the Farm Security Administration, it lent material aid to Puerto Rican birth control efforts. Initiated by two friends of Eleanor Roosevelt, Dorothy Bourne and

Gladys Gaylord, the birth control program remained under the control of feminist social workers and nurses, marking the success of maternalist politics. By December 1935, 24 doctors, 50 nurses, and 70 social aides in Puerto Rico had received instruction on contraceptive methods. By the middle of 1936, this new personnel was employed in 45 clinics, serving a total of 3,404 patients. Staff members made home visits to clients, who received either foam or jelly. In at least one clinic, physicians fitted patients with diaphragms.[10]

Overpopulation provided the logic that justified American financial support for Puerto Rico's birth control program. Emerging in the midst of the Great Depression, debates surrounding the causes of poverty and the role that birth control might play in solving problems of poverty and poor health could be heard on the island much as they could be heard on the mainland. While Puerto Rican Nationalists held that thirty-four years of American intervention were to blame for the island's poverty, many mainland advocates of birth control pointed to overpopulation as the culprit.[11] Washington lawmakers might have been unwilling to provide federal dollars for maternalist politics, financing birth control programs that provided Puerto Rican women with the ability to prevent pregnancy, but they were likely to favor such programs when they were framed as measures to control the size of Puerto Rico's population. Indeed, they were sure to recognize the urgency of the problem when it was couched in terms of overpopulation.

The colonial relationship between the United States and Puerto Rico made birth control in 1930s Puerto Rico a political hot-button issue. Puerto Rico's status first as a colony and then as a commonwealth of the United States eased American influence over Puerto Rican government programs and contributed to a situation in which the discourse about outside support mattered significantly. While the argument that family planning in North Carolina would limit welfare expenses was unlikely to raise opposition even from those who found such arguments offensive, the promotion of family planning in order to control the growth of Puerto Rico's population was much more likely to create opposition. Puerto Rican opponents of family planning argued that birth control was a foreign (that is, American) invention intended to eliminate the island's population. Opponents erased the existence of an independent Puerto Rican birth control movement by placing Puerto Rican family planning in a strictly imperial context. By the late 1930s, both Puerto Rican Catholics and Nationalists conflated motherhood with Puerto Rican identity, insisting that birth control threatened the very existence of the Puerto Rican nation. Thirty years before black nationalists charged family planning clinics on the mainland with racial genocide, opponents of family planning in Puerto Rico held that it threatened national identity and the very survival of Puerto Ricans. When Puerto Rican and mainland Catholics pressured the Roosevelt administration to cease supporting the birth control program during an election year in which the administration was courting the Catholic vote, New Deal administrators withdrew its funding, in effect canceling the fledging program.[12]

Following the cancellation of financial assistance from the federal government, Puerto Rican family planning programs attracted private philanthropic support that allowed for the continuation of the programs but placed family planning into the same research paradigm that emphasized the development of cheap contraceptives over women's reproductive health in domestic programs. Clarence J. Gamble took over the funding of birth control in Puerto Rico, bringing not only his money but also his belief that the distribution and testing of cheap contraceptives should replace programs in which physicians and their trained staff members dispensed advice. His engagement with Puerto Rican family planning coincided with his establishment of contraceptive field tests in Kentucky and North Carolina. Guided by the same principles that shaped his birth control efforts on the mainland, Gamble argued that poor and uneducated women lacked transportation to doctor's offices, feared pelvic exams, and were unable to use diaphragms properly. Thus he argued that rather than employ physicians to fit diaphragms, programs should hire traveling birth control nurses who would dispense foam powder and jellies in women's homes. This strategy, Gamble thought, would save the cost of physicians and ultimately reach more women, thus contributing more to the reduction of the birthrate than physician-centered programs.[13]

Gamble's engagement in Puerto Rico hastened the expansion and institutionalization of birth control and sterilization programs on the island. He encouraged the establishment of a local maternal and child health organization, the Asociación pro Salud Maternal e Infantil, which organized sixty birth control clinics across the island and lobbied for the passage of legislation decriminalizing birth control and sterilization. Following on the heels of similar reform on the mainland, Puerto Rican legislators legalized birth control in 1937. In addition, they passed a sterilization law that established a eugenic sterilization board almost a decade after such measures had been authorized by state legislatures on the mainland. Finally, lawmakers legalized elective sterilization, placing the island far ahead of the mainland in promising women access to sterilization for contraceptive reasons. Over the following decades, the majority of sterilizations performed in Puerto Rico were elective rather than ordered by the island's eugenics board.[14]

Despite the passage of legislation that extended reproductive control to women, Puerto Rican women continued to have trouble obtaining contraceptive advice. Until 1942, the number of rural health units offering birth control continued to increase. With the extension of World War II to the Caribbean, which disrupted shipping of supplies to Puerto Rico and elsewhere, however, it became more difficult for these clinics to provide contraception. At the same time, a new commissioner of health, considerably less excited about birth control than his predecessor had been, began to neglect the service, leaving responsibility in the hands of local officials, who frequently shared his lack of enthusiasm. As a result, the number of women receiving birth control advice at rural health units declined.[15]

As services in government clinics were retracted, women's access to contraceptive advice became increasingly dependent on the availability of contraceptive field trials, which took place outside of government clinics. Just as physicians in places like Watauga County, North Carolina, were frequently unwilling to dispense birth control even though it was legal to do so, Puerto Rican women found their access to birth control restricted by the opposition of local public health officials, leaving women with Gamble's foam powders as their only choice. With Puerto Rican public health officials largely uninterested in birth control, members of the Family Planning Association of Puerto Rico (formerly the Asociación pro Salud Maternal e Infantil) were forced to look elsewhere for supplies. Pharmaceutical companies stepped into this gap. Starting with Gamble in the 1930s and extending to representatives of all the major drug companies that produced contraceptives in the 1940s and 1950s, mainland researchers established a range of contraceptive trials on the island, testing the relative effectiveness of diaphragms, jelly, foam powder, contraceptive foam, condoms, and birth control pills. Members of the Family Planning Association of Puerto Rico served as the local contacts and coordinators for this research activity.

As they did for American women on the mainland, contraceptive research trials denied Puerto Rican women the ability to choose among the best birth control methods available; instead, they swamped them with cheap and unreliable birth control methods and separated the provision of birth control services from the provision of general health care.[16] Between 1954 and 1964, the Family Planning Association of Puerto Rico provided free contraceptive instruction and supplies—principally the contraceptive foam Emko—to about one hundred thousand women on the island. In the late 1950s, physicians at Ryder Memorial Hospital established field tests of the birth control pill and two IUDs, the Lippes loop and the Margulies spiral. Evidence from the trials indicates that most of the simple methods dispensed had a high failure rate. Historian Laura Briggs reports that the jelly and syringe method, for instance, had a failure rate of 40 percent. Many women came to the conclusion that the methods were worthless. Undeterred, Gamble continued to praise their effectiveness in his publications.[17]

Local health professionals struggled to retain control over birth control programs and negotiated with American researchers for better services. For most of the 1940s and 1950s, Puerto Rican feminists, social workers, and Independentistas led the Family Planning Association of Puerto Rico and functioned as medical directors.[18] While they employed eugenic rhetoric, they championed the cause of Puerto Rico's poor, challenging the ineffective methods and the researchers' dismissive attitudes toward participants that characterized the contraceptive trials. Remonstrating Gamble for his shift from diaphragms to foam powder and jellies, one social worker who had previously worked for the health department birth control program objected, "When I was there [working in the clinics], leading physicians were loath to back anything that was not guaranteed a high percent of success."[19] The statistician hired to record the results of Gamble's field trials repeatedly emphasized the superiority of the diaphragm, and the obstetrician whom Gamble tried to recruit as medical director for his program joined with the ABCL in criticizing Gamble's single-minded promotion of simple methods.

The amount of influence Puerto Rican health professionals and social workers were able to exert on American researchers was limited, however. Recognizing that women's access to contraceptives depended on the contributions of pharmaceutical companies, Puerto Rican health professionals cooperated in the collection of statistical data much more enthusiastically than North Carolina's public health officials ever would, thus ensuring that further research trials would be conducted.[20] In at least one case, their repeated criticism of ineffective methods did result in the establishment of a demonstration clinic that offered diaphragms.[21] But evidence also suggests that some contraceptive field tests in Puerto Rico required health professionals to deliver only the method tested: the Sunnen Foundation's Emko foam.[22] It is unclear how common such sponsor restrictions were. As the history of birth control clinics on the mainland illustrates, health officials were occasionally able to exert control over the choice of contraceptive methods offered in field trials. In North Carolina, patients' objections to and health officials' dissatisfaction with foam powder meant that within a couple of years of its introduction most clinics switched to the diaphragm.[23] Only a more detailed long-term analysis of Puerto Rico's clinics will be able to offer insights into the extent to which Puerto Rican health professionals were able to exert similar control over the birth control methods their clinics offered.

Clearly, women's experiences as clients were not just determined by sponsors and sponsor motivation but also—and perhaps more strongly—by the physicians, nurses, and social workers who conducted clinics and advised patients in the use of contraceptives. Even the best staff, however, could not improve the efficiency of substandard contraceptives. Denied the ability to choose among a range of reliable contraceptives offered in the context of general health services, Puerto Rican women's choices were determined by their lack of alternatives. Even if they were not forced to participate in contraceptive field trials, the conditions under which they came to those trials denied them reproductive control.

Puerto Rican trials of the birth control pill demonstrate how closely intertwined population control rhetoric, misogynist research practices, and feminist notions of extending reproductive control to women could be. While population control rhetoric provided the backdrop to the development and testing of the birth control pill, the stimulus for the development of the pill was equally grounded in the feminist conviction that female control of childbearing is a precondition for women's emancipation. The impetus for its development came from Margaret Sanger, with financial support from her friend Katharine Dexter McCormick. Disillusioned with conventional contraceptives, both women wished for a simple, foolproof, female-controlled method.[24] By the 1950s, however, Sanger and McCormick's discussion was also being shaped by contemporary fears of overpopulation and the rhetoric surrounding population control. Thus Sanger explained to McCormick in 1950: "I consider that the world and almost our civilization for the next twenty-five years is going to depend upon a simple, cheap, safe contraceptive to be used in poverty stricken slums, jungles, and among the most ignorant people."[25]

The perception that Puerto Rico continued to suffer from overpopulation and the success of earlier contraceptive field trials made the island an ideal site for trials of the birth control pill. The establishment of a network of birth control clinics during the previous decades had demonstrated that Puerto Rico possessed both competent health professionals willing to cooperate in contraceptive trials and a functioning health care system.

Thus, while Puerto Rico's symbolic role as an overcrowded and under-developed island constituted one factor in its selection for the pill trials, the existence on the island of a well-established family planning movement with a network of clinics and physicians was crucial to the pill's chief researcher, Gregory Pincus, when he chose it as the location for the trials.[26] As a result, when physicians began to recruit the initial group of participants for the pill trials in 1956, they could do so from a pool of women who had already participated in other contraceptive trials and, dissatisfied with the birth control methods they had previously been given, were seeking an alternative.[27] A number of them had sought sterilization through the Family Planning Association of Puerto Rico but had been turned down because they did not meet the association's age-parity formula of having had three children by the age of twenty.[28]

In the pill trials, too, women's lack of access to better contraceptives conditioned their interest in and response to the birth control pill. But the pill trials were unusual in that they represented the first birth control tests in which physically healthy women were subjected—and subjected themselves—to the possibility of harm and a series of invasive medical procedures for the sake of testing. To be sure, women rarely questioned the need for a better contraceptive or faulted the ethics of the human trials. They had their own interests in the trials, and they had decided that the advantages of trial participation outweighed the disadvantages. This is perhaps not surprising, as most of Pincus's American correspondents were desperate to try the pill themselves. And once oral contraceptives had gained FDA approval and became widely accessible, a growing number of women in the United States also came to view the pill as their salvation and chose to tolerate its side effects in exchange for its convenience.[29]

Puerto Rican women flocked to participate in the trials of the birth control pill. Similar to women who encountered the pill in Charlotte, North Carolina, Puerto Rican women took the initiative in approaching health and welfare personnel involved with the trials and requesting to join the group of participants. Nurse Iris Rodriguez reported: "We have more cases than what we can take for our study. Continuously, they are ringing this office asking for the pill, going to see Dr. Rice-Wray and calling on me when I make the visits."[30] Puerto Rican women's eagerness for the pill mirrored the reaction of many women on the mainland who, after learning of the pill trials in Puerto Rico, protested to G. D. Searle and Company, the pharmaceutical company that produced the first birth control pill, that they had no access to the trials.[31] Even in Puerto Rico, not every woman was eligible. Participants had to be younger than forty, to have at least two biological children (as evidence of their fertility), and to be prepared to have a third if the birth control pill failed or the woman was placed in the placebo-only control group.[32]

Once enrolled in the trials, women were active rather than passive participants. In order to obtain accurate test results, the trials demanded a high degree of cooperation on the part of each woman. Large field trials in Río Piedras and at Ryder Hospital in Humacao, Puerto Rico, were preceded by initial small-scale trials in Massachusetts and at a new medical school in Puerto Rico; the participants in these first trials had to follow a set of complicated rules. In addition to taking the pill, they were asked to take their temperature and collect vaginal smears on a daily basis, have monthly biopsies, and collect regular urine samples. Historian Lara Marks concludes, "In asking the women to undertake certain procedures it was clear that women were not merely passive objects, but had an active role in the process of the trials and much depended on their co-operation."[33] Once the trials moved to Río Piedras and Ryder Hospital, trial participants were relieved of many of these onerous requirements. They were, however, expected to take the pill daily, following exact guidelines as to when to stop and what to do if they forgot to take the pill. This meant that women decided on a daily basis whether they were going to continue or stop participation. For a population of women unfamiliar with taking medication every day, such a regimen also emphasized their active participation in the trials. Social workers and nurses visited regularly to help women adhere to the instructions, check whether participants had taken the right number of pills, and provide additional supplies. Moreover, they collected necessary medical information, inquiring about side effects, length of menstrual cycles, and frequency of coitus.[34]

Women carefully weighed the advantages and disadvantages of their participation in the pill trials. As American women had done in the Watauga County condom trials, for instance, Puerto Rican women compared their experiences with the pill with each other, complained to their health care providers about side effects, and based their satisfaction with the pill not only on their own experience with it but also on the experiences of other trial participants. When one woman under Penny Satterthwaite's supervision was hospitalized with a severe headache, others immediately stopped taking the pill even though Satterthwaite—not a person to dismiss women's complaints—considered the headache to be unrelated to the drug. Harking back to Lena Hillard's complaints about the damage of negative publicity, Satterthwaite lamented, "It takes a lot of talking and revisiting to keep the ladies taking the medicine."[35] Her complaint demonstrates that women frequently did vote with their feet by deciding to abandon the trials.

For the duration of the trials, women's responses ranged from compliance to noncompliance with the research protocols. Overall, women found the pill regimen confusing. Some feared that any gap in taking the medication would result in an immediate pregnancy and continued to take the pills without stopping for five days to allow for bleeding between cycles, becoming agitated when the pills ran out and the social worker had not replaced them. Others stopped the medication whenever their husbands went away or presumed that they should consume all the pills at once. Even women who basically followed instructions frequently failed to take the pill every day. Some probably forgot or found it difficult to keep track. Others might have disliked the pill's side effects and hoped that taking a day or two off might offer some relief. Still others might have had conflicts with disapproving husbands, leading them to take the pill on some days but not on others. While it is clear that careful education could eliminate many of these problems, it could not prevent mistakes or conflicts. Marks suggests that a woman's educational background, her individual motivation, and the skill of her instructor were crucial in determining her success with the pill.[36]

Participants who felt that the disadvantages of trial participation outweighed the advantages were free to withdraw from the trial. In fact, attrition rates were high. By June 1957, after fourteen months of testing, 55 percent of the original participants (162 out of 295) had left the trial, although the high dropout rate was offset by a steady stream of new volunteers. Women's reasons for leaving the trial varied. Seventeen percent (28 women) dropped out because of dissatisfaction with side effects, complaining of nausea, dizziness, headaches, stomach pain, and vomiting. Even more women, however, left for nonmedical reasons. Twenty-five women left the Río Piedras trial after the local newspaper denounced the trial as a "neomalthusian campaign" and charged its staff with distributing "sterilizers."[37] Others ceased participation because they moved, separated from their husbands and stopped having sex, were widowed, or had husbands or priests who disapproved of their participation.[38]

Gregory Pincus, like mainland researchers in general, dismissed women's complaints about the pill. In fact, his attitude closely mirrors that of many previous contraceptive researchers who were eager for women's participation in contraceptive trials but ignored their complaints about side effects and fundamentally mistrusted their reports of their experiences as "unscientific." This attitude was further heightened by the physical separation between contraceptive researchers and research subjects, who not only occupied vastly different geographic spaces but were in addition separated by factors such as class, education, and language. However, what really stands out about the pill trials is how ordinary Pincus's attitude toward his research subjects was. Within the context of ethical standards and expectations of the 1950s, the pill trials were considered to be within the bounds of acceptable research practice both by the medical community and—as historian Andrea Tone has pointed out—among women who corresponded with Pincus about the trials. Throughout the period under discussion, the use of human subjects in medical experiments was poorly regulated. Only after revelations about the Tuskegee Syphilis experiment, which lasted until the early 1970s, caused a public scandal did legislators establish stringent legal guidelines for medical research with human subjects.[39] Moreover, Pincus did not choose Puerto Rico rather than the United States as the location of the large-scale field trials because he could only conceive testing the pill on impoverished nonwhite women. Rather, his choice was a response to an "anti-sex" research atmosphere in 1950s America that made the testing of a contraceptive separating sex from reproduction seem untenable on American soil.[40]

In contrast to Pincus, Edris Rice-Wray and Penny Satterthwaite, the Puerto Rican physicians who supervised the pill trials, established themselves as strong patient advocates. They, as well as the nurses and social workers who were in daily contact with trial participants, were well-educated professionals who believed in the importance of reproductive health care and negotiated with Pincus and G. D. Searle and Company in an attempt to minimize the pill's side effects. A ten-milligram dose of the pill Enovid, Rice-Wray complained to Pincus, caused "too many side reactions to be acceptable."[41] Satterthwaite, too, reported repeatedly that she was "a little alarmed by the marked changes" she saw "in the cervices of these women who have been taking the pills."[42] Although Pincus downplayed their concerns, contending that Puerto Rican women's complaints were largely psychosomatic and a result of their "emotional superactivity," both women physicians insisted that their warnings were valid, and both recommended that the pill should not continue to be used further.[43]

Moreover, Rice-Wray and Satterthwaite used the trials to defend women's interest in and access to quality birth control and health services. While they shared Sanger's and McCormick's concern about "overpopulation," they strongly believed that science and modernization would solve Puerto Rico's economic problems.[44] Aware that many of the trial participants lacked access to good health care services, they felt a particular responsibility to offer such care. They gave women complete medical examinations to ensure that they were in good health prior to participation in the trial, and they insisted on frequent medical check-ups as part of the trials—including regular biopsies to test for reproductive cancers, even though these had to be sent all the way to Boston to be analyzed.[45]

Puerto Rican women's lack of access to decent reproductive care conditioned the responses to the trials of both Puerto Rican health care providers and participants. While physicians on the island looked to contraceptive trials as one way to offer some medical services that were otherwise unavailable, Puerto Rican women found that access to the trials offered them some control over reproduction. It did so, however, without providing them with real medical attention and a true commitment to reproductive health care, serving as a temporary Band-Aid solution that might have met physicians and women's short-term interests but left larger structural problems of health care access unsolved.

Feminist activism and women's desire to control their conception also shaped the history of sterilization on the island. Puerto Rican feminists lobbied for the 1937 sterilization bill, and feminist leader and Independentista Carmen Rivera de Alvarado allowed herself to be arrested in order to test the bill's standing under federal law. The passage of the 1937 sterilization law legalized both eugenic and elective sterilization. This gave Puerto Rican women access to sterilization as a form of birth control—the very form of birth control that so many women on the mainland desired and had a hard time obtaining.

Puerto Rican women were clearly interested in sterilization as a permanent form of birth control. While only ninety-seven eugenic sterilizations were carried out between 1937 and 1950, and while the Puerto Rican legislature repealed its eugenic sterilization law in 1960, the number of elective sterilizations performed on the island rose rapidly once the procedure was available.[46] Between 1944 and 1950, the number of sterilizations performed doubled. By the early 1950s, demand for the operation far exceeded capacity to perform it.[47] A significant increase in women's participation in the labor force and the expectation of rising living standards further contributed to a growing demand for effective reproductive control.

As was true for women on the mainland, health concerns, economic constraints, and the desire for improved family life motivated Puerto Rican women to choose sterilization. One survey reported that 57.8 percent of sterilized women gave health factors as their primary reason for choosing the operation, 20.3 percent pointed to economic considerations, and

9.7 percent explained that they sought sterilization for the sake of personal convenience.[48] One woman explained in the opening minutes of Ana María García's documentary *La Operación*: "We didn't have much money, and the doctor told me I couldn't have many children. I talked to my husband, and got myself the operation. . . . Nobody forced me."[49] In addition, in a largely Catholic society, cultural factors contributed to the appeal that sterilization held for Puerto Rican women. Women and their physicians could talk about the surgery without direct reference to the sexual act or sexual organs, easing their discussions. And while the Catholic Church opposed sterilization as much as any other form of birth control, the surgery constituted a one-time violation of Catholic principles rather than a violation that repeated itself every time a woman chose to use a contraceptive. Moreover, especially when it was performed following a delivery, the surgery could easily be kept secret. And unlike abortion, sterilization was legal and lacked the strong associations of immorality that accompanied pregnancy termination.[50]

Despite the legalization of sterilization on the island, however, most poor women did not have access to the surgery. Far from being overwhelmed with unwanted services, most were not getting any health care treatment at all. As was true for women on the mainland, Puerto Rican women's access to elective sterilization depended on their ability to pay for the surgery as well as their proximity to a clinic where a physician was willing to perform it. From the 1930s to the 1960s, a lack of medical infrastructure on the island meant that most medical services were urban, while the majority of the population was rural. Consequently, poor women, regardless of their need for or interest in the surgery, were least likely to gain access to it.[51] Moreover, the same type of age-parity formulas that restricted women's access to sterilization on the mainland also restricted women's access to the procedure on the island. The parity formula at public hospitals required women to have given birth to at least three living children by the age of twenty-five in order to qualify for the surgery. Private hospitals initially tended to be more liberal about granting access to the surgery than government hospitals were. As a consequence, it was women who could afford private care who were able to benefit from sterilization. But as private hospitals sought accreditation, they began to tighten their parity rules, requiring that women have had four children by the age of twenty-five in order to be eligible for the surgery. Although the Family Planning Association of Puerto Rico offered sterilization to a group of lower-class women who had had three living children by the age of twenty, it stopped subsidizing the operation in 1966.

Considering that Puerto Rican families believed that the ideal family had one or two children, the parity formulas meant that women could only gain access to sterilization after they had exceeded the ideal family size. Thus parity formulas denied women their reproductive rights just as coerced sterilization did.

Ironically, it was the attempt to make elective sterilization more widely available to women who were unable to pay for the procedure that contributed to sterilization abuse both in Puerto Rico and in the United States.[52] With the inclusion of sterilization in federally funded family planning programs in the late 1960s, it not only became significantly easier for health and welfare officials to make sterilization available as a form of permanent birth control, it also became much easier to coerce women into accepting sterilizations they might not have chosen on their own. While those who were able to obtain sterilization prior to the late 1960s were overwhelmingly pleased with the results of the surgery, many of the women who were sterilized after the Puerto Rican government made sterilization available for free or for a nominal fee in the late 1960s expressed regret that they had undergone the procedure. Historian Laura Briggs notes, however, that of those who were regretful, only a few implied that they had been misinformed or pressured into having the operation.[53]

In order to evaluate the circumstances that determined women's sterilization experiences, we need a closer analysis of the conditions under which they encountered the surgery and chose the procedure, including a better understanding of the sterilizations performed under Puerto Rico's eugenic sterilization law. It is likely that many of those who received eugenic sterilization did not desire it. Nevertheless, we can expect to find that eugenic sterilization in Puerto Rico was more complex than the statistics reveal and that some individuals might have sought the procedure. Because women on the mainland and on the island operated within a context that denied them full reproductive choices, they were forced to make use of programs in ways that contradicted the intentions of those who designed them. For this reason, it is crucial to our understanding of where abuse did and did not occur to look at where and under what conditions women were able to exert reproductive control.

What sharply differentiated sterilization in Puerto Rico from sterilization on the mainland was the existence of early and persistent vocal opposition to the programs. From the early 1940s through the 1960s, Puerto Rican Nationalists and representatives of the Catholic Church harshly criticized the sterilization of Puerto Rican women, insisting that there was a secret mass sterilization policy being carried out in Puerto Rican clinics and hospitals that was designed to wipe out the Puerto Rican population.[54] Ignoring the fact that the majority of sterilizations were elective procedures, opponents not only conflated elective and eugenic sterilization, they also implied that all sterilizations were involuntary. This conflation, combined with rising sterilization rates, served as prima facie evidence that there was growing sterilization abuse on the island. In the 1970s, mainland socialist feminists adopted this argument about forced sterilization, turning Puerto Rican women whom they imagined were sterilized involuntarily into a symbol of the experiences that poor and nonwhite mainland women had had with involuntary sterilization.[55] While the feminist concern with sterilization abuse on the mainland was valid in some cases, feminists inaccurately conflated the experiences of poor and minority women coerced into sterilization in a number of American hospitals with the experience of Puerto Rican women—or even with the experiences of poor and minority women in the United States in general. By doing so, they reinterpreted women's testimonies to fit a larger narrative about coercive government power, erasing the complex context surrounding women's individual reproductive experiences and women's agency in seeking to control their reproduction.

■ Family Planning in India

If Puerto Rico symbolized the danger overpopulation might pose to a country's economic stability, India came to signify the danger overpopulation might pose to global stability. The construction of India as a Third World country on the brink of a population explosion blamed India's high birthrate not only for the country's poverty but also for pollution and the social and political instability that appeared to threaten the postwar world in general and South Asia in particular. This image was most forcefully popularized in Paul Ehrlich's 1968 book, *The Population Bomb*, in which he described his conversion to population control when riding in a taxi in Delhi:

> As we crawled through the city, we entered a crowded slum area. The temperature was well over 100, and the air was a haze of dust and smoke. The streets seemed alive with people. People eating, people washing, people sleeping. People visiting, arguing and screaming. People thrusting their hands through the taxi window, begging. People

defecating and urinating. People clinging to buses. People herding animals. People, people, people, people. As we moved slowly through the mob, hand horn squawking, the dust, noise, heat, and cooking fires gave the scene a hellish aspect. Would we ever get to our hotel? All three of us were, frankly, frightened. . . . Since that night I've known the feel of overpopulation.[56]

India's and the world's survival seemed to depend on controlling India's population growth. The perceived global importance of India's population policies has placed its family planning programs at the center of scholarly debate.

Although India's adoption of a formal family planning program with support from international agencies only dates back to the early 1950s, the history of birth control in India can be traced to the 1920s. During this decade, Indian economists initiated a sustained public discussion about birth control. At its center stood the question of the meaning birth control should carry for the Indian nation in general and for Indian womanhood in particular. From the very beginning, the relationship between the West and the indigenous birth control movement shaped the debate and placed it firmly in a colonial context.

As in Puerto Rico, population issues and the structure of the family were at the heart of negotiations about Indian independence and nationalism. Indian economists argued that a self-governing India needed a strong and healthy population. But many feared that traditional practices such as child marriage, sati (the self-immolation of widows), and purdah (the physical segregation of women) hampered modernization in India. Child marriage, in particular, contributed to gynecological problems and high maternal mortality rates. Throughout the 1920s, legislators introduced various bills that addressed the age of consent for marriage, none of which passed. In 1927, muckraking American journalist Katherine Mayo published *Mother India*, a devastating attack on Indian customs that berated Indians for their treatment of women of all ages. Drawing on hospital records, official accounts, and personal interviews, Mayo focused particularly on sexual behavior and stories of child brides who were forced prematurely to have sex with their older husbands. Such social customs, she held, accounted for the weakness of the Indian race and signaled that India was not ready for independence.[57] The ensuing controversy culminated in the passage of the Child Marriage Restraint Act two years later, which set the minimum age of marriage for Indian girls at fourteen. Moreover, the controversy surrounding Mayo's book drew attention to the indifference in India to gynecological health and spotlighted the lack of birth control services in the country. It also reminded all involved in the emerging birth control movement of the symbolic place that ideas about gender and science held in the discourse surrounding modernization.

Many feared that India's scientific inferiority contributed to its subjugation by the West. In the 1920s, Indian elites adopted Western scientific discourse and findings in their effort to modernize India and advocated scientific methods of population planning. As controlling reproductive behavior promised to modernize the nation as a whole, urban elites also adopted eugenic science, signaling India's ability to participate in an international scientific discourse and its commitment to solving the population question. Western ideas that linked economic growth and national strength to the control of population growth appealed to Indian elites, who looked to eugenics as a modern way to talk about social problems and propose scientific solutions.[58]

Formulating an identity for the Indian woman suitable for an independent India was crucial to both proponents and opponents of birth control. Such an identity was supposed to both affirm tradition and allow for the development of a modern state while also defining an image that posited India as independent from British and other First World birth control interests. Prior to independence, proponents and opponents of birth control framed their arguments in the context of Indian nationalism. Family planning advocates described birth control as a national responsibility that would preserve mothers' and infants' health and improve the Indian people and nation.[59] Such arguments allowed birth control supporters to link nationalism and traditionalism to an image of modern India. Indian opponents of birth control, like their counterparts in Puerto Rico, feared that the use of contraceptives would rob Indian women of their femininity and "Indian-ness" and lead to the decline of the Indian people and nation. Warning that the use of contraceptives had masculinized British women, one opponent who feared similar consequences for Indian women "shuddered at the thought of Bengalee women reading the binomial theorem, when their housework was being neglected."[60]

The discourse of population control that emerged in the postwar decade threatened to undermine the pre-independence vision of birth control and replace it with one in which birth control became the moral duty of a poor country on the verge of a population explosion. Concerned with the task of industrial development and the provision of food and consumer goods to its citizens, the Indian government saw the establishment of birth control clinics and the reduction of the country's birthrate as an important step toward modernization. As family planning became part of India's agenda for postcolonial development, the ability to limit population size became a sign of modern state planning.[61] Social scientists have described Indian family planning programs as representing both appropriation of and resistance to Western concepts of modernity. They have remained unsure, however, about the precise impact that international aid has had on family planning policies in India. While some note that the Indian government attempted to keep foreign assistance for family planning at arm's length, others have argued that external pressure from the United Nations Fund for Population Activities, the United States Agency for International Development, the International Monetary Fund, and other agencies increased pressure on family planning programs, contributing to their coercive character.[62]

A look at the character of family planning programs in India and women's reception of them presents a decidedly mixed picture. Historians describe the emergence of an indigenous birth control movement in the 1920s that met with reluctance from government health officials but, supported by Western birth control activists, haltingly began to establish birth control services. World War II, however, interrupted these efforts. Investigating Indian family planning after the war, scholars have chronicled a movement toward increasingly coercive policies between the 1950s and the 1970s. Scholars disagree, however, about the duration and extent of coercion and the impact that coercion had on the decision making of individual Indian men and women.

Eager to participate in eugenic discourse and demonstrate scientific sophistication, Indian elites emphasized the importance that reproductive behavior held for national regeneration and modernization. Starting in the 1920s, Indian elites founded eugenic societies that advocated birth control to solve the country's population problems. As in the Puerto Rican case, eugenics societies in India invoked positive eugenic measures, advocating the management of reproduction through birth control and public health voluntarism. In the wake of the *Mother India* controversy, promoting scientific solutions to problems of marriage and women's health took on an even greater urgency. In 1930, for instance, the Sholapur Eugenics Education Society established a "Wives' Clinic" that offered contraceptive services, treatment for venereal disease, and sex counseling. While influenced by Western scientific discourse, Indian elites chose those elements of eugenic science that fit their needs while rejecting elements such as eugenic sterilization that might have been important in the West but failed to appeal in the Indian context.[63]

Unlike their American and European counterparts, few Indian female physicians participated in the public discourse about birth control.[64] Lacking formal instruction about contraception and suffering from the relatively low status of obstetrics and gynecology as a medical specialty, women physicians were both untrained in issues of birth control and hesitant to address a subject that separated sexuality from reproduction. Kinship networks and status concerns further hampered Indian women's birth control activism. While some women physicians pointed to the importance of birth control for maintaining healthy marriages, protecting mothers' health, and promoting eugenic welfare, most medical women in India seemed unwilling to give contraceptive advice. A. P. Pillay, a crusader for birth control in Bombay, concluded in 1937: "No advice [on contraception] is given except in some of the Mission Hospitals, then men doctors are indifferent or timid to take up the work, asserting that Indian women will not practice birth control methods and that there is no demand for the same. The women doctors believe just the contrary but are equally timid to seek the required knowledge and are often domineered by anti–birth control superiors."[65] Those who championed the cause of birth control, then, were elite Indian men and a few women such as Rani Rajwade who looked increasingly to, and cooperated with, foreign female birth control advocates such as Margaret Sanger, Agnes Smedley, Edith How-Martyn, and Marie Stopes.[66]

The growing involvement of foreign birth control supporters in India during the 1920s and 1930s provided an important educational and organizational impetus for the fledging native birth control movement. Indian birth control advocates invited the participation of American and British activists and utilized the information and materials these activists had to offer. Beginning in the early 1920s and cresting in the mid-1930s, foreign birth control advocates toured India to speak to medical and civic associations about contraception and helped to establish birth control clinics. They taught women how to fit diaphragms, spoke to chemists about stocking contraceptives, and often inspired further activism in the towns and villages they visited.[67] As Barbara Ramusack has suggested, foreign birth control activists were able to engage in such activism because they could leave India after stimulating controversy and did not have to suffer the social repercussions of their audacity that Indian women who acted similarly would have faced.[68] In this role, the activists proved committed, aggressive, and effective propagandists in their quest to spread birth control education.

Nevertheless, activists such as Sanger saw Indian medical women and laywomen as crucial in the birth control effort and tried repeatedly to strike up working relationships with them. During the 1920s and 1930s, Sanger and How-Martyn lobbied Indian female physicians and members of the All India Women's Conference who had demonstrated their concern about issues of marriage and women's health when lobbying for the 1929 Child Marriage Restraint Act. And by the early 1930s, with the world-wide economic recession deepening, increasing support for birth control from Indian voluntary associations demonstrated the growing willingness of some Indian women to become active on behalf of birth control. The All India Women's Conference, for instance, passed a number of resolutions in support of birth control, and other voluntary associations followed suit.

Resolutions, however, did not provide women with access to contraceptives. Despite the fact that Indian elites and a number of medical and civic organizations advocated birth control, the implementation of contraceptive services between the 1920s and the 1940s was spotty at best. Government health officials lacked interest in providing medical services for women, and official health statistics were silent on issues of women's health. Although the government established a Women's Medical Service (WMS) in 1914 that was responsible for the treatment of women, the running of women's hospitals, and other tasks relating to women's health, the number of physicians employed in the service was extremely small. Many professional women chose not to stay in India but went to England, where professional opportunities were better. In addition, the WMS was unable to present a unified voice on such contentious issues as birth control. In fact, birth control activists often faced very vocal opposition, with organized protests coming mainly from Catholics and Gandhians.[69] And although international medical research was growing in the 1920s and 1930s with support from the Rockefeller Foundation, funded projects were limited to those that investigated tropical and epidemic diseases. While population issues were high on the private agenda of organizations such as the Rockefeller Foundation, significant funding for contraceptive research was not available until after World War II.[70]

In the early 1920s, the cooperation between Indian and American birth control activists culminated in the establishment of several birth control clinics. Under the cooperative management of the Society for the Study and Promotion of Family Hygiene and the American Birth Control League, birth control clinics opened in the early 1920s in Bombay, Madras, Calcutta, Lucknow, and other cities. By 1935, the American director of the Young Women's Christian Association had opened a birth control clinic at the Nagpada Neighborhood House in Bombay. Located in a mill slum area that had the highest death rate and the highest mortality rate for children under ten in Bombay, the clinic catered to the urban working poor. In addition, Dr. Jean M. Orkney of the WMS established a clinic in Calcutta. By the mid-1930s, physicians associated with several missionary hospitals and medical schools in India were corresponding with Gamble, Sanger, and How-Martyn to secure contraceptive supplies for their patients, and they received material and financial aid in return. How-Martyn estimated the number of birth control clinics in India in 1937 to be close to sixty.[71]

Foreign birth control advocates offered crucial financial and material aid. On her 1935 tour through India, Sanger, for instance, brought two films produced at the Birth Control Clinical Research Bureau in New York, "Biology of Conception" and "Mechanism of Contraception," which she showed to audiences of physicians. In addition, she distributed fifty "gynaeplaques," models of pelvic organs made to open and shut for demonstration purposes of the same type that were used by birth control nurses in the United States. Such innovative techniques allowed Sanger to make use of modern media when instructing her Indian audience and provided Indian medical personnel with the tools to instruct both literate and illiterate groups about contraception. As one missionary physician marveled after using the pelvic model to educate village women on the use of birth control, "I used it yesterday . . . and was amazed to see how easy the model made my explanation; and how clear and plain it seemed to the village women."[72]

International involvement in the early birth control movement in India also included the international pharmaceutical industry that was active in Puerto Rico and the United States. Gamble, Sanger, and How-Martyn promoted a foam powder called Duofoam and distributed it to a number of clinics. Also marketed as "Stoughton Foam Powder" and distributed in the United States, it was by 1937 manufactured in India by Stella and Company of Bombay. In the late 1930s and early 1940s, British Drug House, backed with some financial support from the Eugenics Society of London and the Birth Control International Information Center, developed Volpar Tropical Paste for the Indian market. Volpar, a spermicidal paste designed to be used with diaphragms, was supposed to provide an alternative to spermicidal suppositories, which tended to melt in the hot weather.[73]

Though evidence is limited, sources suggest that Indian women from all urban classes were interested in birth control and asked for contraceptive advice. Like American and Puerto Rican women, they approached their physicians, talked to colleagues and friends, wrote to eugenic societies, and attended talks by birth control activists. One British missionary re- called: "Again and again, women who have been burdened by frequent or constant child bearing, many of whom suffer miscarriages, have come to me begging me to tell them something or to give them something that would release them from this slavery, especially when they get to be about 35 or 40 years of age and are already overburdened with numbers of little children clinging to their skirts, for whom they are unable to provide properly."[74] Those fortunate enough to have access to birth control clinics took advantage of the services provided by Christian missionary doctors and health professionals regardless of the larger political context. Fifteen months after opening in 1935, the clinic in Bombay, for instance, operated every afternoon and advised 107 women. Most of them were female cot- ton mill workers; 55 percent had had six or more pregnancies. While it is unclear from the analyses available whether 107 patients constituted a satisfactory patient load, the Family Hygiene Society's decision to open a second clinic in an industrial area in Bombay indicates that its members considered the clinic a success.[75] And although the Wives' Clinic run by the Sholapur Eugenics Education Society only gave contraceptive advice to married women considered to be "truly in need," the clinic attracted over 40 applications within the first few months of advertising its ser- vices. Between 1929 and 1931, its staff advised about 120 mothers, chiefly ill workers.[76]

Moreover, as in the American and Puerto Rican contexts, women took on an active role in regard to contraception. They not only asked for contraceptive advice but negotiated with their health care providers about birth control and complained about side effects or ineffective methods, arguing, for instance, that the watery Duofoam was unpleasant and caused irritation and burning. At times, women's housing conditions af- fected their ability to properly use the foam powder, further aggravating unpleasant side effects. One physician from the Family Hygiene Society reported in 1936 to How-Martyn that one of her clients had come in with severe inflammation from the Duofoam powder: "It was found that she had emptied nearly half the container onto the sponge because her hous- ing conditions were so bad that she could not see how much powder she was putting on and as her mother-in-law was there she didn't wish to make light. The nurse instructed her to put out in a piece of paper during the daytime just enough powder for one application."[77] At times, Indian physicians also voiced doubts about the suitability of certain methods, recommending jelly and sponge over Duofoam and switching women from one to the other. In addition, they called for the development of better methods and warned others of inferior contraceptives. Pillay reported that one woman "tried unsuccessfully three kinds of contraceptive appliances and, being a cynic, . . . named her three children after the names of these three preparations."[78]

While the existence of these early clinics and the use women made of them demonstrates Indian women's interest in birth control, evidence also suggests that problems endemic to birth control programs everywhere limited the effectiveness of clinics in India as well. As in the United States and Puerto Rico, a lack of publicity, a shortage of staff, and a focus on the distribution of one contraceptive method rather than a range of methods limited women's access to and success with birth control in India. Many of the clinics were small, open only one or two afternoons a week and serving only a handful of women. Services offered by Dr. Jean Orkney of the WMS, for instance, reached thirteen women in 1935 and extended only to an additional thirty-seven and forty women in the following two years. In addition, women did not always learn about the existence of clinics. When the Women's Welfare Society started a birth control clinic at Dufferin Hospital in Calcutta, for instance, the hospital would not allow the clinic to advertise. The clinic was open only one afternoon a week and saw only one to four patients during that time. Organizers eventually severed relations with the hospital and opened an independent clinic. Although Dr. Ruth Young, the British director of India's Maternity and Child Welfare Bureau, indicated that many Indian women might want release from childbearing, she found that most women were not asking for contraceptive information. Moreover, Indian physicians were determined not to offer contraceptive advice through nurses but only through medical doctors. Since many Indian women preferred to consult a female over a male doctor, the lack of female physicians also prevented the effective delivery of birth control.[79]

Fierce competition among foreign birth control activists further complicated the implementation of contraceptive services. At the center of the debate stood the question of which birth control method was most suitable for use in India. Dr. Young cautioned health care providers that no one method of contraception was appropriate for all women. The search for the perfect method, however, dominated the implementation of birth control services in India much as it did in other parts of the world.[80] While Margaret Sanger and Edith How-Martyn favored the distribution of diaphragms, Clarence Gamble continued to maintain that poor women needed an easier birth control method and to take the opportunity to further test and develop jellies and foam powders. Contemptuous of all of these methods, which she criticized as too expensive, Marie Stopes, in turn, advocated the use of a cotton wad soaked in oil, which she thought would be more easily accessible, especially to poor women.[81] Foreign birth control advocates' lack of knowledge about the living conditions of Indian women and the hot and humid climate further aggravated the situation: Indian women lacked access to oil or cotton, contraceptive jelly suppositories melted en route, and foam powder clumped.[82]

Cultural differences created additional problems. Foreign birth control activists walked a fine line between their own strategic impulses and a host environment in which actions appropriate in the West might appear offensive and impolitic. Margaret Sanger and Agnes Smedley tried to be sensitive to the prevailing birth control discourse, emphasizing the improvement of maternal and infant health over arguments for women's reproductive self-determination. Smedley cautioned Sanger in 1924 that when speaking in favor of birth control, it was "better not to stress the woman freedom viewpoint until you have a foothold."[83] But even if foreign birth control activists sought and followed the advice of Indian activists, the latter frequently disagreed with each other over questions of strategy and politics. Contemplating the low number of women seeking contraceptive advice, Dr. Ruth Young argued, for instance, that "women should have the right of deciding the number of children they wish to have and the spacing of these children." A personal rights argument, she concluded, might be more successful in attracting women to India's birth control clinics.[84] In addition, some foreign birth control activists were more sensitive than others to cultural differences and more aware of the political meaning that their advocacy of family planning might have for Indian men and women in a colonial context. At times, however, all sides were baffled and frustrated by their differences of culture and opinion.

World War II interrupted the early movement for birth control in India. Although little is known about the fate of birth control clinics during the war, at least one clinic in Calcutta closed its doors after the Japanese invasion of Burma.[85] When birth control resurfaced as a national issue in the early 1950s, it did so within a postcolonial context that combined the emergence of an international lobby supporting population control in India with the official commitment of the Indian government to family planning.

In 1952, India became the first country in the world to initiate an official population control program, and the Indian government began to commit substantial resources to the expansion of family planning services throughout the country. Appropriations rose from 3 million rupees between 1951 and 1956 to 22 million in the following five-year period to almost 250 million between 1961 and 1966. Despite such substantial allocations, Indian public health officials remained largely hostile to birth control and dragged their feet when it came to the actual establishment of birth control services, spending only half of the allocated funds during the first five-year plan. In fact, in the early years, health officials limited birth control education to already existing services, and by the end of 1956 they had established only 147 new clinics—126 in urban and 21 in rural areas. Moreover, government clinics limited contraceptive education to the rhythm method. At the request of the Indian government, the World Health Organization sent Dr. Abraham Stone, an American expert on family planning, to set up a series of pilot projects to determine the effectiveness of the rhythm method. Stone devised a number of innovative ways to help women keep track of their menstrual cycle and determine their safe period, including the creation of a necklace with twenty-eight colored beads. Variations in women's cycles, however, made the bead project impractical. In addition, some women forgot to move the beads, while others believed that the necklace had magical powers and that its very presence prevented conception. Only after Stone's bead project failed did government clinics begin to include condoms, diaphragms, and jellies in their contraceptive repertoire. Yet even private physicians who were willing to offer mechanical methods of birth control remember the early 1950s for the dearth of contraceptive information and supplies. Most dispensed foam powder and sponges, oil tampons, or contraceptive jellies—the same methods that had been available and deemed largely ineffective before the war.[86]

As in the United States and Puerto Rico, the lack of support from public health officials meant that Indian family planning advocates turned to private philanthropists and contraceptive research in search of money and supplies. Here, too, the artificial restriction of access to contraceptives led to a situation ripe for the establishment of contraceptive field trials that flooded the market with cheap and untested birth control methods. Frustrated with the slow pace of progress and casting about for a better solution, Indian family planning advocates turned to the International Planned Parenthood Federation (IPPF) and private philanthropists for help. The latter were more than willing to promise an infusion of new funds and contraceptives as long as clinic staff were willing to participate in tests of the birth control methods provided. Building on the prewar legacy of cooperation in a context in which patients and health professionals lacked any better alternative, such collaboration seemed like a good solution. As it did in the Puerto Rican context, however, the cooperation with Western philanthropists and pharmaceutical companies paved the way for decades of contraceptive testing and the promotion of birth control services that frequently denied women access to informed and balanced contraceptive advice.

And just like their American and Puerto Rican counterparts, Indian family planning advocates struggled to negotiate for better contraceptives and more comprehensive health care services for their clients. Family planning leaders in India and surrounding countries negotiated with Western birth control activists over the terms and conditions of the help they received and objected to the distribution of inferior contraceptives. One of the first philanthropists to offer his help to India in the postwar period was Clarence Gamble. Between 1950 and 1957, he not only established trials in three Japanese villages to test a range of contraceptive methods, including the diaphragm, jelly, condoms, foam tablets, the rhythm method, and a salt solution, he also began to recruit Christian missionary doctors in India and Pakistan to carry out similar tests.[87] But when Gamble tried to test the contraceptive properties of a salt-based solution in India, Indian and Ceylonese health professionals protested. Issues of race and imperialism quickly took center stage in this debate. Fearing that salt-based contraceptive solutions would irritate women's vaginal walls, Indian and Ceylonese family planning advocates charged Gamble with promoting contraceptive measures for Indian and Ceylonese women that he would not offer American women.[88] Sylvia Fernando, head of the Family Planning Association in Ceylon, explained the problem to Gamble.

> In the east just now there is violent dislike of "white" people telling us about a "better way" especially in regard to so intimate a matter as family planning—of the "whites" the most disliked are the Americans. (I speak frankly as it is the only way to put the thing clearly.) There is the feeling that the American more than any other will suggest things that are good for the world but not for the individual "black." That is why we wanted real tangible data about the salt and sponge. We did not want the idea to get about that we did not mind if the vaginas of poor women were irritated because they were inured to hardship and we should not try to give them a harder but better way.[89]

As it had in earlier relationships between Western birth control advocates and Indian health professionals, a sense of Western cultural superiority aggravated the working relationship between the two groups. Just as

Gamble had resisted hiring African American health care providers for the Birth Control Federation of America's Negro Project in the early 1940s, he resisted hiring native Ceylonese or Indians to work as birth control educators in the early 1950s. Instead, he worked through Western missionaries and insisted on employing a Canadian, Margaret Roots, as a birth control field worker for the region that included India.[90] When Indian family planning advocates objected that Roots lacked medical and contraceptive training, Gamble argued that her position as an "outsider" would make her more effective as a birth control field worker. A lack of modesty, he implied, made even Westerners who lacked training more effective as field workers than native health care providers who were trained in family planning. Dhanvanthi Rama Rau, president of the Family Planning Association of India, protested: "We were also a little upset by your description of her [Margaret Roots:] 'as an outsider she would not suffer from any inhibitions in approaching people with different religion or nationality or social status.' . . . We have been working in this field for several years ourselves, and although we are nationals of the country, believe me, we have not yet been accused of suffering from inhibitions in approaching people with different religion or nationality or social status. I am quite sure that those who are organizing similar work in the countries of our Region, too, would be above such a charge."[91] Finally, Clarence Gamble and his son Richard repeatedly offended their foreign hosts, damaging important political contacts in the process. At a Burmese dinner party, Gamble embarrassed his hosts by insisting on discussing the technicalities of birth control. And when a Singhalese physician explained that patients objected to the messiness of a contraceptive rice-jelly, Richard Gamble responded that he could not understand such criticism, since Singhalese women ate with their fingers.[92]

While IPPF officials and local family planning activists complained about behavior they considered offensive and counterproductive, however, they continued to work with Gamble. Given India's need for family planning and its lack of financial support from other sources, they tried their best to influence his behavior but cooperated with him even when their influence was limited. One IPPF official grudgingly admitted to Margaret Sanger: "We have no-one else to do this work or to finance it, and there is no doubt that he is a tremendous worker—if only he would allow himself to be guided a little more, and realize the effect he has on some people."[93]

Although it is unclear whether Indian and Ceylonese health officials such as Rama Rau shared the sense that cooperation with Gamble was important and valuable despite his shortcomings—most likely officials held a variety of opinions on this topic—it is clear that the family planning services that emerged did so as a product of negotiations between local health officials, family planning advocates, and Western sponsors. In this process of negotiation, Western sponsors did not simply set the terms of the debate while Indian health officials agreed to the plans of sponsors such as Gamble. Rather, local family planning officials criticized those aspects of the sponsors' plans that they found problematic and influenced the decisions of sponsors. Clearly, there were limits to the amount of influence local family planning workers could exert in these negotiations, and if sponsors proved unwilling to compromise, family planning advocates either had to accept the terms of the services or forgo them altogether. To fully understand how services were implemented, however, it is crucial that we carefully analyze these local negotiations and evaluate both the amount of negotiating power different groups had and what each group's interests in the services were.

Evidence also indicates that, just as in other parts of the world, not all Indian health professionals prioritized the protection of women's health over the development and testing of new contraceptives. Indian health professionals and chemists worked feverishly on the development of contraceptive methods, and some dismissed concerns about jeopardizing women's health when it came to the distribution of untested methods. Dr. Chandrakanta Rohatgi, a female gynecologist in Kanpur, for instance, encouraged her brother to manufacture and market Planitab, a pill that produced a spermicidal foam when inserted in the vagina. As Sanjam Ahluwalia argues, "It was [Chandrakanta's] assessment of the general need for a safe and effective contraceptive by women and her awareness of governmental intent to assign the research on contraceptives certain priority that convinced her brother to conduct research in this area."[94] Although Planitab failed to win initial government approval due to its toxicity, the Ministry of Family Planning began to distribute it through its family planning clinics later in the decade. In so doing, government health officials of the postcolonial Indian state demonstrated their lack of concern for Indian women's health.

During the 1950s and 1960s, state financial allocations for family planning rose steadily, climbing from RS 0.05 per capita in 1956 to RS 0.90 in 1970. By 1970, the Indian government had established 45,000 birth control clinics that—at least in theory—offered a range of contraceptive methods, including IUDS and sterilization. Initially, government officials believed that the increased availability of contraceptive information would result in women's increased use of birth control. But if policy makers and health officials expected their efforts to show such tangible results as a decline in population growth and an increase in per capita income, they were disappointed.

Indeed, as a 1950s Harvard School of Public Health study inadvertently indicated, family planning policies frequently failed to meet the needs of poor families. A single-minded concern with overpopulation blinded foreign and Indian family planning advocates to the fact that birth control contradicted the vital interests of many poor villagers. Overpopulation, Harvard researchers postulated in the so-called Khanna study, had to be treated with the techniques of epidemiology; education was crucial. With funding from the Rockefeller Foundation and the Indian government, Indian family planning advocates set out to teach the people of seven Indian villages the value of family planning and to distribute contraceptives to the villagers. While Indian villagers seemed to agree that birth control was important and gratefully accepted the contraceptive devices offered, they failed to use them. Children's labor represented a valuable economic asset to poor farmers. To practice contraception would have meant willfully courting economic disaster.[95] The inability of Harvard researchers to understand that economic and cultural forces might stand in the way of Western family planning goals is indicative of the inability of researchers and health professionals in general to understand the context in which women made decisions about reproduction.

Indeed, by the early 1960s, health officials complained that Indian couples lacked interest in family planning and were not availing themselves of the services, echoing the complaints of public health officials in North Carolina. Evidence indicates that contraceptive services mostly appealed to women at the end of their childbearing years while failing to attract the interest of young married couples. While health and welfare professionals everywhere complained that young women lacked interest in birth control, the high cultural value of motherhood and the importance of sons in Indian society meant that Indian physicians found it especially hard to motivate not only newlywed women to use birth control but also young mothers who had already had one or more daughters but no sons. To those concerned with reducing India's population growth, it was particularly important to convince young couples of the importance of family planning. Indian elites were even more frustrated by the apparent success of China's coercive but reasonably effective one-child policy. The global interest in China's success with population control deeply distressed and impressed Indira Gandhi and her sons, who hoped to catch up to China with an approach that emphasized "targets." Hoping to motivate those who had thus far shown no interest in family planning, they turned to more aggressive policies.

As the Indian government's frustration over the ineffectiveness of state population policies increased, then, the policies became more coercive.[96] Hoping to halve the country's birthrate within the next decade, health officials began in the 1960s to push IUD use and sterilization over all other birth control methods. While other methods were theoretically available, health professionals frequently failed to inform women of alternatives to sterilization. To motivate Indian women and men to choose sterilization and to reward family planning workers for convincing Indian couples to participate in family planning, government officials introduced incentives and goals. States also introduced targets that government health officials were supposed to meet, putting them in competition with each other and stressing statistical results over program quality. By the mid-1970s, state-sponsored birth control efforts culminated in a sterilization campaign so repressive that it eventually led to the fall of the government. Families found they had to agree to sterilization in order to keep their housing and jobs or to receive medical treatment.[97]

Moreover, family planning policies took on the same contradictory character they had in other parts of the world. Since health officials emphasized sterilization as the primary method of family planning, services continued to appeal to women at the end of their childbearing years while essentially depriving younger women of reproductive control. In addition, some physicians targeted women for sterilization or IUD insertion while withholding access to abortion and short-term contraceptive measures. In some hospitals, physicians would only perform an abortion on a woman with one child if she accepted an IUD and on a woman with two or more children if she consented to be sterilized following the abortion.[98] If policy makers were hoping to make family planning more appealing, these policies did the opposite.

Scholars disagree about the reasons why India's family planning program grew more coercive over time. Some have argued that family planning programs adopted coercive measures after failing to appeal to the majority of Indian couples, who desired large families for labor and financial security in old age. Unable to recognize the incompatibility of state family planning policies with women's personal goals, health officials adopted incentives and targets rather than trying to educate clients about the value of smaller families.[99] Others have held that India's reliance on Western models of modernization and its fascination with high-tech contraceptives contributed to an inherently biased approach toward poor and working women.[100] In addition, there is no agreement about the impact that family planning programs had on Indian women and men. Some have argued that women's lack of participation in Indian family planning programs should ipso facto be understood as a sign of resistance to the programs.[101] This discussion has also led to confusion about the question of how to define "choice" and "force" in family planning programs. Particularly in the case of the Emergency, during which sterilization frequently involved some kind of material exchange—a plot of land as a bonus for a sterilization, for instance—some scholars have argued that Indian couples did not necessarily experience financial incentives as a form of coercion. This argument has some validity, as Indian couples frequently deny that they were sterilized by force. One man who chose sterilization in order to obtain a plot of land explains: "No I wasn't pressurized at all. I got sterilized because I wanted the plot."[102] Having investigated the sterilization program in a Bengali refugee community where husbands and fathers were offered material support in exchange for submitting to sterilization, Carolyn Henning Brown concludes that most Bengalis felt the trade-off between material security and vasectomy was fair enough. While she concedes that sterilizations were "heavily sugar coated," she argues that only those already motivated to limit the size of their families actually took advantage of the offer.[103] Others have held, however, that the dichotomy between force and choice is a false one. In accepting sterilization—a process one man described as a "forcible deal"— many Indians were accepting something that they were not in a position to refuse. Emma Tarlo explains: "Notions of force and choice did not so much contradict as reinforce each other. In effect, what people faced were 'forced choices.' "[104] While some Indians might have been motivated to accept sterilization, in other words, they were not motivated by their desire for a permanent form of contraception but by the fact that a sterilization certificate guaranteed them basic necessities such as housing, work, and access to medical care.

In order to understand the extreme represented by coercive population policies, however, it is necessary to understand the implementation of "regular" family planning efforts and their relationship to coercive programs. While studying sterilization abuse holds a kind of gory appeal, we cannot fully understand the meaning of such abuse and the conditions in which it took place if we ignore those reproductive policies that preceded and surrounded it. In fact, most scholars have failed to investigate both the accessibility and the quality of services offered in India at the local level. As a result, they have focused on external rather than internal factors when trying to explain women's lack of interest in family planning, pointing, for instance, to the goals of Western philanthropists, pharmaceutical companies, and international health organizations but ignoring the local family planning professionals who were actually conducting clinics and interacting with patients. While we cannot understand the implementation of family planning services without looking at the motivation of policy makers, we also cannot understand the reception of family planning services without looking at policy implementation. Finally, researchers and policy makers have ignored the importance of women's literacy. Literacy, however, has been a key indicator of success in family planning programs. As literacy rates have gone up, the impact on health and family size has been dramatic. Attention to this wider context, then, is crucial.

Recent studies of Indian family planning programs in the 1990s point to structural problems that limit the effectiveness of birth control services, shedding some light on policy implementation and women's reception of family planning programs in earlier decades and suggesting questions that historians might want to ask when researching the history of family planning in India. Scholars have found that despite an increase in the mid-1990s of almost 20 percent in government per capita expenditures on birth control, women continued either to lack access to family planning services or to have access to inadequate services.[105] Clinics were underfunded, inadequately staffed, and continued to operate under a philosophy that stressed statistical results over the improvement of women's health. Moreover, despite the official government commitment to family planning, vast geographical differences characterized the level and quality of services available.

A lack of frequent contact between family planning workers and clients limited the credibility of the workers in the clients' eyes and hampered their ability to discuss family planning needs effectively. Although the Indian health services theoretically employed outreach workers to visit every household, putting all women in touch with the family planning program, many women never met their outreach worker. Reports of the actual number of households visited ranged from 93 percent in Karnataka to 10 percent in Uttar Pradesh. Moreover, even when outreach workers reached individual households, most visits were extremely short. In one study, almost two-thirds of the respondents reported that the outreach worker had spent less than five minutes during her most recent household visit.[106] Although home visits were supposed to help women establish more personal relationships with their family planning personnel and to ease discussion of their reproductive goals and the benefits of family planning, most women never formed such relationships with the outreach workers.

Moreover, many family planning workers continued to recommend only one birth control method rather than educate women about the range of methods available. Although this practice violated official family planning policy, most health professionals failed to fully inform clients and continued to ignore women's reproductive goals. As Cecilia van Hollen has demonstrated, poor women who seek medical care in government hospitals continue to be pressured to accept an IUD and frequently have an IUD inserted despite their opposition.[107] Erratic supplies of temporary contraceptives and the desire to meet larger family planning targets contributed to health care providers' tendency to push permanent methods of contraception. This tendency, in turn, reaffirmed women's association of contraception with long-term methods, further discouraging young women from seeking birth control counseling. The lack of adequate counseling, moreover, not only deprived women of full contraceptive choice but hindered their ability to anticipate and successfully manage possible side effects.

Despite these problems, Indian women continued to use government family planning services. Wanting contraceptive advice and lacking the financial resources to seek help from private physicians, they took advantage of the government services that were available.[108] At the same time, women tried to exert some influence over the services offered. They complained about health care workers' lack of empathy and respect, their verbal abuse, and their generally substandard care, and they criticized family planning workers for their exclusive focus on birth control at the expense of attention to larger health care issues. As in other contexts, it was women who had the financial resources to consult a private physician who were most likely to gain reproductive control. Poor women could try to gain some control by cobbling public and private services together. Some women who had an IUD inserted at a government hospital, for instance, went to a private hospital to have it removed. Women's ability to do so, however, was limited by their financial resources, and their need to seek private services to achieve reproductive control spoke to the continued denial of such control in public health services. Moreover, it is likely that the lack of accessibility and the poor quality of the services discouraged some women from seeking contraceptive advice in the first place.

While the analysis of family planning in India and Puerto Rico demonstrates the similarity of factors that have impeded women's attempts to control their reproduction worldwide, it also illustrates the need for detailed local analyses to illuminate the problems and opportunities of family planning programs around the world.[109] Local analysis is necessary not only because it provides valuable information about the implementation of family planning programs and policies but also because it reminds us that the impact that family planning services have on women's reproductive decisions depends on the individual situations in which women are trying to control their reproduction. Although we know, for instance, that some health professionals performed postpartum sterilizations or inserted IUDs postpartum without women's knowledge, we cannot conclude that all or even most women who got sterilized or received an IUD after delivery were the victims of coercion. Nor does the data available allow us to draw any conclusions about the extent of such coercion. Programs might deprive some women of reproductive control while allowing others to control their reproduction; they might control a woman's reproduction at one stage of her reproductive life but provide her with much-needed control at another stage. Only a closer analysis of the specific conditions under which individual women made their reproductive decisions will permit us to evaluate whether women were able to exercise reproductive control or were denied such control. This does not mean, however, that we cannot recognize and critique existing family planning structures for their coercive potential and their neglect of women's reproductive health. In fact, investigating the specific conditions surrounding women's reproductive choices will both sharpen our critique and offer valuable insights into the specific factors that make for progressive or coercive programs.

■ Conclusion

Throughout the twentieth century, women sought access to birth control, sterilization, and abortion. They benefited from public health family planning services and contraceptive field trials. Whether they received condoms from Lena Hillard in Watauga County, North Carolina, foam powder in a family planning clinic in Bombay, the birth control pill from Dr. Edris Rice-Wray in Puerto Rico, a sterilization with the help of a Mecklenburg County social worker, or an abortion at North Carolina's Memorial Hospital, they had to negotiate with health and social work professionals for access to reproductive control. Sometimes they were successful and able to conclude that sterilization, birth control, or abortion were indeed "a great thing for poor folks." Often they were forced to compromise or to take advantage of inadequate services. The foam powder burned, the condom required a husband's cooperation, the pill caused side effects and had to be taken every day, the sterilization required a diagnosis of feeblemindedness, and the abortion necessitated a letter from a psychiatrist. Many women did whatever it took to gain reproductive control. They complained about side effects, sought IUDs that their husbands might not detect, tolerated the unpleasant side effects of the pill in exchange for its convenience, and threatened suicide in order to gain access to therapeutic abortion. But sometimes they were unable to get what they wanted. Birth control nurses passed out substandard contraceptives; husbands refused to consent to their wives' sterilization; physicians refused to perform abortions. In these cases, women were denied reproductive control.

While the denial of reproductive control could take many forms, during the 1930s and 1940s it most commonly meant the denial of access to services, though in the case of eugenic sterilization it took on a coercive character. By the 1950s and 1960s, when the state extended welfare services at home and foreign aid abroad, policies were more likely to be coercive. As social workers in North Carolina and elsewhere in the United States began to tie the receipt of welfare services to the insertion of an IUD or to petition for the eugenic sterilization of their clients, as health professionals coerced Puerto Rican women to be sterilized, as Indian physicians forced women to accept IUDs they did not want, and as Indian government officials forced men and women to agree to sterilization or lose their homes, more women experienced the denial of reproductive control by being forced to use unwanted services.

While the development of contraceptives outside women's control provided the necessary precondition for coercive family planning programs, a number of additional factors determined the likelihood of coercion. First, state institutions needed to have an interest in controlling women's reproduction. Governments have always had a financial interest in controlling reproduction. With the extension of the welfare state under the New Deal, the expansion of social services, and the significant rise in commitment to foreign aid during the 1950s and 1960s, however, the notion of controlling expenditures by controlling the reproduction of those supported by welfare programs became a matter of immediate interest to state and federal governments. The expansion of financial commitments carried with it the fear that social programs would lead to the creation of a permanent relief class. In addition, resentment of welfare recipients at home and foreign aid recipients abroad contributed to a punitive approach toward birth control and inspired a desire to control those who were receiving government money.

Second, states needed an ideological framework to justify state control of reproduction. Eugenic theory and, later, the fear of population explosion provided this framework. In the early twentieth century, health and welfare professionals in the United States, Puerto Rico, and India worried about the deterioration of race quality and argued that family planning was essential to prevent the spread of a host of social problems. The meaning of eugenics in Puerto Rico and India differed from the negative eugenic policies that led to eugenic sterilization programs in the United States. Nevertheless, by the postwar era Indian and Puerto Rican elites, inspired by the rhetoric of population control, had joined Western philanthropists, researchers, and government officials in their desire to control the reproduction of the undesirable classes. Research and financial investment in family planning programs geared toward the poor were in all three places based on the assumption that population was spiraling out of control and posing a danger to the social, economic, and political stability of the region and the world. Financial arguments for family planning programs proved so pervasive that even those who defended women's reproductive rights paid lip service to them.

Third, states needed the ability to coerce women—or men—into participating in family planning. An individual's dependence on state services —be they health care, welfare, or housing—gave the state the necessary leverage to do so. Social workers in North Carolina threatened to withhold welfare payments unless clients agreed to be sterilized or fitted with an IUD, health care providers coerced Puerto Rican women seeking health care services into accepting sterilization, and Indian government officials tied the receipt of housing, jobs, and health care to an individual's decision to consent to sterilization.

Fourth, a lack of alternative health and reproductive services left women few choices when they sought reproductive control. Throughout most of the period under discussion, women's access to health and contraceptive services was extremely limited. Opposition by various parties to the dispensing of contraceptive advice created an artificial restriction of family planning programs. Health professionals felt that childbearing and motherhood was women's responsibility, distrusted women's ability to make responsible reproductive decisions, and were suspicious about extending reproductive control to women. Opposition to family planning came from a variety of directions. The U.S. Children's Bureau stifled family planning services during the New Deal era; state public health officials in Raleigh, North Carolina, endorsed public health birth control programs but met with opposition from local health officers; government public health officials in Puerto Rico and India opposed birth control. Officials refused to fund family planning, failed to spend more than a fraction of the money allocated for family planning, refused to advertise existing programs, discredited existing programs, declined to refer patients, and so on. While opposition took many forms, the end result was the same: access to services and general health care was nonexistent or severely restricted. Women lacked choices.

It would not suffice, however, to point to the existence of all of the above factors as proof of the existence of coercive family planning. For even when all of these factors were present, coercion was not a given, but only one of several possibilities. In the end, the individual interactions between patients and health and social work professionals determined how patients experienced family planning services and how much reproductive control they had.

In addition, larger structural problems limited the quality of the services women received. The unequal distribution of access to health care meant that most women—even if they did not experience coercive family planning programs—had only very limited options for controlling their reproduction. Not only were their choices determined by these limited options, but health professionals exploited the fact that women lacked access to alternatives. Women who took advantage of contraceptive field trials might have been thankful to obtain oral contraceptives. Contraceptive field trials frequently extended reproductive control to women who had previously been denied such control. And local health care providers who carried out the trials might have been grateful for access to a new generation of contraceptives and to otherwise inaccessible medical tests for their underserved patients. Nevertheless, the researchers who developed the trials depended on trial groups that had been underserved by reproductive health care services and were in dire need of birth control methods. And because researchers were frequently more concerned with the statistical details of the contraceptive field trials than with women's reproductive health, the trials reinforced the very circumstances that had led to their patients' disadvantaged position in the first place.

Such exploitation of underserved population groups was endemic, and it is still a reality of medical testing in the twenty-first century. While in 1991 80 percent of clinical trials took place in academic medical centers, by 1998 that percentage had fallen by more than half. The majority of trials that are carried out outside academic medical centers still take place in the poorest regions of the world, continuing the trend that was so pervasive in contraceptive research. The same factors that made contraceptive field trials in rural North Carolina, Puerto Rico, and Indian villages appealing still govern the appeal of field trials today. Subjects are likely to come from population groups underserved by and desperately in need of medical services. They are considered more pliable, less likely to ask questions, and less likely to quit the trials than women in developed nations. Moreover, as was the case for contraceptive research, which frequently extended the promise of reproductive control without making any provisions for women's access to birth control once the trials had concluded, today's research trials frequently exploit subjects for research without providing them with any access to long-lasting treatment options. Some local health officials still look to pharmaceutical industries and Western medicine to get access to new treatments. And they continue to find that when the trials have been completed, access to the treatments is again beyond their reach. Research considerations governing trials, then, still win out over basic concerns for a more equal distribution of resources and for the well-being of those who lend their bodies for testing.[110]

In the case of women's reproductive health, such pervasive structural inequities are further compounded by a continued refusal to put women's health and goals at the center of policies. Indeed, many in the population control establishment still assume that the dangers of uncontrolled population growth justify coercion in family planning programs. But if the history of women's reproductive health demonstrates anything, it is that coercive policies are not only inhumane and unethical, they also fail to work, have extremely undesirable consequences—the neglect of Chinese infant girls is only one of the more drastic examples—and in the long run tend to discredit voluntary birth control programs, making people deeply suspicious of the entire movement to control fertility.[111]

Only a dramatic shift in our social priorities will lead to long-lasting changes in the area of women's reproductive health and lives. To improve their choices, women need access not only to comprehensive health care but also to education and participation in the economic and political lives of their communities. During the 1990s, an international coalition of reproductive rights activists participating in the United Nations conferences played a decisive role in replacing the old family planning and population discourse with a broader concept of reproductive and sexual rights that links sexual and reproductive freedom to women's human rights. But present challenges to women's reproductive rights such as

George W. Bush's promotion of the gag rule indicate that the reorientation of family planning policies still has a long way to go.[112] Further progress is not going to take place without the mobilization of the larger women's movement in defense of women's reproductive and sexual rights. This means, however, that the women's movement has to overcome its historically ambivalent attitude toward the reproductive rights of poor women at home and abroad and to demonstrate a willingness to defend the rights of all women, including those who cannot pay for health services.

From the Footnotes to the Headlines

Sterilization Apologies and Their Lessons

On December 8, 2002, the *Winston-Salem Journal* launched a series entitled "Against Their Will" that chronicled the history of North Carolina's eugenic sterilization program, which operated between 1929 and 1975. Under the headline "Lifting the Curtain on a Shameful Era," Kevin Begos, John Railey, and Danielle Deaver inaugurated a series of articles published over the next five days that explored the legacy of state-ordered sterilization in North Carolina.[1] The series culminated in a public apology by North Carolina governor Mike Easley and, in early February 2003, the appointment of a special commission to consider providing restitution to those who were sterilized under the program. In August 2003, Easley approved a list of restitution recommendations, including the provision of education and health benefits to sterilization victims. In this way, North Carolina became the first state in the nation to make any kind of restitution for state eugenic sterilization.[2]

The story behind the newspaper series and the governor's apology is both ordinary and extraordinary. On the one hand, North Carolina was only one of thirty states to have a sterilization program. And by the time Governor Easley issued his public apology, such apologies had become almost routine. The governors of Virginia and Oregon had issued similar apologies earlier that year, and North

Carolina's apology was in turn followed by the apologies of the governors of South Carolina and California for their states' programs.

On the other hand, North Carolina stands out both because of its courageous stand toward its history of eugenic sterilization and because the history itself is unusual. Its willingness to confront its own history did not begin with the governor's apology. It began more than a decade ago, when a staff member at the North Carolina State Archives alerted me to the existence of the Eugenics Board records. This was in the late 1980s, when I was a regular at the archive, where I was researching the history of women's reproductive control. Getting access to the records was not a smooth process. After learning of their existence, I made a formal application to the state attorney general requesting access to the records and promising to protect the privacy of those who were sterilized under the program. Somewhat to my surprise, my request was granted. But if the state attorney general thought I should be able to browse through the files, the archives' staff was less sure about how to interpret the attorney general's letter. Fearing that my perception—that I had full access to the records—was a misunderstanding, they provided me with the papers and correspondence of the Eugenics Board but withheld access to all of the records relating to the more than eight thousand sterilization petitions the board had received. While I was disappointed at this turn of events, I took what I had and went to work. I analyzed the papers I had at hand until they could be analyzed no further and wrote and defended my dissertation.

Six years later, in 1996, I returned to the State Archives for some follow-up work. I had called ahead and let the staff know that I wanted to look at the Eugenics Board material one more time. In preparation for my visit, the archives' staff had again contacted the attorney general, and this time they had received a more liberal interpretation of "access." As I walked into the Search Room, then, I was met by a staff member who handed me three rolls of microfilm. I had no idea what he was giving me. But rather than ask any questions, I marched straight to the microfilm reading room, threaded in the first reel, and this time was faced with a gold mine: the minutes of more than three decades of Eugenics Board meetings. These minutes contained summaries of every sterilization petition considered by the Eugenics Board, records of the board's decisions, and lists of the names of those individuals who were actually sterilized as a result of the board's authorization. What unfolded over the next several weeks was almost surreal. Since I was no longer living in North Carolina, I needed to make copies of the microfilm. The microfilm, however, included all the names of those suggested for sterilization, and while the archives' staff seemed at the moment content with the fact that I was looking at all those names on microfilm, the names had to be eliminated if I wanted to take the material along. This meant I could not just duplicate the microfilm; I had to make paper copies of every page, and the archives' staff had to carefully redact all patient names. Over the course of that summer, then, the entire staff spent weeks patiently taking their black magic markers to the thousands of pages I was copying. By the fall of 1996, I had three large boxes of photocopies sitting on the floor of my office. This was both daunting and exciting.

Faced with this material, I sat down and started reading. I read the eight thousand sterilization petitions, which began in January 1934 and ended in June 1966, several times in a row. Reading these cases was an emotionally devastating experience: they contained summaries of eight thousand individual tragedies of poverty and poor health, sexual and physical abuse, indifference and neglect, all embedded in a context of inadequate social services and equally inadequate health care. I felt as if eight thousand strangers were confiding their individual misfortunes to me and pleading for public recognition of the wrongs done to them. I was outraged by what I read, and I struggled to figure out how to give this history the public recognition it deserved.

Moreover, it became increasingly clear to me that the privacy laws that kept the records of all thirty state sterilization programs closed to protect sterilization victims had another effect: they also kept this history hidden from public view. I was equally aware that my access to these records was an anomaly unlikely to repeat itself. While I knew a number of other historians and lawyers who were researching state sterilization programs in different parts of the country, none of them had ever been able to see the actual records of these programs. And even the North Carolina State Archives had again closed its Eugenics Board records to researchers. From both a scholarly and a political perspective, then, access to these materials came with a unique responsibility: to educate the public about the wrong that had been done. But I was unclear about how to do this. In 2001, after Virginia's governor apologized for his state's sterilization program, I approached the *Raleigh News and Observer*, trying to interest them in the story. The *News and Observer* published an article on the program that questioned whether the governor should issue an apology.[3] But there was no further follow-up. In June 2002, however, Kevin Begos from the *Winston-Salem Journal* called. After talking to him over the course of several weeks, I decided to offer him full access to my yet unpublished research findings and all of the sources I had collected in years of research, including the summaries of the eight thousand sterilization petitions. I felt I had an ethical responsibility toward those who had been sterilized under the program, that I owed them a form of public recognition. A newspaper series would bring the story to the attention of the larger public, and Kevin was the right person to write it: he was persistent and smart, able to appreciate the complexity of the story, and respectful of the concerns I had for the privacy of those who had been sterilized.

■ Eugenic Sterilization in Public Discourse Today

Without a doubt, the media has significant power to shape the debate about and public understanding of the history of eugenic sterilization. In fact, from the very beginning of the *Winston-Salem Journal* series, the paper warned that it was unveiling a legacy that would not go away and suggested ways in which the public might understand and respond to this legacy. The immediate impact of the very first article was extraordinarily powerful. Skillfully drawing from snippets of the sterilization cases, the article portrayed women and men whom the state had sterilized against their will and who had suffered significantly as a result. The inclusion in the article of three named sterilization victims—Elaine Riddick Jessie, Nial Cox Ramirez, and Bertha Dale Midgett Hymes—left no doubt about the human face of sterilization candidates and the devastating consequences the surgery had. These women, the authors made clear, were left with physical and emotional scars that they were still trying to overcome decades later. Nial Cox Ramirez explained: "It's a hell within a hell that you going through. It's like a cancer that eats. . . . I tried to bury it. I tried to get rid of it. I tried to forget all about it. . . . But it comes right back fresh, just like it was yesterday."[4]

How should we understand such a tragedy? The paper offered two frameworks in which to situate it: eugenic science à la Nazi Germany and racism. To illustrate the gravity of science gone wrong, the paper drew comparisons between the eugenic sterilization program and the eugenics programs pursued by Germany under Adolf Hitler. As the son of one of the sterilization victims was quoted as saying in a piece published on the first day of the series, the work of the Eugenics Board was "not far from the thinking of Hitler . . . that same concept when Hitler tried to make this pure race."[5] This link was further reinforced as the series probed the ties between Nazi Germany, the Bowman Gray School of Medicine at Wake Forest College, and North Carolina's sterilization program and speculated about the dangers of the new frontier of genetic testing. The authors pointed out that William Louis Poteat, president of Wake Forest College in the early twentieth century, had been an advocate of eugenic sterilization and had helped to lay the groundwork for the acceptance of eugenic sterilization in North Carolina.[6] During the early 1940s, the Department of Medical Genetics at Bowman Gray had accepted a substantial financial donation from Wickliffe Draper, a philanthropist who had visited a eugenics conference in Nazi Germany and who spent his life and money trying to prove that whites were superior to blacks.[7] And in the 1940s, researchers associated with the Department of Medical Genetics had set up an experimental program of eugenic sterilization in Forsyth County that, the *Winston-Salem Journal* commented, held an eerie resemblance to Nazi experimentation.[8]

And if North Carolina did not have a Jewish population to target, it had an African American population to take its place. Racial bias took center stage as an explanation for how the eugenic sterilization program could have happened in North Carolina. While the first day's articles hinted that the state had authorized the sterilization of Elaine Riddick Jessie and others like her because she was black, on subsequent days the notion that race was at the core of the program was increasingly stressed. On the second day, the article on sterilization victim Nial Cox Ramirez reported that those associated with the Eugenics Board had specifically suggested targeting the black community.[9] When the *Winston-Salem Journal*'s story hit the Associated Press wire, its headline already had the race explanation built into it: "Sterilization program targeted women, blacks in later years," the wire story read as it made its way across the country.[10] A statistical breakdown of the race of sterilization candidates projected over a photograph of civil rights demonstrators suggested that the program could be seen as a state response to the fight for racial equality. Similarly, an article about the use of castration as punishment told about the castration of a black man who had been convicted of indecent exposure, bringing together a familiar and chilling narrative about race and sex.[11] It is no surprise, then, that at least some concluded, in the words of Winston-Salem reverend John Mendez, that the program was "clearly genocide."[12]

Indeed, framing the story of eugenic sterilization as a narrative about race and Nazi eugenics was not particular to news coverage in North Carolina but characterized coverage of state eugenic sterilization programs across the country. Journalists in Virginia, Oregon, and California, too, tied their discussions of their states' eugenic sterilization programs to both racial discrimination and Nazi genocide.[13] Even when details about

Racial shift

While the civil-rights movement gathered momentum in the 1950s and '60s, the North Carolina sterilization program increasingly targeted blacks.

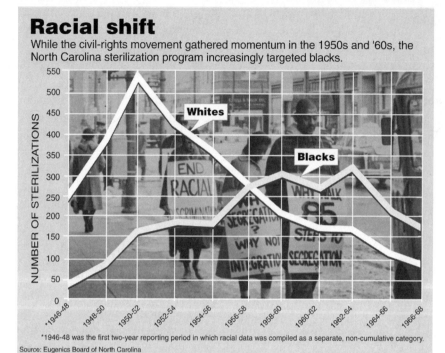

NUMBER OF STERILIZATIONS

Whites

Blacks

*1946-48 was the first two-year reporting period in which racial data was compiled as a separate, non-cumulative category.

Source: Eugenics Board of North Carolina

Racial shift in North Carolina. (©2002 *Winston-Salem Journal*; graphic by Jim Stanley)

the programs were sketchy or unknown, journalists reported that historians expected such links to exist.[14]

Undoubtedly, the *Winston-Salem Journal* series reignited a familiar debate about racial discrimination. In fact, it was a debate that attracted the attention of the NAACP, which was willing to take up the issue. Efforts of NAACP officials kept the history of eugenic sterilization in the public spotlight in North Carolina, contributed to the appointment of the Eugenics Study Commission to consider restitution, and ultimately led to the approval of restitution for those sterilized under the program. The very existence and prolonged nature of this discussion is unprecedented, and it is a tribute to the excellent work of Kevin Begos and his colleagues.

The emphasis on racial discrimination and its relationship to eugenic sterilization, however, came at the expense of attention to the issue of women's reproductive rights. Indeed, while race and the comparisons to genocide and Nazi Germany have evoked the horrors of eugenic sterilization, they have, ironically, also given the impression that policies such as eugenic sterilization can be safely relegated to the past. Nobody would seriously argue that we have to guard against a return of state-level programs of eugenic sterilization like those carried out by the Nazis. And while some might view the development of genetic science as a potential threat of a similar nature, the material realities of health care in the United States are much more likely to make genetic knowledge a luxury of the rich than a threat to the poor.

Women's reproductive rights, on the other hand, and particularly the reproductive rights of welfare recipients, remain a contested issue. In fact, I would suggest that the public discussion following the *Winston-Salem Journal* series centered on race at the expense of reproductive rights because a great many people in this country continue to believe that women should not have children while they are receiving public assistance. The series itself quotes at least two people, Ramirez's surgeon, Dr. A. M. Stanton, and State Senator Wilbur Jolly, who support the notion that women should not have children while on welfare. Although Stanton expressed his regret for Ramirez's sterilization, he went on to comment that the sterilization program "was probably a good thing." He said: "I think some people [had children] on purpose to get a little bit of extra money from the welfare department."[15] Certainly, Stanton and Jolly are not alone in holding this view. In fact, it is likely that many readers of the *Winston-Salem Journal* series, while horrified by the news about North Carolina's sterilization program, agreed with Stanton's misperception that women have children while on welfare in order to grab a larger piece of the welfare pie. What Stanton does not seem to realize is that the women he stereotypes as greedy welfare mothers are precisely those women at the center of eugenic sterilization policies. When Nial Cox Ramirez came to the attention of welfare officials, she was the daughter of a welfare recipient and was pregnant by her boyfriend at the age of seventeen. When Elaine Riddick Jessie came to the attention of welfare officials, she was thirteen, pregnant as the result of a rape, and living with her grandmother because her parents were unable to care for her.

Indeed, I would argue that public attitudes about the reproductive rights of impoverished women have changed little over the last five decades. And it is not only public opinion that remains ambivalent about women's reproductive rights. Government policy, from Bill Clinton's welfare reform to George W. Bush's dismantling of women's reproductive health services, has consistently challenged the reproductive and sexual rights of poor women. Moreover, given public stereotypes toward those receiving government assistance, women of color remain particularly vulnerable. We should ask ourselves, then, if we are inscribing the same attitudes in public policy that shaped state sterilization programs decades ago, only now with a different set of penalties.

Given these political realities, what meaning does an apology for a eugenic sterilization program carry? In the coverage of state sterilization programs, journalists suggested a script that should accompany revelations of sterilization abuse. First, they disclosed the history of the programs and argued that survivors expected an official apology. Second, the state issued an apology. Third, the press rewarded the apology with coverage that included sterilization survivors' comments of appreciation.[16] Public acknowledgment of policies gone wrong—along with sterilization survivors' acceptance of that acknowledgment—quickly became par for the course, providing a clear path from wrongdoing through confession of sin to absolution. But the highly scripted nature of this sequence of events left little room for complications.

Sterilization survivors remain at best ambivalent about state apologies —a fact easily overlooked in the rush to close the ritual by finding a quotable survivor who expresses gratitude. Survivors of the North Carolina program frequently wondered whether state representatives who had issued apologies "really mean[t] it" and criticized the plan for restitution in the form of health and education benefits as too little, too late.[17] "I'm not satisfied with that. They really messed up my life," Ernestine Moore, who was sterilized in 1965, explained.[18] Indeed, if we are to take the stories of sterilization survivors seriously, an acknowledgment of past wrongs means little unless it is accompanied by serious attempts to avoid similar mistakes in the future. Bertha Dale Midgett Hymes, who was sterilized at the age of seventeen, commented after Easley issued his apology that she forgives the state and hopes that it will not "do anybody else like that."[19]

Furthermore, the framework of the apology-absolution sequence makes it tempting to rush through the rituals without really coming to terms with history—in fact, without even finding out much about the people who were supposedly receiving the apologies. As Aaron Zitner from the *Los Angeles Times* commented, Governor Gray Davis issued his apology for California's program before any public discussion about the program had taken place:

> To make amends for a state program that sterilized 7,600 people
> against their will, North Carolina's governor created a panel last year
> to probe the history of the effort, interview survivors, and consider
> reparations. In Oregon, then-Governor John Kitzhaber last year apolo-

gized in person to some of the 2,600 people sterilized there, and he created an annual Human Rights Day to commemorate the state's mistake. On the day Virginia Governor Mark R. Warner apologized, Jesse Meadows and other victims unveiled a roadside marker. . . . Davis offered his apology in a press release. No survivors or disability groups were on hand to accept it. There was no order to probe for more details of a history that, according to scholars, is still largely unexplored and not fully understood.[20]

Indeed, the issuing of apologies has tended to cut off further discussion of the legacy of eugenic sterilization, a development that was clearly intended by a number of governors. The situation was further aggravated by the fact that a number of states took the apology as a sign to close or destroy records that had facilitated the research that preceded published revelations about the sterilization programs and that had been further opened in the immediate aftermath of newspaper coverage. During the months following the publication of the *Winston-Salem Journal*'s series, North Carolina adopted a more relaxed policy of allowing access to the records, but in no other state did publicity lead to an attempt to facilitate further study. In fact, Oregon went so far as to destroy at least a portion of its records.[21] And North Carolina recently joined ranks by again closing access to the Eugenics Board records. Thus states that issued apologies acted to limit further discovery. Despite the fact that researchers and journalists have repeatedly and with great confidence published total numbers of individuals sterilized in given states, for instance, it has so far been impossible to determine the exact sterilization numbers for any state. Even in North Carolina, where access to the Eugenics Board records has allowed me to ask and answer many questions concerning the program, the exact number of those sterilized under it remains unclear, and many more questions are still unanswered.

As is the case when any great wrong is done, it is, of course, difficult to imagine any action that might redress the pain that eugenic sterilization programs have caused. We might begin, though, by reconsidering the significance we attribute to official apologies. Such apologies are certainly necessary, but they are only one component—and not the culmination—of a serious response. Instead, they must be accompanied by sincere attempts to encourage study, to understand the history of state sterilization programs, and to apply the lessons of this history to present-day social policy. How will we, today, guarantee the reproductive rights of poor women? What kind of services are we prepared to offer teenage girls who decide to become sexually active? What kind of services are we prepared to offer rape and incest victims? How will we deal with the question of the sexual self-determination of the mentally ill and mentally retarded? As poor women's ability to exercise their reproductive rights remains under constant attack, it behooves us to remember the legacy of state sterilization programs.

The defense of women's reproductive rights must include efforts to ensure that education about and access to birth control, sterilization, and abortion are available to all women, regardless of their race, class, age, and marital status. Moreover, it must include the acknowledgment that women have the right to decide to use or not use such services—even if we disagree with their decisions. Rights are only as strong as our willingness to tolerate the decisions of others. A full acknowledgment of the suffering of women such as Elaine Riddick Jessie, Nial Cox Ramirez, and Bertha Dale Midgett Hymes must include a spirited defense of their sexual and reproductive rights. It must also include recognition of the responsibility that we, as a society, have to provide them with the health and welfare services that allow them to exercise those rights.

Notes

ABBREVIATIONS

AGR-NCSA	Attorney General's Records, North Carolina State Archives
CB-NA	Children's Bureau Papers, National Archives
CC-SHC	Claude Currie Papers, Southern Historical Collection
CJG-CML	Clarence J. Gamble Papers, Countway Medical Library
CPC-UNC	Carolina Population Center, University of North Carolina
DHR-NCSA	Department of Human Resources, Division of Social Services, Social Services Record Group, North Carolina State Archives
DSS-NCSA	Division of Social Services, Commissioner's Office, Social Services Record Group, North Carolina State Archives
EBM	Eugenics Board Meeting
EB-NCSA	Eugenics Board Papers, North Carolina State Archives
EBW-UNCG	Ellen Black Winston Papers, Jackson Library, University of North Carolina at Greensboro
FA-UNCC	Fred Alexander Papers, Atkins Library, University of North Carolina at Charlotte
HBL-SHC	Human Betterment League Papers, Southern Historical Collection
JWRN-SHC	J. W. R. Norton Papers, Southern Historical Collection
MS-SSC	Margaret Sanger Papers, Sophia Smith Collection
NCF-SHC	North Carolina Fund Papers, Southern Historical Collection
PPFA-SSC	Planned Parenthood Federation of America Papers, Sophia Smith Collection
SBH-NCSA	State Board of Health Papers, North Carolina State Archives
SS-NCSA	Social Services Record Group, North Carolina State Archives
TCP-DUWA	Takey Crist Papers, Duke University Women's Archive

INTRODUCTION

1. Miller, *Worst of Times*, pp. 80–91.

2. It is unclear what surgery, precisely, her physician performed. He might have removed both her ovary and her affected fallopian tube. What is clear is that he was determined to leave the unaffected fallopian tube intact.

3. Quoted in Moya Woodside, *Sterilization and Social Welfare* (Winston-Salem: Human Betterment League of North Carolina, n.d.), p. 1, copy consulted in HBL-SHC.

4. Petchesky, *Abortion and Woman's Choice*, p. 395.

5. See, e.g., Mass, *Population Target*, pp. 91–95; Gordon, *Woman's Body*, pp. 400–402; Angela Davis, *Women, Race, and Class*, pp. 219–21; García, *La Operación*; and Hartmann, *Reproductive Rights*, pp. 244–51.

6. Smith-Rosenberg, "Hysterical Woman"; Smith-Rosenberg, "Abortion Movement and the AMA"; Ehrenreich and English, *For Her Own Good*.

7. Mass, *Population Target*; Dreifus, "Sterilizing the Poor"; Angela Davis, *Women, Race, and Class*; Bock, "Racism and Sexism in Nazi Germany"; Reilly, *Surgical Solution*; Carey, "Gender and Compulsory Sterilization."

8. Shapiro, *Population Control Politics*; Bandarage, *Women, Population, and Global Crisis*; Silliman and King, *Dangerous Intersections*; Hartmann, *Reproductive Rights*.

9. Gordon, *Woman's Body*; Leavitt, *Brought to Bed*; Chesler, *Woman of Valor*; Morantz-Sanchez, "Negotiating Power at the Bedside." See also Gordon, "Family Violence."

10. Rodrique, "Afro-American Community"; McCann, *Birth Control Politics*; Smith, *Sick and Tired*; Ross, "African American Women and Abortion." See also Jones, *Bad Blood*, and Reverby, *Tuskegee's Truths*.

11. Petchesky and Judd, *Negotiating Reproductive Rights*.

12. Petchesky, *Abortion and Woman's Choice* and "Foetal Images." Medical historians also cautioned that we need to understand medicine as a discipline that tries to solve the problems originating in any disease. Even when we study failed therapies, we need to pay close attention to treatment options available at the time. Pressman, *Last Resort*.

13. Reagan, *When Abortion Was a Crime*; Lopez, "Agency and Constraint"; Tone, *Devices and Desires*; Marks, "Cage of Ovulating Females"; Ladd-Taylor, "Saving Babies" and "Politics of Protection"; Briggs, *Reproducing Empire*; Morgen, *Into Our Own Hands*.

14. Beardsley, *History of Neglect*, pp. 128–33.

15. Korstad, "Doctoring the Body Politic," and Beardsley, *History of Neglect*, pp. 128–55. See also Link, "Hookworm Crusade," and Cockrell, "Influenza Pandemic."

16. Korstad has argued that these "underlying economic and racial motivations played an important part in North Carolina's public health campaigns." "Doctoring the Body Politic," p. 9.

17. Badger, *North Carolina and the New Deal*, pp. 40–50.

18. In June 1940, for instance, the average monthly payment for a dependent child on relief in North Carolina was only 29 percent of the payment for a dependent child in New York. Ibid., p. 50. See also Abrams, *Conservative Constraints*.

19. Schulman, *From Cotton Belt to Sunbelt*, pp. 174–205.

20. Ibid.

21. Korstad and Leloudis, "Citizen Soldiers."

22. Ibid., pp. 194–95.

23. "State Adopts Usable Law for Sterilization of Defectives," *Public Welfare Progress* 10, no. 3 (March 1929): 1.

24. For a discussion of the concept of entitlement and its relationship to citizenship, see Gordon, *Pitied but Not Entitled*, pp. 287–306, and Nancy Fraser, "Struggle over Needs."

25. Rodgers, "Age of Social Politics."

26. Gordon, "Family Violence," p. 182. See also Nancy Fraser, "Struggle over Needs."

27. Gordon, *Heroes of Their Own Lives*.

28. Spivak, "Can the Subaltern Speak?"; Sandoval, "U.S. Third World Feminism"; Briggs, *Reproducing Empire*; Theriot, "Women's Voices." A number of recent studies of the history of women's reproductive health have done an admirable job in tracing women's agency. For successful models see, for instance, Lopez, "Agency and Constraint"; Reagan, *When Abortion Was a Crime*; Tone, *Devices and Desires*; Marks, *Sexual Chemistry*; Briggs, *Reproducing Empire*; Theriot, "Women's Voices"; and Morantz-Sanchez, "Negotiating Power at the Bedside."

29. "Mabel Scott" is a pseudonym. Scott, interview.

30. For an excellent example of a multifaceted narrative of agency, see Tarlo, *Unsettling Memories*. On this topic, see also Cronon, "Place for Stories."

31. Petchesky, "Foetal Images."

32. Wailoo, *Drawing Blood*, p. 14.

33. Pressman, *Last Resort*, p. 7.

34. Scott, interview.

35. For a similar patient narrative at odds with science, see Annie Buelin's understanding of her sterilization in Danielle Deaver, "Making Amends," *Winston-Salem Journal*, 28 September 2003.

36. Kevin Begos, John Railey, and Danielle Deaver, "Against Their Will: North Carolina's Sterilization Program," *Winston-Salem Journal*, 8–12 December 2002. The series is presented at <http://againsttheirwill.journalnow.com>, a collaborative project of the *Winston-Salem Journal* and Journalnow.com. Accessed 9 March 2004.

37. "N.C. to Aid Sterilization Victims," *Washington Post*, 29 September 2003.

38. Peter Hardin, "Apology for Eugenics Set: Warner Action Makes Virginia First State to Denounce Movement," *Richmond Times Dispatch*, 2 May 2002; Julie Sullivan, "Legacy of Forced Sterilization Stirs Call for Oregon Apology," *Oregonian*, 30 June 2002; Paul Feist, "Davis Apologizes for State's Sterilization Program: Those with Hereditary Flaws Were Victims," *San Francisco Chronicle*, 12 March 2003; Aaron Zitner, "Davis' Apology Sheds No Light on Sterilization in California," *Los Angeles Times*, 16 March 2003.

39. Kevin Begos, Danielle Deaver, and John Railey, "Easley Apologizes to Sterilization Victims," *Winston-Salem Journal*, 13 December 2002.

1. Quoted in Sylvia Payne to Clarence J. Gamble, 17 November 1941, file 442, box 25, CJG-CML.

2. Gordon, *Woman's Body*; Reed, *From Private Vice*; Chesler, *Woman of Valor*; McCann, *Birth Control Politics*.

3. The chapter draws on the papers of Clarence J. Gamble, which document his philanthropic efforts in the United States and abroad; the papers of North Carolina's Department of Public Health and its Department of Public Welfare; the Margaret Sanger Papers, which chronicle the efforts of Sanger, Lydia DeVilbiss, the Birth Control Federation of America, and the American Birth Control League to promote birth control; and the papers of the Planned Parenthood Federation of America, which document, among other things, the Farm Security Administration's involvement in family planning.

4. See Klein, *For All These Rights*; Hacker, *Divided Welfare State*; and Howard, *Hidden Welfare State*.

5. According to historian Judith Walzer Leavitt, one woman in thirty died over the course of her fertile years. *Brought to Bed*, pp. 25–26.

6. Beardsley, *History of Neglect*, p. 13, quote on 22; Grey, *New Deal Medicine*; Smith, *Sick and Tired*.

7. Brought together through the support of the U.S. Public Health Service and a number of philanthropic organizations, the Committee on the Costs of Medical Care was made up of representatives from medicine, the social sciences, public health, and private philanthropy. Its goal was to develop recommendations that would ensure that all Americans had access to adequate health care at a cost that was within their means to pay. Grey, *New Deal Medicine*, pp. 21–24; Committee on the Costs of Medical Care, *Medical Care for the American People*; Beardsley, *History of Neglect*, pp. 11–74.

8. Quoted in Grey, *New Deal Medicine*, pp. 22, 21. See also Raper and Reid, *Sharecroppers All*.

9. Borst, *Catching Babies*, pp. 101–16. See also Flexner, *Medical Education*, and J. Whitridge Williams, "Medical Education and the Midwife Problem."

10. "Infancy and Maternal Mortality as It Applies to the General Practitioner," ca. 1933–35, series 1924–1935, Dr. G. M. Cooper's file, box 28, SBH-NCSA.

11. Report on Rural Work in North Carolina, November 15th to December 15th, 1916, series 1914–1920, file 4-11-2-7 (North Carolina Progress Report), CB-NA.

12. "North Carolina State-Wide Conference on Better Care for Mothers and Babies, [15 February 1939]," *Child* 3, no. 10 (April 1939).

13. Ladd-Taylor, *Mother Work*, pp. 18–19. See also Meckel, *Save the Babies*.

14. Cooper to Mrs. V. R. Cooke, 22 November 1938, box 23, file 412, CJG-CML. In 1925, North Carolina led the nation with sixty-five hundred midwives, one-seventh of all the midwives in the United States. Lynn Hudson calculates that between 80 and 90 percent of North Carolina's midwives were black. "Twentieth Century Midwives," pp. 2–3, 7–8; Borst, *Catching Babies*; Gertrude Jacinta Fraser, *African American Midwifery*.

15. George Cooper, Untitled paper presented to the North Carolina Federation of Women's Clubs, 1924, 1925, Dr. G. H. Cooper's file, box 28, SBH-NCSA.

16. Beardsley notes that by the early 1920s nearly every county health department in North Carolina employed one or two black nurses. *History of Neglect*, p. 140.

17. Cooper, "Progress." Administered under the Children's Bureau, the Sheppard-Towner Act met with opposition from the American Medical Association (AMA), which feared the establishment of medical authority over child health under lay-women's control. If such services were to be continued, the AMA demanded, they should be placed under the public health services. The Sheppard-Towner Act came up for renewal, moreover, during the presidency of Calvin Coolidge, who was an ally of big business and a critic of a strong federal government. After the act failed to be renewed, a number of states tried to continue maternal and infant welfare work but found themselves under increasing financial constraints. Ladd-Taylor, *Mother Work*, pp. 177–90; Meckel, *Save the Babies*, pp. 212–19.

18. Clarence J. Gamble, "Contraception as a Public Health Measure," *Transactions of the Medical Society of the State of North Carolina*, 1938, box 2, Misc. Papers, JWRN-SHC.

19. The average age at marriage for girls in the rural areas of North Carolina was fifteen years, and maternal deaths were highest among mothers under fifteen. "Medical Indications: Contraception," *Washington Herald*, 19 February 1938, copy consulted in box 2, Misc. Papers, Associations . . . Societies, JWRN-SHC.

20. Tone, *Devices and Desires*, p. 155.

21. Gordon, *Woman's Body*, p. 309.

22. Davidson to Barclay, 5 March 1937, box 190, file 2993, CJG-CML. Emphasis in original.

23. Tone notes that the diaphragm's prescription and successful use entailed four steps: a pelvic examination; measurement of the diameter of the vagina and assessment of its contours; selection of a corresponding diaphragm size; and instruction of the patient in inserting and removing the device by herself. Some doctors insisted on follow-up appointments to double-check patients' technique. *Devices and Desires*, p. 121.

24. Davidson to Barclay, 5 March 1937, CJG-CML. Emphasis in original.

25. On the funding and the development of contraceptive sciences, see Clarke, *Disciplining Reproduction*. On the emergence of a public-private welfare state, see Hacker, *Divided Welfare State*; Howard, *Hidden Welfare State*; and Klein, *For All These Rights*.

26. Reed, *From Private Vice*.

27. See, e.g., Briggs, *Reproducing Empire*; Marks, "Cage of Ovulating Females"; and Harris, "Clinical Trials." Others have acknowledged concerns about such trials but argued that they were part of accepted medical procedure at the time. See Watkins, *On the Pill*, and Tone, *Devices and Desires*. See also Lederer, *Subjected to Science*.

28. See Richter, *Vaccination against Pregnancy*, chapter 4, for this important distinction.

29. Confidential: Survey Report on Foam Powder and Sponge Cases Prescribed by the Maternal Health Clinic, Miami, Florida, March 1935 to February 1937, box 58,

folder 7, PPFA-SSC; Mrs. Zborowski to Mrs. Sanger, memo, 2 August 1935, reel S10, MS-SSC; DeVilbiss to Sanger, 10 September 1935, reel S10, MS-SSC. Ellen Chesler claims that DeVilbiss gave pregnant women capsules containing tiny portions of arsenic and other chemicals, which she encouraged them to take with quinine over a four-day period in order to produce an abortion. I have been unable to substantiate this claim. See *Woman of Valor*, p. 379.

30. DeVilbiss to Sanger, 30 September 1936, reel S11, MS-SSC.

31. DeVilbiss to Sanger, 10 September 1935, MS-SSC.

32. DeVilbiss to Catherine C. Bangs, [1934], box 58, folder 6, PPFA-SSC. Cauterization (referred to as "coagulation" in DeVilbiss's correspondence), in which a cautery is introduced into the uterus to create an inflammation, scarring the fallopian tubes and thus obstructing the passage of eggs to the uterus, was also used by other medical professionals at the time. While not a pleasant procedure—without anesthesia it causes severe cramping similar to bad menstrual cramps or the effects of the insertion of an IUD—it was probably effective, and thus it constituted a permanent form of birth control for women seeking to end their childbearing years. Robert Latou Dickinson and DeVilbiss exchanged information on their experiences with the procedure. The same procedure is still performed today. I am grateful to Takey Crist for this information.

33. Survey Report on Foam Powder and Sponge Cases Prescribed by the Maternal Health Clinic, Miami, Florida, March 1935 to February 1937: Survey of Cases Given Foam Powder but Never Used Method, box 58, folder 7, PPFA-SSC.

34. DeVilbiss to Bangs, [1934], PPFA-SSC. In 1937, DeVilbiss became dissatisfied with the clinic for African Americans and withdrew its funding. She wrote: "Our colored clinic did not turn out the way we thought it would. . . . We shall likely have to re-organize it. I wonder if southern darkies can ever be entrusted with such a clinic. Our experience causes us to doubt their ability to work except under white supervision." Quoted in Gordon, *Woman's Body*, p. 330. The precise cause of DeVilbiss's dissatisfaction with the clinic is unknown.

35. Ella P. Waddill to [Hazel Moore], 5 April 1937, box 23, file 408, CJG-CML.

36. Reed, *From Private Vice*, pp. 225–38.

37. Doone and Greer Williams, *Every Child*, pp. 159–82.

38. Pratt, Travel Narrative, February 1940, box 25, file 432, CJG-CML; Pratt, "Eighteen Months of Health Department Contraceptive Work in North Carolina, 1 April 1937 to 1 October 1938," 1 October 1939, box 2, Misc. Papers, JWRN-SHC.

39. Pratt, Outline Developed in North Carolina State Board of Health for Staff Education Programs for Public Health Nurses in Birth Control Work, 18 October 1939, box 24, file 424, CJG-CML; University News Bureau, "Ninety-three Counties Now Have Contraceptive Services," 24 May 1946, box 26, file 463, CJG-CML.

40. Cooper to Walter W. Point, 28 April 1944, series 3, box 47, folder Birth Control, North Carolina, 1937–1942, PPFA-SSC.

41. From 1935 to 1946, the FSA (and its short-lived predecessor, the Resettlement Administration) provided low-interest loans to impoverished farmers, sharecroppers, and farm laborers to allow them to buy and farm their own land. It established a

broad network of farm labor camps in regions dependent on migrant labor and provided technical and educational support in the hope of eliminating rural poverty. The vigor with which the FSA pursued its mandate established its reputation as one of the most socially conscious of all New Deal programs. The agency was a magnet for highly motivated individuals who shared a passion for social change. Of all the FSA's rehabilitation efforts, perhaps its greatest accomplishments were in the medical care programs established for FSA families. See Grey, *New Deal Medicine*. On the FSA in general, see Baldwin, *Poverty and Politics*, and Hahamovitch, *Fruits of Their Labor*.

42. W. C. Morehead, Outline of Talk Given to FSA Personnel in Special Rural Projects Program, 19 September 1940, series 3, box 45, folder Birth Control, California, FSA Project, 1939–1941, PPFA-SSC.

43. "State Birth Control Program Is Outlined," 30 January 1940, series 3, box 47, folder Birth Control, North Carolina, 1937–1942, PPFA-SSC.

44. Norton, "Health Department" and "Planned Parenthood." See also Maternal Health Project, Second Quarterly Report, 15 November 1937, series 3, box 47, folder Birth Control, North Carolina, 1937–1942, PPFA-SSC; Morehead, Outline of Talk, PPFA-SSC; and Maternal Health Project, First Quarterly Report, 15 July 1937, box 23, file 405, CJG-CML.

45. Quotations in Norton, "Health Department," p. 253.

46. Lawrence, "Something Ought to Be Done about It," 26 April 1935, box 2, Misc. Papers, file Associations . . . Societies, Birth Control Federation of America, JWRN-SHC.

47. W. C. Morehead, "May 1st—The Pioneer Year in Farm Security Special Rural Projects," 8 May 1939, series 3, box 45, folder Birth Control, California, FSA Project, 1939–1941, PPFA-SSC.

48. Quoted in Grey, *New Deal Medicine*, p. 52.

49. One birth control nurse advised FSA agents, "Leading economists and socialists of the country give the four child unit as being the ideal family." Morehead, Outline of Talk, PPFA-SSC.

50. Because they were a contraceptive used by men, condoms had a distinctly unsavory reputation. They were thought to be the chief contraceptive for "sinners" and were closely associated with prostitution, promiscuous sex, vice, and venereal disease. Gordon, *Woman's Body*, pp. 309–10, and Tone, *Devices and Desires*, pp. 183–200.

51. Sylvia Payne to Clarence J. Gamble, 9 February 1942, box 25, file 445, CJG-CML.

52. M. Delp, "My Day: Arizona," 16 January 1940, box 44, file 4, PPFA-SSC. Emphasis in original.

53. Confidential: Survey Report on Foam Powder, PPFA-SSC.

54. Gilbert Beebe, "Watauga County Project: Objectives," 17 August 1939, box 24, file 429, CJG-CML; Weekly Reports on Project in Watauga County, 14 October–11 December 1939, box 24, file 429, and 4 January 1940–7 December 1949, box 25, file 436, both in CJG-CML.

55. Hillard to Claire E. Folsome, 8 April 1942, box 25, file 445, CJG-CML; Payne to Gamble, 17 November 1941.

56. Hillard to Gamble, 14 July 1942, box 25, file 444, CJG-CML.

57. Gamble to Hillard, 9 August 1942, ibid.

58. Gilbert Beebe, "Watauga County Project: Recording Instructions," 19 August 1939, box 24, file 429, CJG-CML.

59. Norton, "Twenty-One Years' Experience."

60. South, Untitled note, 29 September 1937, box 14, file 269, CJG-CML. This is the only reference I have found in which a women expressed any opinion about the testing.

61. Hillard to Youngs Rubber Corporation, 10 February 1941, box 25, file 442, CJG-CML. To distinguish his product from the competition, Merle Youngs, president and treasurer of Youngs Rubber Corporation, began in the mid-1920s to confine Trojan sales to the exclusive drugstore market. He capitalized on a court decision that constructed an erroneous conception of the marketplace in which noble druggists sold condoms to prevent disease, whereas barbers, gas station attendants, and shoe shiners sold them for illicit purposes such as birth control. Only available from "ethical" druggists, Trojans became the country's elite condom. They cost almost twice as much as bargain brands sold at nondrugstore outlets. The primary reason for the high price was the druggists' markup, usually about 300 percent. Tone, *Devices and Desires*, pp. 190–91.

62. Beebe to Cooper, 18 May 1941, box 25, file 442, CJG-CML. Gamble frequently withdrew funding when he had met his research objectives. See, for instance, the description of his jelly project in Berea County, Kentucky, in Louise G. Hutchins, "Three Decades of Family Planning in Appalachia," [1967], folder 437, NCF-SHC.

63. Squier to L. L. Aultz, 7 June 1939, box 44, folder 727, CJG-CML. On the Logan County field trial, see Reed, *From Private Vice*, pp. 247–52.

64. Squier to Aultz, 7 June 1939, CJG-CML.

65. Wulkop to Gamble, 26 September 1936, box 7, folder 135, CJG-CML.

66. Pratt to Gamble, 23 February 1937, box 23, file 403, CJG-CML; Hazel Moore, "Birth Control for the Negro," 1937, box 65, folder 3, PPFA-SSC; "Meeting of the South Atlantic Association of Obstetricians and Gynecologists, 10–11 February 1939," box 24, file 421, CJG-CML; —— to Miss Pratt, n.d., box 2, JWRN-SHC.

67. Frank B. Gilbreth, "State Takes Lead in Birth Control Clinic of South," *Raleigh News and Observer*, 30 June 1940.

68. Wharton, "Birth Control," p. 465. The meaning of this exchange, however, is far from clear. Health officials might have thought about race, or they might have been concerned with high infant and maternal mortality rates. We know neither why state health officials sent county health officers to check their vital statistics nor what county health officials saw when they read those statistics. The only thing we know is that the journalist recounting this incident thought about race.

69. See Beardsley, *History of Neglect*, and Smith, *Sick and Tired*.

70. Of the nine counties in which African Americans made up more than 50 percent of the population, three had no birth control clinics; of the nine counties in which 45 to 50 percent of the population was black, five had no birth control pro-

gram; and of the eighteen counties in which African Americans made up 35 to 45 percent of the population, seven had no birth control clinics. The population figures are taken from the 1940 census.

71. John R. Larkins, "The Negro Population of North Carolina, 1945–1955," North Carolina State Board of Public Welfare, August 1957, North Carolina Collection.

72. Virginia F. South to [Cecil] Damon, 21 October 1937, box 14, folder 269, CJG-CML.

73. Cooper quoted in Roy Norton to Woodbridge E. Morris, 17 November 1939, box 2, JWRN-SHC.

74. Rodrique, "Afro-American Community," pp. 78–79, and Planned Parenthood Federation of America, "A Statement on Behalf of the Planned Parenthood Program for 1945," box 38, file 3, PPFA-SSC. See also Tone, *Devices and Desires*, pp. 85–87.

75. Beardsley, *History of Neglect*, p. 22; Preliminary Annual Report of the Division of Negro Services, reel S62, MS-SSC; Dorothy Boulding Ferebee, Project Reports, 29 January 1942, reel S20, MS-SSC; "Better Health for 13,000,000," [June 1943], box 34, folder 2, PPFA-SSC.

76. Ferebee, Project Reports, MS-SSC.

77. Ibid.

78. Some black intellectuals echoed white eugenicists' concerns about the lower birthrate among the well educated. W. E. B. Du Bois, for instance, disparaged fertility patterns in the black community but opposed the belief that birth control meant race suicide. See "Negroes and Birth Control," April 1939, box 9, folder 4, PPFA-SSC. Others, such as Marcus Garvey, warned that the black race had to be strengthened or it would face elimination. Just as they had exterminated American Indians, Garvey predicted, the "full grown race of white men [would] in turn exterminate the weaker race of black men for the purpose of finding enough room." Such perceptions of the racial struggle made white support for black family planning programs look particularly suspicious. In 1934, Garvey cautioned African Americans not to "accept or practice the theory of birth control." Quoted in Weisbord, *Genocide*, p. 49. See also McCann, *Birth Control Politics*, pp. 154–55.

79. E. Franklin Frazier, "Birth Control for More Negro Babies," *Negro Digest* 3, no. 9 (July 1945), copy consulted in box 34, folder 2, PPFA-SSC.

80. More accurate numbers that would reflect the changes due to the Sheppard-Towner Act are not available. "Public Health Nurses in North Carolina," 10 October 1917, box 1, file Health Officials in North Carolina (lists) 1917–20, DSS-NCSA; Beardsley, *History of Neglect*, p. 140.

81. On black health activism, see Smith, *Sick and Tired*, esp. pp. 58–82.

82. Hazel Moore to Cecil Damon, 14 May 1937, reel S13, MS-SSC.

83. ABCL official to Mrs. Felix Fuld, [1931], box 2, file 6, PPFA-SSC.

84. Sanger to Gamble, 26 November 1939, reel S17, MS-SSC. In fact, offering direct clinic services to African Americans "so that the service [might] be equalized fairly between the whites and the negroes" had already been a goal of the American Birth Control League in the early 1930s. "Southern Conference 1931," box 2, file 6, PPFA-SSC.

85. Gordon, *Woman's Body*, p. 332.

86. Quoted in ibid.

87. Woodbridge E. Morris to John Overton, 6 February 1940, and Morris to Albert D. Lasker, 21 November 1939, both in reel S17, MS-SSC.

88. Sanger to Cecil Damon, 24 November 1939, reel S17, MS-SSC. For further discussion of the differences in the two approaches, see also McCann, *Birth Control Politics*, pp. 161–62.

89. Minutes of Board of Directors Meeting of the Birth Control Federation of America, 7 December 1939, reel S62, MS-SSC; "South Carolina, Moncks Corner, Berkeley County," 10 February 1940, box 36, file 601, CJG-CML; "Better Health for 13,000,000," PPFA-SSC. See also Preliminary Annual Report of the Division of Negro Services, MS-SSC.

90. For eighteen months prior to the establishment of Berkeley County's demonstration project, the county health officer, Dr. William Fishburne, had offered foam powder to women who asked for it, but only 150 women had received contraceptive advice. It is unclear how many of these 150 patients, if any, were African Americans. Additional nurses were added to the Berkeley County public health services to offer birth control at central places throughout the county. In Nashville, John Overton established two additional clinics, one in the Bethlehem Community Center and one in conjunction with Fisk University Settlement House.

91. Planned Parenthood, Untitled pamphlet, [1941], and Minutes of the National Negro Advisory Council Meeting, 9 May 1940, both in reel S62, MS-SSC; "Better Health for 13,000,000," PPFA-SSC.

92. Robert E. Seibels to Sanger, 29 January 1940, reel S17, MS-SSC; Planned Parenthood, [1941], MS-SSC; "Better Health for 13,000,000," PPFA-SSC. These findings mirrored those in other parts of the country. Data from the Harlem Clinic, for instance, indicated that about 50 percent of its patients were found to need medical or surgical treatment. See "Race Leaders Endorse Vitally Important Program," *New York Age*, 11 April 1942, copy consulted in reel S21, MS-SSC.

93. "Better Health for 13,000,000," PPFA-SSC.

94. Ibid.

95. Report on Counties' Participation in Maternal Health Program, n.d., series 3, box 47, file Birth Control, South Carolina, 1939–42, PPFA-SSC.

96. See note above regarding DeVilbiss's dissatisfaction with the birth control clinic she established for African American women in Miami. DeVilbiss to Bangs, [1934], PPFA-SSC, and DeVilbiss to Sanger, 30 September 1936, both in MS-SSC; Gordon, *Woman's Body*, pp. 309–10, 330.

97. Planned Parenthood Federation of America, "A Statement on Behalf of the Planned Parenthood Program for 1945," PPFA-SSC.

98. Of 3,000 African American physicians contacted by 1943, for instance, more than 600 had requested information and volunteered their services. See "Better Health for 13,000,000," PPFA-SSC. Of 5,000 county health officers contacted by the DNS, 300 had requested exhibits and leaflets by 1942. The DNS reported with satis-

faction that the largest response had come from states with large African American populations. "News from the Division of Negro Services," 1942, reel S62, MS-SSC; "Finds Negro Doctors: Health Men Welcome Birth Control Program," [early 1940s], box 9, file 4, PPFA-SSC.

99. John W. Mitchell to Sanger, 18 July 1941, reel S19, MS-SSC.

100. Minutes of the National Advisory Council Meeting, 11 December 1942, reel S65, MS-SSC.

101. Ibid. and Ferebee, Project Reports, MS-SSC.

102. Florence Rose to Sanger, 19 February 1944, reel S23, MS-SSC. On the shift in policy, see McCann, *Birth Control Politics*, pp. 167–68; "Program to Enlist Interest and Cooperation of Negroes," January 1944, box 38, file 3, PPFA-SSC; and D. Kenneth Rose to Mrs. Felix Fuld, 14 July 1943, reel S23, MS-SSC.

103. Edith Turner to Dr. Roy Norton, 8 December 1938, box 2, JWRN-SHC.

104. Ibid.

105. The older that women were, the more likely they were to have used birth control. While only 37.4 percent of women under age twenty reported having used contraceptives, 62.5 percent of women age forty-five or older had tried some method. The average number of pregnancies for contraceptive users in their twenties and early thirties was 3.57, while nonusers had had an average of 3.67 pregnancies. The greatest difference existed among women forty-five years old or older. Nonusers in that age bracket had an average of 8.83 children, while users had an average of 6.9 children. Mildred Delp, "Baby Spacing: A Report on California and Arizona, March–August 1940," box 44, folder 4, PPFA-SSC. See Tone, *Devices and Desires*, for a fuller discussion of contraceptives available outside a physician's office in the 1930s and 1940s.

106. As part of the New Orleans Metropolitan Family Survey, researchers quizzed respondents about their knowledge of reproductive physiology and the ovulation cycle and inquired about their contraceptive usage, desired family size, and feelings about family planning. Eighty-seven percent of the respondents knew nothing about the ovulation cycle, and only half had any knowledge of the union of sperm and ovum. Ward, *Poor Women*, pp. 47–49, esp. p. 48. On ignorance regarding sex education and contraception, see also Crist, "Contraceptive Practices" and "Why Is It."

107. Quoted in M. Delp, "My Day: Arizona," 23 July 1940, box 44, folder 4, PPFA-SSC.

108. Morehead, Outline of Talk, PPFA-SSC.

109. Virginia F. South to [Cecil] Damon, 6 October 1937, box 14, folder 269, CJG-CML, and W. C. Morehead, Rural Projects Program Outline, October 1940, series 3, box 45, folder Birth Control, California, FSA Project, 1939–1941, PPFA-SSC.

110. Morehead, "May 1st," PPFA-SSC.

111. Quoted in James W. Kirkpatrick and Ann Winters, "Planned Parenthood—A Public Welfare Responsibility," May 1967, appendix C, p. 10, unpublished manuscript.

112. South, Travel notes, 4 October 1937, box 14, folder 269, CJG-CML.

113. Morehead, Rural Projects Program Outline, PPFA-SSC.

114. Weekly Reports on Project in Watauga County, 11 September–15 December 1939, CJG-CML.

115. Welch, "Planned Parenthood Services," pp. 146–47. On mistrust of the medical profession, see South, 29 September 1937, CJG-CML. On husbands' opposition, see W. C. Morehead, "Nebraska: Region VII, January 27 to May 18, 1941," series 3, box 47, folder Birth Control, Nebraska, 1941, PPFA-SSC.

116. Morehead, Rural Projects Program Outline, PPFA-SSC.

117. Morehead, Outline of Talk, PPFA-SSC.

118. Delp, "Baby Spacing," PPFA-SSC.

119. "Better Health for 13,000,000," PPFA-SSC.

120. Grey, *New Deal Medicine*, p. 7. See also Morehead, "May 1st," PPFA-SSC, and DeVilbiss to Sanger, 10 September 1935, MS-SSC.

121. Morehead, Outline of Talk, PPFA-SSC.

122. Morehead, "May 1st," PPFA-SSC.

123. Quoted in South to Damon, 21 October 1937, CJG-CML.

124. For an example of health professionals boycotting the distribution of birth control, see Hazel Moore to Gamble, memo, 3 March 1938, box 24, file 418, CJG-CML. On health professionals misinforming patients, see [South] to [Cecil] Damon, 1 October 1937, box 14, folder 269, CJG-CML. On physicians' fear of professional competition, see Gamble to Dr. Hageman, 16 June 1941, box 25, file 442, CJG-CML. On religious opposition, see Morehead, "May 1st" and "Nebraska," both in PPFA-SSC.

125. Reed, *From Private Vice*, pp. 267–68.

126. Quoted in Moore to Gamble, memo, 3 March 1938, CJG-CML. See also McCann, *Birth Control Politics*, pp. 198–200.

127. Tennessee was one state that received such a threat. Because the Children's Bureau distributed Social Security funds, it was a force to be reckoned with. Gamble to Cooper, 23 May 1938, box 24, file 415, CJG-CML.

128. Delp, "Baby Spacing," PPFA-SSC. Delp reports that foam powder units were established following her example both in Mendocino County at the request of the health officer and in the Yuba County Hospital in Marysville, California.

129. Rhode Island Birth Control League, Annual Report, 1935, box 4, folder 6, PPFA-SSC; Delaware League for Planned Parenthood, Inc., Annual Report, 1946, series 3, box 14, folder PPFA—Annual Meeting, State League Reports, 1947, PPFA-SSC; Morehead, Rural Projects Program Outline, PPFA-SSC.

130. H. Curtis Wood Jr., Pennsylvania League for Planned Parenthood: Report to the National Annual Meeting, 21 January 1947, series 3, box 14, folder PPFA—Annual Meeting, State League Reports, 1947, PPFA-SSC.

131. Morehead, "Nebraska," PPFA-SSC.

132. Morehead, "May 1st," PPFA-SSC.

133. Morehead, Rural Projects Program Outline, PPFA-SSC.

134. See, e.g., Cooper to Dr. Cecil A. Damon, 25 January 1938, box 24, file 415, CJG-CML, and Florence Rose to Sanger, 8 December 1942, reel S21, MS-SSC.

135. Norton, "Twenty-One Years' Experience," p. 997.

136. Ibid., p. 998.

137. Gamble to Cooper, 12 August 1940, box 25, file 433, CJG-CML.

138. Doone and Greer Williams, *Every Child*, pp. 137–45.

139. Ibid., pp. 144–45. In 1940, when Gamble ceased to support the program, North Carolina health officials reported that it had 3,233 patients. The number rose to 4,441 patients in 1948 and then fell to almost half that number in the late 1950s. Norton, "Twenty-One Years' Experience."

140. Reed, *From Private Vice*, p. 266, and Grey, *New Deal Medicine*, pp. 9–11.

141. Beardsley, *History of Neglect*, pp. 174–78, 247.

142. By 1960, it was almost unheard of outside of some isolated rural areas for American women to deliver their babies at home. Leavitt, *Brought to Bed*, pp. 171, 174, 194.

143. See Abramovitz, *Regulating the Lives of Women*, pp. 319, 321, and Bell, *Aid to Dependent Children*, pp. 40–56.

144. In Alabama, for instance, the number of new patients quadrupled in eighteen months. Frederick S. Jaffe, "Family Planning and Rural Poverty: An Approach to Programming of Services," June 1967, p. 27, folder 436, NCF-SHC, and Hutchins, "Three Decades of Family Planning," NCF-SHC.

145. Frederick C. McKee, Fund-raising letter, 3 August 1954, reel S44, MS-SSC.

146. By the early 1960s, the U.S. Department of Health, Education, and Welfare had begun to encourage the establishment of family planning programs. The 1962 U.S. public welfare laws, part of the War on Poverty, provided money that could be used for family planning services. In 1965, amendments to the Social Security Act required that state health departments extend services, including family planning, to all areas of the country. State health departments were given a decade to put these services in place. Grants were available for rural poverty pockets and distressed urban areas. The following year, the Department of Health, Education, and Welfare officially encouraged the distribution of birth control through government agencies. And with the passage of the 1967 amendments to the Social Security Act, all state departments of public welfare were required to provide family planning services to welfare recipients. Family planners could exploit this extended eligibility to offer a wide range of maternal and child care services.

147. In 1970, the federal government expanded family planning programs further when it passed the Family Planning Services and Population Research Act, which mandated the development of family planning programs on the state level. Critchlow, *Intended Consequences*, pp. 50–111.

148. Ibid., p. 85.

149. Boger, *Charlotte 23*, pp. 159–71.

150. Kuralt, interview; Cloer, Hicks, and Anderson, interview; Wall, interview.

151. Ward, *Poor Women*, pp. 17, 26.

152. Quoted in ibid., p. 23.

153. Quoted in Kirkpatrick and Winters, "Planned Parenthood," appendix C, p. 3.

154. In 1966, public and private agencies reached only 13 percent of potential family

planning patients among the poor. Research in Louisiana revealed that 68 percent of patients, although still in their early reproductive years, had already reached or exceeded the family size they had thought desirable when first married or pregnant. Frederick S. Jaffe, "Rural Family Planning Programs," May 1967, folder 427, NCF-SHC; Ward, *Poor Women*, p. 49; Darity, "Contraceptive Education."

155. Kuralt, "Public Welfare Agency," p. 8; Ward, *Poor Women*, pp. 24–25. See also Hulka, "How Much Does Family Planning Cost?"

156. Cloer, Hicks, and Anderson, interview.

157. Kuralt to Donald H. Winkler, 20 March 1964, FA-UNCC; Richard C. Bayer, "Mecklenburg and the Pill," *Raleigh News and Observer*, 19 June 1966.

158. While none of the staff members formally told Ward about this practice, comments she collected led her to conclude that staff members made such referrals "rather than see [their patients] go to 'butchers' in desperation." *Poor Women*, p. 58.

159. Shepherd, "Birth Control," pp. 63–67, esp. p. 66; Kuralt, "Public Welfare Agency," pp. 7–8; Ward, *Poor Women*, pp. 56–58; Cloer, Hicks, and Anderson, interview.

160. Since no other statewide program existed in the United States at that time, it is difficult to compare the Louisiana program with other efforts. Ward, *Poor Women*, pp. 62–65.

161. Within three years of its inception, the Mecklenburg County family planning clinic was serving 800 women between the ages of fourteen and forty-seven; two years later, the number had climbed to 2,200 women, and by September 1965, 3,388 women had registered to use the clinic. Kirkpatrick and Winters, "Planned Parenthood"; Corkey, "Birth Control Program," p. 45; Cloer, Hicks, and Anderson, interview; Wall, interview.

162. Kuralt to Winkler, 20 March 1964, FA-UNCC.

163. Quoted in Tom Inman, "Birth Control Working in East," *Raleigh News and Observer*, 10 July 1963.

164. "More than 150 Women Try Experimental Birth Control Device," *Raleigh News and Observer*, 30 January 1964.

165. Tone, *Devices and Desires*, pp. 268–69. On patient interest in the IUD, see also Sheri S. Tepper, "Colorado: Family Planning Programs in Rural Areas," folder 437, NCF-SHC.

166. Inman, "Birth Control Working in the East." See also E. Stewart Allen, "Arkansas: Results of the First Three Years," folder 437, NCF-SHC.

167. Ward, *Poor Women*, pp. 30–31.

168. "Social Work Services in Family Planning: A Course Outline for the Use of Staff Development Personnel in Public Welfare," July 1967, series 1967–68, box 1143, file 4-4-1-1-9, CB-NA.

169. "North Carolina Public Health Department Family Planning Program: Historical Background," [1968], p. 12, box 9, folder Planned Parenthood—World Population, 1968–1973, EBW-UNCG.

170. Jaffe, "Rural Family Planning Programs," NCF-SHC. The report surveyed family planning services in Appalachia, Florida, Colorado, Arkansas, Pennsylvania, North Carolina, and Alabama. In addition, it analyzed services for migrant workers and Native Americans. A 1969 report noted that Mecklenburg County was leading the state of North Carolina in the delivery of birth control services; it had 6,208 family planning clients between 1960 and 1967. Second was Durham County with 1,609, little more than a quarter of Mecklenburg County's caseload. Only seven North Carolina counties carried more than 1,000 family planning clients in the seven years. Twenty-six counties had fewer than 100 clients in their family planning clinics, and two counties had no clients at all. Tyrrell, Gates, and Mecklenburg Counties were leading the state, with Tyrrell County covering 75 percent and Gates and Mecklenburg Counties covering 55 percent of the potential clients between 1960 and 1967. Eighty counties met less than one-quarter of the estimated needs in their area, and thirty-five counties met the needs of fewer than 10 percent of potential clients. James E. Allen, "The Struggle for Institutionalization of Family Planning Care in Guilford County, North Carolina," April 1969, CPC-UNC.

171. Robert H. Browning, "Florida: Bringing the Service to the Patient," folder 437, NCF-SHC.

172. "Tape 22: UNC Infirmary—Coed Requests Pill," [early 1970s], TCP-DUWA. See also Jaffe, "Rural Family Planning Programs," NCF-SHC.

173. See, e.g., "Tape 19: Coed Refused Pills #2"; "Tape 22: UNC Infirmary—Coed Requests Pill"; "Tape 22: Coed Requesting Pill, Boyfriend Brazilian MD"; and "Tape 25: Seventeen-Year-Old Wants Pills," all in TCP-DUWA.

174. "Birth Control Seen as Aimed at Negroes," *Raleigh News and Observer*, 20 November 1968.

175. Elizabeth C. Corkey, "North Carolina: Family Planning in a Rural Maternity Clinic," [1967], folder 437, NCF-SHC, and Ward, *Poor Women*, p. 58.

176. Ward, *Poor Women*, pp. 92–93, and Caron, "Birth Control."

177. Quoted in Caron, "Birth Control," p. 554.

178. Ibid., esp. pp. 559–60.

179. FPI was already a racially and economically integrated workplace. At one time, FPI employed over one thousand people, 81 percent of them women and 52 percent members of racial minorities, largely from the disadvantaged neighborhoods the program served. Members of these groups held 78 percent of all management and professional positions in the organization. By the early 1970s, however, the original management staff of researchers had been replaced with a managerial staff less concerned with open lines of communication. The hiring of black militants further amplified problems of poor communication and allegations of financial abuse, which eventually led to an investigation and the subsequent closing of the foundation. Ward, *Poor Women*, pp. 131–32. For a denial of the charges of financial misdealing, see Russell H. Richardson, "Patterns and Progress in the Promotion of Family Planning in the Southeastern United States" (paper delivered at the 1969 annual meeting of the

Population Association of America, 10 April 1969), box 9, folder Planned Parenthood—World Population, 1968–1973, EBW-UNCG. See also Carl S. Shultz to Arthur J. Lesser, 29 July 1968, series 1967–1968, box 1142, folder 4-4-1-1-9, November 1968, CB-NA.

180. Critchlow, *Intended Consequences*, p. 227.

181. Having demonstrated that family planning services could be delivered en masse to poor women and that the Louisiana model could be exported, Joe Beasley, for instance, received a grant from AID to explore the feasibility of similar programs in a number of Latin American countries. Ward, *Poor Women*, pp. 69–73. See also Tone, *Devices and Desires*, pp. 265–68.

182. Preliminary Annual Report of the Division of Negro Services, MS-SSC, and Rose to Sanger, 8 December 1942, MS-SSC.

183. See Correa and Petchesky, "Reproductive and Sexual Rights," pp. 107–23. While one could correctly argue that most decisions are conditioned by outside factors, Lopez points out that some people have more social space to make decisions than others. "Agency and Constraint," pp. 157–71.

CHAPTER TWO

1. *Cox v. Stanton*, 381 F. Supp. 349 (9th Cir. 1974), Appellant's Brief, p. 3.

2. See Shapiro, *Population Control Politics*; Angela Davis, *Women, Race, and Class*; Dreifus, "Sterilizing the Poor"; Reilly, *Surgical Solution*; Kline, *Building a Better Race*; and Carey, "Gender and Compulsory Sterilization." For a discussion of sterilization in the larger context of fertility control, see also Gordon, *Woman's Body*, pp. 400–402; Hartmann, *Reproductive Rights*, chapter 13; and Petchesky, *Abortion and Woman's Choice*, pp. 178–82.

3. See *Cox v. Stanton*; "Second Suit Hits Sterilization," *Raleigh News and Observer*, 23 January 1974; *Relf v. Weinberger et al.*, 372 F. Supp. 1196 (D.D.C. 1974); *Relf v. Matthews*, 403 F. Supp. 1235 (D.D.C. 1975); *Relf v. Weinberger*, 565 F.2d 722 (D.C. Cir. 1977); Reilly, *Surgical Solution*, pp. 148–52; Shapiro, *Population Control Politics*, pp. 89–94; and Hartmann, *Reproductive Rights*.

4. *Federal Register* 43, no. 217 (8 November 1978): 52146–75, as cited in Petchesky, "Reproduction," p. 312, n. 1. The Committee to End Sterilization Abuse, founded in 1974, and the Committee for Abortion Rights and against Sterilization Abuse are among the organizations that lobbied for legislative guidelines regarding sterilization. On the regulations, see Petchesky, "Reproduction." An international condemnation of sterilization abuse came in 1994 in the form of the United Nations International Conference on Population and Development's *Programme of Action* (par. 7.2), which defined "reproductive rights" as the right of every couple and individual "to make decisions concerning reproduction free of discrimination, coercion and violence, as expressed in human rights documents."

5. *Cox v. Stanton* and Davis, interview. For charges of race genocide, see "N.C. Fam-

ily Planning Needs Aren't Met," *Raleigh News and Observer*, 29 October 1969, and "Sterilization System Rapped," *Raleigh News and Observer*, 15 February 1974.

6. The names in this and all of the following Eugenics Board cases are pseudonyms. See Hearing Case 1, EBM, 28 June 1966, EB-NCSA.

7. Hearing Case 1, EBM, 28 June 1966, EB-NCSA. By giving Shirley's husband the power to veto his wife's decision in favor of sterilization, the Eugenics Board followed the practice of North Carolina's 1963 voluntary sterilization law. Intended to make sterilization more easily accessible, the law permitted anyone twenty-one years of age or older who desired the operation to be sterilized. However, the law required the written consent of a spouse if those seeking sterilization were married. Although the Eugenics Board was not bound by this regulation, it followed the policy in practice, ironically making it more difficult for individuals to seek the surgery over their spouses' opposition. Rhodes, "President's Message."

8. Crist and Hendricks, interview.

9. Petchesky, *Abortion and Woman's Choice*, chapter 5.

10. See, for example, Edward Larson's description of sterilization practices in South Carolina, where county welfare agencies regularly asked the mental health hospital to admit local women for the sole purpose of sterilizing them, and Molly Ladd-Taylor's description of women who were admitted to the State School for the Feeble-minded in Minnesota with the expectation that they would be sterilized and released; Ladd-Taylor emphasizes the central role that social workers played in such cases. Larson, *Sex, Race, and Science*, p. 155; Ladd-Taylor, "Saving Babies," pp. 145–47; Kline, *Building a Better Race*, p. 53. On similar practices in California and Virginia, see Gosney and Popenoe, *Sterilization*, pp. 60–62, and Bishop, "Sterilization Survivors."

11. *Brewer v. Valk*, 204 N.C. 378 (1932), p. 22.

12. Ibid., p. 13.

13. Ibid., pp. 8–9.

14. See Brown, *Eugenical Sterilization*. See also *General Statutes of North Carolina*, 1943, chap. 35, 36, as cited in Bradway, "Legality of Human Sterilization"; *Biennial Report of the Eugenics Board of North Carolina*, serial, 30 June 1934 to 1 July 1968. For general information on *Buck v. Bell*, see Smith and Nelson, *Sterilization of Carrie Buck*; Carey, "Gender and Compulsory Sterilization"; Lombardo, "Eugenic Sterilization"; Reilly, *Surgical Solution*, pp. 88, 129, 137; and Woodside, *Sterilization in North Carolina*, p. 194. Alabama, California, Connecticut, Delaware, Idaho, Indiana, Iowa, Kansas, Maine, Michigan, Minnesota, Montana, Nebraska, New Hampshire, New York, North Dakota, Oregon, South Dakota, Utah, Virginia, Washington, and Wisconsin had all passed eugenic sterilization legislation prior to *Buck v. Bell*. Arizona, Georgia, Mississippi, North Carolina, Oklahoma, South Carolina, Vermont, and West Virginia all passed eugenic sterilization legislation after *Buck v. Bell*.

15. Carey, "Gender and Compulsory Sterilization"; Reilly, *Surgical Solution*, pp. 129, 137, 158; Kline, *Building a Better Race*.

16. Brown, *Eugenical Sterilization*, p. 21.

17. See ibid. and *General Statutes of North Carolina*, chap. 35, art. 7.

18. See Popenoe and Johnson, *Applied Eugenics*, p. 74; Goddard, *Kallikak Family*; and Kevles, *In the Name of Eugenics*, pp. 46–49.

19. Brown, *Definition of a Profession*, and Gould, *Mismeasure of Man*, pp. 146–233.

20. Pernick, "Eugenics and Public Health," p. 1769, and *Black Stork*, pp. 52–53.

21. Ladd-Taylor notes that "incompetent mothering . . . was not only thought to produce feeblemindedness in children; it was also considered evidence of mental 'deficiency' in adults." "Saving Babies," pp. 146–47.

22. Case 5, EBM, 29 August 1934, EB-NCSA.

23. Cases 2, 3, and 4, EBM, 19 October 1934, EB-NCSA. For information on the family history, see Hearing Case 3, EBM, 28 April 1948, EB-NCSA.

24. Case 3, EBM, 13 October 1937, EB-NCSA.

25. Hearing Case 2, EBM, 15 May 1940, EB-NCSA.

26. Hearing Case 3, EBM, 17 March 1943, EB-NCSA.

27. Hearing Case 1, EBM, 26 November 1947, EB-NCSA. Unfortunately, the transcript of this hearing is closed. The only record accessible is the summary of the petition.

28. This decision followed a final hearing at which Tom Bodwin, his lawyer, and his daughter Laura continued to voice their objection. See Hearing Case 5, EBM, 26 May 1948, EB-NCSA.

29. Reports Received since October Meeting of Operations Performed, EBM, 24 November 1948, EB-NCSA.

30. See, e.g., Hearing Case, EBM, 25 July 1945; Hearing Case 1, EBM, 22 January 1936; Hearing Case 1, EBM, 2 December 1936; Hearing Case 2, EBM, 16 March 1938; and Hearing Case 2, EBM, 20 April 1938, all in EB-NCSA.

31. Hearing Case, EBM, 25 July 1945, EB-NCSA.

32. See, e.g., Case 8, EBM, 18 February 1942; Case 8, EBM, 27 September 1944; Hearing Case 4, EBM, 26 May 1948; Case 15, EBM, 25 July 1951; Hearing Case 2, EBM, 16 March 1938; and Hearing Case 2, EBM, 20 April 1938, all in EB-NCSA.

33. I identified 238 families involving 549 individuals whose sterilization petitions were considered by the North Carolina Eugenics Board. It is likely, however, that the number of families targeted was two to three times as high. I tracked family lineage by last name and county of residency. But as soon as a woman got married and adopted her husband's last name, I was no longer able to identify her as a member of her original family group. In most multicase families, two family members were sterilized, but occasionally health and welfare professionals sought the sterilization of entire family groups. I identified several cases in which petitions were filed for the sterilization of five siblings and one case in which petitions were filed for eleven members of the same family group.

34. Hearing Case 3, EBM, 20 April 1938, EB-NCSA.

35. Hearing Case 2, EBM, 20 April 1938, EB-NCSA. See also Hearing Case 1, EBM, 17 August 1938, and Hearing Case 1, EBM, 2 December 1936, EB-NCSA. One mother blamed her daughter's mental troubles on the fact that her husband had been drunk

at the time of conception, thus "marking" the girl. Hearing Case 1, EBM, 28 July 1943, EB-NCSA.

36. Hearing Case 1, EBM, 19 August 1936, EB-NCSA. For a similar argument, see Hearing Case, EBM, 25 July 1945, EB-NCSA.

37. Hearing Case 2, EBM, 16 March 1938, EB-NCSA.

38. Ibid. and Hearing Case, EBM, 25 July 1945, EB-NCSA.

39. Hearing Case 2, EBM, 16 March 1938, EB-NCSA. For the same argument, see Hearing Case, EBM, 20 April 1938, EB-NCSA.

40. Hearing Case, EBM, 21 September 1938, and Hearing Case, 17 August 1938, both in EB-NCSA.

41. On overwork, see Hearing Case, EBM, 25 July 1945. In Hearing Case, EBM, 20 April 1938, a father blamed the mental condition of his daughter on the fact that she was locked up in a room in the county home for fear that she might otherwise associate with the male residents of the home. Both in EB-NCSA.

42. Hearing Case, EBM, 25 July 1945, EB-NCSA.

43. Ibid.

44. "Definitions of Feeblemindedness," General file, box 7, folder Policies and Practices of the Eugenics Board, SS-NCSA. This 1908 definition is taken from the British Royal Commission on the Feebleminded and was provided for North Carolina officials concerned with identifying the feebleminded for sterilization.

45. North Carolina Commission for the Study of the Care of the Insane and Mental Defectives, *Study of Mental Health*, pp. 252–53. See also Degler, *In Search of Human Nature*, p. 40, and DeVilbiss to Sanger, 10 September 1935, reel S10, MS-SSC.

46. George H. Lawrence, "A Study Relating to Mental Illness, Mental Deficiency, and Epilepsy in a Selected Rural County," May 1948, p. 14, General file, box 7, folder Woodside Study, SS-NCSA.

47. A study by eugenicist Paul Popenoe of sterilizations performed in California between 1909 and 1929 shows that "economically dependent" men and women were three times as likely to be sterilized as those who were more prosperous. "Economic and Social Status," p. 24. See also Ladd-Taylor, "Saving Babies," p. 144, and Bishop, "Sterilization Survivors," p. 15.

48. Of 800 sterilization petitions—a sample of 10 percent of the total number of petitions—147 (18.4 percent of the sample) gave information about the candidate's work history. Forty-one households with sterilization candidates (28 percent of the 147 petitions) received ADC payments, while 63 (43 percent) received other benefits. Thirty-nine potential patients (26 percent) were described as unable to work.

49. Information about the physical condition of clients' housing was available in 67 cases (8.4 percent) from the sample in the note above. Fifty-seven candidates (85 percent of the 67 cases) lived in inadequate housing, and 37 (55 percent) lived under overcrowded conditions. In 14 cases (21 percent), houses were in poor repair, and in 11 cases (16 percent) houses were poorly furnished. Six families (9 percent) lacked some or all conveniences.

50. See Case 2, EBM, 28 August 1956, EB-NCSA. For a twenty-five-year-old mother

who lived with her three children in only one room, see also Case 24, EBM, 25 April 1951, EB-NCSA.

51. While overall rates of illiteracy had dropped to 13 percent in 1930, 27.7 percent of African Americans over the age of twenty-one were illiterate. Among the rural farm population, white illiteracy rates stood at 10.4 percent, while rates for African Americans stood at 32.6 percent. Figures compiled from the 1930 census.

52. For a father's inability to pay book rent, see Hearing Case 2, EBM, 20 April 1938. For children who could not attend school because they needed to help with the harvest, see Hearing Case 1, EBM, 21 September 1938. See also Hearing Case 2, EBM, 16 March 1938. All in EB-NCSA.

53. Ladd-Taylor, "Saving Babies."

54. *Brewer v. Valk*, p. 13.

55. DeVilbiss to Sanger, 10 September 1935, MS-SSC. See also EBM, 24 October 1961, 23 and 27 October 1962, EB-NCSA.

56. Hearing Case 1, EBM, 17 August 1938; Hearing Case 1, EBM, 2 December 1936; Hearing Case 2 and 3, EBM, 20 April 1938, all in EB-NCSA.

57. Hearing Case 2, EBM, 2 December 1936, EB-NCSA.

58. Hearing Case 2, EBM, 15 June 1938; Hearing Case 1, EBM, 19 August 1936; Hearing Case 1, EBM, 21 July 1937; Hearing Case 2, EBM, 16 March 1938, all in EB-NCSA.

59. Hearing Case 1, EBM, 27 April 1965, EB-NCSA.

60. Hearing Case 1, EBM, 19 June 1940, EB-NCSA.

61. See, e.g., Hearing Case, EBM, 25 July 1945, and Hearing Case 1, EBM, 19 June 1940, both in EB-NCSA.

62. Hearing Case, EBM, 25 July 1945, EB-NCSA.

63. Ibid.

64. Hearing Case 1, EBM, 27 April 1965, EB-NCSA.

65. Hearing Case 1, EBM, 19 August 1936, EB-NCSA.

66. Kevles, *In the Name of Eugenics*, p. 53, and Davenport, "Feebly Inhibited," p. 608.

67. Rosenberg, *No Other Gods*, p. 94.

68. Dugdale, *Jukes*, pp. 13, 60–61, 64.

69. Marian S. Olden, *The ABC of Human Conservation*, publication no. 31 (Princeton, N.J.: Birthright, [1946]), pp. 6–7, copy consulted in series 1, box 2, folder 77, HBL-SHC.

70. *Report of the Committee on Caswell Training School*, p. 15.

71. Ibid.

72. Lawrence, "Study Relating to Mental Illness," pp. 7, 10, SS-NCSA. Other states mirrored these findings. Seventy-five percent of those sterilized in California, for instance, were considered to be "sex delinquents." Gosney and Popenoe, *Sterilization*, p. 40.

73. Hearing Case, EBM, 25 January 1955, EB-NCSA. It was not unusual for health and welfare professionals across the country to refer promiscuous daughters to welfare departments for sterilization. See, for example, the recommendation by an agent of the FSA to leave such regulation of sexuality to welfare departments: W. C. More-

head, Outline of Talk Given to FSA Personnel in Special Rural Projects Program, 19 September 1940, series 3, box 45, folder Birth Control, California, FSA Project, 1939–1941, PPFA-SSC.

74. One hundred seventy-eight of 800 cases in my sample (22 percent) included information about sexual behavior. One hundred forty-two of those clients were described as sexually promiscuous. In 44 petitions, patients were described as victims of rape or incest or as likely to be taken advantage of. Several cases contain more than one observation about a patient's sexuality.

75. Reilly, *Surgical Solution*, pp. 94–95, 99; Carey, "Gender and Compulsory Sterilization," pp. 84–85 and 101, n. 11; Kline, *Building a Better Race*, p. 53. Other states also had a high percentage of female sterilizations. Seventy-nine percent of individuals sterilized in Minnesota between 1926 and 1946, for instance, were female. Most sterilized women in that state fell into two general categories: they were either sex "delinquents" or older women who had a number of children on welfare. Ladd-Taylor, "Saving Babies," pp. 145, 149, and Bishop, "Sterilization Survivors," p. 14.

76. Hearing Case 3, EBM, 20 April 1938, EB-NCSA. See also Case 3, EBM, 26 April 1966; Case 17, EBM, 24 March 1964; and Case 9, EBM, 26 January 1960, all in EB-NCSA.

77. See, e.g., Case 1, EBM, 26 July 1944; Case 17, EBM, 23 January 1946; Case 5, EBM, 22 January 1947; Case 1, EBM, 26 February 1947; Cases 4 and 15, EBM, 25 February 1948; Case 1, EBM, 26 May 1948; Case 9, EBM, 23 February 1949; Case 2, EBM, 24 February 1954; Case 6, EBM, 22 October 1963; Case 17, EBM, 24 March 1964; and Case 9, EBM, 25 May 1965, all in EB-NCSA.

78. Hearing Case, EBM, 25 July 1945, EB-NCSA. One woman protesting the sterilization of her younger sister assured Eugenics Board members that her sister had behaved well when the two lived together: "She was quiet and worked just like I did. She was very good. She minded me." Hearing Case 2, EBM, 16 March 1938, EB-NCSA.

79. See, e.g., Hearing Case 2, EBM, 20 April 1938, and Hearing Case 1, EBM, 15 June 1938, both in EB-NCSA.

80. Hearing Case 1, EBM, 27 April 1965, EB-NCSA.

81. Ibid., p. 6.

82. Hearing Case 1, EBM, 15 June 1938, EB-NCSA.

83. Hearing Case 2, EBM, 20 April 1938, EB-NCSA.

84. Hearing Case 1, EBM, 15 June 1938, EB-NCSA.

85. Hearing Case 2, EBM, 20 April 1938, EB-NCSA.

86. Hearing Case 1, EBM, 15 June 1938, EB-NCSA.

87. For arguments about savings and earnings, see Hearing Case 1, EBM, 27 April 1965, and Hearing Case 1, EBM, 19 August 1936, both in EB-NCSA.

88. EBM, 27 July 1961, EB-NCSA.

89. Health and welfare authorities across the country looked to sterilization as a model of progressive welfare policy. See, e.g., Margaret Sanger, Address to the Human Betterment Federation of Des Moines, February 1951, reel S72, MS-SSC.

90. Case 39, EBM, 24 May 1955, EB-NCSA.

91. Case 40, EBM, 24 May 1955, EB-NCSA.

92. Case 16, EBM, 26 November 1954, EB-NCSA.

93. Case 19, EBM, 23 June 1954, EB-NCSA.

94. Hearing Case 2, EBM, 20 April 1938, EB-NCSA. See also Hearing Case 3, EBM, 20 April 1938, and Hearing Case 1, EBM, 2 December 1936, both in EB-NCSA.

95. See Case 13, EBM, 27 June 1945; Case 15, EBM, 1 September 1954; Case 5, EBM, 12 June 1959; and Case 12, EBM, 23 January 1952, all in EB-NCSA.

96. Case 2, EBM, 27 October 1964, EB-NCSA.

97. Case 3, EBM, 25 June 1952, EB-NCSA.

98. Case 10, EBM, 25 November 1958, EB-NCSA. For other cases like this, see, e.g., Case 15, EBM, 27 June 1945; Case 21, EBM, 25 January 1950; Case 36, EBM, 28 March 1951; Case 23, EBM, 25 June 1952; and Case 14, EBM, 24 September 1952, all in EB-NCSA.

99. Case 13, EBM, 22 March 1955. See also Case 7, EBM, 22 March 1955. Both in EB-NCSA.

100. Case 28, EBM, 27 September 1950, EB-NCSA.

101. Case 13, EBM, 28 March 1961, EB-NCSA. See also Case 3, EBM, 28 July 1948, and Case 11, EBM, 22 October 1963, both in EB-NCSA.

102. Pressman, *Last Resort*, p. 198. For comparison, see his insightful discussion of the uses of lobotomy in the 1950s, pp. 194–99.

103. Minutes of the EBMs, January 1937–June 1966, EB-NCSA. Similar changes occurred in Virginia, where the incidence of institutional sterilization had drastically declined by the mid-1950s. Only 10 percent of the sterilizations carried out in that state were performed between 1955 and 1971, while 90 percent were performed between 1924 and 1954. Thanks to Paul Lombardo from the University of Virginia for the relevant sterilization statistics. For more information on the growing skepticism of psychiatrists toward eugenic sterilization, see the discussion later in chapter 2.

104. For a more thorough discussion of changes in psychiatric treatment, see Pressman, *Last Resort*, and Grob, *Mad Among Us*.

105. See, e.g., Case 8, EBM, 22 July 1942; Case 28, EBM, 26 July 1950; Case 15, EBM, 22 October 1957; Case 13, EBM, 26 August 1958; Cases 6 and 7, EBM, 23 September 1958; Case 9, EBM, 27 January 1959; and Case 11, EBM, 28 November 1961, all in EB-NCSA. One former Eugenics Board member remembered parents of retarded children who begged the Eugenics Board to authorize the surgery for their children. Koomen, interview. See also Case 20, EBM, 26 January 1965, EB-NCSA.

106. Hearing Case 1, EBM, 21 July 1937, EB-NCSA.

107. Case 14, EBM, 27 October 1964, EB-NCSA. Sterilizations for girls who had been victims of incest were also relatively common. "Even if [the] patient does not seek out men," a social worker argued, "sterilization will protect her against their advances." See Case 5, EBM, 28 April 1964, EB-NCSA.

108. Case 5, EBM, 23 October 1962, EB-NCSA. Another social worker filed a petition for a pregnant eighteen-year-old single girl. The social worker reported that her client had had an "incestuous relationship with the father at age 14" but that "she and

her mother would not testify in court against him[, and] he was found not guilty." The parents refused to attempt to establish paternity, as they did not "want to get messed up in that." The patient and her father consented to the operation. See Case 31, EBM, 26 June 1962, EB-NCSA. Occasionally, Eugenics Board members would pursue incest-related cases to initiate the sterilization of the perpetrator. For a daughter and father who were sterilized, see, e.g., Case 5, EBM, 23 August 1955, and Case 16, EBM, 20 December 1950, both in EB-NCSA. See also Case 12, EBM, 25 September 1961, EB-NCSA.

109. Case 12, EBM, 25 September 1961, EB-NCSA.

110. Hearing Case 1, EBM, 21 July 1937, EB-NCSA.

111. Boys who were incest victims did not come to the attention of the Eugenics Board.

112. Victims of rape and incest, social workers believed, could develop no sense of morality and were unable to resist unwanted sexual advances. As late as 1960, experts still understood incest as a rare sexual perversion, and textbooks described the problem accordingly. Since the assailant was usually the father, prosecuting the perpetrator could result in economic hardship and possible family dependence on ADC; it often met with the resistance of the family, as well. Incest was thus defined as a problem of sexual delinquency on the part of its usually female victims. Blaming the victims of incest, child protectors pointed to the feeblemindedness of victims of sexual assault. The presumed feeblemindedness of these girls also made them bad witnesses and interfered with the prosecution of incest assailants. Social workers considered the victim herself to be sexually polluted and the pollution to be contagious for other children. They attributed disproportionate sexual power to feebleminded girls, who they claimed were able to lead grown men into temptation. Linda Gordon points out that the object of social agencies' work was the family unit, and in this work, attribution of blame was considered destructive. This interpretation was strengthened by assailants' refusal to accept any responsibility for their actions. On social workers' understanding of incest, see Gordon, *Heroes of Their Own Lives*, chapter 7, esp. pp. 213, 216.

113. [Marion Curtis Moser and Jessie M. Stroup], *The Human Betterment League of North Carolina: What It Is and What It Does* (n.p.: Winston Salem, ca. 1945), folder 77, series 1, box 2, HBL-SHC.

114. For geneticists' challenges to pedigree studies, see Morgan, *Evolution and Genetics*, pp. 206–7, and Pearl, "Biology of Superiority." For challenges from psychology, see, e.g., Klineberger, *Negro Intelligence*, and Cravens, "Wandering IQ." For challenges from anthropology, see Boas, *Mind of Primitive Man*, pp. 27, 86–87, 254, 270. For a detailed discussion of Boas's challenge to eugenic science, see Degler, *In Search of Human Nature*. See also Reilly, *Surgical Solution*, pp. 111–27; Kevles, *In the Name of Eugenics*, pp. 112–47; and Larson, *Sex, Race, and Science*, pp. 146–64.

115. Committee for the Investigation of Eugenical Sterilization, *Eugenic Sterilization*. See also Rollins and Wolfe, "Eugenic Sterilization."

116. Osborn, *Future of Human Heredity*; Banfield, *Unheavenly City*; Jensen, "How

Much Can We Boost IQ"; Ehrlich, *Population Bomb*; Kaye, "Birth Dearth"; Hernstein and Murray, *Bell Curve*. See also Rollins and Wolfe, "Eugenic Sterilization."

117. Penrose, *Biology of Mental Defect*.

118. Reilly, *Surgical Solution*, pp. 111–27.

119. The most significant decline in sterilizations took place in California, where new public health officials opposed the practice of eugenic sterilization. The number of eugenic sterilizations performed in California sank from 381 in 1949 to 39 in 1952. Eugenic sterilization laws, however, remained on the books in many states. The American Bar Association concluded in 1961 that it was still legally possible to perform involuntary sterilization in twenty-six states. In six states, the laws theoretically applied to all citizens. Ibid., pp. 137–38.

120. Winston, interview. Winston coauthored *Seven Lean Years* and *The Plantation South*, both studies of the South's economic and social structure during the depression, and *Foundations of American Population Policy*, a study of population problems. She was the American editor of *Nation and Family* by Alva Myrdal, a study of Swedish social welfare programs, and she collaborated on *The Negro's Share* by Richard Sterner, a study of living conditions and relief problems among African Americans.

121. For more information on Gamble, see Reed, *From Private Vice*, and Doone and Greer Williams, *Every Child*.

122. See Larson, *Sex, Race, and Science*, pp. 149–51, and Human Betterment League of North Carolina, "25th Anniversary, 1947—25 years of Human Betterment—1972," series 3, box 4, folder 133 (1968–74), HBL-SHC.

123. During the late 1940s, Clarence Gamble himself published at least twenty articles in professional journals arguing for eugenic sterilization. See bibliography for a partial list of titles. Larson argues that Gamble did as much as any one philanthropist could have done to implement eugenic sterilization programs. *Sex, Race and Science*, pp. 149–50, 155–57.

124. Evangeline Davis, "Alarming Mental Deficiency Rate Confronts State," *Charlotte News*, 27 March 1945.

125. Evangeline Davis, "Crowded Caswell Simply Can't Handle Patients," *Charlotte News*, 28 March 1945.

126. Evangeline Davis, "Sterilization Key in Solving Problem of Feeblemindedness in the State," *Charlotte News*, 29 March 1945. Davis's language shows remarkable similarities to rhetoric used to justify eugenics projects in Nazi Germany. See Proctor, *Racial Hygiene*.

127. *Biennial Report of the Eugenics Board of North Carolina* (1 July 1942–30 June 1944): 7.

128. Speech delivered at Program Institute for Workers Returning from Schools of Social Work, 28 June 1962, folder Speeches on Sterilization, box 7, DHR-NCSA. See also Davis, "Sterilization Key."

129. Marian S. Olden, *The Survival of the Unfittest*, publication no. 28 (Princeton, N.J.: Birthright, [ca. 1947]), p. 14, copy consulted in series 1, files of Marion Moser, box 2, folder 77, HBL-SHC.

130. Minutes, Meeting of the County Boards of Public Welfare and Boards of

County Commissioners, 9 November 1956, box 28C, folder N.C. Association of Public Welfare Officials, 1954–1956, DSS-NCSA.

131. Moynihan, *Negro Family*. See also Kunzel, *Fallen Women*, pp. 155–70, and Solinger, *Wake Up Little Susie*.

132. Case 22, EBM, 24 April 1962, EB-NCSA.

133. While the "culture of poverty" concept was employed both by progressives who sought to draw attention to the continued pervasiveness of poverty and by conservatives who sought to deflect attention from the structural reasons for poverty, it provided sterilization supporters with an intellectual framework that justified eugenic sterilization.

134. See Minutes of the EBMs, EB-NCSA. No comparable data for other states is available.

135. Pax Davis, "Sterilization Funds Urged," *Raleigh News and Observer*, 27 August 1950.

136. Abramovitz, *Regulating the Lives of Women*, pp. 319–21.

137. For an excellent description of the Jezebel stereotype, see White, *Arn't I A Woman*.

138. See, e.g., Kunzel, *Fallen Women*, pp. 161–65; Solinger, *Wake Up Little Susie*, pp. 41–85; and Abramovitz, *Regulating the Lives of Women*, pp. 319–29.

139. Davis, interview.

140. Minutes of the Board of Social Services, 7 November 1958, Assistant to the Commissioner, Minutes of the Board of Social Services, 1946–63, SS-NCSA.

141. In the late 1950s, the North Carolina legislature discussed several bills that would have authorized the eugenic sterilization of women who had had two or more children outside of marriage. The bills defined women with illegitimate children as "grossly sexually delinquent" and prescribed sterilization as a punitive measure. Critics of the 1959 legislative proposal held that it displayed racist assumptions about illegitimacy and aimed specifically to curb the high number of births outside marriage among African American women. The bills died in their respective legislative committees, but the debate about out-of-wedlock births continued. See "Racial Flareup Winds Up Hearing on Sterilization," *Raleigh News and Observer*, 2 April 1959; "Sterilization Bill Hearing Ends in Uproar," *Charlotte Observer*, 2 April 1959; and Ralph Moody to Honorable Malcolm B. Seawell, memo, [1959], box 10, Constitutional folder, AGR-NCSA.

142. Winston to the superintendent of public welfare, 12 December 1951, box 30A, file ADC-Eugenics Program, DSS-NCSA.

143. W. D. Partlow, "Extract from Letter to a State Senator in Alabama," attached to Partlow to Marian Olden, 10 January 1946, cited in Larson, *Sex, Race, and Science*, p. 151. As one social worker argued, a daughter was "greatly influenced by [a] mother's conduct" and tended to follow "the low moral standards in keeping with [her] environment." Case 20, EBM, 28 February 1945, EB-NCSA.

144. Case 3, EBM, 11 June 1964, EB-NCSA. See also Case 12, EBM, 23 June 1964, and Case 1, EBM, 25 August 1964, both in EB-NCSA.

145. Case 19, EBM, 25 February 1964, EB-NCSA.

146. Case 9, EBM, 28 July 1964, EB-NCSA.

147. Case 3, EBM, 22 June 1965, EB-NCSA.

148. See, e.g., Case 8, EBM, 22 July 1942; Case 5, EBM, 22 March 1960; Case 11, EBM, 28 June 1960; and Case 5, EBM, 28 November 1961, all in EB-NCSA.

149. "Sterilization Advocated to Prevent Mental Ills," *Raleigh News and Observer*, 4 July 1948. See also Case 2, Eugenics Board Agenda, 25 November 1969, General file, box 8, SS-NCSA. Jakob Koomen, a former member of the Eugenics Board, described the program's emphasis on the sterilization of young, single women: "Increasingly, we dealt with those kinds of situations where the parent perceived even before this child was pregnant, that here we have a retarded, promiscuous, or potentially promiscuous daughter who was going to get into difficulty and we are not going to be able to protect her." Koomen, interview.

150. [Eugenics Board member,] Speech delivered before the Iredell County Association of Retarded Children, [1967 or later], General file, box 7, folder Speeches on Sterilization, SS-NCSA.

151. Case 15, EBM, 28 March 1961, EB-NCSA. See also Case 1, EBM, 26 March 1963; Case 13, EBM, 22 January 1963; Case 10, EBM, 26 January 1960; Case 11, EBM, 19 December 1961; Case 2, EBM, 30 November 1962; Case 2, EBM, 31 January 1964; Case 6, EBM, 28 March 1957; Case 16, EBM, 28 February 1961; and Case 19, EBM, 28 April 1964, all in EB-NCSA. In some cases, parents had remarried, and their new partners were unwilling to care for a promiscuous daughter. See, e.g., Case 8, EBM, 28 April 1964, EB-NCSA.

152. Moya Woodside, *Sterilization and Social Welfare*, (Winston-Salem, N.C.: Human Betterment League of North Carolina, n.d.), p. 1, copy consulted in HBL-SHC. For a woman who learned about sterilization from her neighbor, see Case 1, EBM, 24 April 1962. For a woman who approached her private physician for sterilization, see Case 16, EBM, 28 August 1962. For a woman who discussed her desire for the operation with public health and public welfare officials, see Case 3, EBM, 24 May 1960. For a husband who sought sterilization for himself, see Case 5, EBM, 26 April 1960. For a husband who secured information for his wife, see Case 10, EBM, 22 May 1962. All in EB-NCSA.

153. The 468 cases constitute about 6 percent of the petitions received by the Eugenics Board between 1937 and June 1966. Studies of sterilization programs in Scandinavia and Puerto Rico have suggested that women in other localities also used eugenic sterilization programs for their own ends. See Broberg and Roll-Hansen, *Eugenics and the Welfare State*, and Briggs, "Discourses."

154. For discussions of health care conditions and services for poor blacks, see Smith, *Sick and Tired*; Beardsley, *History of Neglect*; Jones, *Bad Blood*; Grey, *New Deal Medicine*; and Reagan, *When Abortion Was a Crime*, pp. 204–8.

155. Quoted in Woodside, "Women Who Want," p. 6. See also Case 19, EBM, 26 September 1961, EB-NCSA, and Woodside, *Sterilization and Social Welfare*, HBL-SHC. On the discrepancy between desired and actual family size among the poor, see Darity, "Contraceptive Education," and Ward, *Poor Women*, p. 49.

156. See, e.g., Case 1, EBM, 6 July 1960; Case 1, EBM, 25 June 1963; and Case 5, EBM, 23 November 1965, all in EB-NCSA.

157. Woodside, "Women Who Want," pp. 1–3, 6–7; Woodside, *Sterilization and Social Welfare*, p. 1, HBL-SHC; and Case 2, EBM, 25 May 1965; Case 15, EBM, 22 March 1966; Case 6, EBM, 27 July 1965; and Case 18, EBM, 28 November 1961, all in EB-NCSA.

158. Of the 446 women, 153 (34.3 percent) were married. Of those, only 125 (28 percent) lived with their husbands, some of whom were unable to work, earned too little to support their families, or handled money irresponsibly.

159. Some received income from more than one source.

160. Case 4, EBM, 26 January 1960, EB-NCSA.

161. Of 119 petitions that include information about housing, 9 percent of the petitioners' dwellings lacked all or some conveniences. One-quarter of the petitioners lived in overcrowded conditions; 10 percent of the residences were poorly furnished.

162. Case 14, EBM, 25 August 1948, EB-NCSA.

163. It is likely that physicians referred such cases so that the state, rather than the client, would have to pay for the procedures. See Case 21, EBM, 25 May 1949; Case 14, EBM, 24 April 1956; Case 9, EBM, 26 August 1958; Case 1, EBM, 12 September 1960; Case 28, EBM, 26 September 1961; Case 3, EBM, 18 December 1962; and Case 21, EBM, 1 March 1963, all in EB-NCSA.

164. Case 18, EBM, 25 June 1963, EB-NCSA. See also Case 25, EBM, 23 April 1957, EB-NCSA.

165. Case 5, EBM, 23 January 1962, EB-NCSA. One woman explained to her social worker that she was not interested in marriage, but in men and sexual activity. Case 6, EBM, 26 January 1965, EB-NCSA. See also Case 1, EBM, 23 March 1965, and Case 7, EBM, 18 December 1962, both in EB-NCSA.

166. Case 18, EBM, 28 June 1960. See also Case 15, EBM, 22 September 1964. Both in EB-NCSA.

167. Case 8, EBM, 22 August 1961. See also Case 23, EBM, 25 February 1964. Both in EB-NCSA.

168. Case 11, EBM, 22 March 1966, EB-NCSA. See also Case 25, EBM, 29 April 1959; Case 5, EBM, 26 January 1960; and Case 18, EBM, 25 January 1963, all in EB-NCSA.

169. See, e.g., Case 3, EBM, 28 March 1961; Case 3, EBM, 25 September 1962; Case 1, EBM, 4 November 1964; and Case 3, EBM, 23 November 1965, all in EB-NCSA.

170. See Case 1, EBM, 31 October 1962. See also Case 5, EBM, 24 September 1963. Both in EB-NCSA.

171. Husbands refused consent in Case 15, EBM, 26 January 1949; Case 1, EBM, 23 August 1950; Case 3, EBM, 28 April 1954; and Case 14, EBM, 22 August 1961. Mothers or fathers refused consent in Case 2, EBM, 25 July 1951; Case 4, EBM, 22 August 1951; Hearing Case, EBM, 22 October 1963; Case 9, EBM, 28 January 1964; and Hearing Case, EBM, 24 March 1964. All in EB-NCSA.

172. Case 6, EBM, 19 December 1961, EB-NCSA.

173. Case 15, EBM, 25 February 1964, EB-NCSA.

174. Case 17, EBM, 27 February 1962, EB-NCSA.

175. See, for example, the case of a woman who unsuccessfully applied for steriliza-tion and reapplied in September. Case 21, EBM, 22 June 1971, and Case 4, EBM, 28 September 1971, both in General file, box 8, SS-NCSA. See also Case 30, EBM, 26 September 1961, EB-NCSA.

176. Bradway, "Legality of Human Sterilization," p. 251. See also Woodside, *Steril-ization in North Carolina*, pp. 57–58.

177. No national statistics on therapeutic sterilizations exist. Local data are scat-tered and usually refer to single hospitals, with no comparative statistics available. Data suggests, however, that therapeutic sterilizations were not that common be-tween 1905 and 1935. See Lerner, "Constructing Medical Indications," p. 365. The ear-liest data for North Carolina refers to the 1940s; the head of the obstetrics department of one of the state's teaching hospitals estimated that he alone had per-formed about two hundred sterilizations during the late 1940s. Public welfare depart-ments surveyed between 1945 and 1949 counted 546 therapeutic and 801 eugenic sterilizations. Woodside, *Sterilization and Social Welfare*, HBL-SHC.

178. The percentage of hospital births climbed from 55 percent in 1940 to 88 per-cent in 1950 and reached almost 100 percent by 1960. Leavitt, *Brought to Bed*, pp. 169–95.

179. Lock and Forman, "Postpartum Sterilization." Indications for sterilization also included hypertensive disease, renal disease, eclampsia, tuberculosis, cardiac disease, and a range of constitutional diseases. See Woodside, "Women Who Want," p. 5. These indications were similar to medical indications for abortion and birth control. See Petchesky, *Abortion and Woman's Choice*, pp. 78–84, 125–27; Reagan, *When Abortion Was a Crime*, pp. 193–215; and McCann, *Birth Control Politics*, pp. 62–75.

180. On the blurring of medical and socioeconomic indications, see Lerner, "Con-structing Medical Indications," pp. 372–73.

181. Woodside, *Sterilization and Social Welfare*, pp. 2–3, HBL-SHC. By the late 1940s, even hospitals known for their liberal sterilization policies began to consult the local social service departments to investigate patients' social and psychological situations before performing an operation. Woodside, "Women Who Want," pp. 4–5. See also Reagan, *When Abortion Was a Crime*, pp. 193–215.

182. Reagan, *When Abortion Was a Crime*, pp. 190–91. For a description of postwar domestic ideology, see May, *Homeward Bound*, pp. 58–91, and Solinger, *Wake Up Little Susie*. On demographic changes that contributed to women's increasing demand for reproductive control, see Petchesky, *Abortion and Woman's Choice*, pp. 103–16.

183. The new list of medical indications was much shorter than the old; it included hypertensive cardiovascular disease, evidence of permanent vascular or renal damage, heart disease (for patients with previous congestive failure), tuberculosis, hereditary diseases, repeated C-sections, and multiparity (only for women over the age of thirty with five or more children). In addition, the authors listed a number of conditions that, in their opinion, presented no indication for sterilization, such as Rh incompati-bility, heart murmurs, difficult deliveries, excessive vomiting during pregnancy, re-

peated miscarriages, a lack of desire for children, and a husband's disability. Donnelly and Lock, "Indications for the Sterilization of Women."

184. Reagan points out that such consultation requirements only existed for three operations, "all of them concerning reproduction: first-time cesarean sections, curettages or any procedure in which a 'pregnancy may be interrupted,' and sterilization." *When Abortion Was a Crime*, p. 191.

185. Quoted in Woodside, *Sterilization and Social Welfare*, p. 3, HBL-SHC. Some birth control advocates feared that liberal support of sterilization might backfire and hurt the reputation of the birth control movement in the long run. W. C. Morehead, Rural Projects Program Outline, October 1940, series 3, box 45, folder Birth Control, California, FSA Project, 1939–1941, PPFA-SSC.

186. Only ten hospitals (14 percent) reported no parity requirements, but they might have had age requirements instead. Flowers, Donnelly, and Burwell, "Practice of Tubal Ligation."

187. Ibid., p. 500.

188. Boger, *Charlotte 23*, pp. 159–72. In fact, some of the most progressive social work professionals made extensive use of the eugenic sterilization program. Kuralt, for instance, firmly believed in supporting clients' self-determination and challenged the prevailing wisdom that poor and minority women lacked both interest in family planning and the intelligence to successfully use birth control. By providing women with a wide choice of services, including those of the eugenic sterilization program, his agency demonstrated that women of all ethnic and class backgrounds were interested in taking control of their childbearing capacities. After the passage of the voluntary sterilization bill, Kuralt began to lobby for a reform of North Carolina's abortion law, which passed, albeit in modified form, in 1967.

189. By 1970, four states—Georgia, North Carolina, Virginia, and Oregon—had passed legislation permitting voluntary sterilization.

190. For a woman who was diagnosed with "chronic brain syndrome" and who sought sterilization under the voluntary sterilization law, see Case 11, EBM, 28 May 1968, EB-NCSA. Her petition states, "because of her mental condition the doctors at the hospital will not perform the operation without the authority of the Eugenics Board." The Eugenics Board received forty-two petitions for voluntary sterilization in 1964 and thirty-nine such petitions between 1 January and 30 June 1965. See also Elizabeth C. Corkey, "North Carolina: Family Planning in a Rural Maternity Clinic," [1967], folder 437, NCF-SHC.

191. *Jessin v. County of Shasta*, 274 Cal. App. 2d 737, 79 Cal. Reptr. 359 (Ct. App. 3d D. 1969); U.S. Department of Health, Education, and Welfare, *Family Planning*, pp. 63–69.

192. See Woodside, *Sterilization and Social Welfare*, p. 3, HBL-SHC.

193. Taylor, "Postpartum Sterilization," and Lerner, "Constructing Medical Indications."

194. Woodside, *Sterilization and Social Welfare*, p. 3, HBL-SHC, and Simmons, "Economics of Voluntary Sterilization," pp. 152–53.

195. Woodside, *Sterilization and Social Welfare*, pp. 2–3, HBL-SHC. See also Flowers, Donnelly, and Burwell, "Practice of Tubal Ligation," pp. 494–96.

196. In the 1960s, the welfare department in Caswell County paid physicians fifty dollars per tubal ligation. Other county welfare departments expected surgeons to donate their services, and some physicians refused. O. J. Sikes and Daylon T. Greene, "Sterilization in Caswell County, North Carolina, 1957–68" (Chapel Hill: Carolina Population Center, 1969), CPC-UNC. See also Woodside, *Sterilization and Social Welfare*, p. 2, HBL-SHC.

197. Women were far more likely than men to ask for sterilization. Fearing that any operation involving the reproductive organs might diminish their sexual enjoyment, men typically shied away from the surgery. Fewer than 5 percent of those seeking elective sterilization through the eugenic sterilization program were men. Woodside, *Sterilization and Social Welfare*, p. 2, HBL-SHC. See also Gamble, "Why Fear Sterilization."

198. See, e.g., Case 3, EBM, 24 May 1960; Case 16, EBM, 28 August 1962; and Case 7, EBM, 27 August 1963, all in EB-NCSA.

199. Thirty percent of Hertford County's petitions, 21 percent of Scotland County's petitions, and about 16 percent of Mecklenburg County's petitions were initiated by clients. While 9.4 percent of all Eugenics Board petitions came from Mecklenburg County, 19.2 percent of those classified as petitions for elective sterilizations originated there.

200. Case 30, EBM, 26 September 1961, EB-NCSA, and Kuralt, "Public Welfare Agency," p. 7.

201. Case 1, EBM, 28 May 1963, EB-NCSA.

202. Case 18, EBM, 28 November 1961, EB-NCSA.

203. Reagan, *When Abortion Was a Crime*, pp. 201–3.

204. Case 6, EBM, 27 July 1965, EB-NCSA.

205. Case 20, EBM, 23 April 1963, EB-NCSA.

206. Case 7, EBM, 26 May 1964, EB-NCSA.

207. Case 11, EBM, 26 March 1963, EB-NCSA.

208. In 1950, 31 percent of social workers across the country were male, while 7.2 percent were African American. By 1960, these numbers had climbed to 43 percent and 12.2 percent respectively. See Walkowitz, *Working with Class*, pp. 323, 325. Several interviews with former social workers in Mecklenburg County confirmed that the staff was integrated in terms of both race and gender. Cloer, Hicks, and Anderson, interview, and Wall, interview.

209. Chapin, interview.

210. Quotations in Woodside, *Sterilization and Social Welfare*, p. 1, HBL-SHC, and "Women Who Want," pp. 2–4, 7–9.

211. In several cases, individuals appeared at the Eugenics Board hearings hoping to resolve conflicts among family members regarding the desirability of the surgery. The sister of one sterilization candidate, for example, explained that she supported the operation but that her mother was very upset about the petition. To protect her

mother's feelings, she asked whether the surgery could be postponed until her mother had died. See Hearing Case, EBM, 2 December 1936; also see Hearing Case 1, EBM, 19 June 1940, both in EB-NCSA.

212. See, for example, Hearing Case, EBM, 25 July 1945, EB-NCSA. Elaine Trent, whose illiterate grandmother had signed the consent form without knowing the true nature of the form, later sued the state. See "Second Suit Hits Sterilization." Sometimes family members had unrealistic expectations for the operation when they initially gave consent. One woman thought that sterilization would "give [her son] a new mind" and "make him a perfectly normal person." When she found out this was not the case, she changed her mind regarding sterilization. Hearing Case 1, EBM, 21 July 1937, EB-NCSA.

213. Hearing Case 2, EBM, 20 April 1938, EB-NCSA. For clients who revoked consent, see, e.g., Hearing Case, EBM, 25 July 1945, and Case 7, EBM, 23 September 1958, both in EB-NCSA. It is likely that this happened much more often than I have been able to document. I could only locate such cases if they came up a second time and it was mentioned in the file that the client or family member had revoked consent. In 12 percent of all cases, the surgery was authorized but not performed. The reason is usually not clear in the records, although persistent opposition clearly played a large role in it.

214. Hearing Case 1, EBM, 28 June 1966, and Hearing Case, EBM, 25 July 1945, both in EB-NCSA.

215. For the fear that the patient might die, see Hearing Case, EBM, 19 October 1934, and Hearing Case 3, EBM, 20 April 1938, both in EB-NCSA. For the comparison of sterilization with sterilizing bottles, see James W. Kirkpatrick and Ann Winters, "Planned Parenthood—a Public Welfare Responsibility," May 1967, appendix C, p. 5, unpublished manuscript. For a comparison with veterinary procedures, see Woodside, *Sterilization in North Carolina*, pp. 62, 68.

216. Woodside, *Sterilization in North Carolina*, pp. 62, 68. For women's fears regarding their sexual receptiveness, see Woodside, "Women Who Want," p. 8. For fears that sterilization would increase promiscuity, see also Hearing Case 1, EBM, 17 August 1938. For fears of negative health consequences, see Hearing Case 1, EBM, 19 June 1940; Hearing Case 1, EBM, 21 July 1937; and Hearing Case 3, EBM, 17 March 1943, all in EB-NCSA.

217. Hearing Case 3, EBM, 20 April 1938. See also Hearing Case 1, EBM, 15 June 1938. Both in EB-NCSA.

218. Woodside, *Sterilization in North Carolina*, pp. 77, 207; Hearing Case 2, EBM, 20 April 1938, and Hearing Case 1, EBM, 2 December 1936, both in EB-NCSA.

219. Hearing Case, EBM, 25 July 1945, EB-NCSA.

220. Quoted in Woodside, *Sterilization in North Carolina*, p. 207. See also Hearing Case 1, EBM, 19 June 1940, EB-NCSA.

221. Hearing Case 2, EBM, 15 June 1938, EB-NCSA.

222. Hearing Case 2, EBM, 16 March 1938, and Hearing Case 1, EBM, 19 June 1940, both in EB-NCSA; Replies from County Departments of Public Welfare to Question-

naire Regarding Sterilization, [February 1948], General file, box 7, folder Psychological Services, SS-NCSA; Woodside, *Sterilization in North Carolina*, p. 207. One family argued that the state had no right to treat regular taxpayers this way. Hearing Case, EBM, 25 July 1945, EB-NCSA.

223. Hearing Case 1, EBM, 19 June 1940, EB-NCSA.

224. See, e.g., Hearing Case, EBM, 25 January 1955; Hearing Case 2, EBM, 20 April 1938; Hearing Case 1, EBM, 15 June 1938; and Hearing Case 1, EBM, 17 August 1938, all in EB-NCSA.

225. One wife complained about her husband's operation: "They wanted me to have the operation first[.] I wouldn't[,] and then Mrs. Brown, the welfare worker, said she would see that [the patient] had it before he left hospital. She stopped my check one month. I went to see the county commissioners and they had her send my check." See Hearing Case 1, EBM, 19 June 1940, EB-NCSA. For a social worker who coerced consent by threatening to withhold welfare payments, see also *Cox v. Stanton*. One social worker who in the 1960s worked with ADC mothers recalled a woman who "had been told [by her previous social worker] that she could not have any more children or else all the other children would be taken from home" and she herself would be sterilized. Davis, interview.

226. For claims that sterilization would improve the patient's health and misleading information about the danger of passing syphilis on to the next generation, see, e.g., Hearing Case 3, EBM, 20 April 1938, EB-NCSA. For the claim that the Eugenics Board was required to perform eugenic sterilizations, see Hearing Case 2, EBM, 15 June 1938, EB-NCSA. At least one other board member expressed the understanding that the board authorized sterilizations "because the law obligated [it] to." Koomen, interview.

227. Woodside, *Sterilization in North Carolina*, pp. 61, 204, 209–10. For families who changed their minds, see Case 13, EBM, 28 July 1948; Case 1, EBM, 22 December 1948; Case 23, EBM, 22 February 1950; Case 12, EBM, 19 December 1951; Case 14, EBM, 24 January 1956; Case 7, EBM, 23 September 1958; and Case 16, EBM, 22 May 1962, all in EB-NCSA.

228. Lawrence, "Study Relating to Mental Illness," pp. 10–12, SS-NCSA. For patients who refused to enter the hospital for the operation, see Case 1, EBM, 17 March 1943; Case 11, EBM, 22 September 1948; Case 18, EBM, 26 April 1950; Case 17, EBM, 21 December 1954; Case 18, EBM, 26 November 1957; Case 14, EBM, 24 May 1960; Hearing Cases 1 and 3, EBM, 28 March 1961; Case 3, EBM, 25 September 1962; Case 27, EBM, 25 June 1963; Case 6, EBM, 26 May 1964; Case 1, EBM, 4 November 1964; and Case 3, EBM, 23 November 1965, all in EB-NCSA.

229. Davis, interview.

230. Only 4 percent of the Eugenics Board cases resulted in hearings, and most of those were held not because of opposition to sterilization but because the hearing served as a legal formality in cases in which guardians could not be located.

231. Hearing Case 2, EBM, 20 April 1938; Hearing Case 1, EBM, 15 June 1938; Hearing Case 3, EBM, 17 March 1943; Hearing Case 1, EBM, 19 August 1936; Hearing Case 1,

EBM, 17 August 1938; Hearing Case 1, EBM, 21 September 1938, all in EB-NCSA. Because of the small number of cases that appeared in hearings before the Eugenics Board and the even smaller number of clients who sought legal advice, it is impossible to say whether such actions made a difference in the outcome of the petitions.

232. Hearing Case 2, EBM, 15 June 1938; Hearing Case, EBM, 25 July 1945; Hearing Case 1, EBM, 2 December 1936, all in EB-NCSA. I am unaware of a hearing case ever resulting in a legal suit. While a few women sued the Eugenics Board years after their sterilizations, most clients and family members felt too embarrassed or lacked the financial resources to consider this step.

233. See, e.g., Case 17, EBM, 28 February 1956, and Resolution, EBM, 9 April 1956, both in EB-NCSA. This evidence mirrors similar trends in other state programs. Paul Lombardo reports about Virginia, for instance, that "those who were wealthy enough to afford legal assistance or raised a big enough stink usually didn't get sterilized." Lombardo quoted in Bishop, "Sterilization Survivors," p. 14.

234. See Cox v. Stanton; Bishop, "Sterilization Survivors"; and Hearing Case 1, EBM, 2 December 1936, EB-NCSA.

235. Hearing Case 3, EBM, 20 April 1938. See also Hearing Case 1, EBM, 19 August 1936. Both in EB-NCSA.

236. Hearing Case 2, EBM, 15 June 1938. See also Hearing Case, EBM, 25 July 1945. Both in EB-NCSA.

237. See, e.g., Hearing Case, EBM, 22 March 1955, EB-NCSA. See also Hearing Case, EBM, 19 October 1934, EB-NCSA. In this case, it is unclear whether the father of the sterilization candidate felt intimidated by Dr. Ashby or whether he genuinely respected Ashby's medical knowledge and followed his advice to sterilize his daughter.

238. For a man who wanted to consult a physician about his brother's sterilization, see Hearing Case 1, EBM, 21 July 1937. For a man who sought a certain surgeon for his brother and wished the operation to be performed at a hospital close enough so that his mother could visit, see Hearing Case 1, EBM, 22 January 1936. For a husband who was in prison and worried about help for his wife and children after the surgery, see Hearing Case, EBM, 25 January 1955. All in EB-NCSA.

239. Quoted in Ethel Speas to Dr. Ellen Winston, memo, 9 November 1955, General file, box 7, folder General Correspondence from 1970, SS-NCSA.

240. Quoted in ibid.

241. Quoted in ibid.

242. Koomen, interview.

243. Speas to Winston, memo, 9 November 1955, SS-NCSA.

244. Of 500 board meetings between 1934 and 1966, 244 were attended by only 3 board members, 155 by 4 board members, and 99 by 5 board members. Of the 110 individuals who attended a board meeting as a board member or delegate during this period, 20 came only once and another 27 only two or three times. Seventy came to fewer than 10 board meetings. The members with the highest attendance were Ellen Winston with 169 meetings, R. Eugene Brown with 121 meetings, W. R. Pierce with 111 meetings, and R. D. Higgins with 109 meetings.

245. There is evidence that at least two board members responded this way. Walter A. Sikes, superintendent of the State Hospital at Raleigh and a critical member of the board between 1954 and 1959, attended only four meetings. In 1955, he stopped attending, and he never sent a representative. In 1959, he was replaced by the commissioner of mental health. Robert L. Rollins, superintendent of Dorothea Dix Hospital and a member of the Eugenics Board starting in 1967, also chose not to attend most board meetings because of his opposition to the program. In the early 1970s, Rollins and board member Ann Wolfe introduced fundamental reforms that eventually culminated in the abolishment of the program.

246. Speas to Winston, memo, 9 November 1955, SS-NCSA.

247. Until 1962, 98 percent of sterilization petitions were authorized. Describing his own decision-making process, one former board member recalled that case summaries were followed by a "brisk discussion" and a reflection on his own background. Koomen, interview.

248. Winston to the superintendent of public welfare, 12 December 1951, SS-NCSA. In addition, Winston began to evaluate each county's use of the sterilization program. See Commissioner's Office, box 58, folder Field Representatives, Reports on Territories, 1953–1956, SS-NCSA.

249. Koomen, interview. Koomen explains that the similar ages and academic backgrounds of the board members helped him to overcome his feelings of discomfort with his responsibility on the board.

250. In the early 1960s, the percentage of petitions postponed or rejected began to rise from 8 percent between 1962 and 1964 to 20 percent between 1966 and 1968 to 37 percent between 1971 and 1972. In 1973, the last year for which statistics are available, 60 percent of petitions were postponed or rejected. Sue Casebolt to Winston, memo, 15 May 1962, box 7, folder General Correspondence from 1970, DHR-NCSA.

251. By 1970, Georgia, North Carolina, Virginia, and Oregon had passed voluntary sterilization laws, and Colorado, Arkansas, California, Delaware, Georgia, Kansas, Maryland, New Mexico, North Carolina, Oregon, South Carolina, and Virginia had reformed their abortion laws. Roddey M. Ligon, "North Carolina Voluntary Sterilization Law," p. 2, and John C. Burwell, "The 1963 Sterilization Law," both in series 1, files of Marian Moser, box 2, folder 78 (Sterilization Law), HBL-SHC. See also Sagar C. Jain and Steven W. Sinding, *North Carolina Abortion Law 1967* (Chapel Hill: Carolina Population Center, 1968), p. 16, copy consulted in CPC-UNC, and Reagan, *When Abortion Was a Crime*, p. 222.

252. EBM, 19 December 1972, p. 2, EB-NCSA. See also June P. Stallings to Martha Bovinet, 30 March 1973, box 7, folder Correspondence Eugenics, DHR-NCSA.

253. Critchlow, *Intended Consequences*, p. 145, and Shapiro, *Population Control Politics*, pp. 113–15.

254. *Cox v. Stanton* and "Second Suit Hits Sterilization." Nationally, the most prominent suit involved two African American girls who had been sterilized by a Department of Health, Education, and Welfare–funded program in Montgomery, Alabama, in 1973. *Relf v. Weinberger* (1974).

255. Sue Casebolt to Dr. Norman Polansky, 1 March 1968, General file, box 7, folder General Correspondence from 1970, SS-NCSA.

256. Case 19, Eugenics Board Agenda, 23 April 1963, General file, box 8, SS-NCSA.

257. June P. Stallings to Mrs. Walter B. Cole, 24 January 1974, and Stallings to Josephine W. Kirk, 26 April 1973, both in box 7, folder Correspondence Eugenics, DHR-NCSA.

258. See Grob, *Mad Among Us*, pp. 223, 276–77; Trent, *Inventing the Feeble Mind*, pp. 225–68.

259. EBM; 19 December 1972, General file, box 7, folder Correspondence Eugenics, SS-NCSA.

260. Bob Rollins, "Proposed Eugenics Board Policy," 29 September 1971, General file, box 7, folder Policies and Practices of the Eugenics Board, DHR-NCSA.

261. Robert G. Stewart Jr. to Miss Ellen Douglass Bush, memo, 29 August 1970, General file, box 7, folder General Correspondence from 1970, SS-NCSA. See also Clifton M. Craig to Dr. A. McCray Jones, 2 October 1970, General file, box 7, folder General Correspondence from 1970, SS-NCSA.

262. The state's sterilization law, the *Durham Morning Herald* noted, was "in urgent need of legislative attention." See "Liberalizing Sterilization Law," 25 October 1971. The North Carolina Medical Society and the Human Betterment League also expressed their concern about the Eugenics Board and the existing sterilization statutes. The secretary of the Department of Human Resources described the Eugenics Board of the 1970s as outmoded. Clifton M. Craig to Dr. R. L. Rollins Jr., 27 October 1971, General file, box 7, folder General Correspondence from 1970, SS-NCSA.

263. Wolfe to Colonel Clifton Craig, memo, 10 January 1973, General file, box 7, folder Proposed Revisions of Eugenics Statutes, SS-NCSA.

264. Rollins to June Stallings, 20 December 1972, General file, box 7, folder Proposed Revisions of Eugenics Statutes, SS-NCSA.

265. Jones to Koomen, 19 January 1973, General file, box 7, folder Proposed Revisions of Eugenics Statutes, SS-NCSA.

266. This position was supported by the intense lobbying efforts of the association, which sought a voluntary sterilization law for the mentally incompetent. See Patricia S. Powell, Susan DeStrake, Jane S. Luery [or Query? illegible], Statement of NARC regarding sterilization, ca. 1970, General file, box 7, folder Speeches on Sterilization, SS-NCSA. For opinions of Eugenics Board members, see June P. Stallings, "Sterilization of Persons Mentally Ill or Mentally Retarded," 21 February 1974, General file, box 7, folder Proposed Revisions of Eugenics Statutes, SS-NCSA.

267. Jones to Koomen, memo, 19 January 1973, SS-NCSA.

268. The new legislation required a diagnosis in the form of written reports as well as the written consent or objection of the patient and the next of kin. The law provided the right to counsel at all stages of the procedure and the right to appeal through the superior and appellate courts. It excluded castration as a method of sterilization.

269. See Correa and Petchesky, "Reproductive and Sexual Rights," and Lopez, "Agency and Constraint."

1. Quoted in Miller, *Worst of Times*, pp. 61–64, esp. p. 61.

2. In order to do a D&C, the abortion provider dilated the cervix with metal dilators or gauze tampons and then used a curette, a spoon-shaped instrument, to scrape fetal and placental tissue out of the uterus.

3. Quoted in Miller, *Worst of Times*, p. 63.

4. Quoted in ibid., p. 64.

5. Reagan, *When Abortion Was a Crime*, pp. 14–15.

6. James Mohr and Janet Brodie have analyzed abortion in the nineteenth century and traced the criminalization of the procedure. See Brodie, *Contraception and Abortion*, and Mohr, *Abortion in America*. A range of scholars have examined the period in which abortion was illegal and the impact of legalization with *Roe v. Wade*. See Reagan, *When Abortion Was a Crime*; Solinger, *Abortionist*; Miller, *Worst of Times*; Kaplan, *Story of Jane*; Joffe, *Doctors of Conscience*; Petchesky, *Abortion and Woman's Choice*; and Solinger, *Abortion Wars*. None of the literature has explored the common ties that link the provision of abortion to that of birth control and sterilization.

7. In contrast, in both Nazi Germany and in Communist China, where state supervision over women's reproduction reached an unprecedented height and included, among other things, the registration of pregnancies, eugenic abortions did indeed become reality. See Czarnowski, "Frauen als Mütter der Rasse"; Grossman, *Reforming Sex*, pp. 150–53; Hartmann, *Reproductive Rights*, pp. 157–70; and Greenhalgh, "Controlling Births."

8. "The First One Hundred Cases of the Wake County Birth Control Centers," 23 February 1938, box 23, file 413, CJG-CML. Slippery elm absorbs water. Inserted into the cervix, it will absorb moisture and expand, forcing the cervix to open up and thus causing an abortion. Miller, *Worst of Times*, pp. 73–74.

9. From the viewpoint of the abortionist, there was a slight disadvantage to this second technique. The catheter could not be reused, because the woman left with it. For an excellent description of abortion techniques, see Miller, *Worst of Times*, pp. 323–26.

10. Whenever a foreign object is inserted into the uterus, there is a risk of a life-threatening perforation of the uterine wall. Perforation can cause hemorrhaging and can lead to peritonitis if the object has also punctured the bowel and released fecal material into the body cavity. Such complications caused women to suffer through particularly painful and long deaths. See, for example, the physicians' testimony about the sickness and subsequent death of Mildred Hargrove in *State v. Mitchner*, 256 N.C. 620 (1962). The term "septic abortion" refers to an abortion complicated by an infection. Infections may be localized in the fallopian tubes, ovaries, uterus, or vagina or may spread throughout the body, involving organs outside the reproductive tract. The more widespread the infection, the more dangerous it is. Septicemia is a condition in which infection is so advanced that bacteria or their toxins have invaded the bloodstream and are circulating throughout the body. It is accompanied by chills,

profuse sweating, intermittent fever, and severe weakness. Septic shock occurs when the body is so overwhelmed by infection that there is a general circulatory collapse. Other health risks associated with abortion included air or chemical embolism. Ibid., pp. 327–28. See also Reagan, *When Abortion Was a Crime*, pp. 211, 213.

11. Reagan, *When Abortion Was a Crime*, pp. 19–45; Miller, *Worst of Times*. Naturally, there are exceptions to this rule. Both authors report of women who, in the absence of other alternatives, resorted to repeated abortions to end their childbearing years.

12. Thanks to Dan Pollit at the University of North Carolina School of Law for answering my questions about the functioning of the criminal justice system and the North Carolina Supreme Court.

13. Much of the literature on the history of abortion focuses on urban areas. Reagan's *When Abortion Was a Crime* and Kaplan's *The Story of Jane* look at the history of abortion in Chicago. Solinger's *The Abortionist* tells the story of Ruth Barnett, who practiced in Portland, Oregon. Miller's *Worst of Times* provides recollections of illegal abortions in the Pittsburgh area.

14. *General Statutes of North Carolina*, chap. 351, sec. 1 (1881), as quoted in Sagar C. Jain and Steven W. Sinding, *North Carolina Abortion Law 1967* (Chapel Hill: Carolina Population Center, 1968), appendix A, p. 60, copy consulted in CPC-UNC.

15. Ibid.

16. *State v. Slagle*, 83 N.C. 630 (1880), p. 4. See also Mohr, *Abortion in America*, p. 227; Brodie, *Contraception and Abortion*, pp. 253–56; and D'Emilio and Freedman, *Intimate Matters*, pp. 139–67.

17. Reagan, *When Abortion Was a Crime*, pp. 61–67.

18. The nine cases in which the woman's male partner was indicted are *State v Slagle*; *State v. Crews*, 128 N.C. 581 (1901); *State v. Brady*, 177 N.C. 587 (1919); *State v. Powell*, 181 N.C. 515 (1921); *State v. Martin*, 182 N.C. 846 (1921); *State v. Stewart and Parish*, no. 651, Guilford County (Spring Term 1936); *State v. Baker*, 212 N.C. 233 (1937); *State v. Evans*, 211 N.C. 458 (1937); and *State v. Thompson*, 216 N.C. 800 (1939).

19. *State v. Thompson*, p. 12.

20. Ibid., p. 3 of Brief for State, emphasis mine. For similar cases, see *State v. Slagle*, *State v. Evans*, and *State v. Jordon*, 227 N.C. 579 (1947).

21. *State v. Slagle*, p. 1.

22. Ibid.

23. Ibid., p. 2.

24. *State v. Thompson*; *State v. Evans*, pp. 39–40.

25. See, e.g., *State v. Slagle*; *State v. Shaft*, 166 N.C. 407 (1914); *State v. Powell*; *State v. Thompson*; *State v. Crews*; and *State v. Stewart and Parish*. Worried about their virtue, a number of women emphasized that they had had sexual relations only once. Male relatives swore out indictments in *State v. Crews*, *State v. Brady*, *State v. Powell*, and *State v. Martin*.

26. *State v. Crews*, pp. 3–4; *State v. Shaft*.

27. *State v. Slagle*. See also *State v. Brady* and *State v. Powell*.

28. *State v. Brady*, pp. 6, 8.

29. *State v. Shaft.*

30. *State v. Crews*, pp. 3–4; *State v. Powell*, p. 2.

31. The marriage rate plummeted to an all-time low in the early 1930s, and during that decade limped along below the rate of the 1920s. It was not until 1940 that it began to rise significantly. May, *Homeward Bound*, pp. 7, 39–40. See also D'Emilio and Freedman, *Intimate Matters*.

32. Taussig, *Abortion*, pp. 320–21. See also Reagan, *When Abortion Was a Crime*, pp. 142–59, and Solinger, *Abortionist*.

33. *State v. Brown*, p. 9. In 1947, the *North Carolina Medical Journal*, too, differentiated abortions performed under criminal circumstances "in an undesirable environment" from those in which "asepsis was observed in a hospital." "Maternal Welfare Section," p. 315.

34. *State v. Baker*, p. 9.

35. *State v. Forte*, 222 N.C. 537 (1943), pp. 5–6.

36. The decision argued that Forte had been indicted for performing an operation upon "a woman quick with child" with intent to destroy the child but that the proof tended to show that he had performed an operation upon a pregnant woman not yet quick with child. Ibid.

37. McLennan, *Synopsis of Obstetrics*. Thanks to Chuck deProsse and Takey Crist for their explanations of early pregnancy testing and the infrequency with which these tests were performed.

38. *State v. Forte.* Moreover, the North Carolina Supreme Court called on *State v. Forte* as a precedent when it overturned two additional lower court convictions with the same argument: *State v. Jordon* and *State v. Green*, 230 N.C. 381 (1949). In earlier cases, the fact that a woman was not yet "quick with child" did not become an issue. See *State v. Brady* and *State v. Brown*.

39. *State v. Jordon.*

40. *State v. Dillard*, 223 N.C. 446 (1943), pp. 26–27.

41. *State v. Brown*, p. 10. Bessie Frye got sick and subsequently indicted Dr. Brown.

42. *State v. Stewart and Parish*, pp. 83, 86–89. For other indictments following the death of the woman, see also *State v. Evans*; *State v. Baker*; *State v. Manning*, 225 N.C. 41 (1945); and *State v. Choate*, 228 N.C. 491 (1948).

43. *State v. Brown*, pp. 23–24.

44. Quoted in Miller, *Worst of Times*, pp. 262–63. While the prosecutor quoted above worked in Pittsburgh rather than North Carolina, other historians have found similar patterns of police protection of skilled abortionists. Women in parts of North Carolina were able to benefit from the same system. For similar changes in Portland, see Solinger, *Abortionist*, pp. 149–68. On the role of the police informant, see Miller, *Worst of Times*, pp. 107–8. For North Carolina, see Badie T. Clark to Jesse Helms, 27 January 1981, folder Abortion Reference Index Illustrated—Politics, TCP-DUWA.

45. *State v. Jordon*, p. 11.

46. Ibid., p. 15.

47. Ibid., p. 16. See also *State v. Green.*

48. *State v. Evans*, p. 53.

49. Ibid., pp. 9, 30–31, 35.

50. *State v. Baker*, pp. 10–11.

51. Ibid., pp. 10–11, 20. It is unclear whether "that" refers to Baker's having had sex with Madell, thus impregnating her, or whether it implies an admission that Baker had indeed arranged for Madell's abortion.

52. Smith explained in her dying declaration, "Ollie said I would have to get rid of the youngun. He said it would be no harm. I did not want to do it. He said I would have to." *State v. Stewart and Parish*, p. 30.

53. Ibid., p. 70.

54. *State v. Evans*, p. 28.

55. Ibid., p. 29. See *State v. Thompson* for a similar case. State prosecutors charged the man responsible for the pregnancy with securing an abortion for his girlfriend, who appears to have been entirely passive in court proceedings. But testimony from the abortionist indicates that it was the pregnant woman rather than her boyfriend who sought the abortion and persisted even after the abortionist expressed hesitation due to the advanced stage of her pregnancy.

56. *State v. Evans*, pp. 29–31, 42.

57. *State v. Stewart and Parish*, p. 70. In fact, she was not the only white woman who sought the help of a black physician. See also *State v. Dillard*; *State v. Lee*, 248 N.C. 327 (1958); and *State v. Perry*, 250 N.C. 119 (1959). In two other cases, white women sought abortions from black women, one of whom was a nurse. See *State v. Hoover and Stallworth*, 252 N.C. 1133, and *State v. Brooks*, 267 N.C. 427 (1966).

58. *State v. Stewart and Parish*, pp. 78–79.

59. Quoted in Miller, *Worst of Times*, pp. 112–13.

60. Quoted in ibid., pp. 110–11.

61. Quoted in ibid., p. 102.

62. Quoted in ibid.

63. *State v. Stewart and Parish*, pp. 80–81, 89.

64. Clarence J. Gamble, "Contraception as a Public Health Measure," *Transactions of the Medical Society of the State of North Carolina*, 1938, pp. 2, 8, box 2, Misc. Papers, JWRN-SHC. See also Taussig, *Abortion*.

65. Margaret Sanger and Richard N. Pierson for the BCFA Committee on Public Progress, Form Letter to Members, [1939], reel S62, MS-SSC.

66. Forest M. Houser, "Infancy and Maternal Mortality as It Applies to the General Practitioner," [1933], series State Board of Health, 1924–1935, box 28, folder Dr. G. M. Cooper's file, SBH-NCSA.

67. Reagan, *When Abortion Was a Crime*, pp. 160–64. For an example of the belief that reticence toward pregnancy was a pathological condition, see the research by Dr. Carl T. Javert, an obstetrician at Cornell University Medical College, New York City, as reported in "Fears and Babies," *Newsweek*, 28 December 1953, p. 49, cited in May, *Homeward Bound*, p. 149. See also ibid., pp. 135–61. Somers H. Sturgis and Doris Menzer-Benaron argued in *The Gynecological Patient* that women had to accept the

fact that their emotional and physical happiness depended on their acceptance of their role as mothers and child-bearers. Stuart S. Asch argued that pregnancy was a critical period in feminine development, since it confronted the woman with the undeniable "proof" that she was a woman. See Asch, "Psychiatric Complications," pp. 461–62. See also Ehrenreich and English, *For Her Own Good*, pp. 219–80.

68. Leslie Reagan has characterized the repression of abortion during this period as "new, not normal," and of a kind that "should be incorporated into our understanding of the multifaceted far-reaching effects of 'McCarthyism.'" *When Abortion Was a Crime*, p. 163. For a more general discussion of moral purity campaigns in the 1950s, see D'Emilio and Freedman, *Intimate Matters*, pp. 275–300.

69. Solinger, *Abortionist*, pp. 149–68; Reagan, *When Abortion Was a Crime*, pp. 160–64; Miller, *Worst of Times*, pp. 217, 262–63; Hulka, interview.

70. Miller, *Worst of Times*, p. 122–39, and Clark to Helms, 27 January 1981, TCP-DUWA.

71. DeProsse, interview. See also Hulka, interview; Hendricks, interview; and Miller, *Worst of Times*, p. 112. DeProsse and Hendricks told similar stories about Portsmouth, Virginia, and Columbus and Cleveland, Ohio.

72. Kaplan, *Story of Jane*. Only once did the police raid the group. Seven members were charged with performing illegal abortions, but the group continued to operate as before, and charges against the seven members were eventually dismissed.

73. Miller, *Worst of Times*, pp. 262–63, 141–42, quote on p. 263.

74. *State v. Hoover and Stallworth*, pp. 4–5.

75. The Supreme Court upheld convictions in the following cases: *State v. Furley*, 245 N.C. 219 (1956); *State v. Perry*; *State v. Mitchner*; *State v. Brooks*; *State v. Lee*; *State v. Hoover and Stallworth*. In *State v. Lee* and *State v. Hoover and Stallworth*, it was unclear whether the abortion provider had ended the pregnancy or the very existence of pregnancy was in doubt.

76. *State v. Perry*, pp. 90–91. In *State v. Hoover and Stallworth*, Juanita Rozzell was forced to submit to a gynecological exam to determine whether her abortion had been effective. In *State v. Choate* and *State v. Brooks*, state prosecutors forced a number of women who had obtained abortions from Brooks and Choate to testify against their abortionists. For crackdowns on abortionists in Chicago, see also Reagan, *When Abortion Was a Crime*, pp. 160–73. For crackdowns on abortionists in Wichita and Portland, see Solinger, *Abortionist*, pp. 169–93. For crackdowns in Pittsburgh, see Miller, *Worst of Times*.

77. *State v. Perry*, pp. 75, 77–78.

78. Miller, *Worst of Times*, p. 110.

79. The exception is *State v. Mitchner*, in which Willie Simmons found and hired an abortionist to terminate the pregnancy of his girlfriend, Mildred Hargrove. Despite his role in procuring the abortion, however, Simmons barely appears in the court records. It is possible that he was indicted separately, since Hargrove died as a result of the abortion.

80. *State v. Brooks*, pp. 9–11, 23.

81. See, for instance, the discussions of abortion in Eugenics Board petitions. While only two petitions contained any references to abortion during the first two decades of the eugenic sterilization program, twenty-two petitions submitted between the late 1940s and the early 1960s included references to abortion as proof of women's promiscuity and immorality. See, e.g., Case 13, EBM, 26 March 1947; Case 15, EBM, 19 April 1955; and EBM, 17 January 1963, all in EB-NCSA. See also *State v. Lee* and *State v. Perry*.

82. Reagan, *When Abortion Was a Crime*, pp. 183–85.

83. Dr. Rachel D. Davis to Claude Currie, 26 January 1971, box 1, folder 3, CC-SHC; Reagan, *When Abortion Was a Crime*, p. 208; Solinger, "A Complete Disaster."

84. Reagan, *When Abortion Was a Crime*, p. 186.

85. Ibid., pp. 181–92.

86. DeProsse, interview.

87. Reagan, *When Abortion Was a Crime*, pp. 203–4.

88. Hulka, interview.

89. Ibid.

90. Crist, interview.

91. Quoted in Miller, *Worst of Times*, p. 133.

92. Quoted in ibid., pp. 112–13.

93. *State v. Perry*, p. 75.

94. Ibid., pp. 66–67.

95. Ibid., pp. 109–10. Thanks to Angela Keysor for her help in explaining the procedural details of this legal case.

96. DeProsse, interview.

97. Hulka, interview. All of the physicians I interviewed practiced almost exclusively in large university hospitals and urban areas. None knew any illegal abortionists.

98. Clark to Helms, 27 January 1981, TCP-DUWA. See also Miller, *Worst of Times*, pp. 109–16, for the narrative of Dr. Clay. Clay and his colleagues knew the illegal abortionists in his community outside Pittsburgh. They sent their patients to them and wrote them prescriptions for antibiotics following their abortions.

99. Anonymous to Takey Crist, 16 May 1969, folder Abortion Letters, TCP-DUWA.

100. Crist, "Abortion," p. 348. See also Reagan, *When Abortion Was a Crime*, pp. 193–200, and Miller, *Worst of Times*.

101. *State v. Brooks*, p. 10.

102. Ibid., p. 9. See also *State v. Hoover and Stallworth*, in which police learned about the abortion services of Florence Stallworth after Juanita Hill, unable to pay for her abortion, borrowed money from her employer, who worked as a detective for the Charlotte Police Department. While Hill claimed she did not tell her employer why she needed the money, her employer notified his colleagues, who set a trap for Stallworth.

103. *State v. Choate*, p. 15.

104. Ibid., p. 12.

105. Ibid., p. 15.

106. Ibid., pp. 14–15.

107. Hulka, interview.

108. Hendricks, interview. Physicians interviewed by Carole Joffe expressed similar sentiments. See *Doctors of Conscience*, p. 145. On the lack of interest in reporting patients, see also deProsse, interview.

109. Hendricks, interview.

110. Reagan, *When Abortion Was a Crime*, pp. 209–10.

111. Quoted in Joffe, *Doctors of Conscience*, pp. 60–61.

112. See Reagan, *When Abortion Was a Crime*, 211–13. For a discussion of total numbers, see Leavy and Kummer, "Criminal Abortion," 126. Joffe notes that estimates of death from illegal abortion have been highly contested, with the antiabortion movement, in particular, accusing the pro-choice movement of inflating the figures. Numerous commentators have pointed out how difficult it is to make such an estimate given the likelihood that many abortion deaths were listed as something else in order to mask the shame associated with illegal abortion. *Doctors of Conscience*, p. 216, n. 6.

113. While the number of therapeutic abortions declined during the 1940s and 1950s, the proportion of therapeutic abortions justified on psychiatric grounds increased. Christopher Tietze analyzed therapeutic abortion in New York City between 1943 and 1947 and found that abortions for mental illness "increased steadily" over the period. By 1947, over 19 percent of therapeutic abortions were being induced for psychiatric reasons. Hall's study of sixty of the nation's hospitals found that between 1951 and 1960 psychiatric indications accounted for 43 percent of all abortions. By 1963, 87.5 percent of the therapeutic abortions performed in Buffalo hospitals were being induced for psychiatric indications. Considering these studies, Reagan argues that the growing importance of psychiatric indications arose out of the decline in other medical complications such as heart disease, fibroids, toxemia of pregnancy, and tuberculosis, all of which had disappeared almost completely as indications by the end of the 1950s. *When Abortion Was a Crime*, pp. 201–3.

114. Morris A. Lipton to Charles Hendricks, 7 March 1970, folder Abortion—Psychiatric Letters, TCP-DUWA.

115. Raymond Manson and Donald E. Widmann, Diagnostic Evaluation, 27 May 1970, folder Therapeutic Abortions—Coeds, Jan. 1–June 30, 1970, TCP-DUWA.

116. See, e.g., Malcolm N. McLeod to Takey Crist, 8 October 1971, folder Abortion—Psychiatric Letters, TCP-DUWA. Here, the psychiatrist supported the woman's desire to keep the pregnancy over her boyfriend's wish that she have an abortion: "This 18-year old woman states that her boyfriend . . . wants her to have a therapeutic abortion but she does not want to. In fact, she states that having an abortion would have dire consequences for her. . . . In my opinion this girl shouldn't have an abortion."

117. John A. Ewing to Charles Hendricks, 23 March 1970, folder Abortion—Psychiatric Letters, TCP-DUWA.

118. Wilmer C. Betts to Takey Crist, 18 July 1972, folder Abortion—Psychiatric Let-

ters, TCP-DUWA. For a similar opinion, see also Manson and Widmann, Diagnostic Evaluation, TCP-DUWA.

119. Anonymous to Dr. Crist, [late 1969 or early 1970]. For similar sentiments, see also Anonymous to Dr. Crist, 11 January 1971, and Anonymous to Dr. Noyes, [May 1972]. On difficulties finding a physician who was willing to help, see, e.g., Anonymous to Dr. Crist, 26 March 1970; Anonymous to Dr. Crist, 30 March 1970; Anonymous to Dr. Crist, 14 February 1972; and Anonymous to Dr. Crist, n.d. All in folder Abortion Letters, TCP-DUWA.

120. Don [Widmann] to Takey Crist, 1 April 1970, folder Abortion—Psychiatric Letters, TCP-DUWA.

121. Ibid.

122. See, e.g., Donald E. Widmann, Diagnostic Evaluation, 2 July 1969; Widmann, Diagnostic Evaluation, 24 September 1969; Widmann, Diagnostic Evaluation, 7 January 1970; and Morton Meltzer and Widmann, Diagnostic Evaluation, 24 July 1970, all in folder Abortion—Psychiatric Letters, TCP-DUWA. See also Manson and Widmann, Diagnostic Evaluation, TCP-DUWA. For a discussion of psychiatrists who indicated much greater hostility toward women's ability to choose abortion, see Solinger, "A Complete Disaster."

123. Reagan, *When Abortion Was a Crime*, p. 218; Crist, interview; Hulka, interview; Hendricks, interview; Joffe, *Doctors of Conscience*.

124. The impetus to draft a model abortion law came from complaints from the medical profession about the precarious legal situation regarding abortion. The model abortion law proposed to allow licensed physicians to perform abortions for physical and mental health reasons, because of fetal defects, or if a pregnancy was caused by rape or incest. Reagan notes, however, that legal experts thought it not sensible to propose a general abortion-at-will statute. The model statute thus failed to challenge sexual norms that forbade sex outside of marriage and that used pregnancy and childbearing as a way to punish sexually active unwed women. *When Abortion Was a Crime*, pp. 220–24.

125. For a discussion of the Sherri Finkbine case, see Garrow, *Liberty and Sexuality*, pp. 285–91, 270–334. See also Petchesky, *Abortion and Woman's Choice*, pp. 101–37; Reagan, *When Abortion Was a Crime*, pp. 216–45; and Lader, *Abortion II*, pp. 56–71.

126. North Carolina was one of twenty-eight states in which such a bill was introduced in 1967. For a comprehensive discussion of the passage of North Carolina's abortion law, see Jain and Sinding, *North Carolina Abortion Law*, pp. 3, 15–16, CPC-UNC.

127. Ibid., pp. 17–18.

128. Ibid., p. 19.

129. Ibid., p. 70.

130. See note to chapter 2 above about the proposed legislation. See also "Racial Flareup Winds Up Hearing on Sterilization," *Raleigh News and Observer*, 2 April 1959, and "Sterilization Bill Hearing Ends in Uproar," *Charlotte Observer*, 2 April 1959.

131. Laurie Holder Jr., "Doctors, Ministers Support Abortion Bill," *Raleigh News and Observer*, 29 March 1967.

132. One legislator asked his colleagues to imagine that a pregnant woman whose husband has died decided to have an abortion in order to inherit both her portion of the estate and the portion that would otherwise have gone to her child. Under the new abortion law, he cautioned his audience, this scenario could become reality. "Substitute Abortion Bill Sent to Senate," *Raleigh News and Observer*, 31 March 1967, and "Doctor Says Abortion Bill Would Be License to Kill," *Raleigh News and Observer*, 2 April 1967.

133. Jain and Sinding, *North Carolina Abortion Law*, quotes on pp. 27, 28, CPC-UNC; Holder, "Doctors, Ministers Support Abortion Bill."

134. Quoted in Jain and Sinding, *North Carolina Abortion Law*, pp. 27, 37, CPC-UNC.

135. "Doctor Says Abortion Bill Would Be License to Kill"; Jain and Sinding, *North Carolina Abortion Law*, p. 41, CPC-UNC; Mandetta, "Abortion Legislation."

136. Quoted in Jain and Sinding, *North Carolina Abortion Law*, pp. 32, 36, 56, CPC-UNC.

137. George H. Lawrence to Ellen Winston, 9 November 1945, Correspondence with State Agencies, Boards, and Commissions, 1917–1956, box 30, folder Commission to Study the Laws Relating to Domestic Relations, Correspondence, 1945, DSS-NCSA. For petitions for eugenic abortion, see, e.g., Case 1, EBM, 2 May 1949; Case 12, EBM, 22 November 1950; Case 15, EBM, 24 September 1952; Case 14, EBM, 24 February 1954; and Case 12, EBM, 25 October 1960, all in EB-NCSA.

138. EBM, 27 November 1946, EB-NCSA. For clear denial of abortion requests, see Case 15, EBM, 24 September 1952; and Case 12, EBM, 25 October 1960, continued as Case 8, EBM, 24 January 1961, all in EB-NCSA. For a more thorough discussion of Lawrence's views, see chapters 2 and 3 of this study.

139. Quoted in Garrow, *Liberty and Sexuality*, p. 287.

140. Hendricks, interview.

141. DeProsse, interview.

142. Crist, "Contraceptive Practices."

143. Crist and Hendricks, interview. Hendricks indicated that physicians' personal experiences with unwanted pregnancies of relatives or friends commonly convinced them to aid patients seeking abortions.

144. Crist, "Abortion." While statewide statistics are not available, the number of abortions performed in eleven large hospitals in North Carolina rose from 13 in 1966 to 1,274 in 1970, indicating both a dramatic increase statewide and the leading role that North Carolina Memorial Hospital played in it. William E. Easterling and Charles H. Hendricks, "Pregnancy Termination: The First Five Years at North Carolina Memorial Hospital," 1971, table 2, folder UNC Co-Ed Abortions, TCP-DUWA.

145. Crist, interview.

146. Easterling and Hendricks, "Pregnancy Termination," tables 2 and 3.

147. Hulka, interview. See also Crist, interview.

148. Crist and Hendricks, interview.

149. Quoted in Jaroslav Hulka, *Therapeutic Abortion: A Chapel Hill Symposium* (Chapel Hill: Carolina Population Center, 1967), p. 31, copy consulted at CPC-UNC.

150. Crist, "Abortion," pp. 348–49.

151. There were 1,250 known therapeutic abortions in North Carolina in 1970. Eighty-eight percent of these were performed for psychiatric reasons. See Wilmer C. Betts to Jack Rhyne, 8 April 1971, box 2, folder 18, CC-SHC. For statistics, see Anne Marie Neal, "NC Woman Seeking Abortion Finds Most Doors Closed," *Raleigh News and Observer*, 1970, copy consulted in Clippings File, North Carolina Collection, and Jim Lewis, "No Increase Noted in Number of Hospital Abortions," *Raleigh News and Observer*, 1 October 1967. These findings mirror those in Colorado and California, where abortion reform had a similarly limited impact. See Garrow, *Liberty and Sexuality*, p. 341–42. For suspicions regarding women's motivations for abortion, see Bebe Moore, "No Increase in Abortions Reported," *Raleigh News and Observer*, 19 January 1969.

152. Judith E. Beach to Claude Currie, 8 March 1971, box 1, folder 5, CC-SHC.

153. Crist and Hendricks, interview.

154. See, e.g., Anonymous to Dr. Crist, 24 March 1971, and Anonymous to Dr. Crist, 5 August 1969, both in folder Abortion Letters, TCP-DUWA.

155. On the attempt to challenge the legality of the 1967 abortion bill, see "Law Faces Court Test," *Raleigh News and Observer*, 13 May 1970; "Law Upheld by Judges," *Raleigh News and Observer*, 2 February 1971; and "Ruling on Abortion Law," *Raleigh News and Observer*, 3 February 1971. Among the plaintiffs were the chairmen of the departments of obstetrics and gynecology of Duke University, Wake Forest University, and the University of North Carolina, as well as Dr. Elizabeth Corkey, who ran the Charlotte family planning clinic. For the abortion reform bill of 1971, see "Comparison of Current and Proposed Abortion Laws," March 1971, box 1, folder 7, CC-SHC, and Leslie Wayne, "Liberalized Abortion Bill Triggers Emotional Debate," *Raleigh News and Observer*, 17 January 1971.

156. Wayne, "Liberalized Abortion Bill"; E. A. Schadel to Claude Currie, 25 March 1971, box 1, folder 7, CC-SHC; Mrs. Richard H. Daffner to Currie, 3 March 1971, box 1, folder 4, CC-SHC; Emma Carr Bivins, Mrs. Evelyn Bissell, and Becky S. Bowden to Currie, 4 March 1971, box 1, folder 4, CC-SHC.

157. John R. Marchese, "Abortion: Pure Convenience?" *Charlotte Observer*, 3 October 1971. For similar sentiments, see Davis to Currie, 26 January 1971, CC-SHC. Dr. Rachel Davis's public position advocated, among other things, that any woman seeking a third abortion should be sterilized. Such rhetoric, clearly more in line with the opinions of conservative legislators than with a reproductive rights position, emphasized the conservative arguments for access to abortion, birth control, and sterilization. Takey Crist and Paul Williams, however, remember Dr. Davis as a progressive gynecologist actively involved in extending reproductive control to women. Crist, interview.

158. Charles J. Wells to Claude Currie, 17 March 1971, box 1, folder 6, CC-SHC.

159. Emma J. Drum to Claude Currie, 19 March 1971, box 1, folder 6, CC-SHC. See

also Martha H. Tembath to Currie, 4 March 1971, box 1, folder 4, and James G. Hamilton to Currie, 19 March 1971, box 2, folder 18, both in CC-SHC.

160. Hamilton to Currie, 19 March 1971, CC-SHC.

161. Wells to Currie, 17 March 1971, CC-SHC.

162. Public Health Nurses of the Durham County Health Department to Currie, 18 March 1971, box 1, folder 6, CC-SHC.

163. Jain and Sinding argue that opposition to the 1967 abortion reform bill was entirely Roman Catholic but was organized by laypeople only. No Roman Catholic clergy testified against the 1967 bill. The authors attribute this to the small Catholic population in North Carolina—only 1 percent of the state's population is Catholic—but the explanation is not entirely convincing. It seems likely that opponents from all quarters failed to take the first reform effort seriously. *North Carolina Abortion Law*, pp. 24–25, CPC-UNC.

164. Mrs. Shelby Tyler to Currie, 4 March 1971, box 2, folder 12, CC-SHC.

165. Mrs. Robert Bruce Johnson to Currie, 4 March 1971, box 2, folder 12, CC-SHC. For the comparison to Nazi euthanasia policies, see Patrick A. McKee to Currie, 30 March 1971, box 2, folder 18, CC-SHC, and Jain and Sinding, *North Carolina Abortion Law*, p. 38, CPC-UNC.

166. Johnson to Currie, 4 March 1971, CC-SHC; Captain and Mrs. John P. Galligan to Currie, 2 April 1971, box 2, folder 14, CC-SHC; C. Anthony Ricca to Currie, 15 February 1971, box 2, folder 11, CC-SHC; Rev. Msgr. Frank J. Howard to Currie, 24 March 1971, box 2, folder 13, CC-SHC; Leslie Wayne, "State Senate Defeats Abortion Bill, 25–21," *Raleigh News and Observer*, 7 April 1971; Marchese, "Abortion."

167. Claude Currie to Joseph C. Sloane, 9 April 1971, box 2, folder 18, CC-SHC; Wayne, "State Senate Defeats Abortion Bill"; Bob Brooks, "Did Mountain of Mail Kill the Bill?" *Raleigh News and Observer*, 11 April 1971.

168. See, e.g., "Dr. Takey Crist Interview: High School Couple for AB Coed," tape 26, TCP-DUWA. On the Clergy Consultation Service, see Carmen and Moody, *Abortion Counseling*; Brownmiller, "Abortion Counseling"; Ellsworth, "Contested Space"; and Reagan, *When Abortion Was a Crime*, pp. 241–42. For a more thorough description of the legal battles involved in the establishment of abortion clinics, see Lader, *Abortion II*, pp. 109–21.

169. *Roe v. Wade*, 410 U.S. 113 (1973), pp. 153–54.

170. Petchesky, *Abortion and Women's Choice*, pp. 291–92. The Supreme Court stated in *Roe*: "The decision vindicates *the right of the physician* to administer medical treatment *according to his professional judgment* up to the points where important state interests provide compelling justifications for intervention. Up to those points, the *abortion decision in all its aspects is inherently, and primarily, a medical decision, and basic responsibility for it must rest with the physician*" (emphasis is Petchesky's). See also Glen, "Abortion in the Courts," and Garrow, *Liberty and Sexuality*.

171. Estimates of abortion-related mortality rates prior to *Roe* suggest that between one and five thousand women died annually of illegal abortions and that approx-

imately 1.2 million illegal abortions were performed annually in the years imme-diately preceding *Roe*. Joffe, *Doctors of Conscience*, pp. 4, 29.

172. See, e.g., Fried, "Abortion in the United States."

173. For further discussion of the erosion of medical indications and the conse-quences of this development for funding of abortion, see Petchesky, *Abortion and Women's Choice*, pp. 293–302.

174. Quoted in ibid., p. 293.

CHAPTER FOUR

1. Chesler, *Woman of Valor*, pp. 355–70, 245–46, and Doone and Greer Williams, *Every Child*.

2. Clarke, *Disciplining Reproduction*, p. 57.

3. Kingsley Davis, "Population and Power," p. 356. See also Greenhalgh, "Social Construction"; Reed, *From Private Vice*, pp. 282–83; and Sharpless, "World Population Growth."

4. Quoted in Smith, *Sick and Tired*, p. 115.

5. See Doone and Greer Williams, *Every Child*; Critchlow, *Intended Consequences*; and Reed, *From Private Vice*.

6. See Mass, *Population Target*; Gordon, *Woman's Body*; Angela Davis, *Women, Race, and Class*; and García, *La Operación*. See also Briggs, *Reproducing Empire*, pp. 143–52.

7. Findlay, *Imposing Decency*.

8. Briggs, *Reproducing Empire*, chapter 3, esp. pp. 98–99.

9. Stepan, *Hour of Eugenics*.

10. Ramírez de Arellano and Seipp, *Colonialism*, p. 42, and Briggs, *Reproducing Empire*, pp. 90–96.

11. Ramírez de Arellano and Seipp, *Colonialism*, pp. 34–36, and Briggs, *Reproducing Empire*, pp. 74–102.

12. Briggs, *Reproducing Empire*, pp. 80–81, and Ramírez de Arellano and Seipp, *Colonialism*, pp. 42–44.

13. Briggs, *Reproducing Empire*, pp. 102–8.

14. Ibid., p. 107. Ramírez de Arellano and Seipp note that between 1937 and 1950 a total of ninety-seven sterilizations were carried out under the authority of Puerto Rico's Eugenics Board. See *Colonialism*, p. 204, n. 3. In 1960, the Puerto Rican legisla-ture repealed the eugenic sterilization law. Presser, *Sterilization*, p. 55, n. 26.

15. Briggs, *Reproducing Empire*, p. 123.

16. Ibid., pp. 103, 107–8.

17. Ibid., pp. 127–28.

18. Ibid., pp. 125–27.

19. Gladys Gaylord to Clarence Gamble, 28 October 1936, box 45, folder 733, CJG-CML, quoted in ibid., p. 104.

20. Doone and Greer Williams, *Every Child*, pp. 171–73.

21. Briggs, *Reproducing Empire*, pp. 104–6, and Ramírez de Arellano and Seipp, *Colonialism*, pp. 46–47.

22. Briggs, *Reproducing Empire*, p. 128.

23. Cooper, "Birth Control," p. 466, and Norton, "Twenty-One Years' Experience."

24. Condoms required male cooperation, and, particularly among poor women, the diaphragm had proven to be much less successful than Sanger had hoped. Tone, *Devices and Desires*, pp. 208–9, 211–12, 253.

25. Quoted in ibid., p. 207.

26. In fact, Tone reminds us that Puerto Rico stood in stark contrast to Pincus's home state of Massachusetts, where the dissemination of birth control was still illegal. Ibid., p. 220. For more on Pincus, see pp. 209–26.

27. Presser, *Sterilization*, pp. 30–32, and Marks, "Cage of Ovulating Females," p. 235.

28. Briggs, *Reproducing Empire*, pp. 136–37.

29. Tone, *Devices and Desires*, pp. 220, 227, 258.

30. Quoted in Marks, "Cage of Ovulating Females," p. 237.

31. See Tone on the lengths to which women were willing to go to participate in pill trials. *Devices and Desires*, pp. 225–26.

32. Ibid., pp. 222–23.

33. Marks, "Cage of Ovulating Females," pp. 231, 228, and Briggs, *Reproducing Empire*, pp. 135–36.

34. Marks, "Cage of Ovulating Females," pp. 235–36.

35. Quoted in Tone, *Devices and Desires*, p. 224.

36. Marks notes that over 20 percent of women who participated in the Haiti project forgot to take the pill. There are no comparable statistics for the Puerto Rican women. "Cage of Ovulating Females," pp. 236–37.

37. Quoted in Tone, *Devices and Desires*, p. 223.

38. Ibid., pp. 223–24. See also the discussion about the reasons women left contraceptive trials in chapter 1 above.

39. On the use of human subjects, see Lederer, *Subjected to Science*. On Tuskegee, see Jones, *Bad Blood*.

40. Briggs, *Reproducing Empire*, pp. 124–25, 131–32, and Clarke, *Disciplining Reproduction*, pp. 163–206.

41. Quoted in Tone, *Devices and Desires*, p. 223.

42. Quoted in Briggs, *Reproducing Empire*, p. 218.

43. Ibid., pp. 218–19.

44. Ibid., pp. 137–38.

45. Marks, "Cage of Ovulating Females," pp. 235, 239.

46. Ramírez de Arellano and Seipp, *Colonialism*, p. 204, n. 3, and Presser, *Sterilization*, p. 55, n. 26.

47. Presser, *Sterilization*, pp. 28–29.

48. Ibid., p. 127.

49. Quoted in Briggs, *Reproducing Empire*, p. 145. See also pp. 142–48.

50. Presser, *Sterilization*, p. 50.

51. Briggs, *Reproducing Empire*, pp. 152–56.

52. U.S. Department of Health, Education, and Welfare, *Family Planning*, pp. 63–69.

53. Of 519 women interviewed between three and ten years after they had the surgery, 3 reported that they had learned only later that there were temporary methods of contraception, and 2 felt that sterilization was in conflict with their religious beliefs. Briggs, *Reproducing Empire*, pp. 152–58, esp. pp. 154–56.

54. Ibid., p. 150, and Presser, *Sterilization*, pp. 33, 54.

55. See, e.g., Mass, *Population Target*, pp. 91–95; Gordon, *Woman's Body*, pp. 400–402; Angela Davis, *Women, Race, and Class*, pp. 219–21; García, *La Operación*; and Hartmann, *Reproductive Rights*, pp. 244–51.

56. Ehrlich, *Population Bomb*, p. 15.

57. Forbes, *Women in Modern India*, p. 85, and Mayo, *Mother India*.

58. Dikötter, "Race Culture"; Lal, "Purdah as Pathology"; Arnold, "Official Attitudes"; Hodges, "Indian Eugenics."

59. Some have seen nationalist interest in birth control in a positive light. See, e.g., Ramusack, "Embattled Advocates," and Manna, "Approach towards Birth Control." Others have claimed that the national glorification of motherhood in this discourse allowed the state to opt for cheap baby clinics and health centers while denying women the true empowerment they would have if they were granted their full social, economic, and political entitlement. See Samita Sen, "Motherhood."

60. Satyendranath Vasu quoted in Manna, "Approach towards Birth Control," p. 46.

61. Chatterjee and Riley, "Planning."

62. Ibid.; Hartmann, *Reproductive Rights*, p. 254, also 233–40.

63. Hodges, "Indian Eugenics," and Dikötter, "Race Culture."

64. Ramusack, "Authority and Ambivalence" and "Maternal and Infant Health, Population Control or Eugenics: Reproductive Control in India, 1920–1940," unpublished manuscript.

65. A. P. Pillay, "A Birth Control Educative Tour," *Marriage Hygiene* 4, no. 1 (August 1937): 48–50, quoted in Hodges, "Conjugality," p. 173.

66. Ramusack, "Embattled Advocates."

67. Hodges, "Conjugality," p. 176.

68. Ramusack, "Maternal and Infant Health," pp. 45–46, and "Embattled Advocates."

69. Hodges, "Conjugality," p. 184.

70. Ramusack, "Authority and Ambivalence." David Arnold reports that there were about forty women in active service with the WMS in the 1930s and ten more on leave, compared to nearly a thousand physicians who worked through the Indian Medical Service. See "Official Attitudes." On the funding of contraceptive research, see Clarke, *Disciplining Reproduction*, pp. 207–30.

71. Ramusack, "Embattled Advocates," pp. 37–38; Ramusack, "Authority and Ambivalence"; Arnold, "Official Attitudes"; Ahluwalia, "Controlling Births."

72. Quoted in Ramusack, "Authority and Ambivalence," p. 20.

73. In 1936, a physician at the American Presbyterian Mission in Sharanpur asked Clarence Gamble for help in securing contraceptive supplies for her patients. Gamble also corresponded with Dr. Carol Jameson, who was affiliated with the Missionary Medical School for Women in Vellore, met with her, and later contributed $100 to investigate contraceptives suitable for use in southern India. The Birth Control International Information Center was an investigative center and clearinghouse for birth control information that How-Martyn directed. Hodges, "Conjugality," pp. 175, 194, 196–97; Ramusack, "Embattled Advocates," pp. 37–38; Ramusack, "Authority and Ambivalence"; Arnold, "Official Attitudes"; Ahluwalia, "Controlling Births."

74. Quoted in Ramusack, "Embattled Advocates," p. 40. See also Ahluwalia, "Controlling Births," p. 265.

75. Ramusack, "Embattled Advocates," pp. 46–47, and Manna, "Approach towards Birth Control," pp. 40–42. Recalling her visit to India in 1935 and 1936, Margaret Sanger confirmed women's—especially young women's—interest in contraceptive advice. Sanger, *Autobiography*, pp. 480–81.

76. Hodges, "Indian Eugenics" and "Conjugality," pp. 198–200.

77. Quoted in Hodges, "Conjugality," p. 197.

78. Quoted in ibid., p. 195. See also p. 197.

79. Ramusack, "Embattled Advocates," pp. 45–47; Arnold, "Official Attitudes"; Hodges, "Conjugality," pp. 199–200.

80. Ramusack, "Embattled Advocates," pp. 45–46.

81. Chowdhury, "Instructions."

82. Ibid.; Hodges, "Conjugality," p. 197; H. L. Offerman to Margaret Sanger, 9 February 1951, reel S33, MS-SSC.

83. Quoted in Ramusack, "Embattled Advocates," pp. 37–38.

84. Quoted in ibid., pp. 45–46.

85. Ibid., p. 47.

86. Ledbetter, "Thirty Years," pp. 738–39, and Ahluwalia, "Controlling Births," p. 265.

87. Doone and Greer Williams, *Every Child*, pp. 201–48.

88. Vera Houghton to Margaret Sanger, 27 August 1954, reel S44, MS-SSC. While Gamble argued that the salt solution had also been tested at the Margaret Sanger Clinical Research Bureau, only three women had participated in those tests. It is likely that the staff at the Sanger clinic had reservations about salt-based contraceptives, possibly fueled by the complaints of the three women who had tried the method. Gamble financed tests of the salt solution in Japan as part of the field tests he set up there. Almost all the families who tried the method gave it up quickly. Despite such evidence of the method's unsuitability, Gamble continued searching for sites in which to test it and claimed to critics that the method had shown satisfactory results. Reed, *From Private Vice*, pp. 294–96.

89. Fernando to Gamble, 24 August 1954, reel S44, MS-SSC.

90. Doone and Greer Williams, *Every Child*, pp. 249–51.

91. Rama Rau to Gamble, 14 September 1954, reel S44, MS-SSC.

92. Houghton to Sanger, 27 August 1954, MS-SSC.

93. Ibid.

94. Ahluwalia, "Controlling Births," p. 266.

95. Mamdani, *Myth of Population Control.*

96. As policy makers' desperation grew, their willingness to resort to coercive measures also increased. The resulting picture is one of Indian family planning run amok, with its policies spiraling out of control as the country's population was also spiraling out of control. See, e.g., Chadney, "Family Planning," and Ledbetter, "Thirty Years."

97. Chatterjee and Riley, "Planning"; Ledbetter, "Thirty Years"; Tarlo, *Unsettling Memories.*

98. Srinivasan, "Population Policies," and Van Hollen, "Moving Targets."

99. See, e.g., Ledbetter, "Thirty Years."

100. Chatterjee and Riley, "Planning." See also Vicziany, "Coercion Part 1" and "Coercion Part 2."

101. Chatterjee and Riley, "Planning," pp. 827–28, and Ahluwalia, "Controlling Births."

102. Quoted in Tarlo, *Unsettling Memories*, p. 131.

103. Carolyn Henning Brown, "Forced Sterilization," p. 52.

104. Tarlo, *Unsettling Memories*, p. 177.

105. Srinivasan, "Population Policies," and Koenig, Foo, and Joshi, "Quality of Care."

106. Koenig, Foo, and Joshi, "Quality of Care," p. 3.

107. Van Hollen, "Moving Targets."

108. Koenig, Foo, and Joshi, "Quality of Care," p. 4.

109. Ibid., p. 5.

110. Rothman, "Shame of Medical Research."

111. Amarya Sen, "Population," p. 71.

112. Petchesky and Judd, *Negotiating Reproductive Rights*, p. 3.

EPILOGUE

1. The complete series is now available on a website. See <http://againsttheirwill.journalnow.com> (accessed 9 March 2004).

2. "N.C. to Aid Sterilization Victims," *Washington Post*, 29 September 2003.

3. Bonnie Rochman, "Sterilized by State Order," *Raleigh News and Observer*, 15 April 2001.

4. Quoted in Kevin Begos and John Railey, "Sign This or Else," *Winston-Salem Journal*, 9 December 2002.

5. Quoted in Kevin Begos and John Railey, "Still Hiding," *Winston-Salem Journal*, 8 December 2002.

6. John Railey, "Advocate: WF President Embraced Eugenics Movement," *Winston-Salem Journal*, 9 December 2002.

7. Kevin Begos, "Benefactor with a Racist Bent," *Winston-Salem Journal*, 9 December 2002.

8. Danielle Deaver, "Forsyth in the Forefront," *Winston-Salem Journal*, 9 December 2002.

9. Begos and Railey, "Sign This or Else." See also John Railey, "Wicked Silence," *Winston-Salem Journal*, 11 December 2002.

10. See, e.g., "Sterilization Program Targeted Women, Blacks in Later Years," *Charlotte Observer*, 9 December 2002.

11. Kevin Begos, "Castration: Files Suggest That Punishment Was Often the Aim," *Winston-Salem Journal*, 9 December 2002.

12. Quoted in Railey, "Wicked Silence."

13. Peter Hardin, "Segregation's Era of 'Science' Eugenics Altered Lives, Left Mark in Virginia," *Richmond Times Dispatch*, 26 November 2000; Julie Sullivan, "Facing the Shame," *Oregonian*, 30 June 2002; Mike Anton, "Forced Sterilization Once Seen as Path to a Better World," *Los Angeles Times*, 16 July 2003.

14. Aaron Zitner, "Davis' Apology Sheds No Light on Sterilizations in California," *Los Angeles Times*, 16 March 2003.

15. Quoted in Begos and Railey, "Sign This or Else."

16. See, e.g., John Railey and Kevin Begos, "Still Hiding," *Winston-Salem Journal*, 8 December 2002; Kevin Begos, Danielle Deaver, and John Railey, "Easley Apologizes to Sterilization Victims," *Winston-Salem Journal*, 13 December 2002.

17. Quotation in Begos, Deaver, and Railey, "Easley Apologizes to Sterilization Victims." See also Danielle Deaver, "Making Amends," *Winston-Salem Journal*, 28 September 2003; John Railey, "Offer 'Too Little Too Late,'" *Winston-Salem Journal*, 28 September 2003.

18. Quoted in Railey, "Offer 'Too Little Too Late.'"

19. Quoted in Begos, Deaver, and Railey, "Easley Apologizes to Sterilization Victims."

20. Zitner, "Davis' Apology Sheds No Light." Davis issued his apology following a lecture by Paul Lombardo to a state Senate committee in March 2003.

21. Julie Sullivan, "Eugenics Records Shredded," *Oregonian*, 30 July 2002.

Bibliography

MANUSCRIPT COLLECTIONS

Atkins Library, University of North Carolina at Charlotte,
  Charlotte, N.C.
  Fred Alexander Papers
Carolina Population Center, University of North Carolina at
  Chapel Hill, Chapel Hill, N.C.
Countway Medical Library, Harvard University, Boston, Mass.
  Clarence J. Gamble Papers
Duke University Women's Archive, Durham, N.C.
  Takey Crist Papers
Jackson Library, University of North Carolina at Greensboro,
  Greensboro, N.C.
  Ellen Black Winston Papers
National Archives, Suitland, Md.
  Children's Bureau Papers
North Carolina Collection, Wilson Library, University of North
  Carolina at Chapel Hill, Chapel Hill, N.C.
North Carolina State Archives, Raleigh, N.C.
  Attorney General's Records
  Eugenics Board Papers
  Social Services Record Group Papers
  State Board of Health Papers
Sophia Smith Collection, Smith College, Northampton, Mass.
  Margaret Sanger Papers
  Planned Parenthood Federation of America Papers
Southern Historical Collection, University of North Carolina at
  Chapel Hill, Chapel Hill, N.C.
  Claude Currie Papers
  Human Betterment League Papers
  J. W. R. Norton Papers
  North Carolina Fund Papers

INTERVIEWS

Interviews by the Author

Baker, Elizabeth. 25 April 1990. Cary, N.C.
Bryant, Sarah. 11 June 1997. Charlotte, N.C.
Chapin, Edwin H. 19 June 1997. Charlotte, N.C.
Cloer, Virginia, Dorothy Hicks, and Eleanor Anderson. 11 June 1997. Charlotte, N.C.
Crist, Takey. 20 May 2001. Jacksonville, N.C.
Crist, Takey, and Charles Hendricks. 18 November 2002. Chapel Hill, N.C.
Davis, Elsie. 28 February 1989. Fayetteville, N.C.
DeProsse, Charles. 23 October 2002. Iowa City, Iowa
Hendricks, Charles. 11 October 2001. Chapel Hill, N.C.
Hulka, Jaroslav F. 22 May 2001. Chapel Hill, N.C.
Koomen, Jakob. 2 May 1990. Chapel Hill, N.C.
Kuralt, Wallace. 4 December 1993. Southern Shores, N.C.
Wall, Murlene. 19 June 1997. Charlotte, N.C.
Wolfe, Ann F. 21 May 2001. Wrightsville Beach, N.C.

Jackson Library, University of North Carolina at Greensboro, Greensboro, N.C.

Winston, Ellen. Interview by Annette Smith. 2 December 1974. Raleigh, N.C.

*Southern Historical Collection, University of North Carolina at
Chapel Hill, Chapel Hill, N.C.*

Easely, Eleanor. Interview by Rebecca McCoy. 25 July 1985. Durham, N.C.
Lupton, Caroll. Interview by Mary Murphy. 18 May 1979. Greensboro, N.C.

Unpublished Interviews

Scott, Mabel [pseud.]. Interview by John Railey. 26 August 2002. Atlanta, Ga.

NEWSPAPERS AND PERIODICALS

Asheville Citizen
Biennial Report of the Eugenics Board of North Carolina
Burlington Times News
Charlotte News
Charlotte Observer
Child
Durham Herald News
Durham Morning Herald
Greensboro Daily News
Health Bulletin

Los Angeles Times
New York Times
Oregonian
Public Welfare News
Public Welfare Progress
Raleigh News and Observer
Richmond Times Dispatch
San Francisco Chronicle
Social Services in North Carolina
Washington Herald
Washington Post
Winston-Salem Journal
Winston-Salem Twin City Sentinel

BOOKS, ARTICLES, AND DISSERTATIONS

Abramovitz, Mimi. *Regulating the Lives of Women: Social Welfare Policy from Colonial Times to the Present*. Boston: South End Press, 1988.

Abrams, Douglas Carl. *Conservative Constraints: North Carolina and the New Deal*. Jackson: University Press of Mississippi, 1992.

Ahluwalia, Sanjam. "Controlling Births, Policing Sexualities: A History of Birth Control in Colonial India, 1877–1946." Ph.D. diss., University of Cincinnati, 2000.

Arnold, David. "Official Attitudes to Population, Birth Control, and Reproductive Health, 1926–46." In *Reproductive Health in India: History, Politics, Controversies*, edited by Sarah Hodges. Delhi: Orient Longman, forthcoming.

Badger, Anthony J. *North Carolina and the New Deal*. Raleigh: North Carolina Department of Cultural Resources, Division of Archives and History, 1981.

Baldwin, Sidney. *Poverty and Politics: The Rise and Decline of the Farm Security Administration*. Chapel Hill: University of North Carolina Press, 1968.

Bandarage, Asoka. *Women, Population, and Global Crisis*. London: Zed Books, 1997.

Banfield, Edward C. *The Unheavenly City: The Nature and the Future of Our Urban Crisis*. Boston: Little, Brown, 1970.

Beardsley, Edward H. *A History of Neglect: Health Care for Blacks and Mill Workers in the Twentieth-Century South*. Knoxville: University of Tennessee Press, 1987.

Bell, Winifred. *Aid to Dependent Children*. New York: Columbia University Press, 1965.

Bishop, Mary. "Sterilization Survivors Speak Out." *Southern Exposure* 23, no. 2 (Summer 1995): 12–17.

Boas, Franz. *The Mind of Primitive Man*. New York: Macmillan, 1938.

Bock, Gisela. "Racism and Sexism in Nazi Germany." In *When Biology Became Destiny*, edited by Renate Bridenthal, Atina Grossman, and Marion Kaplan, 271–96. New York: Monthly Review Press, 1984.

Boger, Mary Snead. *Charlotte 23*. Bassett, Va.: Bassett Print Corporation, 1972.

Borst, Charlotte G. *Catching Babies: The Professionalization of Childbirth, 1870–1920*. Cambridge, Mass.: Harvard University Press, 1995.

Bradway, John S. "The Legality of Human Sterilization in North Carolina." *North Carolina Medical Journal* 11 (May 1950): 250–53.

Brandt, Allan M. *No Magic Bullet: A Social History of Venereal Disease in the United States since 1880*. New York: Oxford University Press, 1987.

Briggs, Laura. "Discourses of 'Forced Sterilization' in Puerto Rico." *Differences* 10, no. 2 (1998): 30–66.

——. *Reproducing Empire: Race, Sex, and Science in the U.S. Imperial Project in Puerto Rico*. Berkeley and Los Angeles: University of California Press, 2002.

Broberg, Gunnar, and Nils Roll-Hansen, eds. *Eugenics and the Welfare State: Sterilization Policy in Denmark, Sweden, Norway, and Finland*. East Lansing: Michigan State University Press, 1996.

Brodie, Janet Farrell. *Contraception and Abortion in Nineteenth-Century America*. Ithaca: Cornell University Press, 1994.

Brown, Carolyn Henning. "The Forced Sterilization Program under the Indian Emergency: Results in One Settlement." *Human Organization* 43, no. 1 (1984): 49–54.

Brown, JoAnne. *The Definition of a Profession: The Authority of Metaphor in the History of Intelligence Testing, 1890–1930*. Princeton: Princeton University Press, 1992.

Brown, R. Eugene. *Eugenical Sterilization in North Carolina*. Raleigh: Eugenics Board of North Carolina, 1935.

Brownmiller, Susan. "Abortion Counseling: Service beyond Sermons." *New York Magazine*, 4 August 1969, 1.

Carey, Allison C. "Gender and Compulsory Sterilization Programs in America: 1907–1950." *Journal of Historical Sociology* 11, no. 1 (March 1998): 74–105.

Carmen, Arlene, and Howard Moody. *Abortion Counseling and Social Change: From Illegal Act to Medical Practice; The Story of the Clergy Consultation Service on Abortion*. Valley Forge, Pa.: Judson Press, 1973.

Caron, Simone M. "Birth Control and the Black Community in the 1960s: Genocide or Power Politics?" *Journal of Social History* 31, no. 3 (Spring 1998): 545–69.

Chadney, James G. "Family Planning: India's Achilles' Heel?" *Journal of Asian and African Studies* 22, no. 3–4 (1987): 218–31.

Chatterjee, Nilanjana, and Nancy E. Riley. "Planning an Indian Modernity: The Gendered Politics of Fertility Control." *Signs* 26, no. 3 (Spring 2001): 811–45.

Chesler, Ellen. *Woman of Valor: Margaret Sanger and the Birth Control Movement in America*. New York: Doubleday Anchor Books, 1992.

Chowdhury, Indira. "Instructions for the Unconverted: Birth Control, Marie Stopes, and Indian Women." Paper presented at the Conference on Population, Birth Control, and Reproductive Health in Late Colonial India, School of Oriental and African Studies, University of London, 18–19 November 1999.

Clarke, Adele E. *Disciplining Reproduction: Modernity, American Life Sciences, and the Problems of Sex*. Berkeley and Los Angeles: University of California Press, 1998.

Cockrell, David L. " 'A Blessing in Disguise': The Influenza Pandemic of 1918 and

North Carolina's Medical and Public Health Communities." *North Carolina Historical Review* 73, no. 3 (July 1996): 309–27.

Committee for the Investigation of Eugenical Sterilization, American Neurological Association. *Eugenic Sterilization*. New York: Macmillan, 1936.

Committee on the Costs of Medical Care. *Medical Care for the American People: The Final Report of the Committee on the Costs of Medical Care*. Chicago: University of Chicago Press, 1932.

Cooper, George M. "Birth Control in the North Carolina Health Department." *North Carolina Medical Journal* 1, no. 9 (September 1940): 463–67.

———. "Progress in Maternal and Child Health Work." *Health Bulletin* 52, no. 2 (February 1937): 5–9.

Corkey, Elizabeth C. "The Birth Control Program in the Mecklenburg County Health Department." *American Journal of Public Health* 56, no. 1 (January 1966): 40–47.

Correa, Sonia, and Rosalind P. Petchesky. "Reproductive and Sexual Rights." In *Population Policies Reconsidered: Health, Empowerment, and Rights*, edited by Gita Sen, Adrienne Germain, and Lincoln Chen, 107–26. Cambridge, Mass.: Harvard University Press, 1994.

Cravens, Hamilton. "The Wandering IQ: The Iowa Child Welfare Research Station and Mental Testing, 1935–1940." *Time*, 7 November 1938, 44–46.

Crist, Takey. "Abortion: Where Have We Been? Where Are We Going?" *North Carolina Medical Journal* 32, no. 8 (August 1971): 347–51.

———. "Contraceptive Practices among College Women." *Medical Aspects of Human Sexuality* 5 (1971): 168–76.

———. "Why Is It That with Many Methods of Birth Control So Easily Available, Knowledgeable People Still Become Pregnant When They Don't Want To?" *Sexual Behavior* (September 1971): 4.

Crist, Takey, and Cecil Farrington. "The Use of Estrogen as a Postcoital Contraceptive in North Carolina—Trick or Treatment." *North Carolina Medical Journal* 34, no. 10 (October 1973): 792–95.

Critchlow, Donald T. *Intended Consequences: Birth Control, Abortion, and the Federal Government in Modern America*. New York: Oxford University Press, 1999.

Cronon, William. "A Place for Stories: Nature, History, and Narrative." *Journal of American History* (March 1992): 1347–76.

Czarnowski, Gabriele. "Frauen als Mütter der Rasse: Abtreibungsverfolgung und Zwangseingriff im Nationalsozialismus." In *Unter anderen Umständen: Zur Geschichte der Abtreibung*, edited by Gisela Staupe and Lisa Vieth, 58–72. Berlin: Argon Verlag, 1993.

Darity, William. "Contraceptive Education: The Relative Cultural and Social Factors Related to Applied Health Education with Special Reference to Oral Contraceptives." Ph.D. diss., University of North Carolina at Chapel Hill, 1963.

Davenport, Charles B. "The Feebly Inhibited: I. Violent Temper and Its Inheritance." *Journal of Nervous and Mental Disease* 42, no. 9 (September 1915): 593–628.

Davis, Angela. *Women, Race, and Class*. New York: Vintage, 1981.

Davis, Kingsley. "Population and Power in the Free World." In *Population, Theory, and Policy*, edited by Joseph J. Spengler and Otis Dudley Duncan, 342–56. Glencoe, Ill.: Free Press, 1956.

Degler, Carl N. *In Search of Human Nature: The Decline and Revival of Darwinism in American Social Thought*. New York: Oxford University Press, 1991.

D'Emilio, John, and Estelle Freedman. *Intimate Matters: A History of Sexuality in America*. New York: Harper and Row, 1988.

Dikötter, Frank. "Race Culture: Recent Perspectives on the History of Eugenics." *American Historical Review* 103, no. 2 (April 1998): 467–78.

Donnelly, James F., and Frank R. Lock. "Indications for the Sterilization of Women." *North Carolina Medical Journal* 14, no. 1 (January 1953): 1–5.

Dreifus, Claudia. "Sterilizing the Poor." In *Seizing Our Bodies: The Politics of Women's Health*, edited by Claudia Dreifus, 105–20. New York: Vintage Books, 1977.

Dugdale, Robert L. *The Jukes: Study in Crime, Pauperism, Disease, and Heredity*. 4th ed. New York: Putnam's Sons, 1910.

Ehrenreich, Barbara, and Deidre English. *For Her Own Good: 150 Years of the Experts' Advice to Women*. Garden City, N.Y.: Doubleday, Anchor Press, 1978.

Ehrlich, Paul. *The Population Bomb*. New York: Sierra Club / Ballantine, 1968.

Ellsworth, Elizabeth Stephens. "Contested Space: Illegal Abortion in North Carolina." M.A. thesis, Duke University, 1995.

Findlay, Eileen. *Imposing Decency: The Politics of Sexuality and Race in Puerto Rico, 1870–1920*. Durham: Duke University Press, 1999.

Flexner, Abraham. *Medical Education in the United States and Canada: Report to the Carnegie Foundation for the Advancement of Teaching*. 1910. Reprint, Washington, D.C.: Science and Health Publications, 1960.

Flowers, Charles E., James F. Donnelly, and John C. Burwell. "The Practice of Tubal Ligation in North Carolina." *North Carolina Medical Journal* 20, no. 12 (December 1959): 489–500.

Forbes, Geraldine. *Women in Modern India*. Cambridge: Cambridge University Press, 1999.

Fraser, Gertrude Jacinta. *African American Midwifery in the South: Dialogues of Birth, Race, and Memory*. Cambridge, Mass.: Harvard University Press, 1999.

Fraser, Nancy. "The Struggle over Needs: Outline of a Socialist-Feminist Critical Theory of Late-Capitalist Political Culture." In *Women, the State, and Welfare*, edited by Linda Gordon, 199–225. Madison: University of Wisconsin Press, 1990.

Fried, Marlene Gerber. "Abortion in the United States—Legal but Inaccessible." In *Abortion Wars: A Half Century of Struggle, 1950–2000*, edited by Rickie Solinger, 208–26. Berkeley and Los Angeles: University of California Press, 1998.

Gamble, Clarence J. "Eugenic Sterilization in the United States." *Eugenical News* 34, no. 1–2 (March–June 1949): 1–5.

———. "State Sterilization Programs for the Prophylactic Control of Mental Disease and Mental Deficiency." *American Journal of Psychiatry* 102, no. 3 (November 1945): 289–93.

——. "The Sterilization of Psychotic Patients under State Laws." *American Journal of Psychiatry* 105, no. 1 (July 1948): 60–62.

——. "Trends in State Programs for the Sterilization of the Mentally Deficient." *American Journal of Mental Deficiency* 53, no. 4 (April 1949): 538–41.

——. "Why Fear Sterilization?" *Hygeia* 26 (1948): 22–23, 60.

Gamble, Clarence J., and Gilbert W. Beebe. "The Clinical Effectiveness of Lactic and Jelly as a Contraceptive." *American Journal of the Medical Sciences* 194, no. 1 (July 1937): 79–84.

García, Ana María, director. *La Operación*. VHS. New York: Latin American Film Project / Cinema Guild, 1992.

Garrow, David J. *Liberty and Sexuality: The Right to Privacy and the Making of "Roe v. Wade."* New York: Macmillan, 1994.

Glen, Kristin Booth. "Abortion in the Courts: A Laywoman's Historical Guide to the New Disaster Area." *Feminist Studies* 4, no. 1 (February 1978): 1–26.

Goddard, Henry H. *The Kallikak Family: A Study in the Heredity of Feeblemindedness.* New York: Macmillan, 1921.

Gordon, Linda. "Family Violence, Feminism, and Social Control." In *Women, the State, and Welfare*, edited by Linda Gordon, 178–98. Madison: University of Wisconsin Press, 1990.

——. *Heroes of Their Own Lives: The Politics and History of Family Violence.* New York: Viking, 1988.

——. *Pitied but Not Entitled: Single Mothers and the History of Welfare.* New York: Free Press, 1994.

——. *Woman's Body, Woman's Right: A Social History of Birth Control in America.* New York: Grossman, 1976.

——, ed. *Women, the State, and Welfare.* Madison: University of Wisconsin Press, 1990.

Gosney, E. S., and Paul Popenoe. *Sterilization for Human Betterment.* New York: Macmillan, 1930.

Gould, Stephen Jay. *The Mismeasure of Man.* New York: W. W. Norton, 1981.

Greenhalgh, Susan. "Controlling Births and Bodies in Village China." *American Ethnologist* 21, no. 1 (1994): 3–30.

——. "The Social Construction of Population Science: An Intellectual, Institutional, and Political History of Twentieth-Century Demography." *Comparative Studies in Society and History* 38, no. 1 (1996): 26–66.

Grey, Michael R. *New Deal Medicine: The Rural Health Programs of the Farm Security Administration.* Baltimore: Johns Hopkins University Press, 1999.

Grob, Gerald N. *The Mad Among Us: A History of the Care of America's Mentally Ill.* Cambridge, Mass.: Harvard University Press, 1994.

Grossman, Atina. *Reforming Sex: The German Movement for Birth Control and Abortion Reform, 1920–1950.* New York: Oxford University Press, 1995.

Hacker, Jacob S. *The Divided Welfare State: The Battle over Public and Private Social Benefits in the United States.* New York: Cambridge University Press, 2002.

Hahamovitch, Cindy. *The Fruits of Their Labor: Atlantic Coast Farmworkers and the*

Making of Migrant Poverty, 1870–1945. Chapel Hill: University of North Carolina Press, 1997.

Harris, Heather. "Clinical Trials of Enovid in Kentucky, 1958–1969." Paper presented at the annual meeting of the American Association for the History of Medicine, Toronto, 30 April–3 May 1998.

Hartmann, Betsy. *Reproductive Rights and Wrongs: The Global Politics of Population Control*. 2nd ed. Boston: South End Press, 1995.

Hernstein, Richard J., and Charles Murray. *The Bell Curve: Intelligence and Class Structure in America*. Boston: Free Press, 1994.

Hodges, Sarah. "Conjugality, Progeny, and Progress: Family and Modernity in Twentieth-Century India." Ph.D. diss., University of Chicago, 1999.

——. "Eugenic Maternity." Paper presented at the Conference on Population, Birth Control, and Reproductive Health in Late Colonial India, School of Oriental and African Studies, University of London, 18–19 November 1999.

——. "Governmentality, Population, and the Reproductive Family in Modern India." In *Rocking the Cradle: Essays in India's Reproductive Past*, edited by Sarah Hodges. New Delhi: Permanent Black, forthcoming.

——. "Indian Eugenics in an Age of Reform." In *Reproductive Health in India: History, Politics, Controversies*, edited by Sarah Hodges. Delhi: Orient Longman, forthcoming.

——. "Towards a History of Reproduction in Modern India." In *Reproductive Health in India: History, Politics, Controversies*, edited by Sarah Hodges. Delhi: Orient Longman, forthcoming.

Howard, Christopher. *The Hidden Welfare State: Tax Expenditures and Social Policy in the United States*. Princeton: Princeton University Press, 1997.

Hudson, Lynn. "Twentieth-Century Midwives in North Carolina." M.A. thesis, University of North Carolina at Chapel Hill, 1987.

Hulka, Jaroslav F. "How Much Does Family Planning Cost?" *North Carolina Medical Journal* 29, no. 4 (April 1968): 147–49.

Jensen, Arthur R. "How Much Can We Boost IQ and Scholastic Achievement?" *Harvard Educational Review* 39, no. 1 (Winter 1969): 1–23.

Joffe, Carole. *Doctors of Conscience: The Struggle to Provide Abortion before and after "Roe v. Wade."* Boston: Beacon Press, 1995.

Jones, James H. *Bad Blood: The Tuskegee Syphilis Experiment*. Exp. ed. New York: Free Press, 1993.

Kaplan, Laura. *The Story of Jane: The Legendary Underground Feminist Abortion Service*. New York: Pantheon Books, 1995.

Kaye, Tony. "The Birth Dearth." *New Republic*, 19 January 1987, 20–23.

Kevles, Daniel J. *In the Name of Eugenics: Genetics and the Uses of Human Heredity*. New York: Alfred A. Knopf, 1985.

Klein, Jennifer. *For All These Rights: Business, Labor, and the Shaping of America's Public-Private Welfare State*. Princeton: Princeton University Press, 2003.

Kline, Wendy. *Building a Better Race: Gender, Sexuality, and Eugenics from the Turn of the*

Century to the Baby Boom. Berkeley and Los Angeles: University of California Press, 2001.

Klineberger, Otto. *Negro Intelligence and Selective Migration*. New York: Columbia University Press, 1935.

Koenig, Michael A., Gillian H. C. Foo, and Ketan Joshi. "Quality of Care within the Indian Family Welfare Programme: A Review of Recent Evidence." *Studies in Family Planning* 31, no. 1 (March 2000): 1–18.

Korstad, Robert R. "Doctoring the Body Politic: Public Health Reform in North Carolina, 1909–1925." Paper presented at the Fifty-sixth Annual Meeting of the Southern Historical Association, New Orleans, 3 November 1990.

Korstad, Robert R., and James L. Leloudis. "Citizen Soldiers: The North Carolina Volunteers and the War on Poverty." *Law and Contemporary Problems* 62 (Autumn 1999): 177–97.

Kunzel, Regina G. *Fallen Women, Problem Girls: Unmarried Mothers and the Professionalization of Social Work, 1890–1945*. New Haven: Yale University Press, 1993.

Kuralt, Wallace H. "A Public Welfare Agency Tries 'Prevention of Dependency'!" *Public Welfare News* 31, no. 1 (March 1967): 1–10.

Ladd-Taylor, Molly. *Mother Work: Women, Child Welfare, and the State, 1890–1930*. Chicago: University of Illinois Press, 1994.

——. "Saving Babies and Sterilizing Mothers." *Social Politics* 4, no. 1 (Spring 1997): 136–53.

——. "Sex, the Defective Mother, and the Politics of Protection in Interwar Minnesota." Paper delivered at the Berkshire Conference on the History of Women, Storrs, Conn., 6–9 June 2002.

Lader, Lawrence. *Abortion II: Making the Revolution*. Boston: Beacon Press, 1973.

Lal, Maneesha. "Purdah as Pathology: Medical Research and Reproductive Health in Twentieth-Century India." Paper presented at the Conference on Population, Birth Control, and Reproductive Health in Late Colonial India, School of Oriental and African Studies, University of London, 18–19 November 1999.

Largent, Mark A. "'The Greatest Curse of the Race': Eugenic Sterilization in Oregon, 1909–1983." *Oregon Historical Quarterly* 103, no. 2 (2002): 188–209.

Larson, Edward. *Sex, Race, and Science: Eugenics in the Deep South*. Baltimore: Johns Hopkins University Press, 1995.

Leavitt, Judith Walzer. *Brought to Bed: Childbearing in America, 1750–1950*. New York: Oxford University Press, 1986.

Leavy, Zad, and Jerome M. Kummer. "Criminal Abortion: Human Hardship and Unyielding Laws." *Southern California Law Review* 35, no. 2 (1962): 123–48.

Ledbetter, Rosanna. "Thirty Years of Family Planning in India." *Asian Survey* 24, no. 7 (1984): 736–58.

Lederer, Susan E. *Subjected to Science: Human Experimentation in America before the Second World War*. Baltimore: Johns Hopkins University Press, 1995.

Lerner, Barron H. "Constructing Medical Indications." *Journal of the History of Medicine and Allied Sciences* 49 (July 1994): 362–79.

Link, William A. " 'The Harvest Is Ripe, but the Laborers Are Few': The Hookworm Crusade in North Carolina, 1909–1915." *North Carolina Historical Review* 67, no. 1 (January 1990): 1–27.

Lock, Frank R., and Richard C. Forman. "Postpartum Sterilization." *North Carolina Medical Journal* 4, no. 3 (March 1944): 101–2.

Lombardo, Paul. "Eugenic Sterilization in Virginia: Aubrey Strode and the Case of Buck v. Bell." Ph.D. diss., University of Virginia, 1982.

Lopez, Iris. "Agency and Constraint." In *Situated Lives: Gender and Culture in Everyday Life*, edited by Louise Lamphere, Helena Ragone, and Patricia Zavella, 157–71. New York: Routledge, 1997.

Mamdani, Mahmood. *The Myth of Population Control: Family, Caste, and Class in an Indian Village*. New York: Monthly Review Press, 1972.

Mandetta, Anne. "Abortion Legislation in North Carolina." *Tar Heel Nurse* 33 (March 1971): 8–11.

Manna, Mausumi. "Approach towards Birth Control: Indian Women in the Early Twentieth Century." *Indian Economic and Social History Review* 35, no. 1 (1998): 35–51.

Marks, Lara V. " 'A "Cage" of Ovulating Females': The History of the Early Oral Contraceptive Pill Clinical Trials, 1950–1959." In *Molecularizing Biology and Medicine: New Practices and Alliances, 1930s–1970s*, edited by Soraya De Chadarevain and Harmke Kamminga, 221–47. Reading, UK: Harwood Academic Press, 1997.

———. *Sexual Chemistry: A History of the Contraceptive Pill*. New Haven: Yale University Press, 2001.

Mass, Bonnie. *Population Target: The Political Economy of Population Control in Latin America*. Toronto: Women's Educational Press, 1977.

"Maternal Welfare Section: Abortions and Their Management." *North Carolina Medical Journal* 9, no. 5 (May 1947): 314–15.

May, Elaine Tyler. *Homeward Bound: American Families in the Cold War Era*. New York: Basic Books, 1988.

Mayo, Katherine. *Mother India*. New York: Harcourt Brace, 1927.

McCann, Carol. *Birth Control Politics in the United States, 1916–1945*. Ithaca: Cornell University Press, 1994.

McLennan, Charles E. *Synopsis of Obstetrics*. 6th ed. Saint Louis: C. V. Mosby, 1962.

Meckel, Richard A. *Save the Babies: American Public Health Reform and the Prevention of Infant Mortality, 1850–1929*. Baltimore: Johns Hopkins University Press, 1990.

Miller, Patricia G. *The Worst of Times: Illegal Abortion—Survivors, Practitioners, Coroners, Cops, and Children of Women Who Died Talk about Its Horrors*. New York: Harper Collins, 1993.

Mohr, James. *Abortion in America: The Origins and Evolution of National Policy*. New York: Oxford University Press, 1978.

Morantz-Sanchez, Regina. "Negotiating Power at the Bedside: Historical Perspectives on Nineteenth-Century Patients and Their Gynecologists." *Feminist Studies* 26, no. 2 (Summer 2000): 287–309.

Morgan, T. H. *Evolution and Genetics*. Princeton: Princeton University Press, 1915.

Morgen, Sandra. *Into Our Own Hands: The Women's Health Movement in the United States, 1969–1990*. New Brunswick: Rutgers University Press, 2002.

Moynihan, Daniel P. *The Negro Family: The Case for National Action*. Washington, D.C.: U.S. Department of Labor, 1965.

North Carolina Commission for the Study of the Care of the Insane and Mental Defectives. *A Study of Mental Health in North Carolina*. Ann Arbor, Mich.: Edwards Brothers, 1937.

Norton, J. W. Roy. "A Health Department Birth Control Program." *American Journal of Public Health* 29 (March 1939): 253.

———. "Planned Parenthood." *Living Age*, March 1940, 7.

———. "Twenty-One Years' Experience with a Public Health Contraceptive Service." *American Journal of Public Health* 49, no. 8 (August 1959): 993–1000.

Osborn, Frederick. *The Future of Human Heredity: An Introduction to Eugenics in Modern Society*. New York: Weybright and Talley, 1968.

Pearl, Raymond. "The Biology of Superiority." *American Mercury* 47 (1927): 257–66.

Penrose, Lionel. *The Biology of Mental Defect*. London: Sidgwick and Jackson, 1949.

Pernick, Martin. *The Black Stork: Eugenics and the Death of "Defective" Babies in American Medicine and Motion Pictures since 1915*. New York: Oxford University Press, 1996.

———. "Eugenics and Public Health in American History." *American Journal of Public Health* 87, no. 11 (November 1997): 1767–72.

Petchesky, Rosalind P. *Abortion and Woman's Choice: The State, Sexuality, and Reproductive Freedom*. Boston: Northeastern University Press, 1984.

———. "Foetal Images: The Power of Visual Culture in the Politics of Reproduction." In *Reproductive Technologies: Gender, Motherhood and Medicine*, edited by Michelle Stanworth, 57–80. Minneapolis: University of Minnesota Press, 1987.

———. "Reproduction, Ethics, and Public Policy: The Federal Sterilization Regulations." In *Biology, Crime and Ethics: A Study of Biological Explanations for Criminal Behavior*, edited by Frank H. Marsh and Janet Katz, 292–314. Cincinnati: Anderson Publishing, 1984.

Petchesky, Rosalind P., and Karen Judd, eds. *Negotiating Reproductive Rights: Women's Perspectives across Countries and Cultures*. London: Zed Books, 1998.

Popenoe, Paul. "Economic and Social Status of the Sterilized Insane." In *Collected Papers on Eugenic Sterilization in California*, edited by E. S. Gosney. Pasadena: Human Betterment Foundation, 1930.

Popenoe, Paul, and Roswell Hill Johnson. *Applied Eugenics*. New York: MacMillan, 1922.

Presser, Harriet B. *Sterilization and Fertility Decline in Puerto Rico*. Berkeley: Institute of International Studies, University of California, 1973.

Pressman, Jack D. *Last Resort: Psychosurgery and the Limits of Medicine*. New York: Cambridge University Press, 1998.

Proctor, Robert. *Racial Hygiene: Medicine under the Nazis*. Cambridge, Mass.: Harvard University Press, 1988.

Ramírez de Arellano, Annette B., and Conrad Seipp. *Colonialism, Catholicism, and Contraception: A History of Birth Control in Puerto Rico*. Chapel Hill: University of North Carolina Press, 1983.

Ramusack, Barbara N. "Authority and Ambivalence: Medical Women and Birth Control in India." In *Reproductive Health in India: History, Politics, Controversies*, edited by Sarah Hodges. Delhi: Orient Longman, forthcoming.

———. "Embattled Advocates: The Debate over Birth Control in India, 1920–1940." *Journal of Women's History* 1, no. 2 (Fall 1989): 34–64.

Reagan, Leslie J. *When Abortion Was a Crime: Women, Medicine, and Law in the United States, 1867–1973*. Berkeley and Los Angeles: University of California Press, 1997.

Reed, James. *From Private Vice to Public Virtue: The Birth Control Movement and American Society*. Rev. ed. Princeton: Princeton University Press, 1983.

Reilly, Philip R. *The Surgical Solution: A History of Involuntary Sterilization in the United States*. Baltimore: Johns Hopkins University Press, 1991.

Report of the Committee on Caswell Training School in its Relation to the Problem of the Feebleminded of the State of North Carolina. Raleigh: Capital Printing, 1926.

Reverby, Susan, ed. *Tuskegee's Truths: Rethinking the Tuskegee Syphilis Study*. Chapel Hill: University of North Carolina Press, 2000.

Rhodes, John S. "President's Message: Voluntary Sterilization." *North Carolina Medical Journal* 25, no. 10 (October 1963): 487.

Richter, Judith. *Vaccination against Pregnancy: Miracle or Menace?* London: Zed Books, 1996.

Ringelheim, Joan. "Women and the Holocaust: A Reconsideration of Research." In *Different Voices: Women and the Holocaust*, edited by Carol Rittner and John K. Roth, 373–405. New York: Paragon House, 1993.

Rodgers, Daniel T. "An Age of Social Politics." In *Rethinking American History in a Global Age*, edited by Thomas Bender, 250–73. Berkeley and Los Angeles: University of California Press, 2002.

Rodrique, Jessie M. "The Afro-American Community and the Birth Control Movement, 1918–1942." Ph.D. diss., University of Massachusetts, 1991.

Rollins, Robert L., and Ann Wolfe. "Eugenic Sterilization in North Carolina." *North Carolina Medical Journal* 34, no. 12 (December 1973): 944–47.

Rosenberg, Charles. *No Other Gods: On Science and American Social Thought*. Baltimore: Johns Hopkins University Press, 1961.

Ross, Loretta J. "African American Women and Abortion." In *Abortion Wars: A Half Century of Struggle, 1950–2000*, edited by Rickie Solinger, 161–207. Berkeley and Los Angeles: University of California Press, 1998.

Rothman, David J. "The Shame of Medical Research." *New York Review of Books*, 30 November 2000, 60–64.

Sandoval, Chela. "U.S. Third World Feminism: The Theory and Method of Oppositional Consciousness in the Postmodern World." In *Feminism and "Race,"* edited by Kum-Kum Bhavnani, 261–80. New York: Oxford University Press, 2001.

Sanger, Margaret. *An Autobiography*. 1938. Reprint, New York: Dover, 1971.

Schulman, Bruce J. *From Cotton Belt to Sunbelt: Federal Policy, Economic Development, and the Transformation of the South, 1938–1980*. New York: Oxford University Press, 1991.

Seaman, Barbara. *The Doctor's Case against the Pill*. New York: P. H. Wyden, 1969.

Sen, Amarya. "Population: Delusion and Reality." *New York Review of Books*, 22 September 1994, 62–71.

Sen, Samita. "Motherhood and Mothercraft: Gender and Nationalism in Bengal." *Gender and History* 5, no. 2 (Summer 1993): 231–43.

Shapiro, Thomas M. *Population Control Politics: Women, Sterilization, and Reproductive Choice*. Philadelphia: Temple University Press, 1985.

Sharpless, John. "World Population Growth, Family Planning, and American Foreign Policy." *Journal of Policy History* 7, no. 1 (1995): 72–102.

Shepherd, Jack. "Birth Control and the Poor: A Solution." *Look Magazine*, 7 April 1984, 63–67.

Silliman, Jael, and Ynestra King. *Dangerous Intersections: Feminist Perspectives on Population, Environment, and Development*. Boston: South End Press, 1999.

Simmons, George B. "The Economics of Voluntary Sterilization for the Parent and for the Nation." In *Advances in Voluntary Sterilization*, edited by Marilyn E. Schima, Ira Lubell, Joseph E. Davis, Elizabeth Connell, and Dennis W. K. Cotton, 151–60. Amsterdam: Excerpta Medica, 1974.

Smith, J. David, and K. Ray Nelson. *The Sterilization of Carrie Buck*. Far Hills, N.J.: Horizon Press, 1989.

Smith, Susan L. *Sick and Tired of Being Sick and Tired: Black Women's Health Activism in America, 1890–1950*. Philadelphia: University of Pennsylvania Press, 1995.

Smith-Rosenberg, Caroll. "The Abortion Movement and the AMA, 1850–1880." In *Disorderly Conduct: Visions of Gender in Victorian America*, 217–44. New York: Oxford University Press, 1985.

——. "The Hysterical Woman: Sex Roles and Role Conflict in Nineteenth-Century America." In *Disorderly Conduct: Visions of Gender in Victorian America*, 197–216. New York: Oxford University Press, 1985.

Solinger, Rickie. *The Abortionist: A Woman against the Law*. New York: Free Press, 1994.

——. *Beggars and Choosers: How the Politics of Choice Shapes Adoption, Abortion, and Welfare in the United States*. New York: Hill and Wang, 2001.

——. "'A Complete Disaster': Abortion and the Politics of Hospital Abortion Committees, 1950–1970." *Feminist Studies* 19, no. 2 (Summer 1993): 240–61.

——. *Wake Up Little Susie: Single Pregnancy and Race before "Roe v. Wade."* New York: Routledge, 1992.

——, ed. *Abortion Wars: A Half Century of Struggle, 1950–2000*. Berkeley and Los Angeles: University of California Press, 1998.

Spivak, Gayatri Chakravorty. "Can the Subaltern Speak?" In *Marxism and the Interpretation of Cultures*, edited by Cary Nelson and Lawrence Grossberg, 271–316. Urbana: University of Illinois Press, 1988.

Srinivasan, K. "Population Policies and Programmes since Independence: A Saga of Great Expectations and Poor Performance." *Demography India* 27, no. 1 (1998): 1–22.

Stepan, Nancy Leys. *"The Hour of Eugenics": Race, Gender, and Nation in Latin America.* Ithaca: Cornell University Press, 1996.

Sturgis, Somers H., and Doris Menzer-Benaron. *The Gynecological Patient: A Psycho-Endocrine Study.* New York: Grune and Stratton, 1962.

Tarlo, Emma. *Unsettling Memories: Narratives of the Emergency in Delhi.* Berkeley and Los Angeles: University of California Press, 2003.

Taussig, Frederick J. *Abortion: Spontaneous and Induced; Medical and Social Aspects.* Saint Louis: C. V. Mosby, 1936.

Taylor, John C. "Postpartum Sterilization." *North Carolina Medical Journal* 11, no. 6 (June 1950): 283–85.

Theriot, Nancy M. "Women's Voices in Nineteenth-Century Medical Discourse: A Step toward Deconstructing Science." *Signs* 19, no. 1 (Autumn 1993): 1–31.

Tone, Andrea. *Devices and Desires: A History of Contraceptives in America.* New York: Hill and Wang, 2001.

Trent, James W. *Inventing the Feeble Mind: A History of Mental Retardation in the United States.* Berkeley and Los Angeles: University of California Press, 1994.

United Nations International Conference on Population and Development. *Programme of Action of the International Conference on Population and Development.* UN doc. A, Conf. 171/13, 18 October 1994. <http://www.unfpa.org/icpd/docs/index.htm> (accessed 14 May 2004).

U.S. Department of Health, Education, and Welfare, Public Health Service. *Family Planning, Contraception, and Voluntary Sterilization: An Analysis of Laws and Policies in the United States, Each State, and Jurisdiction.* Rockville, Md.: Health Services Administration, Bureau of Community Health Services, National Center for Family Planning Services, 1974.

Van Hollen, Cecilia. "Moving Targets: Routine IUD Insertion in Maternity Wards in Tamil Nadu, India." *Reproductive Health Measures* 6, no. 11 (May 1998): 98–105.

Vicziany, Marika. "Coercion in a Soft State: The Family-Planning Program of India; Part 1, The Myth of Voluntarism." *Pacific Affairs* 55, no. 3 (1982): 373–402.

———. "Coercion in a Soft State: The Family-Planning Program of India; Part 2, The Sources of Coercion." *Pacific Affairs* 55, no. 4 (1982): 557–92.

Wailoo, Keith. *Drawing Blood: Technology and Disease Identity in Twentieth-Century America.* Baltimore: Johns Hopkins University Press, 1997.

Walkowitz, Daniel J. *Working with Class: Social Workers and the Politics of Middle-Class Identity.* Chapel Hill: University of North Carolina Press, 1999.

Ward, Martha C. *Poor Women, Powerful Men: America's Great Experiment in Family Planning.* Boulder, Colo.: Westview Press, 1986.

Watkins, Elizabeth Siegel. *On the Pill: A Social History of Oral Contraceptives, 1950–1970.* Baltimore: Johns Hopkins University Press, 1998.

Weisbord, Robert G. *Genocide? Birth Control and the Black American*. Westport, Conn.: Greenwood Press, 1975.

Welch, Grace Woodward. "Planned Parenthood Services in Four North Carolina Health Departments." M.A. thesis, University of North Carolina at Chapel Hill, 1946.

Wharton, Don. "Birth Control: The Case for the State." *Atlantic Monthly*, October 1939, 463–67.

White, Deborah Gray. *Arn't I A Woman? Female Slaves in the Plantation South*. New York: Norton, 1985.

Williams, Doone, and Greer Williams. *Every Child a Wanted Child: Clarence James Gamble, M.D., and His Work in the Birth Control Movement*. Boston: Francis A. Countway Library of Medicine, distributed by Harvard University Press, 1978.

Williams, J. Whitridge. "Medical Education and the Midwife Problem in the United States." *Journal of the American Medical Association* 58 (1912): 1–7.

Woodside, Moya. *Sterilization in North Carolina: A Sociological and Psychological Study*. Chapel Hill: University of North Carolina Press, 1950.

——. "Women Who Want to Be Sterilized." *Woman's Life*, Fall 1950, 6.

Index

Aid to Families with Dependent Children (AFDC), 61, 68, 190–91
Alabama, 33, 110
All India Women's Conference, 221
American Birth Control League (ABCL), 28, 58, 207, 221
American College of Surgeons, 117–18
American Indians, 259 (n. 78)
American Law Institute (ALI), 179–80, 181
American Medical Association (AMA), 118, 255 (n. 17)
American Neurological Association, 104
Anderson, Annie, 173–74
Applewhite, C. C., 128
Arizona, 39–40
Asia, 199
Asociasión pro Salud Maternal e Infantil, 205
Atlanta Tuberculosis Association, 47

Baker, Melton, 158
Bangladesh, 6, 76
Barclay, Elizabeth, 28
Beasley, Joe, 24, 65, 67, 70, 71, 73
Beebe, Gilbert, 42–43
Begos, Kevin, 18–19, 241, 243–44, 246
Belk, Lucile, 150, 158, 159
Bennett, Mildred, 157
Birth control: ease of use, 28–29, 30, 34, 44; and eugenic theory, 81; lack of interest in, 58–59; legalization of, 22; opposition to, 22, 57–58, 221, 238; men's attitudes towards, 55–56; misconceptions about, 54–55; Puerto Rican legalization of, 205; reliability of, 53, 130; and reproductive control, 193–94, 237; side effects of, 234; sterilization as, 113, 117, 118–19, 121–22, 123, 124, 136, 213, 215; women's use of, 53, 113, 261 (n. 105). *See also* Contraceptive access; Contraceptive distribution; Contraceptive field trials
Birth Control Clinical Research Bureau, 29

Birth control clinics: and clients' apathy, 54–55; clients' experiences of, 73–74; and DeVilbiss, 31–32, 256 (n. 34); and Gamble, 35, 37; and gynecological checkups, 54; in India, 221–25; in Puerto Rico, 203, 206–8
Birth Control Federation of America (BCFA), 24, 42, 45, 47–51, 163
Birth control movement, 21–22, 197, 279 (n. 185)
Birth control pills: access to, 2–3, 16; development of, 62, 130, 208; difficulties in using, 114; field trials for, 30, 199, 207, 208–11; and Kuralt, 64; in Puerto Rico, 207–8; side effects of, 78, 210, 211, 212, 236
Birth control programs: for African Americans, 44–45, 47, 48–50, 258–59 (n. 70); health and social services integrated with, 24, 53, 66, 72; international programs, 197, 198–99; lack of publicity for, 59, 60; maternal and child health services separated from, 59, 68, 206; and population control, 44, 59, 73, 204; and public health clinics, 33, 37–38, 71; in Puerto Rico, 203, 207; waning interest in, 60
Birth defects, 143, 180, 184, 195
Birthright, 107, 108
Black militants, 70
Black nationalists, 6, 46
Blacks. *See* African Americans
Boas, Franz, 104
Bourne, Dorothy, 203–4
Brady, Charles, 151
Brazil, 6, 76
Brewer, Mary, 81, 82, 90–91
Briggs, Laura, 207, 215
Brodie, Janet, 286 (n. 6)
Brooks, Thelma, 173
Brown, Carolyn Henning, 232
Brown, J. R., 153, 156
Brown, R. Eugene, 128, 129
Bryson, Eva, 149–51
Buck, Carrie, 82

12, 64, 80, 130, 140, 141, 142, 143, 145, 147, 155, 179–93, 195, 293 (n. 124); and eugenic sterilization, 81–84, 104, 130, 132, 274 (n. 119), 285 (n. 262); and Puerto Rican sterilization law, 205; and voluntary sterilization law, 3, 7, 12, 64, 80, 119–20, 130, 136, 180, 267 (n. 7)
Lee, Dorothy, 164
Lenroot, Katharine, 57–58
Louisiana, 24, 53, 65, 66, 67, 68, 70

Marks, Lara, 210, 211
Maternal health: and African Americans, 45–46; and family planning programs, 22, 59, 201, 218, 225; improvement in, 23, 26, 60; and public health clinics, 27, 71; and spacing births, 23, 45–46, 49, 51
Maternal mortality, 3, 25, 26, 27–28, 45, 255 (n. 19); and abortion, 145, 161, 163, 175, 176, 180, 183, 193, 292 (n. 112), 296–97 (n. 171); and India, 217; and spacing births, 31, 45–46, 71, 163
Mauney, A. A., 166
Mayo, Katherine, 217–18
McClure, Elmer, 154, 155
McCormick, Katharine Dexter, 208, 212
Meadows, Jesse, 249
Medicaid, 195–96
Medical technology: contraceptive technology, 62, 72; and developing countries, 199–200; and India, 231–32; meaning of, 15–17; and reproductive control, 7; and sterilization, 79; women's access to, 6
Men: and abortion cases, 142, 148, 149–52, 157, 158, 159, 166–67, 290 (n. 79); attitudes towards birth control, 55–56; and condoms, 21, 78, 236, 257 (n. 50), 298 (n. 24); and contraceptive field trials, 211; and elective sterilization, 113, 116, 120, 280 (n. 197); and eugenic sterilization, 99, 102, 103, 120; and reproductive control, 77–78, 200, 257 (n. 7); and sterilization access, 78, 236; and vasectomies, 31

Mendez, John, 245
Mental illness: and abortion, 140, 143, 164, 176–79, 188, 191–92, 195, 236, 292 (nn. 113, 116); causes of, 89, 90; and elective sterilization, 115; and eugenic sterilization, 75, 82, 95, 98–99, 100, 103, 107, 123, 132, 134–35; as hereditary, 88, 108; medication for, 100, 131; and motherhood, 99; and sexuality, 92–93, 95, 98; and therapeutic sterilization, 118; understanding of, 130, 131
Mental retardation: causes of, 104; and eugenic sterilization, 98, 123, 132, 134–35; and heredity, 108; and motherhood, 99–100; and sexual abuse, 101–3, 272 (n. 107); understanding of, 131. *See also* Feeblemindedness
Merritt, Donna Lee, 166–67, 173
Midwives, 23, 26–27, 60–61, 117, 141, 160–61, 168–69, 254 (n. 14)
Migrant labor camps, 37, 54, 257 (n. 41)
Modernization: of India, 217, 218–19, 231–32; and population control, 198, 199; of Puerto Rico, 202–3, 212
Mohr, James, 286 (n. 6)
Moore, Ernestine, 248
Morehead, Willie C., 54, 55–56, 57, 58–59
Mortality rates, 48. *See also* Infant mortality; Maternal mortality
Motherhood, 8, 37, 52–53, 57, 99, 113, 138, 268 (n. 21); and India, 230; pathologized, 163, 289–90 (n. 67); and Puerto Rican identity, 204–5
Mothers' Health Clinic, 31
Mueller, Herbert, 104
Myerson, Abraham, 104

National Association for Retarded Children, 133
National Association for the Advancement of Colored People (NAACP), 51, 246
National Committee for Maternal Health (NCMH), 29, 30, 43
National Council of Negro Women, 51
National Negro Health Movement, 46

Nazi Germany, 105, 191, 244, 245, 246–47, 274 (n. 126), 286 (n. 7)
Nebraska, 56
New Deal era: and birth control movement, 22; and birth control programs in Puerto Rico, 203, 205; and family planning programs, 24, 237–38; programs, 10, 23, 37, 236, 256–57 (n. 41)
New York, 25
New York City, 8
Norplant, 73
North Carolina: and abortion law, 180, 181, 187; and birth control services, 33, 34–35, 36, 37, 47, 60, 263 (n. 139); early concern for public health, 9; and contraceptive field trials, 30, 42–43, 60, 205; eugenic sterilization program of, 7, 80, 82–83, 84, 90, 94, 105–6, 107, 112–13, 121, 128–30, 133–34, 241–42; and family planning programs, 68, 265 (n. 170); and restitution to sterilization survivors, 19
North Carolina Bureau of Maternity and Infancy, 26, 27
North Carolina Department of Public Welfare, 12, 100, 112
North Carolina Eugenics Board: attendance of board members, 128–29, 283 (n. 244), 284 (n. 245); and authorization of petitions, 129, 130, 132, 135, 284 (nn. 247, 250); and causes of feeblemindedness, 18, 88–89, 107; dissent within, 128, 129, 132–33; dissolution of, 133; and elective sterilization, 113–14, 116, 117, 120, 121–22, 124, 131, 138; establishment of, 82; and eugenic abortion, 183–84; and patients' opposition to sterilization, 126–27, 131, 282 (n. 226), 283 (n. 232); patients' suing of, 130–31; records of, 242, 249; and sterilization for sexual behavior, 94–96, 102, 111–12, 276 (n. 149); and sterilization of families, 88, 91–92, 96–98, 268 (n. 33); and sterilization petitions, 84–86, 242

North Carolina Fund, 11
North Carolina Human Betterment League, 80
North Carolina Medical Society, 119
North Carolina Office of Economic Opportunity, 130
North Carolina State Board of Health, 4, 9, 10, 26, 27, 33, 35, 43
North Carolina State Board of Public Welfare, 10
North Carolina Supreme Court, 145–46, 147, 154, 155–56, 165, 166
Norton, Roy, 42, 59–60
Nurses: and abortion, 164, 171; African American, 27, 44, 46, 51; and maternal and infant health, 27, 59; public health, 18, 21, 23, 35, 37, 44, 46, 144; in Puerto Rico, 205, 208, 210, 212; skills of, 25–26; visiting, 31

Office of Negro Health Work, 46
Ogburn, William, 105
Oregon, 241, 245, 249
Orkney, Jean M., 222, 224
Overpopulation, 8, 29, 208; fears of, 62, 208, 237; and India, 216–17, 230; and Puerto Rico, 204; and Sanger, 208, 212
Overton, John, 260 (n. 90)

Pakistan, 227
Parish, Ollie, 158–59
Park, Robert, 105
Pathfinder Fund, 71
Patient education, 28, 37, 54, 55, 56–57, 60, 66, 68, 72, 211; and India, 220, 226, 227, 228, 230, 231, 234
Pennsylvania, 58
Penrose, Lionel, 104
Pernick, Martin, 83–84
Perry, A. E., 169–70
Petchesky, Rosalind, 3, 193
Pharmaceutical companies: and birth control access, 206, 207, 239; and India, 222
Philanthropists, 3, 4, 18, 22, 44, 107; and

Public health clinics: and birth control, 3, 33, 37–38, 57, 71; equal access to, 9–10; and family planning, 22; and maternal and infant health, 27; and reproductive policies, 130; and segregation, 44–45; and sterilization, 121

Puerto Rican Nationalists, 204, 215

Puerto Rican Socialist Party, 203

Puerto Rico: and birth control programs, 203, 207; and contraceptive field trials, 30, 199–200, 206, 209–10; modernization of, 202–3; opposition to family planning programs, 204–5, 238; and reproductive policies, 13, 198; and sterilization, 199, 205–6, 213, 214, 215–16; and sterilization abuse, 6, 76, 215, 236

Quickening, 141, 154, 155

Quinacrine, 73

Race and racism: and abortion, 168–70; anthropologists' criticism of term, 103–4; and birth control, 32, 67, 70, 256 (n. 34); racial equality, 9, 105, 245; and reproductive control, 5, 80, 237; and sterilization, 79, 108, 119, 134, 244, 245

Racial discrimination, 6–7, 9, 11, 17, 46, 72, 108, 138, 246

Racial genocide, 69, 76, 245, 246

Racial politics, 24, 30, 69–70

Railey, John, 241

Rajwade, Rani, 220

Rama Rau, Dhanvanthi, 228

Ramusack, Barbara, 220

Rankin, Watson Smith, 9–10, 26, 46

Rape, Lillie Mae, 166, 169–70

Raper, Arthur, 25

Reagan, Leslie, 141, 148, 153, 163, 167, 292 (n. 113), 293 (n. 124)

Reid, Ira, 25

Religion, 126, 191, 205, 214, 215, 221

Reproductive control: and abortion, 45, 53, 140, 141, 142, 144, 145, 182, 184–85, 189, 192, 194, 195, 196; and birth control, 59, 72, 193–94, 237; and class, 5, 67, 237; conflicts over, 5, 133–34; and contraceptive field trials, 30, 208, 213, 238; in developing countries, 200–201; and family planning programs, 12, 63, 65, 73; in India, 218; and international programs, 202; and intrauterine devices, 23–24, 67, 73, 236; meaning of, 8; and men, 77–78, 200, 257 (n. 7); and physicians, 67, 73; and poverty, 3, 4, 23, 130, 145, 203, 237; in Puerto Rico, 203; and sterilization, 76, 77–78, 79, 118–19, 120, 124, 125, 134, 135, 137, 142, 143, 144, 193–94, 213, 237; and women's agency, 7, 216; and women's rights, 4, 12, 23; women's struggles with, 1–3

Reproductive policies, 3–4, 6, 11, 13, 80, 104, 109, 181, 198, 201, 239. *See also* Coercive reproductive policies

Reproductive technologies, 15–16

Rhythm method, 226

Rice-Wray, Edris, 212, 235

Riddle, Estelle Massey, 51

Rivera de Alvarado, Carmen, 213

Rivers, Eunice, 200

Rockefeller, John D., III, 201

Rockefeller Foundation, 12, 221, 230

Rockefeller Sanitary Commission, 9

Rodman, William, 128

Rodriguez, Iris, 209

Roe v. Wade (1973), 141, 175, 193, 194, 195, 196, 296 (n. 170)

Rohatgi, Chandrakanta, 229

Rollins, Robert L., 132, 284 (n. 245)

Roman Catholics, 191, 205, 214, 215, 221

Roosevelt, Eleanor, 58, 203

Roosevelt, Franklin D., 10, 203, 205

Roots, Margaret, 228

Rose, D. Kenneth, 58

Ross, Robert A., 182–83

Rozzell, Juanita, 165–66, 290 (n. 76)

Russell Sage Foundation, 13

Samarcand Training School, 87, 88

Sanford, Terry, 11

Sanger, Margaret: and contraceptive distribution, 22, 29; and India, 197, 220–21, 222, 224, 225, 228; and international programs, 13, 197, 198, 201; and Negro Project, 47, 48, 51; and overpopulation, 208, 212; and reproductive control, 37, 208

Satterthwaite, Penny, 210, 212

Seagle, Clarence W., 173–74

Segregation, 44–45, 46, 69

Seibels, Robert, 49–50

Sexuality: and abortion, 146, 149, 150, 151, 157, 287 (n. 25); and feeblemindedness, 76, 83, 93–94; and incest, 101–3, 272 (n. 108), 273 (n. 112); and India, 217; and mental illness, 92–93, 95, 98; and modernization of Puerto Rico, 202–3; outside of marriage, 141, 181–82, 195, 293 (n. 124); and sterilization, 94–96, 98, 102, 103, 108, 110–11, 115, 123, 125, 132, 134, 137, 271 (n. 74)

Sexual promiscuity, 3, 92, 103, 109, 122, 125, 126, 138, 167, 190, 192

Shaft, Elizabeth, 150, 151

Sheppard-Towner Act (1921), 27, 46, 57, 255 (n. 17)

Sherrill, J. L., 150, 151

Sholapur Eugenics Education Society, 219, 223

Sikes, Walter A., 284 (n. 245)

Sinclair, Polly, 151

Slagle, Jacob, 149–51

Smedley, Agnes, 220, 225

Smith, Ethel, 156, 158–60, 161

Social Security Act (1935), 27

Social Security Act amendments, 62, 263 (n. 146)

Social workers: African Americans as, 124, 280 (n. 208); and birth control, 33, 64–65, 66; and coercive reproductive policies, 131, 237; and elective sterilization, 114–15, 116, 121–24, 131; and eugenic sterilization, 92, 98–99, 101–2, 107–8, 110–13, 136, 272 (n. 107); and incest, 101–3, 273 (n. 112); in

Puerto Rico, 207, 208, 210, 212; and sterilization petitions, 83, 86, 122–24, 126, 132, 138; and teenage girls, 110, 111–12

Society for the Study and Promotion of Family Hygiene, 221, 223

South, the, 8–12, 25, 47

South, Virginia, 42, 55, 57

South Carolina, 33, 47, 48–49, 242, 260 (n. 90), 267 (n. 10)

Speas, Ethel, 129

Spencer, Robert Douglas, 164

Squier, Raymond, 43

Stallworth, Florence, 165–66

Stanton, A. M., 247

State: prosecution of abortion, 141, 146, 147, 152–58, 161, 163–79, 181, 194; and reproductive policies, 2, 133–34, 194, 236, 237

State governments, 22, 26, 58, 61–62, 71, 82, 105, 263 (n. 146)

State mental institutions, 100

States' Rights Party, 67

State v. Evans (1937), 150

State v. Forte (1943), 154

State v. Jordon (1947), 157

State v. Thompson (1939), 150

Stepan, Nancy, 203

Sterilization: and abortion, 140, 143–44, 167, 193–94, 214, 231; compulsory sterilization, 181–82; and consultation requirements, 118, 279 (n. 184); and DeVilbiss, 31, 32, 256 (n. 32); elective sterilization, 112–24, 142, 205–6, 213–16; eugenic sterilization law, 81–84, 104, 130, 132, 274 (n. 119), 285 (n. 262); and feeblemindedness, 75–76, 82, 83, 93, 101–2, 104, 107, 236; in India, 229, 231, 232; indications for, 75, 117, 118, 119, 120, 153, 214–15, 278–79 (nn. 179, 183); involuntary, 6, 76, 113, 216; meaning of, 79–80, 125, 281 (n. 212); and noninstitutional sterilizations, 109–10; opposition to, 125–33; in Puerto Rico, 205, 213–14; and reproductive control,

Gender and American Culture

Choice and Coercion: Birth Control, Sterilization, and Abortion in Public Health and Welfare, by Johanna Schoen (2005).

Closer to Freedom: Enslaved Women and Everyday Resistance in the Plantation South, by Stephanie M. H. Camp (2004).

Masterful Women: Slaveholding Widows from the American Revolution through the Civil War, by Kirsten E. Wood (2004).

Manliness and Its Discontents: The Black Middle Class and the Transformation of Masculinity, 1900–1930, by Martin Summers (2004).

Citizen, Mother, Worker: Debating Public Responsibility for Child Care after the Second World War, by Emilie Stoltzfus (2003).

Women and the Historical Enterprise in America: Gender, Race, and the Politics of Memory 1880–1945, by Julie Des Jardins (2003).

Free Hearts and Free Homes: Gender and American Antislavery Politics, by Michael D. Pierson (2003).

Ella Baker and the Black Freedom Movement: A Radical Democratic Vision, by Barbara Ransby (2003).

Signatures of Citizenship: Petitioning, Antislavery, and Women's Political Identity, by Susan Zaeske (2003).

Love on the Rocks: Men, Women, and Alcohol in Post–World War II America, by Lori Rotskoff (2002).

The Veiled Garvey: The Life and Times of Amy Jacques Garvey, by Ula Yvette Taylor (2002).

Working Cures: Health, Healing, and Power on Southern Slave Plantations, by Sharla Fett (2002).

Southern History across the Color Line, by Nell Irvin Painter (2002).

The Artistry of Anger: Black and White Women's Literature in America, 1820–1860, by Linda M. Grasso (2002).

Too Much to Ask: Black Women in the Era of Integration, by Elizabeth Higginbotham (2001).

Imagining Medea: Rhodessa Jones and Theater for Incarcerated Women, by Rena Fraden (2001).

Women Artists and the Development of Modern American Art, 1870–1920, by Kirsten Swinth (2001).

Remaking Respectability: African American Women in Interwar Detroit, by Victoria W. Wolcott (2001).

Ida B. Wells-Barnett and American Reform, 1880–1930, by Patricia A. Schechter (2001).

Taking Haiti: Military Occupation and the Culture of U.S. Imperialism, 1915–1940,
  by Mary A. Renda (2001).
Before Jim Crow: The Politics of Race in Postemancipation Virginia, by
  Jane Dailey (2000).
Captain Ahab Had a Wife: New England Women and the Whalefishery, 1720–1870,
  by Lisa Norling (2000).
*Civilizing Capitalism: The National Consumers' League, Women's Activism, and
  Labor Standards in the New Deal Era,* by Landon R. Y. Storrs (2000).
Rank Ladies: Gender and Cultural Hierarchy in American Vaudeville, by
  M. Alison Kibler (1999).
Strangers and Pilgrims: Female Preaching in America, 1740–1845, by
  Catherine A. Brekus (1998).
Sex and Citizenship in Antebellum America, by Nancy Isenberg (1998).
Yours in Sisterhood: Ms. Magazine and the Promise of Popular Feminism, by
  Amy Erdman Farrell (1998).
We Mean to Be Counted: White Women and Politics in Antebellum Virginia, by
  Elizabeth R. Varon (1998).
*Women Against the Good War: Conscientious Objection and Gender on the
  American Home Front, 1941–1947,* by Rachel Waltner Goossen (1997).
Toward an Intellectual History of Women: Essays by Linda K. Kerber (1997).
*Gender and Jim Crow: Women and the Politics of White Supremacy in North
  Carolina, 1896–1920,* by Glenda Elizabeth Gilmore (1996).
*Delinquent Daughters: Protecting and Policing Adolescent Female Sexuality in the
  United States, 1885–1920,* by Mary E. Odem (1995).
U.S. History as Women's History: New Feminist Essays, edited by Linda K.
  Kerber, Alice Kessler-Harris, and Kathryn Kish Sklar (1995).
*Common Sense and a Little Fire: Women and Working-Class Politics in the United
  States, 1900–1965,* by Annelise Orleck (1995).
How Am I to Be Heard?: Letters of Lillian Smith, edited by Margaret Rose
  Gladney (1993).
Entitled to Power: Farm Women and Technology, 1913–1963, by Katherine
  Jellison (1993).
Revising Life: Sylvia Plath's Ariel Poems, by Susan R. Van Dyne (1993).
Made From This Earth: American Women and Nature, by Vera Norwood (1993).
Unruly Women: The Politics of Social and Sexual Control in the Old South, by
  Victoria E. Bynum (1992).
The Work of Self-Representation: Lyric Poetry in Colonial New England, by
  Ivy Schweitzer (1991).
Labor and Desire: Women's Revolutionary Fiction in Depression America, by
  Paula Rabinowitz (1991).

Community of Suffering and Struggle: Women, Men, and the Labor Movement in Minneapolis, 1915–1945, by Elizabeth Faue (1991).

All That Hollywood Allows: Re-reading Gender in 1950s Melodrama, by Jackie Byars (1991).

Doing Literary Business: American Women Writers in the Nineteenth Century, by Susan Coultrap-McQuin (1990).

Ladies, Women, and Wenches: Choice and Constraint in Antebellum Charleston and Boston, by Jane H. Pease and William H. Pease (1990).

The Secret Eye: The Journal of Ella Gertrude Clanton Thomas, 1848–1889, edited by Virginia Ingraham Burr, with an introduction by Nell Irvin Painter (1990).

Second Stories: The Politics of Language, Form, and Gender in Early American Fictions, by Cynthia S. Jordan (1989).

Within the Plantation Household: Black and White Women of the Old South, by Elizabeth Fox-Genovese (1988).

The Limits of Sisterhood: The Beecher Sisters on Women's Rights and Woman's Sphere, by Jeanne Boydston, Mary Kelley, and Anne Margolis (1988).